"In *African American Readings of Paul*, Lisa Bowens ably proves how a select set of African American interpreters of Paul from the 1700s through the 1900s wrestled Paul from the grips of pro-slavery and anti-Black interpretations. Bowens demonstrates how these African American authors interpreted Paul in subversive, disruptive, and revolutionary ways."

— DAVID D. DANIELS
McCormick Theological Seminary

"What happens when African Americans are at the center of Pauline interpretation? This book provides an answer by tracing African American interpretation of Paul from the mid-eighteenth century to the end of the twentieth. Here we find not the Paul used by slaveholders or white racists who calls for submission and blind obedience, but Paul the liberator, the spiritual guide to the third heaven, and the champion of bodily integrity. While not all African American interpreters embraced Pauline texts, Bowens shows how many of them did, employing Paul's words in provocative and powerful ways. Students and faith leaders will welcome this text for the fresh insights it gives into Paul's letters."

— SHELLY MATTHEWS
Brite Divinity School

"In this singular work on the reception history of Paul among African Americans from the eighteenth to the twentieth century, Dr. Bowens has provided us with a densely packed treasure-trove of information, analysis, and insight. Bowens elegantly and compellingly demonstrates the central role Paul plays in the struggle for African Americans to confront white supremacy and the dehumanization of black bodies across centuries. If you are looking for one book that will bring you up to date on African American hermeneutics, this is it. Bowens has taught me new knowledge and has provided me a way to draw students into the study of Paul in a gripping, relevant way."

— JAIME CLARK-SOLES
Perkins School of Theology

African American Readings of Paul

RECEPTION, RESISTANCE, AND TRANSFORMATION

Lisa M. Bowens

WILLIAM B. EERDMANS PUBLISHING COMPANY
GRAND RAPIDS, MICHIGAN

Wm. B. Eerdmans Publishing Co.
4035 Park East Court SE, Grand Rapids, Michigan 49546
www.eerdmans.com

26 25 24 23 22 21   2 3 4 5 6 7

ISBN 978-0-8028-7676-8

Library of Congress Cataloging-in-Publication Data

A catalog record for this book is available from the Library of Congress.

Excerpts from the following sources are used by permission:

God Struck Me Dead: Voices of Ex-Slaves, ed. Clifton H. Johnson, © 1969 Pilgrim Press.

"God and Time: Exploring Black Notions of Prophetic and Apocalyptic Eschatology," pages 213–24 in *T & T Clark Handbook of African American Theology,* ed. Antonia Daymond, Frederick Ware, and Eric Williams, © 2019 Marilyn Dunn, published by T&T Clark, an imprint of Bloomsbury Publishing Plc.

Cover credits:

Front cover: African American Man. Photo by Thomas Eakins, ca. 1884. The Metropolitan Museum of Art. www.metmuseum.org/art/collection/search/285842

Front flap: daughter of Mrs. D. Saggus, FSA (Farm Security Administration) borrower. Greene County, Georgia. Photo by Jack Delano, 1941. Library of Congress. www.loc.gov/item/2017794954/

Back flap: full-length portrait of an African American woman seated holding an African American infant. Photo by A. D. Jaynes, Corning, NY, between 1860 and 1870. Library of Congress. lccn.loc.gov/2010647820.

For my entire family, especially my parents, Reginald and Eunice Bowens, and in memory of my grandparents, Lawrence and Martha Bowens, Irving and Nettie McKoy. Also, in memory of Otis Lockett Sr., a spiritual father, and Joseph Bordeaux, a modern-day John Jea, who would often testify about how God taught him to read. And finally to my great-grandfather Bowens born in slavery, my ancestors, and the millions who perished in the Middle Passage. May you never be forgotten.

CONTENTS

Contents

FOREWORD

Liberation for all people has been the central political debate in the development of the democratic nation formed as the United States. African American agency has been key to this discussion from the beginning, even if this part of the story is less reported and less well known in the country's central myths. Since the civil rights movement, scholarly efforts have been directed more intentionally toward the original sources of the formidable black thinkers from the eighteenth century onward. In the treatment of this literature, scholars of religion have often divided many of the early African American sources into two categories, those interested in political liberation and those engaged in spiritual liberation. Lisa Bowens has discovered an odd—but significant—link between these two prominent understandings of freedom: the words and writings of the first-century Jew Paul of Tarsus. The author provides a wide-ranging study guiding the reader through a variety of genres—political speeches, essays, sermons, autobiographies, and conversion stories—in order to make her case that most, if not all, of these interpreters saw themselves—along with and through the words of Paul—as "divine mouthpieces bridging the gap between the divine and human."

African American Readings of Paul makes the case that reading Scripture as identity formation, group enhancement, survival literature, and world construction was part of early African American thinking, even while religious and political institutions opposed to the humanity of black folks utilized the same collection of sacred texts.

Readers will be pleased to discover many gems within this volume. Let me mention only four:

- The use of early (eighteenth-century) petitions: Bowens demonstrates that during the American Revolutionary period, many such petitions rhetorically negotiated "Pauline" texts to enhance their arguments for claims for freedom. Bowens is to be commended for locating these petitions and analyzing them for their use of biblical passages as excellent early resources for African American interpretation. Outside of traditional sources (e.g., sermons), these "petitions" represent early *oral* expression within these communities.

- Recognition of the historical backdrop to the myth of white superiority: with the use of Josiah Priest and many others (including leading white biblical theologians such as Samuel May and Charles Hodge), Bowens provides key discussions on select writers and their arguments in support of the myth of white superiority as instrumental to the prominent ideologies of the time. While many white abolitionists argued for the freedom of blacks, the same abolitionists were developing plans to establish separate communities for the formerly enslaved in colonized spaces. Even as African Americans argued for their civil rights one century after formal emancipation, many white religious communities called for patience, not believing wholeheartedly in the full humanity of their fellow citizens of a darker hue.

- The hermeneutical appeal to the Spirit: the author includes several stories in which it is claimed that the Spirit spoke to empower and to instruct when legal stipulations were in place to hinder literacy and leadership. There are a number of striking accounts herein, including John Jea's vision of an angelic figure with a big Bible in its hands—as the Spirit spoke to him, even when the Bible did *not*!—or Jarena Lee's vision of a pulpit with a Bible on it, or Zilpha Elaw's vision confirmed by a milking cow. As Bowens emphasizes from these (final two) accounts, black women were doubly criticized for their race in a white supremacist society and for their gender in a patriarchal ecclesial setting. They utilized these "visions" to interpret their Bibles, and not the other way around; an emphasis on the *Spirit* who allows them necessary agency to become critical interpreters of their contexts despite institutional constraints. As Bowens puts it succinctly: "Although they may have been denied access to education, they did have access to God and God had access to them, access that no law could contravene."

- The emphasis on a "body hermeneutic": Bowens shows repeatedly that the "body" is a contested site throughout these investigations. During the early period, black bodies were oftentimes enslaved bodies, under the control of someone else, yet blacks read *with their bodies* and, as Bowens's insightfully argues, used their bodies as a way to interpret Paul. During the civil rights period of the mid-twentieth century, they offered their bodies—in King's words, following Romans 12:1—"as a sacrifice" for others. They employed a sophisticated theology of the body (and the embodied) in order to reread and reclaim Paul and to expose the Spirit's infusion of their bodies as fully human in the sight of God. They were writing and speaking their fleshly, black bodies into existence.

These pro-Paul interpreters did not utilize his words to accept the status quo. Rather, as Bowens has carefully shown, these engaged interpreters have called many things into question: white supremacy, human bondage, trading in human bodies, black dehumanization, and patriarchal leadership roles within black ecclesial circles. These folks used Paul to make change within their surroundings rather than accept a socially conservative reading of the ancient apostle—still common today in many African American settings.

Readers will also discover extensive citations of many primary sources. Though necessarily selective in its referencing to representative texts, *African American Readings of Paul* does not shy away from those individuals whose interpretation of Paul would have clashed with others, even while fighting on the same side for black human dignity. Bowens recognizes the significance, for example, of Howard Thurman's and Albert Cleage's preference for Jesus (over against Paul). Despite these outliers, the project reveals an extensive African American (and proto-womanist) tradition engaged in the practice of reclaiming Paul from white supremacist and black patriarchal discursive modes.

EMERSON B. POWERY

PREFACE

I am thankful to many people who have encouraged me along the writing and teaching journey regarding this monograph. Special appreciation goes to J. Ross Wagner, whose work has influenced me greatly and who, when this subject was in its inchoate stages during my PhD coursework, encouraged me to pursue it as a topic. Along with him, I offer thanks to George Parsenios and Yolanda Pierce, who also advised me to continue with this project.

I have also been encouraged by conversations with Eric Barreto, Shane Berg, Ashley Byrd, Caryl Chambers, Mark Chironna, David Daniels, Hannah Eagleson, J. Louis Felton, Priscilla Felton, Jeannine Fletcher, Chris Greene, Geddes Hanson, Andy Johnson, Sarit Kattan, Jacqueline Lapsley, Cleo LaRue, Martin Mittlestadt, Dennis Olson, Peter Paris, Michael Peppard, Raynard Smith, Larry Welborne, my Rev22 sisterhood group, the Princeton University Graduate IV Group, and SPS conference members. I am thankful to each of you for your presence during this process. The following people read drafts of this project during its various stages and offered feedback, suggestions, and corrections, and for that I am deeply appreciative: Stephanie Bowens, Presian Burroughs, Febbie Dickerson, Sherry Sherrod DuPree, Jennifer Kaalund, Mark Noll, Angela Parker, Emerson Powery, Shanell Smith, and Shively Smith. I am also deeply grateful for the grant support from the Louisville Institute, which provided the resources for a sabbatical leave to work on this book. Conversations with Edwin Aponte, Executive Director, Don Richter, Associate Director, and my colleagues at the Louisville Winter Seminar were truly uplifting experiences. I am thankful to Princeton Theological Seminary for granting release from teaching and committee responsibilities so that I could do the research and writing necessary to complete this project. In addition, I extend my appreciation to Patricia Goodall, Special Collections Librarian; Evelyn Frangakis, Managing

Director of the Library; and Chip Dobbs-Allsopp, James Lenox Librarian; all of Princeton Seminary, as well as Darrin Rodgers and the Flowers Pentecostal Heritage Center for their help in locating and sharing resources. I am thankful to the current congregation of Ida B. Robinson's church, Mount Olive Holy Temple, especially Brenda McKune and the church's current pastor, Thomas J. Martin, for providing me with an important monograph on Ida Robinson. I must also thank my students who have been in the first iterations of my African American Pauline Hermeneutics course at Princeton Theological Seminary: Richard Anderson, Aliya Browne, Gerald Cameron, Dennis Carroll, Theron Cook, Callie Crowder, Lee Enochs, Jamel Flag, Barbara Florvil, Jacqueline Fowler, Darius Fowlkes, Brian Fox, Jennifer Herold, Thomas Hurst, David Jefferson, Enoch Kuo, Kelsey Lambright, Chris Lane, John Francis Maher III, Christina Manero, Gabrielle Martone, Latasha Milton, Garrett Mostowski, Adam Munshaw, Andre Samuels, Nahed Selwanes, Kalina Smith, William Stell, Romee St. John, Taylor Street, Marcus Tillery, Heelee Joo Velez, Christopher Waks, Yedea Walker, and Daryl Winston. Our conversations about race, racism, the church, and Paul have been rich, provocative, and deeply engaging. You are an inspiration.

Special appreciation goes to my former editor, Michael Thomson, for encouraging me to write and publish this monograph. I am especially grateful to my present editor, Trevor Thompson, for his ongoing reassurance, patience, and expertise. Your presence during this journey has been instrumental. I am also thankful for the assistance of Linda Bieze, Laura Hubers, Tom Raabe, and all of those at Eerdmans who have helped shepherd this book through the publication process. I am also extremely grateful to my research assistants, Jessica Croneau, Charles Gilmer, Sean Tripline, and Heelee Joo Velez, who helped me at various stages of the project. Thank you for your time, your diligence, and your willingness to assist me. To Judith Attride and Teresa Reed I offer a word of thanks as well for your assistance during different phases of the book. I extend deep gratitude to Emerson Powery and Beverly Roberts Gaventa, who have written the foreword and afterword for this book. Thank you so very much.

For the interpreters that appear in this volume with whom I have rejoiced, lamented, and celebrated as I read your stories of joy, pain, and triumph, I give thanks. They have taught me so much, and my hope is that what I write here will, in some small measure, demonstrate my gratitude. Their stories affirm that we are surrounded with so great a cloud of witnesses.

I am eternally grateful to Reggie, Vonnie, Anna, Stephanie, and all of my family members (Bowens and McKoy), especially my parents, Reginald and

Eunice Bowens, for whom words cannot express my abiding love and appreciation. My family's constant support gives me life. We have been through so much together, especially these last couple of years, but your steadfast faith in the midst of everything encourages me to "press on" and to "hold on." I love you deeply.

And to God, the author and finisher of my faith, I offer praise. For from you, and through you, and to you are all things. To you be the glory forever. Amen.

African American Pauline Hermeneutics

Paul speaks in my text [Acts 20:24] of finishing his course. We are all on a journey, travelling into another world.[1]

When discussing the relationship between African Americans and Paul's letters, one often hears the account of Howard Thurman and his grandmother, Nancy Ambrose. The following excerpt from Thurman's *Jesus and the Disinherited* merits full citation:

> During much of my boyhood I was cared for by my grandmother, who was born a slave and lived until the Civil War on a plantation near Madison, Florida. My regular chore was to do all of the readings for my grandmother—she could neither read nor write. Two or three times a week I read the Bible aloud to her. I was deeply impressed by the fact that she was most particular about the choice of Scripture. For instance, I might read many of the more devotional Psalms, some of Isaiah, the Gospels again and again. But the Pauline epistles, never—except, at long intervals, the thirteenth chapter of First Corinthians. My curiosity knew no bounds, but we did not question her about anything.
>
> When I was older and was half through college, I chanced to be spending a few days at home near the end of summer vacation. With a feeling of

---

1. Excerpt from Lemuel Haynes's speech "The Sufferings, Support, and Reward of Faithful Ministers Illustrated: Being the Substance of Two Valedictory Discourses, delivered at Rutland, West Parish, May 24th, A.D. 1818," in *Sketches of the Life and Character of the Rev. Lemuel Haynes, A.M., For Many Years Pastor of A Church in Rutland, VT and Late in Granville, New-York*, ed. Timothy Mather Cooley (New York: Harper & Brothers, 1837), 179.

great temerity I asked her one day why it was that she would not let me read any of the Pauline letters. What she told me I shall never forget. "During the days of slavery," she said, "the master's minister would occasionally hold services for the slaves. Old man McGhee was so mean that he would not let a Negro minister preach to his slaves. Always the white minister used as his text something from Paul. At least three or four times a year he used as a text: 'Slaves, be obedient to them that are your masters, as unto Christ.' Then he would go on to show how it was God's will that we were slaves, and how, if we were good and happy slaves, God would bless us. I promised my Maker that if I ever learned to read and if freedom ever came, I would not read that part of the Bible."[2]

This poignant selection illustrates how slaveholders and white ministers often used Paul's words to justify the cruel practice of enslaving African Americans. In their atrocious misappropriation, Scripture sanctioned slavery for blacks and linked their identity to that of chattel. The narrative also demonstrates some blacks' rejection of Paul because of the way whites preached and interpreted his texts. Thurman's grandmother echoed the words of the minister: "It was God's will that we were slaves." How could the God of the Bible sanction such atrocity? And how could African Americans utilize Paul to argue against such interpretive postures? This book aims to explore the complicated relationship that African Americans have with the apostle and to reveal and uncover the ways in which blacks did employ Paul to resist and protest the readings exemplified by the white minister in Nancy Ambrose's powerful account. The white minister in this narrative is by no means an anomaly; such sermonic interpretations were endemic to the culture and indicative of the sentiments of the time. This reality makes it all the more astonishing that many blacks utilized Paul in their own work, repossessing and reappropriating him as a voice for liberation and freedom. The surprisingly provocative and powerful ways in which African Americans "rescue" Paul from the clutches of white supremacy speak in profound ways to the power of black faith, the ability of black resilience, and the fortitude of black intelligentsia.

2. Howard Thurman, *Jesus and the Disinherited* (Richmond, IN: Friends United, 1981; original Nashville: Abingdon, 1949), 19–20.

What Is African American Pauline Hermeneutics?

The topic of this monograph is African American Pauline hermeneutics, and upon first glance the nomenclature raises a couple of issues. First, what is hermeneutics and what does that word signify? Second, what does it mean to assert that African Americans have particular hermeneutics when reading Paul? The term "hermeneutics" derives from the Greek word *hermeneus*, which denotes an interpreter or explicator.[3] The Greek god Hermes (Roman god Mercury) was believed to be the interpreter or messenger of the gods, carrying forth to humans the communications and mysteries from the divines of Olympus.[4] David Jasper characterizes Hermes's role in the following way: "With his winged sandals Hermes was able to bridge the gap between the divine and human realms, putting into words those mysteries which were beyond the capacity of human utterance. Without such a messenger how would these two realms communicate with each other, and how would the gap in the understanding between the gods and humankind be overcome? His task was to bridge this gap and to make that which seems unintelligible into something meaningful and clear to the human ear."[5]

Jasper's comments regarding Hermes's duties resonate well with the African American hermeneutics encountered in this monograph. In their essays, sermons, autobiographies, and conversion stories, the interpreters discussed in this book see themselves as divine mouthpieces bridging the gap between the divine and the human, uttering interpretations of Paul that defy the prevalent oppressive interpretive trajectories of the apostle as exemplified by the "master's minister" in Nancy Ambrose's narrative. For these interpreters, a gap in understanding Paul existed, and they sought to rectify this reality in their speeches, in their petitions, and in their work overall. Rather than messengers of the gods of Olympus, however, they were messengers of the God of the Bible, the God that spoke through Paul and who now spoke through them, providing them with true understandings of the apostle that were to be shared with the world. Hermeneutics, then, for the

3. David Jasper, *A Short Introduction to Hermeneutics* (Louisville: Westminster John Knox, 2004), 7.

4. Jasper, *A Short Introduction to Hermeneutics*. Cf. Michael Gorman, *Elements of Biblical Exegesis: A Basic Guide for Students and Ministers*, rev. and expanded ed. (Peabody, MA: Hendrickson, 2009), 140.

5. Jasper, *A Short Introduction to Hermeneutics*, 7.

purposes of the present discussion, can be defined as the art of interpretation, an interpretive posture or perspective.[6]

Regarding the second question, what it means to assert that African Americans have particular hermeneutics when reading Paul, the subject matter assumes that African Americans have different and unique ways of reading and interpreting Paul and his writings. African Americans offered ways of reading Paul that were historically counter to the way many white Americans read the apostle. Nancy Ambrose's story illuminates the intersections of the experiences of chattel slavery, the resulting suppression and dehumanization of African Americans, and how such realities shape the way African Americans read, interpret, and respond to Paul. The "distinct Black experience in America"[7] affects black interpretations of the apostle, and so black Pauline hermeneutics address to a great extent "the Black man's condition, and [are] committed to changing that condition."[8] Thus, in many instances African American Pauline hermeneutics are resistance or protest hermeneutics in which blacks employ Paul to protest the oppressive structures of society and to resist whites' interpretations of the apostle. To be sure, African American history informs blacks' interpretive postures when reading Pauline Scriptures.

In a true sense, African American Pauline hermeneutics are intricately tied to *Geschichte*, or history. The two cannot be divorced. How African Americans read Paul is influenced by how Paul was read and presented to them in the past. The dominant white presentation of the apostle to blacks included preaching the repeated sermon topic of "Slaves, obey your masters" from select Pauline passages by white ministers. Accordingly, the unethical behavior of whites who venerated and read Paul presented a faulty portrait of the apostle to the enslaved Africans. Thus, the actions of slaveholders and their ministers shaped African American interpretations of Paul, for many blacks saw the hypocrisy in the behavior of whites who loved and preached the apostle. For example, white preachers were often giving admonitions not to steal. Yet enslaved Africans argued that they themselves were stolen property, and so to them such words dripped

---

6. Gorman, *Elements of Biblical Exegesis*, 26.

7. Henry H. Mitchell, *Black Preaching* (San Francisco: Harper & Row, 1979), 57.

8. Mitchell, *Black Preaching*, 30. Although Mitchell's comments regarding a black hermeneutic occur in relationship to his discussion on black preaching, they are also appropriate for delineating African American Pauline hermeneutics. In addition, Mitchell's comments should be construed for the sake of this monograph as gender inclusive, "black people's condition."

with hypocrisy. Many black interpreters countered what they considered to be hypocritical depictions by choosing to act and react in more faithful ways to the apostle's words.

It is important to note, however, that the African American community is not monolithic by any means. There is no one way that African Americans interpret and understand Paul; hence, the pluralization of "hermeneutics" in the topic under discussion. The *Weltanschauung* (worldview) of African Americans is diverse and multivalent, and Paul plays a significant role in African American reflection in the midst of all its diversity. African American Pauline hermeneutics—that is, the use and interpretation of Pauline Scripture by blacks—have impacted the religious thought and experience of many African Americans and have been employed by them to resist oppression and to protest dehumanization. The ensuing exploration will examine the various interpretive lenses that blacks utilize to understand the apostle and to apply his words to their lives and circumstances. For example, in the narratives and autobiographies of the enslaved, readers will get a sense of these authors' precarious existences and catch glimpses into how some enslaved Africans weave Paul's writings into the fabric of their lives, how they weave him into their own stories, and how they weave him into their own contexts. In the depths of pain, sorrow, torture, and dehumanization, many African Americans reach for Paul's words, seize his language to give language to their own voices, and take up his writings to give meaning to their own horrid stories. The subsequent discussion will allow us, by glimpsing their lives, to understand how Paul fits into their realities, how they fit into Paul's story, and at the same time how they transform Pauline texts and make them their own.

The Significance of Pauline African American Interpreters in Reception History

Why does this book focus only on Paul and not on the use of Scripture in its entirety by African Americans? The letters of Paul played an enormous role in justifying slavery and promoting slavery as a Christian practice. Paul's words were central to the debate between those who advocated slavery and those abolitionists who fought against slaveholding. Because his words were used to justify their enslavement, blacks have had a complex relationship with the apostle, with some choosing to reject this part of Scripture altogether and others deciding to read his words in a more liberative way. Even today this complicated relationship remains, and the apostle continues to have a great deal of influence in African American Christian communities.

Historically, many blacks felt connected to Paul and his writings, for they perceived in his words language that spoke to their own life circumstances, which enabled them to endure but also resist the status quo. African Americans engaged in a reclamation or resistance hermeneutic in which they reclaimed Paul for themselves in their fight and struggle against injustice and asserted their use of him in their resistance of racism. The enormous amount of attention black authors gave to Paul, as seen by the many citations and echoes of his work in their writings, underscores the pivotal place the apostle played in the debate about slavery as well as these authors' own beliefs in his letters as Holy Scripture, which needed and called for their reflections and expositions. This combination of the massive number of references to Paul or his letters and blacks' identification of these writings as sacred makes African American interpretations of Paul and his epistles significant resources for historical, religious, theological, and biblical conversations in contemporary discussions.

Exploring African American interpretations of Paul and his writings is a noteworthy undertaking both for what we can learn from these interpreters and because of the increase in reception history discussions in biblical scholarship. One of the tenets of *Wirkungsgeschichte*, or reception history, is that "biblical texts not only have their own particular backgrounds and settings but have also been received and interpreted, and have exerted influence or otherwise have had impact in countless religious, theological, and aesthetic settings."[9] The analysis of the interpretation of Paul and his influence among African Americans is an important aspect of the biblical reception project and will contribute greatly to this growing field of study. Thus, to extend *Wirkungsgeschichte* of Paul to African American interpreters is a necessary development in light of the historical presence of the apostle in black thought and reflection. Due to Paul's towering presence in black writings, these compilations deserve substantial consideration and investigation. Moreover, this project is needed because, to date, no monograph has been devoted exclusively to analyzing the use of Paul's letters among blacks with a historical, theological, and biblical focus. Such a project is important for documenting the intersection of black religious life with American religious life because black religious life and experience are deeply woven into the

---

9. Hans-Josef Klauck, ed., *Encyclopedia of the Bible and Its Reception* (Berlin: de Gruyter, 2009), ix.

fabric of American religious life. If this issue is not examined, an important piece of American religious history will be ignored, since Paul's words appear throughout history in various documents, essays, and narratives written by black Americans.

' *Previous Scholarship*

African Americans have been studying and utilizing the Bible for hundreds of years. Yet with the rather recent increase in the number of African Americans entering the academy to study Scripture in the guild, important volumes on black scriptural interpretation have been written and have extensively shaped the academic landscape of biblical studies. Charles Copher, one of the founders of African American biblical interpretation, established the African presence in the Bible perspective, and in the 1980s monographs by Renita Weems, *Just a Sister Away: A Womanist Vision of Women's Relationships in the Bible*, and Cain Hope Felder, *Troubling Biblical Waters: Race, Class, and Family*, addressed biblical interpretation through black women's experiences and black scriptural interpretation regarding the issues of race, class, and family, respectively.[10] These three scholars' groundbreaking works help set the course of subsequent black biblical interpretation. *Stony the Road We Trod: African American Biblical Interpretation*, published in 1991, consists of a collection of articles written by black scholars that reveal the wide variety of hermeneutical strategies utilized by African American biblical scholars as well as the emerging questions and issues specific to black scholars and the black church.[11]

In the beginning of the twenty-first century, several additional significant monographs appeared. In 2000, a notable massive tome entitled *African*

10. Charles B. Copher, "Three Thousand Years of Biblical Interpretation with Reference to Black Peoples," in *African American Religious Studies: An Interdisciplinary Anthology*, ed. Gayraud S. Wilmore (Durham, NC: Duke University Press, 1989), 105–28; Charles B. Copher, *Black Biblical Studies: An Anthology of Charles B. Copher; Biblical and Theological Issues on the Black Presence in the Bible* (Chicago: Black Light Fellowship, 1993); Renita J. Weems, *Just a Sister Away: A Womanist Vision of Women's Relationships in the Bible* (San Diego: LuraMedia, 1988); Cain Hope Felder, *Troubling Biblical Waters: Race, Class, and Family*, Bishop Henry McNeal Turner Studies in North American Black Religion, vol. 3 (Maryknoll, NY: Orbis, 1989); see also Cain Hope Felder, *Race, Racism, and the Biblical Narratives* (Minneapolis: Fortress, 2002).

11. Cain Hope Felder, ed., *Stony the Road We Trod: African American Biblical Interpretation* (Minneapolis: Fortress, 1991).

Americans and the Bible: Sacred Texts and Social Structures was published.[12] In this collection of essays, edited by Vincent Wimbush, a variety of scholars address the role of the Bible in African American culture and how blacks have utilized the Bible in diverse ways in different arenas of their lives, such as in music and literature. In 2003, Randall Bailey edited and published *Yet with a Steady Beat: Contemporary U.S. Afrocentric Biblical Interpretation*, which includes a collection of essays on scriptural interpretation and the many interpretive strategies employed by black biblical scholars at the turn of the century.[13] *Blackening of the Bible: The Aims of African-American Biblical Scholarship*, by Michael Joseph Brown, published in 2004, provides a vital introduction to the field of black biblical interpretation, and Allen Callahan's innovative project, *The Talking Book: African Americans and the Bible*, published in 2006, provides four themes that he believes shape African Americans' experiences with Scripture: exile, exodus, Ethiopia, and Emmanuel.[14] *True to Our Native Land*, another consequential volume, appeared in 2007. Edited by Brian Blount, Cain Hope Felder, Clarice J. Martin, and Emerson Powery, it is the first African American New Testament commentary, analyzing each New Testament book from an African American perspective.[15] This substantial work includes a number of black scholars and interpretive postures, including womanist biblical hermeneutics. *The Africana Bible*, published in 2010, covers the Hebrew Bible, Pseudepigrapha, and apocryphal writings from African and African diasporic perspectives.[16] Most recently, two additional, important monographs appeared. In *The Genesis of Liberation: Biblical Interpretation in the Antebellum Narratives of the Enslaved*, Emerson Powery and Rodney Sadler examine the ways in which enslaved Africans interpreted Scripture and the role of the Bible in the slave debate.[17] And Stephanie Crowder explores maternity throughout the Old

12. Vincent Wimbush, ed., *African Americans and the Bible: Sacred Texts and Social Structures* (New York: Continuum, 2000).

13. Randall Bailey, ed., *Yet with a Steady Beat: Contemporary U.S. Afrocentric Biblical Interpretation*, Semeia Studies (Atlanta: Society of Biblical Literature, 2003).

14. Michael Joseph Brown, *Blackening of the Bible: The Aims of African-American Biblical Scholarship* (Harrisburg, PA: Trinity Press International, 2004); Allen Dwight Callahan, *The Talking Book: African Americans and the Bible* (New Haven: Yale University Press, 2006).

15. Brian Blount et al., eds., *True to Our Native Land: An African American New Testament Commentary* (Minneapolis: Fortress, 2007).

16. Hugh Page and Randall Bailey, eds., *The Africana Bible: Reading Israel's Scriptures from Africa and the African Diaspora* (Minneapolis: Fortress, 2010).

17. Emerson Powery and Rodney Sadler, *The Genesis of Liberation: Biblical In-*

and New Testament through a womanist lens in *When Momma Speaks: The Bible and Motherhood from a Womanist Perspective.*[18]

Chapters, essays, and articles about African American interpretations of Paul and his letters appear in many of the works identified above, all of which focus more broadly on black scriptural interpretation. The present monograph is needed because most discussions of African Americans' interpretations of Paul and his epistles occur within larger works on African American biblical hermeneutics. The focus on Paul is limited in these works by the structure and scope of the various projects. The current examination is indebted to the aforementioned studies and will interact with some of them at various points in the subsequent analysis.

Additionally, two monographs, written by two African American New Testament scholars, Brad Braxton and Love Sechrest, focus explicitly on Paul. In *No Longer Slaves: Galatians and African American Experience*, Braxton concentrates on liberating and empowering aspects of the Galatian text for black communities. Utilizing a reader-response methodology, he argues that Paul's language in the letter centers on Christian unity in the midst of difference. Thus, Paul's rejection of the need for gentile circumcision means that gentile identity continues and that in this new creation there is no "obliteration of difference but obliteration of dominance,"[19] for unity does not mean sameness. Paul, then, affirms blackness in all its forms and at the same time rejects racial hierarchies and supremacy.

In her book *A Former Jew: Paul and the Dialectics of Race*, Love Sechrest looks at almost five thousand ancient Jewish and non-Jewish texts in regard to ethnic and racial identity. Using historical and literary methodologies, she presents an analysis of ancient understandings of race and ethnicity and how these perspectives shape Paul's own understanding of race. One of her primary arguments is that Paul operates with a different understanding of "the nature of ethnic and racial identity" than what is found in modern discourse.[20] She then brings the evidence of this research into conversation with modern understandings of race, contending that scholars often un-

---

terpretation in the Antebellum Narratives of the Enslaved (Louisville: Westminster John Knox, 2016).

18. Stephanie Crowder, *When Momma Speaks: The Bible and Motherhood from a Womanist Perspective* (Louisville: Westminster John Knox, 2016).

19. Brad Braxton, *No Longer Slaves: Galatians and African American Experience* (Collegeville, MN: Liturgical Press, 2002), 90, 94.

20. Love Sechrest, *A Former Jew: Paul and the Dialectics of Race* (New York: T&T Clark, 2009), 226.

derestimate the "radical nature of the transformation of identity in Pauline thought."[21] In fact, the transformation of identity is so radical in Paul that he believes those who follow Christ "suspend the bonds of allegiance to their birth identity" and become part of a new race, that of Christian.[22] The work of Braxton and Sechrest makes significant contributions to understanding Paul in terms of race and identity, particularly from the perspectives of two African American specialists in the New Testament field of Pauline studies.

The present analysis differs methodologically and in scope of content from Braxton, Sechrest, and all the works listed above, for none of these previous compositions provides a comprehensive study that traces a historical trajectory of black thought and reflection upon the apostle from the 1700s to the mid-twentieth century, as this project will do. This book (1) consists of a historical trajectory from the 1700s to the mid-twentieth century, (2) concentrates solely on African American Pauline hermeneutics, and therefore can be more in-depth in this regard, and (3) engages the use of Paul's language in enslaved Africans' conversion experiences. These previous significant studies contribute to the conversation about African American interpretations of Paul and lay the foundations for the subsequent work through their engagement of black biblical interpretation. Although building upon these works in a number of ways, the current study differs from them in method, focus, and scope.

Methodology

The core question this study seeks to address is how African Americans have interpreted Paul and the Pauline epistles from the 1700s to the mid-twentieth century. Thus, this investigation will not present one correct reading of Paul from an African American perspective but rather will shed light on the many insights of black interpreters who read, preached, and studied Paul's letters and will allow their voices and ideas to come to the forefront. This analysis, then, delineates African American interpretive postures to the apostle and his epistles on their own terms and in their own expressions as much as possible. Hence, the citation of primary texts is central to the present project, and so the reader will find extensive quotations from these primary sources in what follows. These citations are necessary for understanding these au-

---

21. Sechrest, *A Former Jew*, 226.
22. Sechrest, *A Former Jew*, 230–31. See especially 113–31.

thors' use of Paul, the Scriptures they cite and echo, and the portrait of Paul they paint in their own words. Moreover, these excerpts bear witness to the eloquence and sophisticated textures of these interpreters' voices.

As will be observed repeatedly in this book, however, often these writers do not explain their interpretive processes or their hermeneutical decisions. In some cases, genre plays a role in the absence of this information, such as in the writing of petitions. Yet there are occasions in the African American literature where writers do explain how they interpret Paul's letters and what their aims entail, and we will observe these hermeneutical considerations when they appear. Nonetheless, in many instances, because of the environment in which these writers lived and worked, they simply asserted their use of Paul with no exegetical or hermeneutical explanations of their interpretive processes. Reasons for these omissions range from the types of documents written, to the urgency of the moment in which they were written, to the danger of writers losing their lives if they did explain how they were interpreting Paul. One significant example of the latter is Jupiter Hammon, who preached to mixed audiences, consisting of both enslaved Africans and slaveholders, and so had to be careful about how he preached and interpreted Paul to his audiences. He often had to be clever enough in his preaching that blacks would understand the nuances of what he was saying while white slaveholders would miss his subtle calls for freedom and equality.[23] Accordingly, in light of the variety of circumstances of the authors discussed in this book, another important aim of this work is to reveal the various portraits of Paul found within these authors' texts and to showcase the multifaceted ways the apostle has been understood throughout the years in black communities in terms of their own historical locations, theological beliefs, and biblical interpretations.

The current analysis revolves around a central tenet that most of these authors raise in their Pauline hermeneutics, that is, the relationship between their rich, provocative, and defiant adoptions and adaptations of the apostle Paul and the way in which they understood his letters as sacred Scripture—as texts to be engaged, examined, and proclaimed as protests against evil and injustice. The sacredness of these letters mattered to these interpreters and provided the divine impetus to utilize the apostle to resist and protest injus-

---

23. Sondra O'Neale, *Jupiter Hammon and the Biblical Beginnings of African-American Literature* (Metuchen, NJ: ATLA and Scarecrow Press, 1993), 2–4; Arien Nydam, "Numerological Tradition in the Works of Jupiter Hammon," *African American Review* 40, no. 2 (Summer 2006): 209.

tice and oppression. Just as the sacredness of these letters mattered to these interpreters, these interpreters, in seeing themselves in Pauline Scripture, understood that they too mattered in God's divine economy and that this understanding had ethical, social, and political implications.

The subsequent research demonstrates the overwhelmingly positive role that Paul plays in African American Pauline hermeneutics. Again and again we will see how black interpreters take up Paul's voice and use him to protest and resist injustice. However, we will meet two interpreters who, in the vein of Howard Thurman's grandmother, choose to resist Paul and Pauline Scripture. They, too, are a part of African American Pauline hermeneutics, for their rejection of him is based upon their interpretation of who he is and what he has meant for black communities throughout history. These figures notwithstanding, this monograph will focus primarily upon what is most common in African American autobiographies, essays, sermons, and petitions, that is, the positive adoption and adaptation of Paul and blacks' use of his words in the protest tradition.

Many of the authors chosen for this monograph are thought provoking and subversive when it comes to the apostle Paul and his letters. They utilize his work to protest and resist white supremacy, slavery, the slave trade, black dehumanization, and male-centered readings that prohibit women preachers, and in doing so, they select Paul as a source to speak to black and black female identity in a positive way. These authors are representatives of their period regarding the types of subversive readings of Paul taking place in their historical contexts. Many engage in subversive ways of reading Paul that were revolutionary for their own time, place, and audience. Furthermore, many were significant personalities in American history working to effect change through their voices. The interpreters selected have written or dictated substantial prose works, either autobiographies, sermons, essays, conversion stories, or books, that facilitate a context in which to understand how they employ the apostle in their writings in a radical manner. Each work or person included is introduced with some brief historical information, if available, and selected material follows with interpretive analysis. If necessary, additional historical information may appear in order to add context to the work and or person discussed.

Not all the black hermeneuts that meet the above criteria are included in the following pages. As stated above, I have chosen representative figures of subversive readings of Paul. Numerous individuals and writings that interpret Paul in subversive ways, specifically in regard to racism against African Americans, have been omitted from detailed analysis due to space and time.

As research for this project unfolded, it became clear that there simply was no way to include every author and every writing that employs Paul and his letters. Such omissions do not in any way reflect a lack of significance on their part. They do, however, represent, to this author's mind, the vast amount of work yet to be done in African American Pauline hermeneutics. This monograph attempts to contribute to the overall conversation about Paul and African Americans and to illustrate the historical legacy of subversive Pauline hermeneutics by blacks as well as spur more interest and research in this field. This book can be thought of as an introductory volume to the field of African American Pauline hermeneutics.

The book proceeds in the following manner: chapter 1, "Early Eighteenth Century to Early Nineteenth Century," begins by exploring the historical, biblical, and theological landscape of early America and continues by examining enslaved Africans' petitions and analyzing their authors' use of Paul in their government documents. The discussion then turns to early African American interpreters, Jupiter Hammon, Lemuel Haynes, John Jea, and David Walker, who in many ways forge the foundation for later black scriptural hermeneutics in their use of Paul to defy many of the oppressive interpretations of Paul occurring during this time. This chapter also analyzes the use of Paul by early black women preachers Jarena Lee and Zilpha Elaw, who, because of their gender and race, faced dangerous circumstances but risked their lives anyway to preach the gospel. Their important writings anticipate a long trajectory in viewing Paul as an ally to female preachers.

As the debates over slavery in this country became increasingly caustic and contentious, the stories of slavery from African Americans who were able to escape it became all the more critical because they informed the world of the horrors taking place in this practice. Chapter 2, "Mid-Nineteenth Century to Late Nineteenth Century," discusses how such escapees from slavery, such as James Pennington and Harriet Jacobs, use Pauline language to tell their stories in profound ways. It also discusses Daniel Payne, a free black, who heads north because of the South's slavocracy. In addition, during this time black women preachers like Maria Stewart and Julia Foote continue the traditions of Jarena Lee and Zilpha Elaw in employing Paul to sanction their right and call to preach.

Once slavery is abolished, African Americans are forced to reckon with its legacy in a variety of forms, including Jim Crow and segregation. In the group of writings discussed in chapter 3, "Late Nineteenth Century to Mid-Twentieth Century," authors such as Howard Thurman and Albert Cleage speak candidly about their rejection of Paul because of his use in the slave debate, whereas others, like Reverdy Ransom, William Seymour, Charles Harrison Mason, Ida B. Robinson, and Martin Luther King Jr., employ him fervently to argue against racism, segregation, and lynching. Seymour, Mason, and Robinson also contend that Paul's words about the Spirit can bring new life, healing, and racial unity. Paul was instrumental in Mason's protest against war.

In chapter 4, "Pauline Language in Enslaved Conversion Experiences and Call Narratives," accounts by ex-slaves of their conversion experiences and their call to preach are analyzed in regard to Pauline language. We find these powerful narratives in a volume entitled *God Struck Me Dead*, in which formerly enslaved Africans tell of their dramatic conversions to Christianity and God's call upon their lives to proclaim the gospel.

Chapter 5, "African American Pauline Hermeneutics and the Art of Biblical Interpretation," raises and answers several important questions: What does reception history look like for African Americans when it comes to Paul and his writings? What common themes emerge in this study, and how do these themes impact biblical interpretation at large? What are some possible next steps in engaging African American Pauline hermeneutics, this important aspect of biblical reception history? This area is a rich and unmined field full of potential, and so the last section of this chapter will explore briefly some of these possibilities.

With all this in mind, this research examines an array of primary source material from a range of African American authors whose writings are political, theological, biblical, historical, and rhetorical. The beauty of these texts is that many of them combine all these elements, which enables one to see the hermeneutical features so prominent in these authors' works. Readers will gain a sense of these authors' times and places and gain a glimpse into their world and how the apostle Paul affects it and how it affects the apostle Paul. For these black hermeneuts, Pauline hermeneutics is not a neutral undertaking where reading Paul is a leisure activity or an exercise. Rather, in many cases reading, writing about, or preaching Paul had life-or-death consequences with significant implications in the authors' lives and in the lives of those in their respective communities. Hence, engaging Paul was neither a mere intellectual endeavor nor a hobby to pass the time, but it had real-life consequences that spoke to current debates that affected African American existence.

CHAPTER 1

Early Eighteenth Century
to Early Nineteenth Century

But God hath chosen the weak things of the world to confound the mighty.
Divine goodness raised me and honoured me as an angel of God.[1]

During the eighteenth and early nineteenth centuries, a variety of laws and legislation were passed to subjugate blacks and to enforce the belief that blacks were either less than human or, if human, of an inferior lot.[2] For instance, in 1787 the US Constitution declared an enslaved African to count as three-fifths of a person, and between 1830 and 1860, Southern states increasingly prohibited manumission, expelled freed blacks, eliminated black churches, and ignored penalties for hurting or killing blacks.[3] Views of black inferiority and black inhumanity were propagated widely and believed by many people across the spectrum of society. Indeed, many who adhered to such understandings taught that Scripture, which was central to the discussion about slavery at the time, upheld these perspectives. As discussed above in the introduction, proponents of slavery employed Paul's words

1. *Memoirs of the Life, Religious Experience, Ministerial Travels and Labours of Mrs. Zilpha Elaw, an American Female of Colour: Together with Some Account of the Great Religious Revivals in America [Written By Herself]* (London: Published by the authoress, 1846) (hereafter Elaw, *Memoirs*), reprinted in *Sisters of the Spirit: Three Black Women's Autobiographies of the Nineteenth Century*, ed. William L. Andrews (Bloomington: Indiana University Press, 1986), 92.

2. Portions of this chapter appear in Lisa Bowens, "Liberating Paul: African Americans' Use of Paul in Resistance and Protest," in *Practicing with Paul: Reflections on Paul and the Practices of Ministry in Honor of Susan G. Eastman*, ed. Presian Burroughs (Eugene, OR: Wipf & Stock, 2018), 57–73.

3. Yuval Taylor, introduction to *I Was Born a Slave: An Anthology of Classic Slave Narratives*, vol. 1, *1772–1849*, ed. Yuval Taylor (Chicago: Lawrence Hill Books, 1999), xxvi.

to justify slavery, but a common belief during this time was that the story of Ham in Genesis 9:18–27 sanctioned slavery as well. Proponents of slavery proclaimed that Ham was the originator of the black race and that the curse Noah pronounced upon Canaan referred to God's ordination of blacks' enslavement. In *Slavery as It Relates to the Negro or African Race*, written in 1843, Josiah Priest, a proslavery advocate, represents well the prevalent sentiments of the time regarding this passage of Scripture. Priest writes:

> The appointment of this [Negro] race of men to servitude and slavery was a judicial act of God, or in other words was a divine judgment. There are three evidences of this, which are as follows:
>
> First—The fact of their being created or produced in a lower order of intellectuality than either of the other races . . . is evidence of the preordination of their fate as slaves on the earth as none but God could have done or determined this thing.
>
> Second—The announcement of God by the mouth of Noah, relative to the whole race of Ham, pointing out in so many words in the clearest and most specific manner, that they were adjudged to slavery . . . that they were foreordained and appointed to the condition they hold among men by the divine mind, solely on account of the foreseen character they would sustain as a race, who, therefore were thus judicially put beneath the supervision of the other races.
>
> Third—The great and everywhere pervading fact of their degraded condition, both now and in all time . . . that the negro race as a people, are judicially given over to a state or peculiar liability of being enslaved by the other races.[4]

Priest captures the white supremacist scriptural hermeneutics of his period in these passages. Because blacks descended from Ham, as this interpretation goes, their slavery was ordained and appointed by God, and the evidence of this preordained status is their intellectual inferiority, the prophetic utterance of Noah's curse, and their degraded condition, which demonstrates that their enslavement lasts for all time. Priest repeatedly affirms the lasting nature of this curse in his work, writing that the curse "not only covered the person and fortunes of Ham, but that of his whole posterity also, to the very end of time."[5]

---

4. Josiah Priest, *Slavery as It Relates to the Negro or African Race* (Albany, NY: C. Van Benthuysen & Co., 1843), 83.

5. Priest, *Slavery as It Relates*, 78.

Priest's interpretation of this passage also reinforced another prevalent stereotype of the period, which was the inferior and evil character of blacks. He states: "The curse, therefore, against Ham and his race was not sent out on the account of that *one* sin only. But . . . was in unison with his *whole* life, character, and constitutional make *prior* to that deed, the curse which had slumbered long was let loose upon him and his posterity . . . placing them under the ban of slavery, on account of his and their foreseen characters."[6] Priest contends that Ham's character was always deficient and that his act merely brought about the inevitable curse. In an interesting "exegetical" move here, Priest aligns Ham's character with that of his descendants. Just as Ham's character was always evil and morally corrupt, so too is the character of all his posterity. According to Priest, Noah uttered this curse through the power of the Holy Spirit, demonstrating God's knowledge of Ham's character and that of all his future generations. Therefore, God's ordination of blacks' enslavement is just because their character necessitates it. The ramifications for perception of blacks in these interpretations are significant, for such interpretations promote the notions that blacks are unintelligent, evil, and cursed by divine decree to eternal enslavement. Corresponding to this view, many Southern preachers proclaimed that the curse of Canaan was a curse of black skin as well as perpetual slavery. Augustin Calmet related, in his popular dictionary, that Ham's skin became black upon Noah's pronouncement of a curse on Canaan and Ham.[7]

One cannot underestimate the prevalence of such beliefs in society during this time. For example, a group of Southern petitioners wrote in their document that "We of the South understand the Negro character. We know that naturally they are indolent, lazy, improvident, destitute of forethought, and totally incapable of self government."[8] John Saffin, considered today one

6. Priest, *Slavery as It Relates*, 79.
7. Augustin Calmet, *Calmet's Great Dictionary of the Holy Bible*, vol. 4 (Charlestown: Samuel Etheridge, 1812), 21. An earlier edition, 1797, of this dictionary is quoted in Emerson Powery and Rodney Sadler, *The Genesis of Liberation: Biblical Interpretation in the Antebellum Narratives of the Enslaved* (Louisville: Westminster John Knox, 2016), 86. Another common interpretation of this period was the belief that the mark God placed upon Cain in Gen. 4:15 was black skin. This belief was so common that Priest, *Slavery as It Relates*, refers to it in his book: "Others have imagined that the mark set upon Cain by the Divine Power, for the crime of homicide, was that of jet, which not only changed the color of his body, but extended to the blood and the whole of his physical being, thus originating the negro race" (iv).
8. Race, Slavery, and Free Blacks petition, South Carolina Department of Archives and History, Columbia, South Carolina, https://library.uncg.edu/slavery/petitions/details.aspx?pid=1645.

of the important minor poets in Massachusetts in the seventeenth century who is also well known for his debate with Samuel Sewell over slavery, wrote a poem published in 1701 that captures well the perceptions of blacks that permeated the culture. The poem, entitled "The Negroes Character," reads as follows:

> Cowardly and cruel are those blacks innate,
> Prone to revenge, imp of inveterate hate.
> He that exasperates them, soon espies
> Mischief and murder in their very eyes.
> Libidinous, deceitful, false and rude,
> The spume issue of ingratitude
> The premises consider'd, all may tell
> How near good "Joseph" they are parallel.[9]

Saffin, like Priest, forefronts common beliefs of the period that blacks are inherently vicious, hateful, and full of everything that those traits entail, such as being murderous and prone to lying. Saffin contradicts Sewell, his conversation partner, who had rejected slavery because he believed adhering to slavery was akin to Joseph's brothers selling him into slavery (Gen. 37). Saffin argues against Sewell, sardonically stating that blacks cannot be compared to "good 'Joseph.'" Their character precludes such an association.

Underlying the scriptural exegesis of people like Priest and the perspectives of the Southern petitioners and Saffin was a deep-seated belief in the inferiority of blacks. Thomas Jefferson shared such views, writing of blacks, "Comparing them by their faculties of memory, reason, and imagination, it appears to me, that in memory they are equal to the whites; in reason much inferior, as I think one could scarcely be found capable of tracing and comprehending the investigations of Euclid; and that in imagination they are dull, tasteless, and anomalous."[10] And again he states, "I advance it therefore as a suspicion only, that the blacks, whether originally a

---

9. John Saffin, *A Brief and Candid Answer*, http://global.oup.com/us/companion.web sites/fdscontent/uscompanion/us/static/companion.websites/9780199338863/whitting ton_updata/ch_2_saffin_a_brief_and_candid_answer.pdf. Also quoted in Sondra O'Neale, *Jupiter Hammon and the Biblical Beginnings of African-American Literature* (Metuchen, NJ: ATLA and Scarecrow Press, 1993), 25.

10. Thomas Jefferson, *Notes on the State of Virginia* (Philadelphia: Pritchard & Hall, 1787), 149, https://docsouth.unc.edu/southlit/jefferson/jefferson.html#p138.

distinct race, or made distinct by time and circumstances, are inferior to the whites in the endowments both of body and mind."[11] Consequently, for Jefferson both color and faculty cast doubt on the possibility of freedom for the slaves, as he asserts, "This unfortunate difference of colour, and perhaps of faculty, is a powerful obstacle to the emancipation of these people."[12] As indicated by these quotes, Jefferson adhered to the idea of white superiority. Moreover, the idea of black inferiority coupled with depictions of blacks as dangerous, as seen in the Saffin poem, meant that for whites black movement needed supervision and monitoring. In 1786 a Delaware group petitioned the legislature "to more rigorously regulate the movements of people of color" because "many idle and evil-disposed slaves throughout this County" move throughout the area, "some with and some without passes or Certificates." These petitioners asked for the creation of a law that forbade blacks from traveling from one county to another without some sort of written or printed pass, or certificate.[13] The notions that blacks were not only inferior but also dangerous permeated the body politic. The *Democratic Standard*, a newspaper in Concord, New Hampshire, summed up all these convictions well: "To us, the proposition that the negro is equal by nature, physically and mentally, to the white man, seems to be so absurd and preposterous, that we cannot conceive how it can be entertained by any intelligent and rational white man."[14] These statements of Jefferson, the newspaper quote, along with the words of Priest, the Delaware and Southern petitioners, and Saffin provide salient snapshots into the environment of the time regarding racism and slavery.[15] In such an atmosphere, laced with this prevalent type of scrip-

11. Jefferson, *Notes on the State of Virginia*, 153.

12. Jefferson, *Notes on the State of Virginia*, 154. At the same time that Jefferson believed in the superiority of whites and the differences between the two races, he also believed that if blacks were freed, they would have to be colonized "to such place as the circumstances of the time should render most proper" (147).

13. Loren Schweninger and Robert Shelton, eds., *Race, Slavery, and Free Blacks: Series I, Petitions to Southern Legislatures, 1777–1867*, microfilm project of University Publications of America (Bethesda, MD). Petition cited is from Reel 1.0014.

14. *Democratic Standard* (Concord, NH), September 8, 1860, quoted by Eugene H. Berwanger, "Negrophobia in Northern Proslavery and Antislavery Thought," *Phylon* 33, no. 3 (Fall 1972): 268.

15. The idea of black inferiority was not limited to Southern white society but was shared by many white Northerners as well, even among those who advocated the abolishment of slavery. See the discussion in James Oliver Horton and Lois E. Horton, "The Affirmation of Manhood: Black Garrisonians in Antebellum Boston," in *Courage and Con-*

tural exegesis and attitudes about blacks, Paul's admonition of "Slaves, obey your masters" (Eph. 6:5; Col. 3:22) cohered well. Whites depicted the apostle as merely endorsing what was "evident" from Genesis and sanctioning common beliefs about African Americans' character and nature.

Slavery advocates' distorted use of Scripture and the laws they implemented, which they believed to be sanctioned by the Bible, sought to prevent or limit enslaved Africans' access to Scripture and thereby underscored "one of the greatest fears of slaveholding society: that religion, if taught honestly, was full of revolutionary possibilities."[16] Although sometimes slaveholders permitted black ministers to preach to the enslaved Africans, more often than not white ministers preached to them, and the message they proclaimed was "Slaves, obey your masters." When black preachers did preach to the slaves, they had to be careful what they proclaimed, as indicated in the following testimonial of Anderson Edwards, an enslaved preacher: "I been preachin' the Gospel and farmin' since slavery time. . . . When I starts preachin' I couldn't read or write and had to preach what massa told me and he say tell them [n——] iffen they obeys the massa they goes to Heaven but I knowed there's something better for them, but daren't tell them 'cept on the sly. That I done lots. I tell 'em iffen they keeps prayin' the Lord will set 'em free."[17] This black preacher dared to proclaim the true gospel to his fellow enslaved Africans because he "knowed" there was more to the gospel than what the slave owner wanted him to proclaim. That slaveholders tried to derail and control African Americans' access to the Bible testifies to the liberating potential of the scriptural text.

Remarkably, despite the repeated attempts of slaveholders to drill into the hearts and minds of enslaved Africans, through Scripture, that God appointed slavery for them, many enslaved Africans refused to believe it. Albert Raboteau writes about enslaved Africans' resolve regarding this issue: "In opposition to the slaveholder's belief, the slave believed that slavery was surely contrary to the will of God. John Hunter, a fugitive from slavery in Maryland, attested to this belief: 'I have heard poor ignorant slaves, that did

science: Black and White Abolitionists in Boston, ed. Donald M. Jacobs (Bloomington: Indiana University Press, 1993), 137–38, and Berwanger, "Negrophobia," 266–75.

16. Yolanda Pierce, *Hell without Fires: Slavery, Christianity, and the Antebellum Spiritual Narrative* (Gainesville: University Press of Florida, 2005), 41.

17. George P. Rawick, ed., *The American Slave: A Composite Autobiography*, 41 vols. (Westport, CT: Greenwood, 1972), part 2, vol. 4:9; also quoted in Albert Raboteau, *Slave Religion: The "Invisible Institution" in the Antebellum South* (New York: Oxford University Press, 1978), 232.

not know A from B, say that they did not believe the Lord ever intended they should be slaves, and that they did not see how it should be so.'"[18]

In the midst of Pauline interpretations that repeatedly deemed them as destined for slavery and designed for such a life, blacks resisted by engaging in their own hermeneutical delineations, for "African Americans have struggled for more than two centuries to reinterpret and revise a distorted gospel received from White Christians."[19] Part of this reinterpretation and revision involved snatching Paul from the hands of white slaveholders and employing him in the liberation fight.

In her essay "Paul and the African American Community," C. Michelle Venable-Ridley states that one of her goals is "not to redeem but to reclaim the writings of Paul as a religious source for the African American community."[20] The present project reveals that historically many African Americans considered Paul's words to be a redemptive force, and so he became a religious as well as a political resource for them. For these interpreters the religious and the political were intricately linked and could not be separated, and Paul's words provided spiritual nourishment and the biblical basis to protest unjust laws and to resist the dehumanization of slavery promulgated by the distorted gospel of white Christian slaveholders and preachers. These rich, early interpretive trajectories of African American Pauline hermeneutics provide an important glimpse into Paul's significance in the black struggle for justice.

Early Petitions for Freedom and Liberty That Cite Paul

As early as 1774, enslaved Africans interpreted Paul to argue their case for freedom and liberty. Below is a petition written to the governor, council, and representatives of Massachusetts, with Pauline references italicized:

18. Raboteau, *Slave Religion*, 309.

19. C. Michelle Venable-Ridley, "Paul and the African American Community," in *Embracing the Spirit: Womanist Perspectives on Hope, Salvation, and Transformation*, ed. Emilie M. Townes (Maryknoll, NY: Orbis, 1997), 214.

20. Venable-Ridley, "Paul and the African American Community," 214. See also Abraham Smith's insightful essay on Paul and African Americans in "Paul and African American Biblical Interpretation," in *True to Our Native Land: An African American New Testament Commentary*, ed. Brian Blount et al. (Minneapolis: Fortress, 2007), 31–42; Abraham Smith, "Putting 'Paul' Back Together Again: William Wells Brown's *Clotel* and Black Abolitionist Approaches to Paul," *Semeia* 83–84 (1998): 251–62.

The Petition of a Grate Number of Blackes of this Province who by divine permission are held in a state of Slavery within the bowels of a free and christian Country Humbly Shewing

That your Petitioners apprehind we have in common with all other men a naturel right to our freedoms without Being depriv'd of them by our fellow men as we are a freeborn Pepel and have never forfeited this Blessing by aney compact or agreement whatever. But we were unjustly dragged by the cruel hand of power from our dearest frinds and sum of us stolen from the bosoms of our tender Parents and from a Populous Pleasant and plentiful country and Brought hither to be made slaves for Life in a Christian land. Thus are we deprived of every thing that hath a tendency to make life even tolerable, the endearing ties of husband and wife we are strangers to for we are no longer man and wife then our masters or mestreses thinkes proper marred or onmarred. Our children are also taken from us by force and sent maney miles from us wear we seldom or ever see them again there to be made slaves of for Life which sumtimes is vere short by Reson of Being dragged from their mothers Breest Thus our Lives are imbittered to us on these accounts By our deplorable situation we are rendered incapable of shewing our obedience to Almighty God *how can a slave perform the duties of a husband to a wife or parent to his child* How can a husband leave master and work and cleave to his wife *How can the wife submit themselves to there husbands in all things. How can the child obey thear parents in all things. There is a grat number of us sencear . . . members of the Church of Christ how can the master and the slave be said to fulfil that command Live in love let Brotherly Love contuner and abound Beare yea onenothers Bordenes How can the master be said to Beare my Borden when he Beares me down whith the Have chanes of slavery and operson against my will* and how can we fulfill our parte of duty to him whilst in this condition and as we cannot searve our God as we ought whilst in this situation Nither can we reap an equal benefet from the laws of the Land which doth not justifi but condemns Slavery or if there had bin aney Law to hold us in Bondege we are Humbely of the Opinon ther never was aney to inslave our children for life when Born in a free Countrey. We therefor Bage your Excellency and Honours will give this its deu weight and consideration and that you will accordingly cause an act of the legislative to be pessed that we may obtain our Natural right our freedoms and our children be set at lebety at the yeare of Twenty one for whoues sekes more petequeley your Petitioners is in Duty ever to Pray.[21]

21. Founders' Constitution, *Slave Petition*, 3:432–33. Portions of this petition are also

The disruptive nature of the gospel is evident in the enslaved Africans' powerful argument that slavery and Christianity are irreconcilable. How do these enslaved Africans argue for this incompatibility? They utilize Pauline language. Echoing Paul's call in Galatians 6:2 to believers to "Bear ye one another's burdens,"[22] they forcefully declare that slavery prevents the fulfillment of the apostle's words. By placing burdens upon enslaved Africans and creating the heavy chains of slavery and oppression, white slaveholders do the opposite of what the apostle commanded. Through their citation and interpretation of Galatians 6:2, these petitioners adamantly decree that slavery counteracts Christian behavior, for whites do not carry the burdens of their black brothers and sisters; instead they create them. Additionally, while slaveholders often begin and end their scriptural exegesis with Ephesians 6:5-6, Colossians 3:22-24, or 1 Timothy 6:1-2, these enslaved Africans maintain that true scriptural exegesis begins in Ephesians 5:22 (cf. Col. 3:18-20) with instructions to wives and continues until 6:4 with instructions to fathers. The practice of slavery, which separates family members from one another, violates all the household admonitions set forth by the apostle. Slavery, these petitioners exclaim, impedes husbands from loving their wives, wives from submitting to their husbands, and children from obeying and being instructed by their parents. The enslaved Africans skillfully raise the question of how they can love their wives and their children if they are taken from them. Slavery prohibits them from obeying almighty God in carrying out their Christian duties to their families. And these petitioners argue that serving God is the priority, not serving the slaveholder. In addition, freedom is a natural right, one they never forfeited. The apostle's words, these writers reason, condemn slavery and the actions of the white slaveholders; they do not condone them.

As the writers of the petition state, separation of black families was a painful norm for enslaved Africans. Henry "Box" Brown's account of this event in his own life provides a graphic description of enslaved Africans' reality. Upon learning that his family has been sold, he relates the following:

---

cited by Raboteau (*Slave Religion*, 290-91) and discussed in Allen Dwight Callahan, *The Talking Book: African Americans and the Bible* (New Haven: Yale University Press, 2006), 34-35. See also *A Documentary History of the Negro People in the United States*, ed. Herbert Aptheker, 3 vols. (New York: Citadel, 1951), 1:8-9. Pauline language appears in italics in this petition and in subsequent citations from primary texts.

22. Biblical quotations in this book come from the King James Version, unless otherwise indicated. This is the version used by all the interpreters in this book.

I received a message, that if I wished to see my wife and children, and bid them the last farewell, I could do so, by taking my stand on the street where they were all to pass on their way for North Carolina. I quickly availed myself of this information, and placed myself by the side of a street, and soon had the melancholy satisfaction of witnessing the approach of a gang of slaves, amounting to three hundred and fifty in number, marching under the direction of a methodist minister, by whom they were purchased, and amongst which slaves were my wife and children. . . . These beings were marched with ropes about their necks, and staples on their arms, and, although in that respect the scene was no very novel one to me, yet the peculiarity of my own circumstances made it assume the appearance of unusual horror. This train of beings was accompanied by a number of wagons loaded with little children of many different families, which as they appeared rent the air with their shrieks and cries and vain endeavours to resist the separation which was thus forced upon them, and the cords with which they were thus bound; but what should I now see in the very foremost wagon but a little child looking towards me and pitifully calling, father! father! This was my eldest child, and I was obliged to look upon it for the last time that I should, perhaps, ever see it again in life. . . . Thus passed my child from my presence—it was my own child—I loved it with all the fondness of a father; but things were so ordered that I could only say, farewell, and leave it to pass in its chains while I looked for the approach of another gang in which my wife was also loaded with chains. My eyes soon caught her precious face, but, gracious heavens! that glance of agony may God spare me from ever again enduring! My wife, under the influence of her feelings, jumped aside; I seized hold of her hand while my mind felt unutterable things, and my tongue was only able to say, we shall meet in heaven! I went with her for about four miles hand in hand, but both our hearts were so overpowered with feeling that we could say nothing, and when at last we were obliged to part, the look of mutual love which we exchanged was all the token which we could give each other that we should yet meet in heaven.[23]

23. *Narrative of the Life of Henry Box Brown, Written by Himself*, ed. John Ernest (Chapel Hill: University of North Carolina Press, 2008; original Manchester: Lee & Glynn, 1851), 80–81. Henry "Box" Brown received that nomenclature because of his extraordinary escape from slavery in a box that was shipped to the North. His riveting escape is recounted in his autobiography.

This vivid account of Brown's forced separation from his family provides a snapshot into what African Americans experienced routinely and provides a backdrop to the petitioners' use of Pauline family language in Ephesians and Colossians. They believed that this type of separation and dehumanization neither cohered with the apostle's words regarding family life nor aligned with God's plan for familial structure. Interestingly, all of this Pauline language occurs after the writers designate this country as "free and Christian." Such language frames their subsequent use of Paul. If this country is "free and Christian," then it is neglecting the apostle's words regarding the family. These writers resisted the prevalent notion that it was God's will for them to be enslaved and that they had to obey their masters by protesting whites' interpretation and use of Paul to justify enslaving them. Rather, they interpreted the apostle's words for themselves. We can extrapolate from both the historical environment of the time and the specific words of Paul that these writers chose to include in their requisition that their act of interpreting Paul on their own terms was an act of resistance and protest; an act that can be delineated for heuristic purposes in three ways: (1) They began their interpretation of Scripture where *they* wanted to begin (Eph. 5:22; Col. 3:18–20) and not where their white enslavers chose to begin. This meant they were "seizing hermeneutical control" of Pauline Scripture.[24] (2) They engaged in "exegetical reversal," disputing whites' ownership of Paul to sanction slavery, and instead proclaimed that Paul condemns slavery with his very words. (3) They appealed to familial language to undercut "slaveholding religion."[25]

This familial language resonated in two spheres: in the natural family and in the Christian family. The enslaved Africans insisted that their identity as members of biological families was primary; their identity as husbands, wives, and children negated American slave status. When Paul spoke of families, he included them, and so they insisted that the apostle recognized them as human beings with families that needed nurture and love like any other. Black families mattered, and by insisting on this truth they asserted their personhood and their humanity. In terms of the Christian family, these

---

24. Brad Braxton, *No Longer Slaves: Galatians and African American Experience* (Collegeville, MN: Liturgical Press, 2002), 12.

25. This phrase comes from Frederick Douglass, "Narrative of the Life of Frederick Douglass, an American Slave, Written by Himself," in *I Was Born a Slave*, 1:592, who makes a profound distinction between the Christianity of Christ and "slaveholding religion."

petitioners cited Hebrews 13:1: "Let brotherly love continue."[26] How can brotherly love coexist with the wretched practice of slavery? The two, these enslaved Africans contended, are mutually exclusive. In a similar vein, these writers recognized that their enslavement prohibited them from having a genuine Christian relationship with the slave owners, asking, "How can we fulfill our parte of duty to him whilst in this condition?" They recognized that slavery destroys natural familial relationships and Christian familial relationships, and this destruction is another dimension of the nullification of the Scripture "Let brotherly love continue." These authors maintained that the apostle supported their natural right to freedom, upheld their declaration that they should not be enslaved to anyone, and recognized the significance of blacks' familial relationships, both biological and Christian. To petition the governor and other governmental leaders with the apostle's words, the same apostle used to justify their enslavement, was a bold move for these early writers to make. It demonstrated that they recognized their agency in interpreting Scripture for themselves and their right to claim and proclaim this Holy Writ.

Similar to the petitioners in 1776, the slaves in Fairfield County, Connecticut, requested freedom from slavery in their state in 1779. The request reads as follows, again with references to Paul italicized:

> To the Honbl General Assembly of the State of Connecticut to be held at Hartford on the Second Thursday of Instant May
>
> The Petition of the Negroes in the Towns of Stratford and Fairfield in the County of Fairfield Who are held in a State of Slavery humbly sheweth—
>
> That many of your Petitioners, were (as they verily believe) most unjustly torn, from the Bosoms of their dear Parents, and Friends, and without any Crime, by them committed, doomed, and bound down, to perpetual Slavery; and as if the Perpetrators of this horrid Wickedness, were Conscious (that we poor Ignorant Africans, upon the least Glimmering Light, derived from a Knowledge of the Sense and Practice of civilized Nations) should Convince them of their Sin. they have added another dreadful Evil of holding us in gross Ignorance, so as to render Our Subjection more easy and tolerable. may it please your Honours, we are most grievously affected, under the Consideration of the flagrant Injustice;
>
> Your Honours who are nobly contending, in the Cause of Liberty,

---

26. During this time Paul was believed to be the author of Hebrews. Paul will be assumed to be the author of Hebrews throughout the book.

whose Conduct excites the Admiration, and Reverence, of all the great Empires of the World, will not resent our thus freely animadverting, on this detestable Practice; altho our Skins are different in Colour, from those who we serve, yet Reason & Revelation join to declare, that we are the Creatures of that *God who made of one Blood, and Kindred, all the Nations of the Earth*; we perceive by our own Reflection, that we are endowed, with the same Faculties, with our Masters, and there is nothing, that leads us to a Belief, or Suspicion, that we are any more obliged to serve them, than they us, and the more we Consider of this Matter, the more we are Convinced, of our Right (by the Law's of Nature and by the whole Tenor, of the Christian Religion, so far as we have been taught) to be free; we have Endeavoured rightly to understand, what is our Right, and what is our Duty, and can never be convinced, that we were made to be slaves Altho God almighty, may justly lay this, and more upon us, yet we deserve it not, from the hands of Men. we are impatient under the grievous Yoke, but our Reason teaches us, that it is not best for us, to use violent measures, to cast if off; we are also Convinced, that we are unable to extricate ourselves, from our abject State; but we think we May with the greatest Propriety, look up to your Honours, (who are the fathers of the People) for Relief. And We not only groan under our own Burden, but with Concern & Horror, look forward & Contemplate, the miserable Condition, of our Children, who are training up, and kept in Preparation, for a like State of Bondage, and Servitude. we beg leave to submit to your Honours serious Consideration, whether it is Consistent with the Present Claims, of the united States to hold so many Thousands, of the *Race of Adam, our Common Father*, in perpetual Slavery. Can human Nature endure the Shocking Idea? can your Honours any longer Suffer, this great Evil to prevail, under your Government? we entreat your Honours, let no Considerations of Publick Inconvenience, deter your Honours, from interposing in Behalf of your Petitioners; who ask for nothing, but what we are fully persuaded, is ours to Claim. we beseech your Honours, to weigh this Matter, in the Scale of Justice, and in your great Wisdom and Goodness, apply such Remedy, as the Evil does require; and let your Petitioners. rejoice with your Honours, in the Participation, with your Honours, of that inestimable Blessing,

Freedom and your Humble Petitioners, as in Duty bound, shall Ever pray & c. dated in Fairfield the 11th Day of May AD 1779.[27]

27. *Petition of 1779 by Slaves of Fairfield County*, Revolutionary War Papers, Connecticut State Library, 1:37:232.

Of the numerous significant insights offered by this powerful petition, several speak to our present purposes. First, the writers state unequivocally that they are "Creatures of that God who made of one Blood, and Kindred, all the Nations of the Earth." This statement echoes Paul's words in Acts 17:26, where the apostle declares to his audience the unity in God's creation of human beings, a declaration that became known as the "one blood doctrine."[28] A common refrain throughout African American protest literature, the apostle's words make an early appearance here in 1779. Emerson Powery and Rodney Sadler also note the prominence of this Pauline phrase in black literature.[29] Unlike modern scholars who make distinctions between the Paul of Acts, the Paul of the undisputed Pauline letters, and the Paul of the disputed Pauline letters, these writers and other black interpreters make no such distinctions. For them, all of these writings, including Hebrews, are legitimately Pauline. Thus, this Pauline passage enables the writers of this petition to claim that since God has made of one blood, and kindred, all the nations of this earth, God stands opposed to any white supremacy contention for black inferiority. Since God has unified all peoples, all blacks of this period could boldly declare, just as these writers did, that they have the "same faculties, with our Masters." For the enslaved to make such assertions and to place themselves on the same level as their masters was bold and risky.[30] Indeed, in contradistinction to Priest, Saffin, and others who held to their racist ideologies, these petitioners insisted that Paul's words undermined the prevalent claims of black subservience.

Second, the enslaved Africans challenged the predominant ideas that they were ordained to slavery by God, arguing that they "can never be convinced, that we were made to be Slaves." They maintained that perhaps God could put them into slavery but men could not, for they did not deserve slavery from other men. Here these enslaved Africans demonstrate an important distinction between human and divine will in the slave trade. Although whites were constantly asserting that the slave trade was God's

---

28. Callahan, *The Talking Book*, 115–16; Emerson Powery, "'Rise Up, Ye Women': Harriet Jacobs and the Bible," *Postscripts* 5, no. 2 (2009): 176; Demetrius Williams, "The Acts of the Apostles," in Blount, *True to Our Native Land*, 236–38.

29. Powery and Sadler, *The Genesis of Liberation*, 140–42.

30. Janet Duitsman Cornelius, *When I Can Read My Title Clear: Literacy, Slavery, and Religion in the Antebellum South* (Columbia: University of South Carolina Press, 1991), in her brief discussion of this petition notes that the writers link "freedom and knowledge" and that they see one of the horrors of slavery as "the master's deliberate withholding of knowledge from them" (23–24).

will, these enslaved Africans insisted that what was happening to them had nothing to do with God but was a system created by human beings, and they "deserve it not, from the hands of Men." They saw the slave trade as originating from the human realm and not the divine sphere; this hermeneutic rejected the interpretations of proslavery advocates. These African Americans were able to distinguish between a human-made institution and a divine mandate.

Third, the writers appealed to a common Adamic ancestry, for they too were of the "Race of Adam, our Common Father."[31] Whereas whites were intent on emphasizing blacks' descendancy from Ham, these writers focused on the creation story and Adam as the father of both blacks and whites. Since both races have a common father, one race enslaving the other is illogical. For these writers, shared paternity trumps any interpretive move that made central the supposed subsequent curse by Noah. Noah's curse cannot negate Adamic origin.

Finally, fourth, the authors of this petition boldly call slavery evil, wicked, and a sin. While many blacks and abolitionists used such language to describe slavery, many whites refused to see slavery and the slave trade in such terms. Rather, they chose to believe that the converse was true. For example, Alexander Stephens, proslavery advocate and vice president of the Confederacy, argued that the Old and New Testaments sanctioned slavery and that "The relation of master and slave, even in a much more abject condition than existed with us, is not founded in sin."[32] In the midst of such sentiments, these early interpreters, as indicated by their use of Paul in the petition, understood that the apostle's words dismantled the basis for the slave trade. Black and white were made of one blood, one kindred, and descended from one common ancestor, Adam. In the eyes of these interpreters, such truths meant that any basis for slavery and the slave trade was inconsistent with the Pauline message.

These petitions were written during the period of the American Revolution when talk of freedom and liberty abounded. The authors of these documents and other slave petitions believed that this was the time to seize their own right to freedom and to ask for such actions on their behalf. After all, as these writers determined, surely the leaders of a country who argued

---

31. This language could also echo Paul's statements in Rom. 5:14 and 1 Cor. 15:22, 45.

32. Quoted by John R. McKivigan and Mitchell Snay, introduction to *Religion and the Antebellum Debate over Slavery*, ed. John R. McKivigan and Mitchell Snay (Athens: University of Georgia Press, 1998), 2.

for and valued freedom to such an extent as to wage war against Great Britain would extend this same value of freedom to those enslaved within its own borders. That this was the case is evident in another petition by the enslaved submitted in Boston, where the authors write, "We expect great things from men who have made such a noble stand against the designs of their fellow men to enslave them."[33] Similarly, as indicated in the 1779 petition, the writers appeal to the "Honours" "who are nobly contending, in the Cause of Liberty" and whose actions for freedom garnered the admiration of "all the great Empires of the World." In another petition to the Massachusetts government, the creators employ the language of a "natural and unalienable" right to assert that the freedom the Americans fought for from Britain included the enslaved Africans' freedom as well.[34]

Needless to say, such eloquent cries for freedom were denied, and slavery continued. Yet the writers of the 1776 and 1779 petitions discussed in detail here demonstrate the powerful ways in which Paul's words were used to advocate for justice, freedom, and liberty. These brave writers risked their lives to engage in a counterhermeneutic or a resistance and protest hermeneutic in which they refused to allow the prevalent error-filled ideas about their existence to stand. They were not intellectually inferior, neither were they created to live in slavery, but as children of Adam, with families and the human right to be free, they also had the right to interpret Scripture for themselves and not to rely upon any white supremacist interpretive strategy. Furthermore, such petitions indicate the intricate links between the Bible, theology, and politics in the minds of the originators. The writers' use of Pauline language in a government document indicates their beliefs that Scripture matters, particularly Pauline Scripture, and that Scripture had ethical and societal implications. It is noteworthy that these writers wrote these petitions prior to the intensification of the modern abolition movement in America, which began to rise in prominence in the early 1830s;[35] this makes these writers' words and use of Paul all the more formidable and impressive. Jupiter Hammon, another early African American figure, employs Paul in revolutionary and controversial ways as well.

33. Slave Petition for Freedom during the Revolution, 1773–1779, Petition (b), Boston, April 20, 1773.

34. Slave Petition for Freedom during the Revolution, 1773–1779, Petition (d), January 13, 1777.

35. McKivigan and Snay, introduction to *Religion and the Antebellum Debate*, 6; Berwanger, "Negrophobia," 273.

Jupiter Hammon (1711–[1790–1806?]):
The First Published African American Poet

Jupiter Hammon,[36] a preacher, poet, and bookkeeper for his owners, bears the title of the first published black poet in America.[37] An enslaved African his entire life, about eighty years, he became a Christian during the Great Awakening, and his writings are filled with biblical language and echoes indicating his love and passion for the Christian faith.[38] Hammon's owners allowed him to learn to read and write in order to assist them in their business in Long Island, New York. Sondra O'Neale describes Hammon's work as the "most comprehensive, statement of Black theology as well as the earliest antislavery protests by a Black writer in all of American literature."[39] In her opinion, "Hammon's dual commitment to Christianity and freedom has been either undervalued or ignored," and he "has been one of the least understood writers in two hundred years of minority authorial experience."[40] Critics of Hammon believe that he is weak, and that instead of fighting for freedom in the present world, he admonishes his enslaved African audience to look to heaven as their escape and liberation. In the views of these critics, his otherworldly stance did more harm than good.[41]

Yet O'Neale cautions against the complete dismissal of Hammon's importance to the legacy of African American writing. For her, Hammon's work makes significant contributions to black protest literature because he emphasizes blacks' ancient identities; employs a convincing, subtle challenge to whites' consciences; provides proof that an enslaved African could write and publish; and becomes an example of enslaved African leadership through public speaking and written works for mixed audiences of enslaved Africans and slaveholders.[42] Whichever side of this debate one finds one-

36. Jupiter Hammon's death date is difficult to determine. Historians estimate his death took place between 1790 and 1806. See Margaret Brucia, "The African-American Poet, Jupiter Hammon: A Home-Born Slave and His Classical Name," *International Journal of the Classical Tradition* 7, no. 4 (2001): 515–17; O'Neale, *Jupiter Hammon*, 1; Philip Richards, "Nationalist Themes in the Preaching of Jupiter Hammon," *Early American Literature* 25, no. 2 (1990): 123.

37. Brucia, "The African-American Poet," 515; O'Neale, *Jupiter Hammon*, 1; Richards, "Nationalist Themes," 123.

38. O'Neale, *Jupiter Hammon*, 2.

39. O'Neale, *Jupiter Hammon*, 1.

40. O'Neale, *Jupiter Hammon*, 1.

41. O'Neale, *Jupiter Hammon*, 1–39.

42. O'Neale, *Jupiter Hammon*, 2–3. See also Arien Nydam, "Numerological Tradition in the Works of Jupiter Hammon," *African American Review* 40, no. 2 (Summer 2006): 207–20.

self, it will be clear in the subsequent examinations of a few of his writings, "A Winter Piece," "An Evening's Improvement," and "An Address to the Negroes in the State of New York," that Hammon employs Paul a great deal and utilizes the apostle in provocative, albeit subtle, ways to advocate for freedom and justice.[43] Although O'Neale does not focus on or analyze Hammon's use of Paul, the subsequent analysis will demonstrate that the subtlety she identifies as aimed at white consciences appears also in relation to Hammon's black audience.

One of the causes of Hammon's subtle antislavery protest message is that enslaved Africans in New York faced general police-state conditions, and so any overt opposition would not have been tolerated.[44] Accordingly, Hammon shrewdly employs Paul to speak to his black audiences, his "brethren," and to address the black desire for liberation. Arien Nydam views this tactic of Hammon's as "subtextual, encoded resistance."[45] As this discussion of Hammon's work will reveal, he engages in Pauline interpretation to emphasize divine grace, righteous living, and black agency. Along with these themes, he also takes up Pauline language to reject notions of black appearance as evil and to critique those in power, the wealthy white slaveholders.

"A Winter Piece"

Some of the major themes of Hammon's essay "A Winter Piece," published in 1782, are the need for repentance before God, allowing Christ to come and transform one's life, and holy living. Hammon opens the essay by quoting Matthew 11:28: "Come unto me, all ye that labour and are heavy laden." As O'Neale notes, many enslaved Africans viewed this verse as speaking to

43. Additional works by Hammon include "An Evening Thought, Salvation by Christ, with Penitential Cries" (poem), "An Address to Phyllis Wheatley Ethiopian Poetess in Boston" (poem), "An Essay on the Ten Virgins" (nonextant), "A Poem for Children with Thoughts on Death," "The Kind Master and Dutiful Servant" (poem). In 2011, Julie McCown, a graduate student, discovered a previously unpublished and unknown poem by Hammon entitled "An Essay on Slavery, with Submission to Divine Providence, Knowing That God Rules over All Things," dated November 10, 1786, which means it was written around the same time as "Address to the Negroes in the State of New York." See Cedrick May and Julie McCown, "'An Essay on Slavery': An Unpublished Poem by Jupiter Hammon," *Early American Literature* 48, no. 2 (2013): 457–71, who call this latest discovery "the most outspoken antislavery statement by this often-neglected eighteenth century writer" (457).

44. O'Neale, *Jupiter Hammon*, 8.

45. Nydam, "Numerological Tradition," 209. See also O'Neale, *Jupiter Hammon*, 3–4.

their own harsh labor under enslavement and as Christ's offering of comfort during such oppression. Although Hammon may be pointing to this common understanding, his primary concern is to emphasize that "We are to come with a sense of our own unworthiness to confess our sins before the Most High God, to come by prayer and meditation, and we are to confess Christ to be our Savior and Mighty Redeemer."[46] For Hammon, salvation is central since people should come "laboring and heavy-laden with a sense of our lost and undone state," and he quotes Paul in Ephesians to emphasize that by grace salvation comes through faith; it is God's gift (2:8). Philip Richards likewise recognizes that in this, his first homily, Hammon, using the format of an evangelical sermon, attempts to convert his fellow enslaved Africans.[47] At the same time that he focuses on salvation and holy living, he also suggests in several places that physical freedom from slavery concerns him as well. He writes:

> My brethren, many of us are seeking a temporal freedom and I wish you may obtain it; remember that all power in heaven and on earth belongs to God. If we are slaves, it is by the permission of God; if we are free, it must be by the power of the Most High God. Stand still and see the salvation of God. Cannot that same power that divided the waters from the waters for the children of Israel to pass through make way for your freedom? I pray that God would grant your desire and that he may give you grace to seek that freedom which tendeth to eternal life.[48]

Hammon states that the same God who freed Israel can also free blacks from the American slave system. He was the first black Christian to link Israel's bondage to enslaved Africans in writing, but the theme is ubiquitous in subsequent black American literature and theology.[49] One sees quite

---

46. Hammon, "A Winter Piece," in O'Neale, *Jupiter Hammon*, 97. All of Hammon's essays cited in this volume appear in O'Neale, *Jupiter Hammon*, and the page references are to O'Neale.

47. Richards, "Nationalist Themes," 125.

48. Hammon, "A Winter Piece," 102–3.

49. O'Neale, *Jupiter Hammon*, 85. Scholars have long noted the prominence of the exodus motif in black writings. Among them are Callahan, *The Talking Book*; Eddie Glaude, *Exodus! Religion, Race, and Nation in Early Nineteenth-Century Black America* (Chicago: University of Chicago Press, 2000); Herbert Marbury, *Pillars of Cloud and Fire: The Politics of Exodus in African American Biblical Interpretation* (New York: New York University Press, 2015); Albert Raboteau, *A Fire in the Bones: Reflections on African-American Religious History* (Boston: Beacon, 1995), 17–36, 57–76.

poignantly Hammon's struggle with the existence of enslavement—is it by divine ordination, as people like Josiah Priest believed, or just permitted by God? Interestingly, Hammon does not adhere to the notion, such as found in Priest's work, that slavery was ordained by God, but he does use the language of permission, which differentiates his views from slave advocates like Priest and Saffin. Whereas interpreters like Priest believed that slavery was ordained by God for all time, Hammon sees it as permitted, which indicates an expected end whenever God chooses to display divine salvation and make way for the enslaved Africans' freedom, as God did for Israel. Such a subtle but important distinction in this interpretation makes sense in light of what Hammon writes a few lines later: "This we know, my brethren: '. . . *that all things work together for good to them that love God . . .*'" (Rom. 8:28).[50] This quote, in light of the context, indicates that Hammon expects God to liberate his fellow Africans just as God liberated Israel. Addressing his fellow enslaved Africans as brethren, Hammon encourages them to trust in God's power to work out all things for their good, including their spiritual and physical freedom.

Hammon prefaces his statements about Israel and blacks' salvation from slavery with Peter's declarations in Acts 10:34–35, in which Peter avers that "God is no respecter of persons: but in every nation he that feareth him, and worketh righteousness, is accepted with him."[51] Quoting Peter's comments at this point indicates Hammon's emphasis on God's inclusion of blacks in salvation and their inclusion in God's liberative mission. God's call is open to all, and so they too are included in God's story of redemption, for Hammon states unequivocally, "Come my dear fellow servants and brothers, Africans by nation, we are all invited to come."[52] In a society built upon black exclusion, Hammon emphasizes God's inclusion. Thus, Hammon makes an impressive array of connections in this part of the essay. He acknowledges blacks' identity as Africans, connects this identity with God's acceptance of them, links blacks' plight with that of Israel's bondage, and links Israel's de-

---

50. Hammon, "A Winter Piece," 103.

51. Hammon, "A Winter Piece," 102.

52. Hammon, "A Winter Piece," 102. O'Neale, *Jupiter Hammon*, insightfully writes as follows regarding Hammon's use of the phrase "Africans by nation": "In addition to 'my brethren,' Hammon calls his fellow slaves 'Africans by nation' or 'Ethiopians.' Although born in America, Hammon was the first African to leave printed evidence that slaves recognized the treachery of cultural alienation. He refers to his brethren as 'ancient' in order to uplift his fellow servants with a sense of inclusion in a history older than that of their British masters" (86). Hammon uses these phrases throughout the essay.

liverance with the enslaved Africans' own future liberation. Hammon, then, does not totally disregard physical freedom and its importance but associates spiritual freedom with physical freedom. For him spiritual freedom may be more significant in the grand scheme of things, but the need and desire for physical freedom do not go unrecognized. If it is to come, then it must come, in Hammon's view, from God's divine hand.

Although at several places in this essay Hammon quotes Paul to speak about the beauty of salvation and to reinforce righteous living,[53] he also employs the apostle to counter some of the prevailing views of blacks during this time. In several instances Hammon pointedly calls attention to the enslaved Africans as agents in their own salvific process:

> My brethren, it is your duty to strive to make your calling and election sure by a holy life [2 Pet. 1:10], *working out your salvation with fear and trembling* [Phil. 2:12], for we are invited to come without money and without price.[54]

> We should be always preparing for the will of God, *working out our salvation with fear and trembling* [Phil. 2:12]. *O may we abound in the works of the Lord* [1 Cor. 15:58]. . . . *Let us then be pressing forward to the mark, for the prize of the high calling of God is Christ Jesus* [Phil. 3:13–14].[55]

Hammon uses Pauline language here to underscore enslaved Africans' agency and their ability to work out their salvation. Such a view counters that of many white slave owners and advocates of slavery who declared that enslaved Africans' salvation rested on their obedience to slaveholders and that only if they did what the slave owners instructed would they experience redemption.

For example, Peter Randolph, in his writing *Sketches of Slave Life*, narrates an episode in which a Baptist minister, named James L. Goltney,

---

53. Hammon's utilization of Paul to encourage a moral life include the following passages: 1 Cor. 10:31 (p. 101); 2 Cor. 5:17 (p. 103); Acts 24:16 (p. 104); Rom. 6:22, 23 (p. 105); 2 Cor. 7:10 (p. 111). In addition, Hammon echoes Paul's language in Rom. 5:8, writing, "My brethren, here we see the love of God plainly set before us: *that while we were yet sinners,* he sent his Son to die for all those that come unto him" ("A Winter Piece," 109 [emphasis added]).

54. Hammon, "A Winter Piece," 101; scriptural citations that appear in brackets in direct quotations in this monograph are my authorial insertions; these references do not appear in the actual quotations.

55. Hammon, "A Winter Piece," 108.

preaches to enslaved Africans using as his text, "Servants, obey your masters." Randolph describes this episode in a most telling manner: "[Goltney] would try to make it appear that he knew what the slaves were thinking of,—telling them they thought they had a right to be free, but he could tell them better,—referring them to some passages of Scripture. 'It is the devil,' he would say, 'who tells you to try and be free.' And again he bid them be patient at work, warning them that it would be his duty to whip them, if they appeared dissatisfied,—all which would be pleasing to God! 'If you run away, you will be turned out of God's church, until you repent, return, and ask God and your master's pardon.' In this way he would continue to preach his slaveholding gospel."[56] The "slaveholding gospel" that Randolph describes puts God on the side of the slaveholder, even sanctioning the cruel beatings that slaves receive at the hands of their enslavers, which Randolph has previously narrated. What is more, instead of liberation originating from God, in the slaveholding gospel freedom is demonic and the desire for it comes from Satan, not God. Accordingly, if enslaved Africans were to pursue freedom by running away, they would in effect be excommunicated from the church, acquiring reinstatement only if and when they returned, asked for, and received forgiveness from God *and* their masters. This idea that freedom was demonic and that slaves who pursued it by running away were no longer welcomed by God was common, with some enslaved Africans unfortunately believing it.[57]

Hammon, however, resists this prevalent view and, by using the language "My brethren," insists to the blacks in his audience that God invites *them* to come and this invitation does not depend upon the permission of slaveholders. He frames the scriptural citations from Isaiah and Matthew with the Pauline texts of Philippians and 1 Corinthians and employs Paul's words as divine invitations specifically given to the enslaved Africans. When

56. Peter Randolph, *Sketches of Slave Life; or, Illustrations of the "Peculiar Institution" by Peter Randolph, An Emancipated Slave* (Boston: Published for the author, 1855), reprinted in *"Sketches of Slave Life" and "From Slave Cabin to the Pulpit,"* ed. Katherine Clay Bassard (Morgantown: West Virginia University Press, 2016), 62.

57. Occasionally, slave owners hired a preacher who did not preach these types of sermons but more liberative ones. These ministers, however, did not last long, as Randolph, *Sketches of Slave Life*, indicates: "Mr. L. Hanner was a Christian preacher, selecting texts like the following: 'The Spirit of the Lord is upon me, because he hath anointed me to preach deliverance to the captives, he hath sent me to bind up the brokenhearted.' But Hanner was soon mobbed out of Prince George's County, and had to flee for his life, and all for preaching a true Gospel to colored people" (62).

quoting Romans 10:10, Hammon continues his concentration on enslaved Africans' agency, writing that "'for with the heart men believeth unto righteousness; and with the mouth confession is made unto salvation' (Rom. 10:10). Here we see that there is something to be done by us as Christians."[58] Enslaved Africans have their own agency and can believe, confess, and act on their own faith.

Furthermore, their social status does not preclude them from salvation; they can come without money and receive God's good news. Not only do the enslaved Africans have agency but this agency does not depend upon social status or economics. In the midst of a society that denies them agency and the freedom to do and think for themselves, Hammon admonishes his audience to recognize their agency and to use it to abound in good works and to press forward to the mark—all usages of Pauline language to encourage enslaved Africans' agency and action. This focus on blacks' agency appears again in Hammon's statement that God created blacks as "rational creatures," a statement that contradicts some white perceptions of blacks as animals, intellectually inferior, and nonhuman.[59] Hammon refutes such views, reminding his listeners that God created them as people with thinking faculties, and his assertions here align with the enslaved petitioners' claims above that blacks have the same faculties as their enslavers.

Hammon's zeroing in on enslaved Africans' agency is part of a larger conversation taking place in society during this time regarding whether or not blacks could experience salvation and whether or not they had souls. His pointed affirmation of blacks' rational capability and agency in the salvific process, and his repeated call in the essay to rely upon God's power and Spirit, indicate Hammon's desire to empower his audience, to affirm publicly their humanity, and to encourage their agency despite their toxic surroundings.

Equally important is Hammon's repeated emphasis on the power of sin and its universal effect. He writes: "My brethren, it is not we servants only that are unworthy; but all mankind by the fall of Adam became guilty in the sight of God (Gen. 2:17)."[60] Here Hammon implicitly rejects the notion of blacks' descendancy from Ham and "the curse's connection to African racial identity, and its implications of God's preordination of slavery. Certain

58. Hammon, "A Winter Piece," 107.
59. Hammon, "A Winter Piece," 106. See such comments by proslavery advocates in the previous section.
60. Hammon, "A Winter Piece," 106.

revelation could thwart white theologians' attempts to laden Africans with abnormal guilt."[61] Citing Genesis, but no doubt echoing Paul as well (Rom. 5:12–19; 1 Cor. 15:22), Hammon proclaims that it is not just enslaved Africans that are unworthy but whites also, since Adam's sin affects everyone. Hammon makes a stark distinction between the so-called inherited sinful nature of Ham peculiar to blacks and sin that affects all persons, regardless of color. Scripture, from Hammon's perspective, pronounces the nonexistence of the Hamic curse upon blacks, since all fell in Adam and all suffer because of him. Hammon, therefore, grasps Paul's emphasis on the deep power of sin and its effects upon the entire human race.

Hammon understands the universal nature of sin as well as the universal nature of Christ's power to rescue and redeem all, for he quotes Paul, who declares that *"since by man came death, by man came also the resurrection of the dead. For as in Adam all die, even so in Christ shall all be made alive"* (1 Cor. 15:21–22).[62] Just as sin's power affects all, both white and black, so too Christ's redemptive power delivers all, both black and white. Blacks cannot only experience spiritual salvation and physical liberation in the here and now, which affirms their personhood, including the fact that they possess souls, but they can also experience God's resurrecting power in the future.

"An Evening's Improvement"

In his essay "An Evening's Improvement," published in 1783, Hammon returns to some of the themes of "A Winter Piece," such as repentance, receiving God's gift of salvation through Christ, and the agency of the enslaved Africans. In regard to this last theme, he repeats his use of Pauline language from Philippians 2:12, 1 Corinthians 15:58, and Romans 8:28. Although Pauline citations and expressions permeate the essay, several distinct uses of the apostle's words appear in this document and will focus the present discussion. Hammon emphatically directs his audience's attention to their new identity in Christ as children of God led by the Spirit of God. He empowers his hearers by reminding them of their transformed identity:

There is such a depravity in our natures that we are not willing to suffer any reproach that

---

61. O'Neale, *Jupiter Hammon*, 94.
62. Hammon, "A Winter Piece," 108–9.

may be cast on us for the sake of our religion; this, my brethren, is because *we have not the love of God shed abroad in our hearts* [Rom. 5:5]; but our hearts are set too much on the pleasures of this life, *forgetting that they are passing away* [1 Cor. 7:31]; but the *children of God are led by the Spirit of God. Therefore, brethren, we are debtors, not to the flesh to live after the flesh. For if ye live after the flesh, ye shall die: but if ye through the Spirit do mortify the deeds of the body, ye shall live. For as many as are led by the Spirit of God, they are the sons of God* (Rom. 8:12–14). Here, my brethren, we see that it is our indispensable duty to conform to the will of God in all things, not having our hearts set upon the pleasures of this life; but we must prepare for death, our great and last change.[63]

A few pages later he returns to Romans 8: "But there must be a saving change wrought in our hearts, and we must become as new in Christ Jesus. *We must not live after the flesh but after the Spirit* [Rom. 8:1, 4]. *'For as many as are led by the Spirit of God, they are the sons of God'*" (Rom. 8:14).[64] Hammon urges his audience to look beyond the pleasures of this life and to allow the Spirit within them to lead them, for their new identity means a new focus. His comments illustrate to the enslaved Africans that God's Spirit grants them a new way of being and that they are not children of Ham but children of God. What is more, their identity does not derive from whom they belong to on earth but originates from their heavenly Father. Hammon establishes divine sonship for African Americans, refuting beliefs that they were beasts, nonhumans, or inferior human beings. The presence of God's Spirit affirms their humanity and God's divine call upon their lives, thereby negating any views that would relegate them to subordinate status. In addition, Hammon's use of Paul encourages his audience to live a Christian life that surpasses that of their white enslavers. This emphasis by Hammon is an early example of the tendency among blacks to counter the racist behavior of their white owners by living a superior moral life.

Earlier in the essay Hammon echoes 1 Thessalonians 5:22, writing, "And we should put our whole trust in the Lord at all times; we should strive to live a religious life, to *avoid the very appearance of evil*, lest we incur the wrath of God."[65] Hammon asserts here that the religious life avoids the appearance of evil, and he employs Pauline language to establish that evil is not found in

63. Hammon, "An Evening's Improvement," 163.
64. Hammon, "An Evening's Improvement," 169–70.
65. Hammon, "An Evening's Improvement," 167.

blackness or enslaved Africans' black skin but in how one lives. Hammon's interpretive move is important in light of the views of the time. Josiah Priest recapitulates the beliefs of the period regarding black skin: "As to the intrinsic superiority of a white complexion over that of black, there is no question; for by the common consent of all ages among men, and even of God himself in heaven, there has been bestowed on white the most honorable distinction. White has become the emblem of moral purity and truth, not only on earth, but in eternity also."[66] He continues, writing, "Black, in all ages, has been the sign of every hateful thing."[67]

Priest sums up the prevalent views about black bodies and black skin that permeated the culture in this period. For black slaves, "skin color alone was enough to identify them as that which has no value."[68] That Hammon is aware of such views can be seen most poignantly in his remark, "For if we love God, Black as we be and despised as we are, God will love us."[69] These words illustrate Hammon's somber acquaintance with the painful reality of black bodies and black lives in America. His adoption and adaptation of Paul's words about the *religious life* avoiding the appearance of evil contest the idea of black skin being evil and black bodies being wicked. Instead, what is evil is how one lives. Hammon protests erroneous views of black bodies and simultaneously launches a critique against white slave owners, who attempt to attach evil solely to black bodies while living lives that betray the Christianity they confess. In Hammon's view, these slave owners are the ones who have an appearance of evil because they are not living a moral religious life. Such a reading corresponds to Hammon's repeated terminology in this essay regarding punishment for the wicked and impending judgment.

Hammon returns to the judgment theme at the end of the essay by quoting Paul's words in 2 Corinthians 5:10 (cf. Rom. 14:10). He writes, "My brethren, we know not how soon God may send the cold hand of death to summon us out of this life to a neverending eternity, there to appear before the *judgment seat of Christ. 'For we must all appear before the judgment seat of Christ.'*"[70] Affirming the universality of judgment, noting that all must appear before God, both black and white, Hammon closes the essay with

66. Priest, *Slavery as It Relates*, 136.

67. Priest, *Slavery as It Relates*, 138.

68. Shanell T. Smith, *The Woman Babylon and the Marks of Empire: Reading Revelation with a Postcolonial Womanist Hermeneutics of Ambivalence*, Emerging Scholars (Minneapolis: Fortress, 2014), 165.

69. Hammon, "An Evening's Improvement," 171.

70. Hammon, "An Evening's Improvement," 173.

one explicit Pauline citation and one Pauline echo. He encourages his audience regarding judgment by citing all of 1 Corinthians 15:51–53, including the apostle's words that *"we shall all be changed."* These words recall Hammon's earlier insistence that death is the final great change.[71] Hammon's appeal to an apocalyptic transformation of the body, a body that in the case of an enslaved African had endured so much, underscored that black bodies belonged to God, not the white slaveholder, and that the bodily transformation prophesied by the apostle included black bodies too. Although one may construe Hammon's words as pie-in-the-sky language that is so otherworldly as to have no earthly significance, one can also maintain that this language both denied whites ownership of black bodies and affirmed the existence of black souls, two important statements to make in this time period.

"An Address to the Negroes in the State of New York"

Written in 1787 near the end of his life, "An Address to the Negroes in the State of New York" is Hammon's final essay and perhaps his most controversial publication.[72] It is also, according to some, his most published work. Hammon begins the essay by taking on the persona of the apostle Paul, who in Romans 9 lamented over his fellows Jews and their rejection of the gospel. Similarly, Hammon grieves over the plight of his fellow enslaved Africans, mourning over their current existence. He states in his opening salvo:

> When I am writing to you with a design to say something to you for your good and with a view to promoting your happiness, I can with truth and sincerity join with the Apostle Paul, speaking in his own nation, the Jews, and say: *"That I have great heaviness and continual sorrow in my heart . . . for my brethren, my kinsmen according to the flesh"* (Rom. 9:2–3) [cf. Rom. 10:1]. Yes, my dear brethren, when I think of you, which is very often, and of the poor, despised, and miserable state you are in as to the things of this world, and when I think of your ignorance and stupidity and the great wickedness of the most of you, I am pained to the heart. It is at times almost too much

---

71. Hammon, "An Evening's Improvement," 163.

72. This writing is his final prose address. However, in 2011 a graduate student, Julie McCown, found an unpublished poem by Hammon, which she dates at the same time of this essay, speculating that Hammon probably intended the poem to circulate along with "An Address." It was Hammon's practice to append poems to his written essays. See above, n. 43.

for human nature to bear, and I am obliged to turn my thoughts from the subject or endeavor to still my mind by considering that it is permitted thus to be by that God who governs all things, who setteth up one and pulleth down another.[73]

Hammon's words here are interesting on several levels. First, in an ironic move, he takes on the mantle of the apostle Paul, as it were, the one whose words are used during this time to justify his enslavement. Yet, despite this reality, he connects with the apostle's love for his Jewish contemporaries and perceives in Paul's writings a way to express his own care for his fellow enslaved Africans. Paul assists him in telling his story regarding his deep longing for his people and his recognition of their "poor," "despised," and "miserable" state. The apostle's lament, then, becomes a means by which Hammon demonstrates concern and distress over his fellow Africans, for he sees in Paul a companion in sorrow and "joins with the Apostle" in mourning over his own kinsmen according to the flesh.

Second, as Hammon's statements reveal, his distress derives from slavery's effects upon his fellow blacks: "ignorance," "stupidity," and "wickedness." Hammon fleshes out in the body of the essay what he means by these harsh descriptors. The enslaved Africans' "ignorance" and "stupidity" stem from not being permitted to learn and to read for themselves, especially not being able to read the Bible, and their "wickedness" derives from not following the commands of the Bible and not living a religious life superior to that of their masters. Each of these descriptors, then, describes a reality that is the fault not of the enslaved Africans but of their current predicament, a recognition that leads Hammon to resort to the language of permission, in which God permits all of this to be. At the same time, Hammon tacitly concedes that even the language of divine permission does not mollify the condition of blacks' enslavement for him, for he continues, "While I have been thinking on this subject, I have frequently had great struggles in my own mind and have been at a loss to know what to do."[74] Like Paul, who wrestled in anguish about what to do regarding his people because their lack of response to the gospel seemed to defy his human logic, Hammon wrestles with the complex competing realities of an almighty God and the horrid existence of slavery. With utmost honesty and transparency, he admits his frequent loss at what to do about this complicated and horrendous situation.

73. Hammon, "An Address," 230–31.
74. Hammon, "An Address," 231.

Admitting that his own ignorance and inadequacy in teaching had often prohibited him from speaking to his fellow enslaved Africans, he nevertheless decides in this final essay to speak to them, writing, "I have wanted exceedingly to say something to you, to call upon you with the tenderness of a father and friend, and to give you the last and, I may say dying, advice of an old man who wishes your best good in this world and in the world to come." Hammon believes that this essay will transmit his final wishes to those he cares about so much, promising that he will tell the enslaved Africans "what he really thinks is in your best interest and is your duty to comply with."[75] These declarations make Hammon's first piece of advice all the more controversial, for he dwells on the enslaved's duty to obey the slaveholder. Hammon quotes all of Ephesians 6:5–8 to remind his fellow enslaved Africans that they are to obey their masters according to the flesh. After citing Ephesians, he writes, "Here is God's plain command for us to obey our masters. It may seem hard for us, if we think our masters wrong in holding us slaves, to obey in all things, but who of us dares dispute with God! He has commanded us to obey, and we ought to do it cheerfully and freely."[76] Hammon's adoption of proslavery advocates' use of Paul earned him the title of "Uncle Tom" and the castigation of many black scholars, for in their view Hammon becomes the black version of the white minister in Nancy Ambrose's narrative.

He goes on to state that enslaved Africans should obey their masters not just because God commands it but because the enslaved Africans' "own peace and comfort depend upon it. As we depend upon our masters for what we eat and drink and wear and for all our comfortable things in this world, we cannot be happy unless we please them. . . . If a servant strives to please his master and studies and takes pains to do it, I believe there are but few masters who would use such a servant cruelly. Good servants frequently make good masters."[77] Hammon then admonishes his fellow enslaved Africans to refrain from stealing from their masters and from swearing by taking the Lord's name in vain.

On one level, one can argue that Hammon's advice to enslaved Africans to follow the apostle's words of obedience to their masters was advice aimed

---

75. Hammon, "An Address," 231.

76. Hammon, "An Address," 232.

77. Hammon, "An Address," 232. Hammon's statements can be considered rather naïve because enslaved autobiographies and narratives document that it was a common practice for masters to treat enslaved Africans cruelly, no matter how "good" the enslaved Africans behaved.

at the enslaved Africans' survival, to make their harsh lives easier. This is, in fact, what O'Neale argues, writing that "Hammon readers today assume that he was delivering Tommish advice in support of the slave system. . . . Yet history shows that he was not merely calling for Christian submissiveness; he was trying to keep slaves alive and out of jail. All of the seemingly petty societal infringements that Hammon warns of in this essay were serious crimes for which slaves were flogged, jailed, put in stocks, otherwise abused, and sometimes executed."[78] Moreover, the existence of general police-state conditions in New York for enslaved Africans may have facilitated Hammon's comments, in that obeying the slave owner may be difficult but increases chances of survival.[79] For them to obey increased the likelihood of their "best good in this world."

Not only is it feasible to argue the possibility of survival as Hammon's reasoning here, it is also feasible to say that Hammon firmly believed that good enslaved Africans could change the character of their enslavers, even if their enslavers were cruel and wicked. He writes, "If you are humble and meek and bear all things patiently, your master may think he is wrong: if he does not, his neighbors will be apt to see it and will befriend you and try to alter his conduct."[80] Hammon, therefore, believes that enslaved Africans, through their submissive actions, have the ability to transform slaveholders' hearts, a belief, however, that is not substantiated by the historical evidence. Nonetheless, he admits that if this does not work, the enslaved African must resort to prayer and to divine intervention.

Though Hammon adopts proslavery uses of Paul that reinforce the status quo, in these essays he employs the apostle in some subtle, subversive ways.

---

78. O'Neale, *Jupiter Hammon*, 249.

79. O'Neale, *Jupiter Hammon*, 8. O'Neale's observations about the reasoning behind Hammon's statements resonate with Shively Smith's *Strangers to Family: Diaspora and 1 Peter's Invention of God's Household* (Waco, TX: Baylor University Press, 2016) interpretation of the author of 1 Peter, whose language is often interpreted as ordaining slavery, racism, and patriarchy. Yet Smith writes, "The author of 1 Peter was not persuading his Christian sisters and brothers to see their plight as domestic slaves, inferior people, and subjects of imperial control as God's created order. . . . The author commands submission not because it was God's way but because it was his way of mitigating the conspicuousness of his community and *keeping members alive*. The writer of 1 Peter did not want Christian sisters and brothers to die any more than he wanted them to abandon the faithful community altogether. Yet he recognized that they were targets for verbal assault, social ostracism, and even susceptible to random or systematic acts of capital punishment. Even if it could not be entirely remedied or avoided, the intention of the letter is to lessen the suffering the communities experienced" (165 [emphasis added]).

80. Hammon, "An Address," 233.

For instance, in his admonition to enslaved Africans to cease swearing and taking God's name in vain, he says those who do such things are under the power of Satan, who "as a roaring lion, walketh about, seeking whom he may devour" (1 Pet. 5:8), and who is also "the prince of the power of the air, the spirit that now worketh in the children of disobedience." According to Hammon, Satan takes captive people who swear and take the Lord's name in vain because they are being *"taken captive by him at his will"* (Eph. 2:2; 2 Tim. 2:26). At first Hammon directs this language to the enslaved Africans in his audience, but he implicitly aims this censure to the white masters too, since he openly acknowledges that they swear and take God's name in vain. He writes further on that the enslaved Africans' excuse that because their masters swear they can do it also does not legitimate the action. In this censure he tacitly chastises his white addressees who do swear and so underscores his own argument that they are under the power of the devil and that Satan has taken them captive, since all "who are profane are serving the devil."[81] This "all," Hammon declares, includes the white slave owners. In fact, then, it is not blacks who are de facto children of the devil, as some in the proslavery camp believed, but whites themselves who, through their actions, demonstrate their own captivity to this inimical being. Hammon urges his fellow Africans to resist following in the slaveowners' footsteps and to demonstrate a higher religious life. That Hammon views the white owners as under the power of the devil is clearly seen in his appeal to an eschatological judgment by which he encourages his audience, both black and white, to take heed to his words:

> To [God] we must give an account for every idle word that we speak. He will bring us all, rich and poor, white and black, to his *judgment seat* [Rom. 14:10; 2 Cor. 5:10]. . . . Our slavery will be at an end, and though ever so mean, low, and despised in this world, we shall sit with God in his kingdom, as kings and priests, and rejoice forever and ever. Do not then, my dear friends, take God's holy name in vain or speak profanely in any way. Let not the example of others lead you into sin, but reverence and fear that great and fearful name, the Lord our God.[82]

Again Hammon advises his fellow enslaved Africans not to follow the example of the slaveholders ("Let not the example of others lead you into

81. Hammon, "An Address," 235.
82. Hammon, "An Address," 235–36.

sin") but to adhere to a higher ethic of being. In a sense, Hammon encourages his fellow enslaved Africans once again to use their agency. They should act and live a different way of life than the slave owners do. Philip Richards correctly observes that "Hammon's disapproval of whites carries over into a number of implicit criticisms of their morality as well as into explicit exhortations for blacks to act independently of their 'superiors,' their white masters. Hammon exhorts his black audience not to use profanity although the white masters may do so. . . . The upshot of this criticism is that blacks must strive for moral regeneration despite what may be the bad example of their white masters."[83] Paul's words enable Hammon to introduce a cosmic element of satanic influence and dominion, a subversive notion of whites being under the control of Satan, and the picture of an eschatological reckoning in which all, regardless of race and societal status, stand equal before God.

Furthermore, in his repeated recommendations in this essay that enslaved Africans, if given the chance, learn to read, Hammon insists that the purpose of acquiring this skill is to be able to read the Bible.[84] For him, the Bible is the most important book and the only book worth reading. In it enslaved Africans find comfort, assurance, happiness, and encouragement in the midst of their own dire circumstances. Janet Duitsman Cornelius notes this desire to read by the enslaved: "A desire to read the Bible was a powerful motive for slaves to gain literacy; in New York and in the Carolinas, Huguenot missionaries described the eagerness with which slaves embraced the few opportunities they had to learn to read Bibles and hymn books."[85] In one portion of his essay, Hammon's advocacy for reading the Bible utilizes a Pauline passage, 1 Corinthians 1:26–29. His argument at this point, with Pauline echoes and references italicized, is worth quoting at length:

> Now, my dear friends, seeing that the Bible is the word of God and everything in it is true and that it reveals such awful and glorious things, what can be more important than that you should learn to read it? And when you have learned to read, that you should study it day and night? There are some things very encouraging in God's word for such ignorant persons as we are. *For God hath not chosen the rich of this world. Not many rich, not many*

83. Richards, "Nationalist Themes," 133.
84. See the discussion in Callahan, *The Talking Book*, on the deep desire many African Americans had for learning to read during this time, particularly so that they could read Scripture for themselves (1–20).
85. Cornelius, *When I Can Read My Title Clear*, 17.

noble are called, but God hath chosen the weak things of the world, and things which are not, to confound the things that are [1 Cor. 1:26–28]. And when the great and rich refused to come to the gospel feast, the servant was told to go into the highways and hedges, and compel those poor creatures that he found there to come in. Now, my brethren, it seems to me that there are no people that ought to attend to the hope of happiness in another world so much as we. Most of us are cut off from comfort and happiness here in this world and can expect nothing from it. Now seeing this is the case why should we not take care to be happy after death? . . . We cannot plead so great a temptation to neglect religion as others. Riches and honours, which drown the greater part of mankind, who have the gospel, in perdition, can be little or no temptation to us.[86]

Prior to this passage, Hammon has already censured the rich (white slave owners) in his audience by stating that the "rich and great gentlemen swear and talk profanely" and that all those who swear are under satanic power, which implicitly includes the slave owners. In addition, he has also earlier reminded whites and the enslaved Africans that all, rich and poor, will stand before God's judgment seat and that the rich will be saved not by their wealth but by a holy life lived before God and others. When Hammon returns to a critique of the rich whites in his audience by utilizing Paul, he transforms the apostle's words to state that God does not choose the rich of this world but the weak. Paul speaks of the wise and how not many wise men after the flesh are called, but where "mighty" appears in the original Pauline text, Hammon substitutes "rich" to continue his biting critique of the white slave owners, who were rich and profiting by forced labor.[87] Riches, he declares, drown a large part of humanity, even though they may have the gospel.

86. Hammon, "An Address," 239.

87. Hammon's substitution gets to the point that Paul makes in this passage. Paul draws a distinction between the powerful, mighty, and those of noble birth and those who have no or little power in society. In other words, Paul makes a distinction between the wealthy and the poor in the Corinthian congregation to underscore the radical nature of the new creation in which God often chooses those whom society frequently rejects. See the classic study, Gerd Theissen, *The Social Setting of Pauline Christianity: Essays on Corinth*, edited and translated with an introduction by John H. Schütz (Philadelphia: Fortress, 1982). See also my discussion of Paul and the poor in "Spirit-Shift: Paul, the Poor, and the Holy Spirit's Ethic of Love and Impartiality in the Eucharist Celebration," in *The Holy Spirit and Social Justice Interdisciplinary Global Perspectives: Scripture and Theology*, ed. Antipas Harris and Michael Palmer (Lanham, MD: Seymour, 2019), 218–38.

Here one sees Hammon's veiled attack upon whites in his audience who are rich and have the gospel but remain lost. The alteration that Hammon makes to Paul's words cannot be overstated, for this change coheres with the gospel parable (Luke 14:15–24) he echoes right after this Pauline passage. In Hammon's reading of this parable, the wealthy that God invited to the feast refused the invitation, so others were called in their stead. Hammon views his current situation as similar to that of the parable: God does not choose the rich but the weak, an affirmation that aligns with the enslaved Africans' own poor and miserable status to which he referred in the beginning of the essay. Though poor and weak, they are invited to come share in God's divine feast. Such revelations as these are why Hammon encourages his fellow enslaved Africans to learn to read. By doing so, they will be able to discover for themselves the truth about who they are, that God chooses them, and that they are loved by the Divine. By reading for themselves, they will see that there is more in Pauline Scripture than "Slaves, obey your master."

A complex, enigmatic figure in many respects, Jupiter Hammon uses Pauline texts in ways that are both controversial and innovative, conventional and subversive. He employs the apostle to critique those in power and, at the same time, falls in line with the powers that be, proslavery advocates who see in Paul a companion in their own thirst for power and continued subjugation of black bodies. To focus only on Hammon's statements of acquiescence to slavery does not do him justice, however, for as our examination of his essays reveals, especially his last writing, Hammon is a struggling human being attempting to make sense of his world. In this last essay he relates his unfulfilled hopes that God would open the eyes of whites as they fought for their own liberty in the Revolutionary War, and that they would have remembered the blacks and granted them freedom as well.[88] Of course, this did not happen, and it seems Hammon resigned the situation to God's hands, writing that "If God designs to set us free, he will do it in his own time and way."[89] At the same time, to focus only on Hammon's subversive uses of Paul does not tell the whole story either, since his use of Paul is both conventional for Hammon's time and resistance oriented. Though Hammon is not as radical in his use of Paul as some other black writers, he does employ

88. Hammon, "An Address," 236. He writes, "That liberty is a great thing we may know from our own feelings, and we may likewise judge so from the conduct of the white people in the late war. How much money has been spent and how many lives have been lost to defend their liberty! I must say that I have hoped that God would open their eyes, when they were so much engaged for liberty, to think of the state of the poor blacks and to pity us" (236).

89. Hammon, "An Address," 240.

the apostle in a number of important, subversive ways: (1) to underscore black agency, (2) to critique the white wealthy and powerful, (3) to make the charge that whites were under satanic influence, (4) to assert blacks as rational human beings, (5) to proclaim blacks' humanity and identity as sons of God, not Ham, and (6) to lament over his fellow enslaved Africans. To dare to interpret Paul in such ways in public places and spaces secures Hammon's position as one of the important starting points for African American Pauline hermeneutics.

Lemuel Haynes (1753–1833): The First Ordained Black American

Another important early black Pauline exegete is Lemuel Haynes. Haynes, a child of a white mother and black father, both of whom abandoned him, grew up as an indentured servant in a Christian foster home.[90] His indenture ended near the time of the American Revolution, and he joined the Minutemen and served with the Continental army.[91] After his war service, Haynes studied for the ministry, learning Latin and Greek, and became licensed to preach on November 29, 1780.[92] After preaching and pastoring for five years, Haynes was officially ordained on November 9, 1785, becoming the "first black to be ordained by any religious organization in America."[93] Haynes was a pastor and a popular and well-known preacher, speaker, and writer. He became the pastor of a Congregational church in Rutland, Vermont, in 1788, and many of his publications were sermons or speeches he gave there.[94]

90. Helen MacLam, "Introduction: Black Puritan on the Northern Frontier; The Vermont Ministry of Lemuel Haynes," in *Black Preacher to White America: The Collected Writings of Lemuel Haynes, 1774–1833*, ed. Richard Newman (Brooklyn, NY: Carlson Publishing, 1990), xix; Richard Newman, "Preface: The Paradox of Lemuel Haynes," in *Black Preacher to White America*, xi; portions of this section appear in Bowens, "Liberating Paul," 57–73.

91. Newman, "Preface," xii; MacLam, "Introduction," xx.

92. MacLam, "Introduction," xxi.

93. MacLam, "Introduction," xxi.

94. John Saillant, *Black Puritan, Black Republican: The Life and Thought of Lemuel Haynes, 1753–1833* (New York: Oxford University Press, 2003), 3; John Saillant, "'Remarkably Emancipated from Bondage, Slavery, and Death': An African American Retelling of the Puritan Captivity Narrative, 1820," *Early American Literature* 29 (1994), notes the popularity of Haynes's writing: "Haynes was a noted figure in New England Congregationalism, since he was a veteran of the Revolution, the first ordained black American, the leader of several successful revivals, the first black American to receive a college degree (Middlebury College, honorary, 1804), and a champion of orthodoxy in theological disputes. Haynes's renown is

Although he pastored a white congregation in Rutland for thirty years, it was ultimately prejudice against his race that terminated his pastorship there: "The people in Rutland, where he preached thirty years, at length began to think they would appear more respectable with a white pastor than a black one, and therefore, or at least measurably on that account, dismissed him."[95]

Lemuel Haynes's Use of Paul to Critique the Ham Myth

Yet, long before he was dismissed, a young Haynes, writing around 1776, penned an essay entitled "Liberty Further Extended: Or Free thoughts on the illegality of Slave-keeping; Wherein those arguments that Are useed [sic] in its vindication Are plainly confuted. Together with an humble Address to such as are Concearned in the practise," in which he argues insightfully against slavery, utilizing political, theological, and moral arguments.[96] As the essay's title intimates, Haynes contends that the idea of liberty fomented by the American Revolution should be extended to black enslaved Africans within the United States.[97] He emphasizes the "hypocrisy of Americans who complained of English oppression while they tolerated slavery in their own land."[98] Like the enslaved African writers of the petitions discussed above, Haynes attempts to seize this moment in American history to launch a comprehensive attack against the reasons for approval of and participation in slavery and the slave trade. Haynes critiques the use of the Ham story in Genesis by white Christian proslavery proponents, who used it extensively to justify slavery. Katie Cannon observes that the belief that enslaving blacks

indicated in the extravagant success of his 1805 sermon pamphlet, Universal Salvation . . . which appeared in over seventy editions, more than fifty of them within Haynes's lifetime, as well as in his invitation in 1814 to offer a sermon in Timothy Dwight's Yale College chapel, the epicenter of New England theology" (123).

95. MacLam, "Introduction," xxxiv.

96. MacLam, "Introduction," xxv.

97. Newman, "Preface," xii. Mark Noll's observation that this essay draws as much upon the Declaration of Independence as upon the Scriptures is important, especially in light of the enslaved petitioners above who seek to connect their desire for freedom with the American Revolution. It also important to note that even though this essay was not published while Haynes was alive, Saillant states that it "should not be considered private. His manuscripts were preserved by white people with whom he studied, to whom he preached" (*Black Puritan, Black Republican*, 15).

98. John Saillant, "Lemuel Haynes and the Revolutionary Origins of Black Theology, 1776–1801," *Religion and American Culture* 2, no. 1 (1992): 79.

was a "judicial act of God" and "necessary to the veracity of God Himself" enabled whites to see blacks as nonhuman property.[99] With this basic belief system in place, it became easy to portray "people with Black skin as demonic, unholy, infectious progenitors of sin, full of animality and matriarchal proclivities."[100] As Cannon indicates, the Ham story provided biblical sanction for blacks' slavery, and for some whites it even provided the idea that part of the curse was a curse of blackness. Enslaved Africans' black skin proved that they were evil descendants of Ham deserving subjugation.

Haynes, however, was skeptical of whites' use of the Ham passage, stating that "Whethear the Negros are of Canaans posterity or not, perhaps is not known By any mortal under Heaven. But allowing they were actually of Canaans posterity, yet we have no reason to think that this Curs Lasted any Longer than the comeing of Christ: when that Sun of riteousness arose this wall of partition was Broken Down [Eph. 2:14]."[101] And again, he declares that "Our glorious hygh preist hath visably appear'd in the flesh, and hath Establish'd a more glorious Oeconomy. . . . It is plain Beyond all Doubt, that at the comeing of Christ, this curse that was upon Canaan [Gal. 3:13], was taken off."[102] As illustrated by these quotations, part of Haynes's critique of this story's interpretation lies in recognizing the improbability of knowing the identity of Canaan's descendants.[103] Yet his resistance to this interpretation of the narrative also rests upon echoing Paul's words in Ephesians 2:14 and Galatians 3:13. In Ephesians 2:14, where Paul discusses Christ's destruction of the wall between Jew and gentile, Haynes understands the partition as the one prevalent in his day, the wall erected between black and white, slave and free, and insists that Christ destroyed these humanly instituted barriers also. Moreover, in Galatians 3:13 the apostle states, "Christ hath redeemed us from the curse of the law, being made a curse for us: for it is written, Cursed is

99. Katie Cannon, "Slave Ideology and Biblical Interpretation," *Semeia* 47 (1989): 12.

100. Cannon, "Slave Ideology and Biblical Interpretation," 12.

101. Lemuel Haynes, "Liberty Further Extended: Or Free thoughts on the illegality of Slave-keeping; Wherein those arguments that Are useed [*sic*] in its vindication Are plainly confuted. Together with an humble Address to such as are Concearned in the practise," in Newman, *Black Preacher to White America*, 24. All of Haynes's essays cited in this volume appear in Newman, *Black Preacher to White America*, and the page references are to Newman. See John Saillant's important discussion of Haynes and other early black exegetes in "Origins of African American Biblical Hermeneutics in Eighteenth-Century Black Opposition to the Slave Trade and Slavery," in *African Americans and the Bible: Sacred Texts and Social Structures*, ed. Vincent L. Wimbush (New York: Continuum, 2000), 236–50.

102. Haynes, "Liberty," 25.

103. Saillant, "Origins," 238.

everyone that hangeth on a tree." Using the apostle's language, Haynes grants that even if blacks were descendants of Canaan, Christ's death removes this curse and therefore delegitimizes the use of the Ham narrative. By employing both of these Pauline passages, Haynes maintains that the "curse" and, as a result, slavery were eradicated by Christ's advent.

Haynes's Reading of 1 Corinthians 7:21

Haynes also confronts those who applied Paul's words in 1 Corinthians 7:21 ("Art thou called, being a servant? care not for it; but if thou mayest be made free, use it rather") to sanction the slave trade and slavery. He believes that although slaves existed in the apostle's day, in this verse Paul advocates for their freedom if at all possible:

> So that the Apostle seems to recommend freedom if attainable, q.d. "if it is thy unhappy Lot to be a slave, yet if thou art Spiritually free Let the former appear so minute a thing when compared with the Latter that it is comparitively unworthy of notice; yet Since freedom is so Exelent a Jewel, which none have a right to Extirpate, and if there is any hope of attaining it, use all Lawfull measures for that purpose." So that however Extant or preval[e]nt it mite Be in that or this age; yet it does not in the Least reverse the unchangeable Laws of God, or of nature; or make that Become Lawfull which is in itself unlawfull.[104]

Here Haynes claims that spiritual freedom is more important than physical freedom, but that does not mean that physical freedom is insignificant or unnecessary, for the apostle urged those in his audience to acquire it. As John Saillant correctly observes, "the proslavery interpretation of this verse was inverted by Haynes," who argues that this verse does not condone slavery but rather emphasizes the direct opposite, the right of every person to be free.[105] Furthermore, Haynes insists that just because slavery existed in Paul's day does not mean that slavery is right; its existence in Paul's time and in Haynes's society does not change the "unchangeable Laws of God," since people in all ages have deviated from God's laws due to their sinful natures.

104. Haynes, "Liberty," 25–26.
105. Saillant, *Black Puritan, Black Republican,* 34; Saillant, "Lemuel Haynes and the Revolutionary Origins," 83–84.

Haynes believes that every African has "an undeniable right to his . . . Liberty," and that "Consequently, the practise of Slave-keeping, which so much abounds in this Land is illicit."[106] Haynes views liberty as a gift given by God to every human being, and if anyone attempts to destroy that gift, he or she violates a God-given right. "Every privilege that mankind Enjoy have their Origen from god; and whatever acts are passed in any Earthly Court, which are Derogatory to those Edicts that are passed in the Court of Heaven, the act is *void*. If I have a perticular previledg granted to me by god, and the act is not revoked nor the power that granted the benefit vacated, (as it is imposable but that god should Ever remain immutable) then he that would infringe upon my Benifit, assumes an unreasonable, and tyrannic power." For Haynes, the court of heaven's declaration of liberty to every human being supersedes any earthly court or laws that would deny a human being's divine rights of freedom. No human court can overthrow what the divine tribunal has put in place. In addition, God's immutability means that the benefits enacted by the Divine will not be revoked by the God who granted them. Therefore, anyone who would presume to nullify a divine gift becomes a tyrant and presumes to stand in God's place.

Haynes quotes Acts 17:26, arguing that since God makes of one blood all nations of men, the same laws and the same "aspiring principles" exist in every nation. Paul's statements in Acts underscore the unity of the human race in its creation, including its innate desire and love for liberty. "Therefore we may reasonably Conclude, that Liberty is Equally as pre[c]ious to a Black man, as it is to a white one, and Bondage Equally as intollarable to the one as it is to the other: Seeing it Effects the Laws of nature Equally as much in the one as it Does in the other."[107] God's creation of humanity from one blood means that all human beings share a common existence, a common bond, and a common divine privilege of freedom. No race has a monopoly on liberty, and no race has the right to withhold it from another. Haynes also argues that color cannot be a decisive factor in determining whether or not someone deserves to be free. The one blood the apostle declares negates color as a criterion. The Englishman has no "hygher Descent" compared to the African and is not above the African in "Natural privilege." In fact, Haynes, echoing Paul's language regarding Adam's sin, insists that the Fall is the source of this "insatiable thurst after Superorety one over another" and

---

106. Haynes, "Liberty," 19.
107. Haynes, "Liberty," 19.

that the ubiquity of this practice does not mean it is legitimate or approved by God.[108]

In addition to quoting Paul in this portion of the essay, Haynes reminds his audience of the words of Jesus, "As you would that men should do unto you, do you Even so to them." Paul's words and Jesus's words, Haynes declares, should convict the slave traders and all who participate in this enterprise, since they make clear that what a person does not want imposed upon himself or herself should not be executed upon someone else.

Haynes Challenges the Idea of the Divine Providence of Slavery

Haynes's work also protested the idea of the slave trade as an action of divine providence, for it was argued that through enslavement Africans were "Christianized" and "civilized." Some whites contended that the slave trade really was a blessing to the Africans because it allowed them to be freed from their savage lands and customs in order to experience "civilization." Most of all, slavery permitted them to live in a "Christian" nation. Nehemiah Adams, a proslavery minister, believed that God used whites "as the chief instruments of good to the African race."[109] And Joseph Lovejoy wrote in a letter to his brother, that "American slavery is a redemption, a deliverance from African heathenism,"[110] and that "The best thing that could be done for Africa, if they could live there, would be to send [to Africa] a hundred thousand American Slaveholders, to work [the Africans] up to some degree of civilization."[111]

Not only was this view preached and advocated from American pulpits but it appeared in media outlets as well. Eugene Berwanger captures the prevailing spirit of such views in newspapers at the time: "John Van Evrie, editor

108. Haynes, "Liberty," 20.

109. Nehemiah Adams, *A South-Side View of Slavery, or Three Months at the South in 1854* (Boston: T. R. Marvin and B. B. Mussey & Co., 1854), 209. Also quoted by Berwanger, "Negrophobia," 269. In another part of his book, Adams, *A South-Side View of Slavery*, argues that the South should be left alone, should be defended "against interference" and left "to manage their institution," and as a result "American slavery will cease to be any thing but a means of good to the African race" (201).

110. Joseph C. Lovejoy, *The North and the South! Letter from J. C. Lovejoy, Esq to His Brother, Hon. Owen Lovejoy, M. C., with remarks by the Editor of the Washington Union* (Washington, DC, 1859), 5. Also quoted by Berwanger, "Negrophobia," 270.

111. Lovejoy, *The North and the South!*, 6.

of the New York Day-Book, was so convinced of slavery's Divine Mission that he accused abolitionists of 'impiety to God' for opposing the institution. 'Christian slavery,' claimed the New York Morning Express, brought 'the redemption of the African from Heathenism, Idolatry and Savagery,' and thus became his 'blessing not his curse.' In Ohio, the Cleveland Daily Plain Dealer characterized American slavery as a 'Godsend to the African Race' for it had raised Negroes 'morally, socially, and religiously far above what they would have been had they been left in their native wilds.'"[112]

Despite the ubiquitous nature of this perspective, the brutality of slavery belied the view of slavery as a "Divine Mission." A couple of citations make this clear. David Walker states:

> But Christian Americans not only hinder their fellow creatures, the Africans, but thousands of them will absolutely beat a coloured person nearly to death, if they catch him on his knees, supplicating the throne of grace.... Yes, I have known small collections of coloured people to have convened together for no other purpose than to worship God Almighty, in spirit and in truth, to the best of their knowledge; when tyrants, calling themselves patrols ... would burst in upon them and drag them out and commence beating them as they would rattle-snakes—many of whom, they would beat so unmercifully, that they would hardly be able to crawl for weeks and sometimes for months.[113]

Also, Frederick Douglass relates the following:

> For between the Christianity of this land, and the Christianity of Christ, I recognize the widest possible difference—so wide, that to receive the one as good, pure, and holy, is of necessity to reject the other as bad, corrupt, and wicked. To be the friend of the one, is of necessity to be the enemy of the other. I love the pure, peaceable, and impartial Christianity of Christ: I therefore hate the corrupt, slaveholding, women-whipping, cradle-plundering, partial and hypocritical Christianity of this land. Indeed, I can

112. Berwanger, "Negrophobia," 269.

113. David Walker, *Walker's Appeal, In Four Articles, Together with A Preamble To The Coloured Citizens of the World, But in Particular and Very Expressly, to Those of The United States of America, Written in Boston, State of Massachusetts, September 28, 1829* (Boston: Revised and published by David Walker, 1830), reprinted in *David Walker's Appeal: In Four Articles* (Mansfield Centre, CT: Martino Publishing, 2015), 37. See the discussion of Walker in the final section of this chapter.

see no reason, but the most deceitful one, for calling the religion of this land Christianity. I look upon it as the climax of all misnomers, the boldest of all frauds, and the grossest of all libels.[114]

The unspeakable horrors captured in these passages and endured by many enslaved Africans contradict any notion of slavery as a blessing to the enslaved. Walker underscores the hypocrisy of the idea of a Christian nation when enslaved Africans were not even permitted to pray, and if they were caught doing so, suffered egregiously. Anderson Edwards, a former enslaved African, also speaks about the danger enslaved persons faced when they prayed: "When the darkies prayed in slavery they darsn't let the white fo'ks know 'bout it or they beat them to death. When we prayed we turned a wash pot down to the ground to catch the voice. We prayed lots in slavery to be free and the Lord heard our prayer."[115]

Similarly, the Douglass quote underscores the preposterous idea of slavery as a blessing to enslaved Africans, for he contends that the Christianity practiced in this country does not correspond at all with the Christianity of Christ. He vehemently declares that if one holds to the Christianity of this country, one cannot hold to the Christianity of Christ, and if one holds to the Christianity of Christ, one cannot follow the Christianity of this country, for the two are diametrically opposed. Furthermore, in his writings Douglass laments the hypocrisy of ministers who whip and steal; who preach about purity yet prostitute their slaves; who proclaim family values yet destroy black families without hesitation, separating mothers from fathers and children from parents. Both Walker and Douglass deny the beneficence of slavery or any notion of its "Divine Mission."

The belief that divine providence approved of the slave trade so that enslaved Africans could find salvation is ludicrous to Haynes as well. To refute the notion of slavery's benefit, Haynes uses the apostle's words in Romans 3:8 and 6:1-2 that declare, respectively, "And not rather, (as we be slanderously reported, and as some affirm that we say,) Let us do evil, that good may come? whose damnation is just," and "What shall we say then? Shall we continue in sin, that grace may abound? God forbid." By drawing on these texts, Haynes demonstrates that, just as in Paul's day when some were exclaiming, "Let us do evil so that good may come," some whites want to

---

114. Douglass, "Narrative of the Life of Frederick Douglass," 1:592.

115. George P. Rawick, ed., *The American Slave: A Composite Autobiography*, 41 vols. (Westport, CT: Greenwood, 1972), supplement 2, vol. 4:1262.

commit evil in promoting the slave trade so that "good" (civilizing Africans and causing them to become Christians) may result.[116] Haynes avers that the apostle's answer to his readers in the first century is the same answer the apostle gives to Haynes's audience: μὴ γένοιτο (God forbid!). In his use of Paul here to condemn whites' view of slavery, Haynes calls slavery sin ("Shall we continue in sin?"), a move that many white Christians at the time could not and would not make.[117] Haynes asserts that instead of slavery being a blessing to the African, it is the exact opposite. It is sin that God through Paul forbids continuing. For those who do engage in it, their damnation is a righteous one, as evidenced by the apostle's words.

Haynes closes the essay by appealing to Romans 2:21–23 ("Thou therefore which teacheth another, teachest thou not thyself? thou that preachest a man should not steal, dost thou steal? Thou that sayest a man should not commit adultery, dost thou commit adultery? thou that abhorrest idols, dost thou commit sacrilege? Thou that makest thy boast of the law, through breaking the law dishonourest thou God?"). Here Paul critiques those in his

116. Haynes, "Liberty," 26.

117. Even leading academics of the day did not believe that slavery was sinful. Samuel Miller, Princeton Seminary's second professor, did not consider the practice sinful, as his son wrote of Miller, "But greatly as he disliked the institution [of slavery], he did not, we have seen, consider slaveholding in itself, of necessity, a sin; and even during the earlier part of his residence in New Jersey, at different times, held several slaves under the laws providing in that state for the gradual abolition of human bondage." Samuel Miller, *The Life of Samuel Miller, D.D. LL.D.*, 2 vols. (Philadelphia: Claxton, Remsen & Haffelfinger, 1869), 2:300. At other times Miller, *The Life of Samuel Miller*, criticized slavery, such as in his 1797 speech for the New York Society for the Manumission of Slaves, in which he states, "In this country, from which has been proclaimed to distant lands, as the basis of our political existence, the noble principle, that 'ALL MEN ARE BORN FREE AND EQUAL,'—in this country there are slaves!—men are bought and sold! Strange, indeed! that the bosom which glows at the name of liberty . . . should yet be found leagued on the side of oppression" (1:92). A few years later he called slavery an "evil," but an evil that could not be ended at once, but its termination "must be a work of time" (Samuel Miller, *A Sermon Preached at March 13th, 1808, For the Benefit of the Society Instituted In The City of New York, For The Relief Of Poor Widows With Small Children* [New York: Hopkins & Seymour, 1808], 7). For Miller, the American Society for Colonization was the solution for abolitionism, for he believed that if left in the United States, freed blacks could "never . . . associate with the whites on terms of equality. . . . They will be treated and they will feel as inferiors" (13). Since whites and blacks could not live together in one society if blacks are freed, "Coloured people must be colonized. In other words, they must be severed from the white population, and sent to some distant part of the world" (15). See also Samuel Miller, *A Sermon Preached at Newark, October 22d, 1823 Before the Synod of New Jersey* (Trenton, NJ: George Sherman, 1823).

audience who engage in the very actions they teach against. Haynes once again sees a parallel between Paul's audience and those in his own audience. Whereas Americans have a magnanimous spirit regarding their own natural right for freedom and will not tolerate despotism and tyranny from Britain, they in turn take on these characteristics, which they seem to loathe, when it comes to the enslaved Africans in their own country. Thus, Haynes sees white Americans as similar to those in Paul's audience who participate in the very sins they teach others not to commit. Using the apostle's words, Haynes admonishes his readers to undo the "heavy burdens" of their black brothers and sisters and "let the oppressed go free." If they fail to do so, he predicts judgment, for "god will not hold you guiltless."[118] Paul becomes a way for Haynes to hold up a mirror to his audience so that they may see their reflections in the apostle's words, beholding their own hypocritical mask that cries out liberty at the same time it withholds freedom from others and systematically destroys bodies and lives.

John Saillant calls Haynes "a founding father of Black Theology" and states that "Haynes demonstrates the uniquely American source of Black Theology, which, by the late twentieth century, is clearly part of a worldwide liberation theology."[119] Haynes's hermeneutical audacity in his use of Paul is both penetrating and ingenious and grants insight into Saillant's epithet, making Haynes a worthy recipient of the title "a founding father of black theology." Utilizing the apostle, he proclaimed that Christ destroyed any curse (if there ever was one) that white believers maintained existed upon the black race and abolished every dividing wall. He also argued that God bestowed upon every human being in creation the universal law and right to freedom. Furthermore, the practice of slavery in the apostle's day did not legitimate the practice, since human beings throughout time deviate from the mandates in God's heavenly court system. The existence of a practice does not mean God sanctions it. The apostle's advice to enslaved Africans to pursue liberty if possible suggests that Paul recognized slavery's existence but also understood physical freedom to be the preferred state. Additionally, Paul exposes the double standard of white Americans who advocate "justice and liberty for all" but in reality limit it to whites only. And, in response to the argument that the slave trade blessed blacks, Haynes reversed the whites' practice of having the apostle preach to the enslaved Africans ("Slaves, obey your masters"). Rather, Haynes depicts the apostle as preaching to the white

118. Haynes, "Liberty," 30.
119. Saillant, "Lemuel Haynes and the Revolutionary Origins," 80.

slave owner and minister, "Shall you continue in sin, that is, participate in slavery and the slave trade? μὴ γένοιτο (God forbid)!"

John Jea (1773–1817[?]): The African Preacher and Miracle of Literacy

In the beginning of his narrative *The Life, History, and Unparalleled Sufferings of John Jea, The African Preacher. Compiled and Written by Himself*, which was published in 1811, John Jea reveals that he was born in 1773 in Old Callabar in Africa and that he and his family were stolen, shipped to America, and sold as enslaved Africans in New York to a Dutch couple, Oliver and Angelika Triebuen.[120] He describes the treatment that he and the other enslaved Africans received:

> Our labour was extremely hard, being obliged to work in the summer from about two o'clock in the morning, till about ten or eleven o'clock at night, and in the winter from four in the morning, till ten at night. The horses usually rested about five hours in the day, while we were at work; thus, did the beasts enjoy greater privileges than we did. We dared not murmur, for if we did we were corrected with a weapon an inch and-a-half thick, and that without mercy, striking us in the most tender parts . . . often they treated the slaves in such a manner as caused their death, shooting them with a gun, or beating their brains out with some weapon, in order to appease their wrath, and thought no more of it than if they had been brutes: this was the general treatment which slaves experienced. After our master had been treating us in this cruel manner, we were obliged to thank him for the punishment he had been inflicting on us, quoting that Scripture which saith, "Bless the rod, and him that appointed it." But, though he was a professor of religion, he forgot that passage which saith, "God is love, and whoso dwelleth in love dwelleth in God, and God in him." . . . Conscience, that faithful monitor, (which either excuses or accuses) caused us to *groan, cry, and sigh, in a manner which cannot be uttered* [Rom. 8:22–23, 26].[121]

120. There is some discussion regarding the date of publication, and nothing is known about the circumstances of Jea's death. See Graham Russell Hodges, ed., *Black Itinerants of the Gospel: The Narratives of John Jea and George White* (Madison, WI: Madison House, 1993), 34; Pierce, *Hell without Fires*, 38–39.

121. All excerpts taken from John Jea, *The Life, History, and Unparalleled Sufferings of John Jea, the African Preacher*, Documenting the American South, University of North Carolina at Chapel Hill Digitization Project, https://docsouth.unc.edu/neh/jeajohn/jeajohn

As this excerpt indicates, early on in his narrative Jea lays out three significant motifs that appear in the rest of his story: (1) his connection of Scripture to his horrible experiences as an enslaved person, (2) his identification of the stark contrast between the Christianity professed and practiced by his enslavers and the Christianity espoused by Scripture, and (3) the importance of Paul to his narrative. From the beginning of his exposition, Jea links Scripture to his atrocious existence as an enslaved African. He recounts how he and the other enslaved Africans had to cite Scripture in response to the harsh treatment they received from their owner, a Scripture the slave owner selected that, in his view, condoned his behavior in afflicting such cruelty upon them. They, in taking up Scripture's voice, had to bless the rod and the slaveholder who used it. In reflecting upon this treatment, Jea realizes the slaveholder's perverse tendency—utilizing Scriptures that sanction the despicable treatment of the enslaved and omitting Scriptures that would prohibit such behavior. Although his enslaver professes Christianity, he does not act or live in love as God is love. The stark dichotomy between his owner's actions and the Christianity his owner professes to follow is a distressing issue for Jea, as indicated in several places in his autobiography.

In addition, in these opening paragraphs Jea echoes Paul, signifying the importance of the apostle to his own narrative. The brutality he describes causes enslaved Africans to groan, cry, and sigh in a manner that cannot be uttered. Echoing Romans 8:22–23, where creation groans and is in travail and in pain, and Romans 8:26, where the Spirit makes intercessions with groanings that cannot be uttered, Jea merges the groanings of the enslaved Africans with those of creation and the Spirit. In doing so, he unites the enslaved's woeful cries with creation's travail and the Spirit's speech, suggesting a fused discourse of pain that incorporates creation, the enslaved, and the Spirit. Thus, the enslaved Africans' voices are not lost but taken up into the

---

.html. Hereafter, page references from this work will be given in parentheses in the text. Stephen Butterfield, *Black Autobiography in America* (Amherst: University of Massachusetts Press, 1974), writes about the importance of the autobiographies of the enslaved, stating that "Even in the antislavery movement [blacks] were often urged into mere support roles for white activists and discouraged from developing their own powers of speech and thought. The slave narratives fight these forms of oppression too, testifying to the mental capacities of the slave, arguing tirelessly for his humanity, . . . demanding equal treatment for black people in all areas of public life, and wrestling with the mental devils of self-doubt and despair. And little by little, book by book, they construct the framework of black American literature. Autobiography in their hands became so powerful, so convincing a testimony of human resource, intelligence, endurance, and love in the face of tyranny, that, in a sense, it sets the tone for most subsequent black American writing" (12).

language of Scripture, indeed, into a Pauline passage that recognizes the existence of anguish in the world.

Despite professing Christianity, Jea's enslaver taught him and other enslaved Africans that "when we died, we should be like the beasts that perish; not informing us of God, heaven, or eternal punishments" (5), and that "we poor slaves had no God" (7). In addition, Jea reports that "Frequently did they [masters] tell us we were made by, and like the devil, and commonly called us black devils" (9).[122] Due to the violent treatment Jea receives, he despises Christianity, writing, "From my observations of the conduct and conversation of my master and his sons, I was led to hate those who professed themselves christians, and to look upon them as devils; which made me neglect my work, and I told them what I thought of their ways. On this they did beat me in a most dreadful manner; but instead of making me obedient, it made me the more stubborn, not caring whether I lived or died" (9–10).[123]

Yolanda Pierce insightfully observes the "powerful rhetorical reversal" present in Jea's language here. Though told that he and other enslaved Africans were devils and made by the devil, Jea "appropriates the devil figure from whites for his own use. Through appropriation and reversal, Jea illustrates how slavery inverts given meanings: the 'black devil' figure is really an enactment of white devilry."[124] To Jea, his enslavers' actions demonstrate that they are devils and belong to the devil, not Jea and the other enslaved Africans. Jea rejects any notion that links his existence to the demonic. It is not the color of one's skin that suggests satanic ties but rather one's actions and beliefs, as indicated by his owners' behaviors.

Because Jea despises religion so greatly, his enslaver sends him to church every Sabbath as a punishment, and Jea abhors every minute of it. Nonetheless, Jea, upon hearing the minister one Sabbath urging the congregation to pray for God's presence, decides to do so, by frequently retiring to secret places to pray. When he does not get an answer from God, Jea believes that he is too wicked to receive salvation. Because of his repeated prayers and no answer from God, Jea experiences such distress that even the slaveholder and the slaveholder's wife notice the change in his behavior. When he relates to them the sinful state of his soul and his fear of being killed by God

---

122. See a similar account told in the narrative of Henry "Box" Brown, a former enslaved African, in *Narrative of the Life of Henry Box Brown*, 91–92.

123. As Pierce, *Hell without Fires*, 39, notes, Jea foreshadows Frederick Douglass, who spoke of the great chasm between "slaveholding Christianity" and the Christianity of the Bible.

124. Pierce, *Hell without Fires*, 40.

on account of his sin, they respond that the minister had put the devil in Jea and they were going to beat the devil out of him. They, in fact, do beat Jea, and from then on refuse to let him attend church. Yet Jea continues to attend church despite the floggings he receives. What had at one time been a punishment became for him a necessity so that he could "hear the word of God and seek instruction for my soul" (16). In addition to going to church, Jea divulges that he would often sneak out at night to talk and pray with the minister, that he may be saved (14).

After five or six weeks of this, Jea experiences conversion; he describes the event: "During five or six weeks of my distress, I did not sleep six hours in each week, neither did I care to eat any victuals, for I had no appetite, and thought myself unworthy of the least blessing that God had bestowed on me. . . . And while I was thus crying, and begging God to have mercy on me, and confessing my sins unto him, it pleased God to hear my supplications and cries, and came down in his Spirit's power and blessed my soul" (17). Jea's conversion does not lessen or stop the beatings he receives from his owners, but the Spirit comforts him and enables him to endure. He describes his state before and after conversion with the words of Paul as found in 1 Corinthians 12:3: *"Wherefore I give you to understand, that no man speaking by the Spirit of God calleth Jesus accursed: and that no man can say that Jesus is the Lord, but by the Holy Ghost"* (24). Before receiving salvation, Jea called Jesus and Christians accursed, but now, by God's Spirit, he calls Jesus Lord, a confession only possible through divine enablement.

Jea is only fifteen when he receives conversion, and after his conversion he commences to preach to his enslaver, his enslaver's wife, and his own family members, declaring to them that they could "be saved by grace, through faith in the Lord Jesus Christ" (Eph. 2:8–9) (25). All of them reject Jea's preaching, believing him to have lost his mind, and his enslaver continues to persecute him. Jea's response to their reaction to him contains several Pauline echoes and citations.

> But being taught and directed by the Spirit of God, I told my master, mistress, mother, sisters, and brothers, that there was nothing too hard for the Almighty God to do, for he would deliver me from their hands, and from their tyrannical power; *for he had began the work of grace in my heart, and he would not leave it unfinished, for whatsoever grace had begun, glory would end* [Phil. 1:6] . . . and he gave me power over my *beseting sins* [Heb. 12:1], to cast them from me, and to despise them as deadly poison. *He armed me with the whole armour* of divine grace, whereby I *quenched all the fiery darts*

of the wicked [Eph. 6:16], and compelled Satan to retreat; and put him to flight by faithful and fervent prayer. In addition to these he gave me power over *the last enemy, which is death* [1 Cor. 15:26]; that is, I could look at it without any fear or dread. (25)

Jea prophesies boldly his future freedom with the language of Philippians, for the grace that God began in him that God will complete includes deliverance from "their hands, and from their tyrannical power." Jea links the liberation of his soul that God began with grace to the liberation of his physical body; the two for him are intricately connected. Thus, his words align with what so many African Americans believed during this time—that spiritual salvation includes physical liberation. In addition, utilizing Pauline language, Jea fights a battle with physical people, such as the slave owner, and a battle with sin, which God grants him power over. Fitted with battle armor, Jea goes up against Satan and triumphs through prayer, and so Jea bears witness to a two-tiered understanding of spiritual struggle—believers contend with spiritual forces as well as with physical people.[125] The power with which Jea fights against these entities comes from God and enables him to gain power over death, the last enemy, through his refusal to fear it. To support this contention, Jea quotes Paul, writing, "And St. Paul expresses himself, 'Through fear of death were all their lifetime subject to bondage'" (Heb. 2:15), indicating that he interprets Paul as citing fear as part of death's ability to keep people in bondage. But Jea, refusing to be afraid of death, triumphs over it.

In Jea's case, the fear of death would be monumental, because he was an enslaved African, and death came frequently for enslaved Africans at the hand of their owners. But also now he was a *converted enslaved African*, which some church laws prohibited during this time. As Pierce notes, Jea's owners were members of the conservative Dutch Reformed Church, which opposed slave conversion during this period. In 1792, however, the church changed this prohibition, but as she states, the change did not always affect actual practice.[126] Many slave owners considered conversion dangerous, for it could encourage insubordination and disobedience, as it did in Jea's case— Jea continues to go to church even though his owner forbade it. Jea's enslaver punishes him severely for church attendance, praying, and preaching to him as well as to other enslaved Africans. Some white slave owners knew that

125. See also the discussion in Pierce, *Hell without Fires*, 44–45.
126. Pierce, *Hell without Fires*, 40.

conversion had the potential to limit a slaveholder's rule and authority, as the following episode from Jea's autobiography demonstrates.

> At other times when kept without victuals, in order to punish me, I felt the love of God in me, that I did not regard the food. . . . At other times when they gave me any refreshment, I acknowledged that it came from the immediate hand of God, and rendered unto him humble and hearty thanks in the best manner I could, as the Spirit gave me utterance [Acts 2:4], which provoked my master greatly, for his desire was that I should render him thanks, and not God, for he said that he gave me the things, but I said, no, it all came from God, for all was his; that the Spirit of God taught me so; for I was *led, guided, and directed by the Spirit* [Rom. 8:14], who taught me all things which are of God, and opened them unto my understanding. (20)

This episode reveals the desire of Jea's owner to be viewed as the sole cause of Jea's provision; the owner did not want God to take his place as Jea's source. This incident illustrates that one of the essential foundations of slavery was that enslaved Africans believe in their owners' total claim to their bodies, minds, and souls and believe that their existence rested upon the slaveholders alone. Conversion, however, disrupts this totalizing claim, demonstrating that enslaved Africans do not belong to the slaveholders but to God, whose Spirit transforms them and, by extension, affirms their existence as human beings.[127] The Spirit bestows agency upon them, including the power to resist slave owners' totalizing claims. Indeed, Jea takes hold of the Spirit's teaching him, which is an act of resistance to the doctrine taught to him by his enslaver that he had no god. God's Spirit instructs him, and in doing so reveals the falsehood of his enslaver's words. In addition, Jea becomes another example of the Spirit becoming a resource for resistance.[128] Despite his enslaver's teaching him and the other enslaved Africans a slaveholding gospel, the Spirit grants Jea insight into God's liberating purpose for him.

The reaction that Jea's enslaver exhibits toward Jea giving God thanks aligns with the statements Jea makes early in his narrative about how some enslaved Africans, including himself, were at one time led to "look up unto him as our god" (4), and that enslaved Africans "were often led away with

127. See chap. 4, which discusses in detail some conversion stories of the enslaved.
128. The Holy Spirit is a resource for resistance in Jupiter Hammon's work. See above discussion.

the idea that our masters were our gods" (5). Although to modern ears such thoughts may seem absurd, the absolute control many slaveholders had over the enslaved Africans, often a control parsed out through floggings and torture, with no accountability for such actions, made owners appear godlike, able to do what they wanted, when they wanted, and how they wanted.[129] Conversion, however, meant that slaveholders' authority was not all-encompassing and that they too had to answer for their deeds. Equally significant, conversion meant that God cared about the enslaved Africans' plight and they had not been forgotten.

But Jea was not just a converted slave but a converted slave who preached, which caused his afflictions to increase, afflictions so harsh they could easily have led to death. But Jea's divine encounter empowers him to such an extent that he says, "From the fear of death it pleased the Lord to deliver me by his blessed Spirit; and gave me the witness of his *Spirit to bear witness with my spirit* [Rom. 8:16], that I was passed from death unto life, and caused me to love the brethren. At the time I received this full evidence and witness within me, I was about seventeen years of age, then I began to love all men, women, and children, and began to speak boldly in the name of the living God, and to preach as the oracles of God, as the *Spirit and love of God constrained me* [2 Cor. 5:14]" (31). Jea takes up Paul's understanding of the power of Christ's love to generate unwavering devotion to service and to living for God. Jea's bold preaching compelled by the Spirit and God's love cannot be impeded. Here a distinct juxtaposition appears in Jea's narrative. Before his conversion he did not care whether he lived or died, because the harsh treatment by his masters facilitated a sort of fearlessness on his part. But after his conversion, not fearing death derived from his faith and the freedom it bestowed.

His release from fear of death enables Jea to preach boldly and leads to his sale by three different slaveholders who believe he is harming other enslaved Africans with his preaching and talking (32). While with the last slaveholder, Jea runs to the church and receives baptism. Upon learning of this matter, the slave owner becomes irate, beats Jea, and threatens to beat the minister for performing the exercise. The slaveholder then has Jea examined by the magistrates, who, upon examination, perceive that he is a believer and inform him that he is "free from [his] master, and at liberty to leave him" (33). At this time, Jea writes, "It was a law of the state of the city of New York, that if any slave could give a satisfactorily [*sic*] account

---

129. See similar views in *Narrative of the Life of Henry Box Brown*, 53–54.

of what he knew of the work of the Lord on his soul he was free from slavery, by the Act of Congress, that was governed by the good people the Quakers, who were made the happy instruments, in the hands of God, of releasing some thousands of us poor black slaves from the galling chains of slavery" (39).[130] Refusing to let him leave, however, his enslaver and his enslavers' sons tell Jea that the Bible commands slaves to obey their masters in everything, whether the master is right or wrong, and that Jea had to submit to these words. Their use of the Bible makes a profound impact upon Jea, whose description of these discussions is worth quoting in its entirety:

> But my master strove to baffle me, and to prevent me from understanding the Scriptures: so he used to tell me that there was a time to every purpose under the sun, to do all manner of work, that slaves were in duty bound to do whatever their masters commanded them, whether it was right or wrong; so that they must be obedient to a hard spiteful master as to a good one. He then took the bible and showed it to me, and said that the book talked with him. Thus he talked with me endeavouring to convince me that I ought not to leave him, although I had received my full liberty from the magistrates, and was fully determined, by the grace of God, to leave him.... My master's sons also endeavoured to convince me, by their reading in the behalf of their father; but I could not comprehend their dark sayings, for it surprised me much, how they could take that blessed book into their hands, and to be so superstitious as to want to make me believe that the book did talk with them; so that every opportunity when they were out of the way, I took the book, and held it up to my ears, to try whether the book would talk with me or not, but it proved to be all in vain, for I could not hear it speak one word, which caused me to grieve and lament, that after God had done so much for me as he had in pardoning my sins, and blotting out my iniquities and transgressions, and making me a *new creature* [2 Cor. 5:17; Gal. 6:15], the book would not talk with me; but the Spirit of the Lord brought this passage of Scripture to my mind, where Jesus Christ says, "Whatever ye shall ask the Father in my name, ye shall receive. Ask in faith nothing doubting: for according unto your faith it shall be unto you. For unto him that believeth, all things are possible." (33–34)

130. It is not certain to which law Jea refers in his narrative, for it is unclear when such a law existed. See discussions in Hodges, *Black Itinerants*, 19, 22; Pierce, *Hell without Fires*, 40–41.

Jea's enslaver attempts to utilize Scripture to continue his authority over Jea, echoing Pauline words that servants have to obey their masters in everything. He asserts that the Bible communicates with him, which he contends grants him ultimate control over Jea, although Jea is legally and spiritually free. As this excerpt shows, Jea believes that the Bible does talk with the slaveholder, and he desires the same access. Since God had forgiven his sins and made him a new creature, Jea is bitterly disappointed when the book does not speak to him.[131] He asks God to give him the ability to read the Bible for himself and to "speak it in the Dutch and English languages, that I might convince my master that he and his sons had not spoken to me as they ought, when I was their slave" (34). Although the book would not talk, the Spirit would and did ("the Spirit of the Lord brought this passage of Scripture to my mind"), bringing to Jea's mind an important passage of Scripture that facilitates his prayer request to God. After five or six weeks of prayer, God miraculously grants Jea's petition by sending him an angel "with a large bible in his hands" (35):

> Thus the Lord was pleased in his in finite mercy, to send an angel, in a vision, in shining raiment, and his countenance shining as the sun, with a large bible in his hands, and brought it unto me, and said, "I am come to bless thee, and to grant thee thy request," as you read in the Scriptures. Thus my eyes were opened at the end of six weeks, while I was praying, in the place where I slept; although the place was as dark as a dungeon, I awoke, as the Scripture saith, and found it illuminated with the light of the glory of God, and the angel standing by me, with the large book open, which was the Holy Bible, and said unto me, "Thou has desired to read and understand this book, and to speak the language of it both in English and in Dutch; I will therefore teach thee, and now read"; and then he taught me to read the first chapter of the gospel according to St. John; and when I had read the whole chapter, the angel and the book were both gone in the twinkling of an eye, which astonished me very much, for the place was dark immediately; being about four o'clock in the morning in the winter season. (35)

The angel teaches Jea to read the first chapter of the Gospel of John, and when the angel disappears, Jea is not sure whether the event is real or

---

131. Henry Louis Gates Jr., *The Signifying Monkey: A Theory of African-American Literary Criticism* (New York: Oxford University Press, 1988), identifies this motif as the "trope of the talking book," which appears in other narratives of early African American writers such as James Gronniosaw, John Marrant, Olaudah Equiano, and Ottobo Cugoano (127–69).

not. Nevertheless, the Spirit speaks to him and assures him that he is able to read. Jea proceeds to praise God for this supernatural deliverance and speaks to his minister about this miracle, proclaiming to the minister that he can read. Refusing to believe him, the minister brings him a Bible, and Jea reads the Scripture to him, prompting the minister to ask Jea how he learned to read. Jea remarks that the Lord taught him. Since Jea could not read any other books the minister presented to him and could not spell, the minister and his wife become convinced that the Lord had indeed taught Jea to read only the Bible.[132]

News of this miraculous deed spread, and Jea was once again brought before the magistrates, who ask him if he can read. After answering affirmatively, they give him a Bible, and upon hearing him read, they ask how he learned to do so. As he had answered his minister, so Jea answers the magistrates, "The Lord had taught me" (37). Believing that this occurrence was a work of the Lord, the magistrates declare that Jea should be free indisputably, for as Jea recounts, "they believed that I was of God, for they were persuaded that no man could read in such a manner, unless he was taught of God. From that hour, in which the Lord taught me to read, until the present, I have not been able to read in any book, nor any reading whatever, but such as contain the word of God" (38).[133]

Recall that earlier in Jea's autobiography he says the Bible talks and tells Jea's enslavers that he should remain a slave. Yet one of the striking features of the narrative is that the Lord teaches Jea to read the very book his enslavers use to try to convince him of his permanent enslavement. Jea recognizes his former enslaver's role in attempting to prevent him from understanding Scripture and to keep him in bondage; therefore, the prevention of understanding Scripture is linked with slavery. The actions of the slaveholder demonstrate that one of the important elements of slavery was to control enslaved Africans' access to Scripture by keeping them illiterate, by making them believe that the book only talked to whites, and that God had no concern for them except for creating them for slavery. Jea's ability

---

132. There are accounts of other miraculous instances of African Americans being taught to read by God, such as Jean McMahon Humez, ed., *Gifts of Power: The Writings of Rebecca Cox Jackson, Black Visionary, Shaker Eldress* (Amherst: University of Massachusetts Press, 1981), 108.

133. Some historians question the accuracy of Jea's account regarding his miracle of literacy and subsequent freedom. See discussions in Pierce, *Hell without Fires*, 59; John Saillant, "Traveling in Old and New Worlds with John Jea, the African Preacher, 1773–1816," *Journal of American Studies* 33 (1999): 488.

to read the Bible, however, overcomes all these obstacles established by slavocracy, solidifies his freedom once and for all, and enables him to travel around preaching the good news to enslaved Africans and to all who would listen. As Henry Louis Gates observes, Jea "literally reads his way out of slavery."[134] Through Jea's miraculous experience of literacy the liberating power of Scripture is given physical expression through Jea's physical liberation from slavery. This extraordinary occurrence provides the impetus for Jea's preaching "from house to house, and from plantation to plantation" (38).[135] Eventually Jea joins another black preacher and some white friends to erect a meetinghouse where blacks could worship.

God's divine intervention on Jea's behalf bestows agency upon Jea, who now has power over his own body. As the use of his Pauline language of "new creation" signifies, Jea experiences a total transformation, that is, spiritual freedom, physical freedom, and, with the ability to read, mental freedom. As he reflects upon his converted state, Jea remarks, "It pleased *God to send the Spirit of his Son into my heart* [Gal. 4:6], to *bear witness with my spirit that I was a child of God* [Rom. 8:16]" (74). Jea saw his life as transformed, in which God's Spirit resided in him and affirmed his humanity, thereby establishing that, contrary to what his former owner taught him, he was neither created by the devil nor a devil himself but was a child of God, his Creator. Jea's use of Paul's words resists the distorted ideology of the slaveholders and asserts that the apostle's language gave him the words to communicate his personhood and dignity. Moreover, whereas before he experienced beatings whenever he went to church, now Jea becomes part of a "church-planting team," as it were, that opens a church for African Americans. And, contrary to the earlier part of his life where he needed to sneak out at night to pray and talk with the minister, Jea is a minister free to proclaim the gospel. After continuing to serve as a preacher in this church for four years, Jea leaves for Boston to preach there and travels elsewhere in the United States and the world to proclaim the gospel, including New Orleans, the East Indies,

---

134. Gates, *Signifying*, 163.

135. Jea's preaching carries over into his narrative. At moments his autobiography becomes a sermon in which he addresses the reader to get saved and receive God's grace. For example, in one place he writes, "I would, therefore, advise you, my dear reader, to endeavour, if you have not, to seek the Lord" (23). In addition to his various direct addresses of the reader to seek salvation, he exhorts the reader to read certain Scriptures. Once his "mini-sermons" conclude, he returns to the narrative with a cue to the reader, "But, to resume my narrative . . ." (25). Even in his autobiography, Jea sees an opportunity to share the gospel, indicating his preacher's heart and his desire for everyone's salvation.

Holland, France, Germany, Ireland, England, and Asia.[136] In his narration of his reasons for embarking upon these preaching tours around the world, he declares that the *love of God has constrained him*, and so he invokes Paul's language in 2 Corinthians 5:14 to indicate that God's love is foundational to his gospel proclamation.[137] In addition, in describing his reasons for traveling to the East Indies, he cites in full 1 Corinthians 10:24–33, focusing upon Paul's statements in these verses that believers ought not to seek their own wealth but the wealth of others (10:24), believers are to do all things for the glory of God (10:31), and they are to seek the salvation of all (10:33). His powerful interpretation of these verses appears in what follows:

> This was my motive in going to the East Indies, that *whatsoever I did, to do it for the honour and glory of God* [10:31]; *not to seek mine own interest* [10:24, 33], but the interest of my Lord and Master Jesus Christ; not for the honour and riches of the world, but the riches and honours of that which is to come: I say, not for the riches of this world, which fadeth away; neither for the glory of man; nor for golden treasure; but my motive and concern was for the sake of my Lord and Master, who went about doing good, in order to save poor wicked and sinful creatures. (77)

As indicated by this citation, proclaiming the gospel's transformative power became Jea's life and focus. Although during his travels he experiences a great deal of suffering, ranging from illness to gross racist mistreatment from the staff onboard the ships, he presses on. Utilizing the language of James, Acts, Romans, 2 Thessalonians, and 2 Corinthians, Jea describes his response to the suffering he endures: "I counted it all joy [James 1:2] that *I was worthy to suffer for the glory of God* [Acts 5:41; 2 Thess. 1:5]; *for our trials and tribulations which are but for a moment* [2 Cor. 4:17] *are not worthy to be compared with the glory that shall be given us hereafter* [Rom. 8:18]" (65). Moreover, Jea believed that the words of the apostle Paul and Barnabas,

---

136. Saillant, "Traveling in Old and New Worlds," 476.

137. Jea, *Life*, writes: "After this the love of God constrained me to travel into other parts to preach the gospel" (49); "The love of God constrained me to preach to the people at Liverpool, as I had done to those in North America" (55); "After that I was constrained by the love of God to take another journey abroad" (66); "I was constrained by the Spirit of God, to take a journey into a foreign country" (75). Paul writes in 2 Cor. 5:14: "For the love of Christ constraineth us; because we thus judge, that if one died for all, then were all dead." Though Jea substitutes "God" and "Spirit of God" for "Christ" in his recitation of this verse, his inclusion of the phrase demonstrates his view that his ministry originates in divine love.

that it is through many trials and tribulations that believers enter into the kingdom of God, characterize his life story as well (Acts 14:22) (75). Yet Jea's sufferings do not diminish his desire to spread the gospel but only increase his eschatological expectations. While his sufferings are great, his heavenly reward is much greater. When he is threatened by a sea captain who would not pay him his earned wages, Jea describes the victory he receives over this situation as a divine deliverance that comes to him because "*There is no condemnation to them which are in Christ Jesus, who walk not after the flesh, but after the Spirit* [Rom. 8:1]" (79). Jea understands God to be on the side of the oppressed, and thus on his side. And so every victory comes about because God delivers those who follow after the divine call.

That Jea views himself and his travels in Pauline terms comes to the fore in the way he portrays his preaching ministry. Like Paul, he proclaims Jesus and him crucified (1 Cor. 2:2) (79), sees his labor as not in vain (1 Cor. 15:58) (56, 75), and describes his preaching as weak, though God's power manifests miracles for those who hear him (1 Cor. 1:27, 2:1-4) (82).[138] Even when he faces opposition to his preaching, he characterizes those that oppose him with Pauline language. For example, when he preaches in Sunderland, two preachers contest his presence and one attempts to berate him before the congregation, chastising the people for coming out to hear Jea speak. In his autobiography, Jea describes this man as not being "*led by the Spirit of God* [Rom. 8:14]" and as operating in the "*works of the flesh*" and not in the "*fruit of the Spirit*" (62).[139]

Furthermore, he deliberately patterns his itinerant ministry after Paul by seeking employment when traveling in order to earn his own money. He writes, "I had engaged myself on board of the above ship [*The Prince of Boston*], as cook, for seventeen Spanish dollars per month, in order that I should not be burdensome to the church of God; and this was the way I acted whenever I travelled; for, as St. Paul saith, '*I would rather labour with my hands than be burdensome to the church*'" (79).[140] Jea models himself after the apostle, working with his own hands so that he may not cause the church undue stress.

138. See also Jea's description of one of his sermons preached in Liverpool taken from 1 Cor. 10:1-15 (71-73), his use of Heb. 4:1-6, 11 (85-86), and his use of 2 Cor. 13:11 to bid farewell to his friends (88).

139. Although Jea cites this as Gal. 4:18-24, it is actually Gal. 5:18-23.

140. Here Jea refers to Paul's words in 2 Cor. 11:7-10; 12:13-14, where the apostle discusses how he preaches the gospel free of charge to the Corinthians to keep himself from being a burden to the church.

Jea's extraordinary encounters with the divine realm lead to a preaching career that spans several countries. He employs Pauline passages in a number of ways in his narrative, to describe suffering, salvation, his ministry, the Spirit, and those in opposition to him. To be sure, Jea incorporates a number of other biblical passages in his narrative, for Scripture itself is central to his story. Yet Paul and his words take on special roles in Jea's book, for he sees himself, like Paul, engaged in spiritual battle and laboring in behalf of the church.

At first Jea rebels against Christianity, at least the version practiced by his enslavers, but yet ultimately ends up embracing the faith because he encounters a God who embraces him and makes God's self real to him through conversion. He eventually recognizes that the Christianity adhered to by his enslavers was not real Christianity, describing their misuse of the faith in Pauline terms: "*Their hearts being carnal, as the Scriptures saith, were at enmity with God, not subject to the law of God, neither indeed could be* [Rom. 8:7], *for they gave themselves up to the works of the flesh, to fulfil it in the lusts thereof* [Rom. 13:14; Gal. 5:19]" (8). His enslavers' carnal hearts revealed that although they attended church, their hearts were not subject to God but instead were focused on their own desires, which led them to act in destructive ways. Moreover, Jea, an enslaved African whom his enslavers declared "had no god," proves the falsehood of this declaration, for God saves him, teaches him how to read, calls him to preach, and enables him to travel the world proclaiming the gospel.

Jea's deep desire to read the Bible and the literacy miracle that he receives constitute a miracle that defies everything slavocracy stands for: inferiority of African Americans, the supremacy of white Americans, God's so-called appointment of black slavery for all time, and the idea that God had no concern for those trapped in slavocracy's shackles. Henry Louis Gates insightfully remarks, "Jea's desire, satisfied by divine intervention when all other merely mortal avenues had been closed off by the evils of slavery, was for a bilingual facility with the text of God, a facility that he is able to demonstrate upon demand of the skeptical. It is the mastery of the text of God, alone of all other texts, which leads directly to his legal manumission."[141] As we have seen, this "text of God" flows throughout Jea's story, shaping his narrative in profound ways.

Significantly, Paul is a means by which Jea interprets his life and the lives of his former enslavers. In regard to the slaveholders, the apostle becomes a way to attempt to explain and to try to understand the incomprehensible—the cruelty they exhibited toward him and the other enslaved Africans. Their "car-

141. Gates, *Signifying*, 164.

nal hearts" made it evident that they "did not believe the report God gave of his Son," which means they could not love, could not see the enslaved Africans as human beings, and so could not rightfully claim and proclaim the title of Christian. In addition, Paul provides the language of judgment, for Jea quotes 2 Corinthians 5:10, *"The time is drawing nigh when we must all appear at the bar of God, to give an account of the deeds done in the body"* (22). The time of judgment pertains to all who do not repent, including his former enslavers.

As for Jea, Paul enables him to reinterpret his life and demonstrate for the slave "who had no god" the reality of God, the God who comes to him and saves him by grace through faith (Eph. 2:8–9) (25) and makes him a new creature (2 Cor. 5:17) (34). This reinterpretation of his life leads to a reinterpretation of his purpose. He goes forth in an apostolic role with Paul's language providing the means to describe his apostolic wanderings and sufferings for the sake of the gospel. Jea's experience provides a stunning move from the Paul used to keep him in slavery to the Paul he reappropriates as a preaching companion and a conveyor of freedom and liberation.

Jarena Lee (1783–1850[?]): One of the First Black Women Preachers in the African Methodist Episcopal Church

As some enslaved Africans cited Paul in petitions and others, like Hammon, Haynes, and Jea, used the apostle to argue on multiple levels for black identity, black agency, and black liberation, a prominent black woman preacher named Jarena Lee claimed Paul's voice to validate her call to proclaim the gospel.[142]

Jarena Lee's Conversion and Sanctification in Pauline Language

In her narrative *The Life and Religious Experience of Jarena Lee, A Coloured Lady, Giving An Account of Her Call to Preach the Gospel. Revised and Corrected from the Original Manuscript, Written by Herself*, Lee relates that she

---

142. Jarena Lee's specific date of death is unknown, but she is believed to have died in the 1850s. See "Jarena Lee," in *Preaching with Sacred Fire: An Anthology of African American Sermons, 1750 to the Present*, ed. Martha Simmons and Frank A. Thomas (New York: Norton, 2010), 160; "Jarena Lee," in *Can I Get a Witness? Prophetic Religious Voices of African American Women, an Anthology*, ed. Marcia Riggs (Maryknoll, NY: Orbis, 1997), 6. See also the discussion of Jarena Lee in Bettye Collier-Thomas, *Daughters of Thunder: Black Women Preachers and Their Sermons, 1850–1979* (San Francisco: Jossey-Bass, 1998).

was born free on February 11, 1783, in Cape May, New Jersey, and that at seven years old she separated from her parents and became a servant maid to the Sharp family—being hired out was a common practice among poor blacks—who lived about sixty miles from her birthplace.[143] Later she moved to Philadelphia, where she has a dramatic conversion experience, an experience facilitated by a deep sense of her sin and unworthiness. At first, the weight of her sin causes her to contemplate suicide by drowning, but the "unseen arm of God" mysteriously stops her.[144] She subsequently hears Pastor Richard Allen of the Bethel African Methodist Episcopal Church preach and decides to join his congregation. Three weeks after this decision she hears another sermon and is "gloriously converted to God." She describes the event:

> Three weeks from that day, my soul was gloriously converted to God, under preaching, at the very outset of the sermon . . . when there appeared to my view, in the centre of the heart one sin; and this was malice, against one particular individual, who had strove deeply to injure me. . . . At this discovery I said, Lord I forgive every creature. That instant, it appeared to me, as if a garment, which had entirely enveloped my whole person, even to my fingers ends, split at the crown of my head, and was stripped away from me, passing like a shadow, from my sight—when the glory of God seemed to cover me in its stead. . . . That moment, though hundreds were present, I did leap to my feet and declare that God, for Christ's sake, had pardoned the sins of my soul. Great was the ecstasy of my mind, for I felt that not only the sin of malice was pardoned, but all other sins were swept away together. That day was the first when *my heart had believed, and my tongue had made confession unto salvation* [Rom. 10:9-10]. . . . For a few moments I had power to exhort sinners, and to tell of the wonders and of the goodness of him who had clothed me with his salvation. During this, the minister was silent, until my soul felt its duty had been performed, when he declared another witness of the power of Christ to forgive sins on earth, was manifest in my conversion. (29)

143. Joy Bostic, *African American Female Mysticism: Nineteenth-Century Religious Activism* (New York: Palgrave Macmillan, 2013), 49.

144. *The Life and Religious Experience of Jarena Lee, A Coloured Lady, Giving An Account of Her Call to Preach the Gospel. Revised and Corrected from the Original Manuscript, Written by Herself* (Philadelphia: Printed and published for the author, 1836), reprinted in Andrews, *Sisters of the Spirit*, 28. Hereafter, page references from the reprinted edition will be given in parentheses in the text.

In her narration of her conversion, Lee portrays an ecstatic encounter with God and employs Pauline language to depict a fusion of divine and human wills. The glory of God covers her and empowers her, as demonstrated by her physical response. She physically leaps and proclaims publicly her salvation, illustrating an empowerment of her own agency in the salvific process, a process that involves both an inner and an outer transformation, for she believes in her heart and confesses with her mouth. God removes the sin of malice that once covered her like a garment and transforms her life.

Three months after her conversion, Lee learns about the gift of sanctification, which she understands as the "entire sanctification of the soul to God" (33). This "special sense of empowerment" was called the second blessing in the Methodist tradition.[145] According to John Wesley, the founder of Methodism, once an individual repented, conversion happened.[146] After conversion or justification, then the believer received the gift of sanctification, which included "cleansing, empowerment, and habitation" of the Spirit.[147] Desiring this beautiful gift, Lee begins to call upon the Lord to show her all that was in her heart that was not right with God, for she wants to "know more of the right way of the Lord" (33). After seeking God in prayer for almost three months, Lee receives the gift of sanctification, despite what she believes is Satan's attempt to stop her from receiving it. The following citation illustrates the spiritual struggle Lee undergoes to experience this new level of intimacy with God.

> But when this voice whispered in my heart, saying, "Pray for sanctification," I again bowed in the same place, at the same time, and said, "Lord sanctify my soul for Christ's sake?" That very instant, as if lightning had darted through me, I sprang to my feet, and cried, "The Lord has sanctified my soul!" There was none to hear this but the angels who stood around to witness my joy—and Satan, whose malice raged the more. That Satan was there, I knew; for no sooner had I cried out, "The Lord has sanctified my soul," than there seemed another voice behind me, saying, "No, it is too great a work to be done." But another spirit said, "Bow down for the

145. Andrews, introduction to *Sisters of the Spirit*, 14.
146. Andrews, introduction to *Sisters of the Spirit*, 14–15.
147. David D. Daniels III, "'Doing All the Good We Can': The Political Witness of African American Holiness and Pentecostal Churches in the Post–Civil Rights Era," in *New Day Begun: African American Churches and Civic Culture in Post–Civil Rights America* (Durham, NC: Duke University Press, 2003), 167. We will see in chap. 3 that Pentecostals believe in a third grace or blessing—baptism of the Holy Spirit.

witness—I received it—thou art sanctified!" The first I knew of myself after that, I was standing in the yard with my hands spread out, and looking with my face toward heaven. I now ran into the house and told them what had happened to me, when, as it were, a new rush of the same ecstasy came upon me, and caused me to feel as if I were in an ocean of light and bliss. During this, I stood perfectly still, the tears rolling in a flood from my eyes. So great was the joy, that it is past description. There is no language that can describe it, except that which was heard by St. Paul, *when he was caught up to the third heaven, and heard words which it was not lawful to utter* [2 Cor. 12:4]. (34)

Lee's reception of the gift of sanctification is such a powerful experience for her that she describes it in cosmic and supernatural terms. The divine power felt like lightning going through her body, and her sensitivity to the spirit world is evident in that she experiences this divine engagement in the presence of angels as well as Satan. Supernatural forces, both good and evil, witness her divine episode. Moreover, although she tries to describe the ecstatic encounter as an ocean of light and bliss, she recognizes the limitations of human words to depict this foray into the divine realm. In fact, she recognizes that her experience parallels that of Paul, who, when he traveled to the third heaven, heard things that were not lawful to speak. Similar to the apostle, Lee's journey into the divine intimates a chasm between human and divine speech, a chasm that cannot be completely overcome, for the language of the holy realm cannot be fully expressed in the earthly sphere. Nevertheless, Paul's language functions as a way for Lee to attempt to articulate her conversion and sanctification experiences, episodes that demonstrate a transport to another realm where human and divine meet and the human being is forever transformed. Part of this transformation is, as Joy Bostic notes, indicated in the imagery of lightning in Lee's mystical experience, for the lightning signifies the "intensity and pervasiveness of divine illumination" that Lee experiences. Additionally, the mystical event bestows a new consciousness of herself that is not "bound by the controlling images or narrow constructs generated out of the matrix of domination," for now Lee views herself and her life as directed by God's purpose and mission.[148]

---

148. Bostic, *African American Female Mysticism*, 70. For a christological reading of Lee's sanctification experience, see J. Kameron Carter, *Race: A Theological Account* (New York: Oxford University Press, 2008), 333–39.

Lee's Call to Preach in Pauline Terms

After narrating her conversion and sanctification, Lee relates another divine encounter that transforms her life and provides the basis for her call to preach. She hears a voice that says, "Go preach the Gospel!" and she replies, "No one will believe me." The voice then responds, "Preach the Gospel; I will put words in your mouth, and will turn your enemies to become your friends" (35). Interestingly, Lee believes that this voice may have come from Satan, because she had read that "[*Satan*] *could transform himself into an angel of light,* for the purpose of deception" (35). This Pauline text, 2 Corinthians 11:14, becomes the basis for her doubt that the call she receives is real and from God. The apostle's recognition that Satan disguises himself as an angel of God compels Lee to guard against any type of deceit and to seek confirmation of what she hears.

Consequently, she goes into a secret place and asks God whether or not she is being deceived. God answers by giving her a vision of a pulpit and a Bible laying upon it being presented to her. This confirmation causes Lee to speak to Richard Allen, the aforementioned pastor in charge of the Methodist African Society, regarding her experience, and he tells her that the Methodist discipline "did not call for women preachers" (36). At his words she felt relief for a moment and then realized that the "holy energy which burned within [her] as a fire, began to be smothered." She then proceeds to chastise church government and bylaws that do not correspond to the divine will or the divine word, for Lee declares:

> O how careful ought we to be, lest through our by-laws of church government and discipline, we bring into disrepute even the word of life. For as unseemly as it may appear now-a-days for a woman to preach, it should be remembered that nothing is impossible with God. And why should it be thought impossible, heterodox, or improper, for a woman to preach? seeing the Saviour died for the woman as well as the man. If a man may preach, because the Saviour died for him, why not the woman? seeing he died for her also. Is he not a whole Saviour, instead of a half one? as those who hold it wrong for a woman to preach, would seem to make it appear. (36)

Lee echoes Scripture to proclaim that although God does the impossible, a woman preaching should be considered a natural phenomenon since Christ died for both women and men, and as a result both should be able to proclaim the good news. If one holds that only men can preach, then

Christ must have died only for men, which contradicts Holy Scripture. Thus, she speaks out against church tradition that contradicts the Word of God and lifts up Mary as the first preacher: "Did not Mary *first* preach the risen Saviour, and is not the doctrine of the resurrection the very climax of Christianity—hangs not all our hope on this, as argued by St. Paul [1 Cor. 15:12–22]? Then did not Mary, a woman, preach the gospel? for she preached the resurrection of the crucified Son of God" (36).[149] Lee argues here that Mary is the first preacher, since Paul in 1 Corinthians 15 contends that the resurrection is central to the Christian faith and that believers' hope rests upon this fact. Since this is the case, Mary, a woman, becomes the first proclaimer of the gospel because she declares Jesus's resurrection. In an ironic twist, Lee utilizes the apostle, often employed to disavow a woman's right to preach, to condone and sanction women preaching, for Mary proclaims what is in the apostle's eyes the very heart of the gospel. Lee argues that God can inspire a female to preach the birth, death, and resurrection of Jesus just as well as God can inspire a man. In fact, that God calls women is evidenced in Lee's own ministry, for when she proclaims the gospel, sinners are awakened and converted. She reveals that many families have come to her and professed that through her they came to receive the gospel, and she confesses that God speaks through her, a "poor coloured female instrument" (37).

Despite these powerful affirmations of her ministry, Lee describes a time in her life when she was afflicted by an inner turmoil that consisted of the fear of losing her soul and falling from grace (37). She constantly prayed about this torment and finally received a vision from God that set her at ease about the state of her soul:

There appeared a form of fire, about the size of a man's hand, as I was on my knees; at the same moment, there appeared to the eye of faith a man robed in a white garment, from the shoulders down to the feet; from him a voice proceeded, saying: "Thou shalt never return from the cross." Since that time I have never doubted, but believe that god will keep me until the day of redemption. *Now I could adopt the very language of St. Paul, and say that nothing could have separated my soul from the love of god, which is in Christ Jesus* [Rom. 8:35–39]. From that time, 1807, until the present, 1833, I have

149. See also the discussion of this passage in Valerie Cooper, *Maria Stewart, the Bible, and the Rights of African Americans* (Charlottesville: University of Virginia Press, 2011), 135–36; Carter, *Race*, 339–42.

> not yet doubted the power and goodness of God to keep me from falling,
> through sanctification of the spirit and belief of the truth. (37–38)

The cross, which is central to Paul's understanding of the gospel, becomes the means by which Lee's assurance regarding her soul takes place; she can "never return from the cross." The cross is God's power for her salvation and her deliverance from her tormenting fears, and it solidifies her stance before God, enabling her to proclaim that now she "could adopt the very language of St. Paul," to declare the inability of her soul to become separated from God's love. The apostle's words, then, become her own, empowering her to articulate the depth of God's love for her, a love that removes her fears, silences her doubts, and refuses to let her go.

Eight years after her first request to preach, Lee makes another appeal to Richard Allen, who had in the meantime become Bishop Allen. She writes, "It was now eight years since I had made application to be permitted to preach the gospel, during which time I had only been allowed to exhort, and even this privilege but seldom" (42). Lee describes a significant moment in her life that changes her ministerial status. During a service at Bethel church in which Rev. Richard Williams was the designated preacher, Lee ends up preaching the sermon because, when Williams begins to speak from Jonah 2:9,

> he seemed to have lost the spirit; when in the same instant, I sprang, as by an altogether supernatural impulse, to my feet, when I was aided from above to give an exhortation on the very text which my brother Williams had taken. I told them that I was like Jonah; for it had been then nearly eight years since the Lord had called me to preach his gospel to the fallen *sons and daughters of Adam's race* [Rom. 5:14–19; 1 Cor. 15:22], but that I had lingered like him, and delayed to go at the bidding of the Lord, and warn those who are as deeply guilty as were the people of Nineveh. During the exhortation, God made manifest his power in a manner sufficient to show the world that I was called to labour according to my ability, and the *grace given unto me* [Rom. 12:3; 15:15; cf. 1 Cor. 3:10; Eph. 3:2, 7], in the vineyard of the good husbandman. I now sat down, scarcely knowing what I had done, being frightened. I imagined, that for this indecorum, as I feared it might be called, I should be expelled from the church. But instead of this, the Bishop rose up in the assembly, and related that I had called upon him eight years before, asking to be permitted to preach, and that he had put me off; but that he now as much believed that I was called to that work, as any of the preachers present. These remarks greatly strengthened me. (44–45)

The "supernatural impulse" that empowers Lee to speak during this service is the same supernatural impulse that enabled her to speak publicly years earlier about her conversion. In that earlier instance, during Lee's proclamation, "the [male] minister was silent" (29), and here again, Lee's divine empowerment mutes the male minister, which represents a divine interruption of the status quo.[150] Echoing Paul's belief in the universal effect of Adam's action ("the fallen sons and daughters of Adam's race"), Lee believes that her ministry is universal as well; God calls her to preach to all people, black, white, male, and female. Here Lee connects her calling to Jonah as well as to Paul, demonstrating that for her both figures help to depict her preaching mission. As God bestowed grace upon Paul, now this grace rests upon Lee to proclaim the good news to "the fallen sons and daughters of Adam's race" who are similar to the guilty "people of Nineveh." After this incident Allen permits Lee to preach and hold prayer meetings in her home, and in other homes upon invitation, yet interestingly enough he never ordains her.[151] Lee's ministry, however, expands from meetings in homes to more public places, such as schools, and she preaches to racially mixed audiences with diverse socioeconomic backgrounds.

Lee as Paul: The Colored Woman Preacher Sent to Jerusalem and "Operations of the Spirit"

Throughout her autobiography, along with narration of divine encounters, Lee discloses a life filled with chronic illness and battles with various sicknesses. In addition, tragedy permeates her story for, in a span of six years, five members of her family die, including her husband, which leaves her widowed with two small children to support. However, she writes of her dependence upon God, who said, "I will be the widow's God, and a father to the fatherless" (Ps. 68:5) (41). In the midst of such hardships, she proclaims the gospel and travels as far as Canada and the Northwest Territory and becomes well known for her powerful sermons.[152] In 1835 she confesses that she has "traveled over seven hundred miles and preached almost the same number of sermons."[153]

---

150. See also Bostic, *African American Female Mysticism*, 67.
151. "Jarena Lee," in *Preaching with Sacred Fire*, 161–62.
152. "Jarena Lee," in *Preaching with Sacred Fire*, 162.
153. Andrews, introduction to *Sisters of the Spirit*, 6.

In the final pages of her autobiography, Lee discloses how, after fourteen years, she desires to return to Cape May, the place of her birth. She compares her return to Cape May to Paul, writing that "the Lord sent me, as Saul of Tarsus was sent to Jerusalem, to preach the same gospel which he had neglected and despised before his conversion" (46). Her ministry in Cape May, though meeting with some opposition, flourishes, and lives are transformed by her preaching. People come with "curiosity to hear the coloured woman preacher" (46), and she preaches to mixed congregations consisting of "both coloured and white" (47). In fact, she encounters a man, a slaveholder, who believes that black people do not have souls, but through her preaching his mind is changed, although "whether he became a converted man or not" she did not know (47). In her closing remarks, Lee recognizes that her narrative is filled with supernatural encounters and "operations of the Spirit," and that such narrations may seem improper or incredulous to some who read her story (48). Yet she maintains that just as a blind person is able to use other senses more acutely than can a person with sight, so has Lee developed her "Spirit" sense, if you will, and is able to discern and feel the Spirit's leading in a way that differs from those who do not develop this capacity. She develops this ability by watching "the more closely the operations of the Spirit" and consequently learns how the Spirit leads. The Spirit, she insists, always leads her in concert with the Scriptures, as she understands them. She concludes this section with Pauline language, declaring that "*For as many as are led by the Spirit of God are the sons of God*—Rom. viii.14" (48). Her inclusion of this passage proclaims that this Pauline language describes her identity: she is a child of God to whom and through whom the Spirit speaks. The Spirit of God leads her, authorizes her, and demonstrates that she belongs to God.

William L. Andrews writes that Jarena Lee's autobiography argued for women's spiritual authority that challenged the conventional female roles of her day in slave and free states, among blacks and whites.[154] In fact, the "American 'cult of true womanhood'" defined a woman's place as in the home, and activity outside of that realm that could interfere with her duties to her husband and children was considered dangerous.[155] The idea of a woman's place carried over to the organization of the church, and women were given specific positions considered "suitable" for them. For example, when Lee first approached Allen about her call to preach, he informed her that "women had done much good by way of exhortation," which meant that

154. Andrews, introduction to *Sisters of the Spirit*, 2.
155. Andrews, introduction to *Sisters of the Spirit*, 13.

he saw her in the role of an exhorter, a position given to women because it was not empowered with the authority of ordination. Exhorters held the lowest status in the church's hierarchical structure, and led Sunday school and prayer meetings, but in church services they only spoke in response to the biblical text chosen that day by the presiding minister. Consequently, "as exhorters women remained dependent on the male leadership of the church for access to the ears of a congregation and to the Bible itself."[156] Yet Lee's autobiography demonstrates that her ministry expanded beyond this imposed status.

Lee's narrative, therefore, is significant because it contends for women's spiritual authority and challenges conventional ideas about womanhood, but also because it is the "earliest and most detailed firsthand information we have about the traditional roles of women in organized black religious life in the United States and about the ways in which resistance to those roles began to manifest itself."[157] This earliest and most detailed account, as we have seen, is fertile ground in ascertaining how Paul's language early on becomes a tool to resist these conventional female roles as well as racist beliefs and stereotypes. Exploring Lee's groundbreaking autobiography provides a glimpse into how she faced resistance to her noncompliance of traditional women roles and how she employed Paul's language to resist the resistance.

For Jarena Lee, Pauline language allows her to narrate her divine encounters and her life as a Spirit-filled woman whose life and call God orchestrates and ordains. The apostle's language becomes her own, for she claims it and transforms it through her experiences as a black woman daring to proclaim the gospel in the midst of a society that opposes her. The Spirit's work in her ministry allowed her to change minds, such as that of the slaveholder who believed that blacks had no souls, and the Spirit, through her, demonstrated that colored females spoke for the Divine as well. That she, a black woman, could have an ecstatic experience similar to Paul's meant that such experiences were not limited to Paul alone, or by extension, to men alone, but women, including black women, were admitted to the divine realm, and not just admitted but welcomed. God's words ring loud and clear to Lee's readers, "Thou art sanctified!" Lee's use of the apostle's words signify the reality of divine interruptions that can take place in the midst of human oppression.

156. Andrews, introduction to *Sisters of the Spirit*, 14.
157. Andrews, introduction to *Sisters of the Spirit*, 2.

Zilpha Elaw (1790[?]–?): Renowned Early Black Woman Preacher

Like Jarena Lee, Zilpha Elaw is a black woman preacher who appears on the American landscape during this period.[158] Elaw was born free around 1790 near Philadelphia but became a servant to a Quaker couple and endured "harsh fieldwork on an early nineteenth-century farm."[159] She was one of the few black women during her time to proclaim the gospel in the midst of great adversity from both women and men because of her gender and race. Elaw appeared with her fellow sister preacher, Jarena Lee, at least on one occasion,[160] and although she preached numerous sermons, unfortunately none of them survive. In her autobiography, *Memoirs of the Life, Religious Experience, Ministerial Travels and Labours of Mrs. Zilpha Elaw, an American Female of Colour: Together with Some Account of the Great Religious Revivals in America [Written By Herself]*, in which she details her conversion, her call to preach, and her subsequent ministry, she extensively adopts and adapts Paul's language.[161] Throughout her narrative she describes various supernatural encounters with God, what some today would call mystical experiences.

The Pauline Contours of Zilpha Elaw's Autobiography

From the beginning of her autobiography until the end, Elaw consistently employs Pauline language to describe her life and her profound supernatural episodes, and repeatedly depicts her call and her ministry in terms of Paul and his ministry. Indeed, the verse displayed on the cover of her autobiography, 2 Corinthians 3:5 (*"Not that we are sufficient of ourselves to think any thing as of ourselves; but our sufficiency is of God"*), presages the extensive use of Pauline language that follows.[162] That she views herself in relationship

---

158. Elaw's death date is difficult to determine since information about her after 1846 is not known. See "Zilpha Elaw," in Simmons and Thomas, *Preaching with Sacred Fire*, 168.

159. Pierce, *Hell without Fires*, 90; cf. 89; "Zilpha Elaw," in Simmons and Thomas, *Preaching with Sacred Fire*, 167.

160. "Zilpha Elaw," in Riggs, *Can I Get A Witness?*, 11. According to Andrews, *Sisters of the Spirit*, "Lee met Zilpha Elaw while both were proselytizing in western Pennsylvania. Lee recalls that they 'enjoyed good seasons together' as a temporary preaching team" (6).

161. Elaw includes over one hundred Pauline citations and echoes in her autobiography.

162. Elaw, *Memoirs*, reprinted in Andrews, *Sisters of the Spirit*, 49. Hereafter, page numbers from this work, as found in the Andrews volume, will be given in parentheses in the text.

to the apostle appears prominently in the way she writes the dedication of her narrative. She dedicates her autobiography to her friends in England and writes the prefatory dedication in the form of a Pauline epistle. She begins the dedicatory letter with a Pauline greeting and closes it with a complete quotation of 2 Corinthians 13:14. In addition, the content of the letter employs several significant Pauline Scriptures. Elaw describes herself as an example of power in weakness (2 Cor. 12:9), and, as one called by God, she takes on the mantle of the apostle to exhort her English friends to "*walk worthy of the high vocation wherewith you are called*" (Eph. 4:1) (51), to "*renounce the love of money, for it is the root of all evil*" (1 Tim. 6:10), and to build their foundation upon Jesus, "*the chief cornerstone*" (Eph. 2:20) (51–52). This prefatory letter, along with her choice of 2 Corinthians 3:5 for the title page verse, indicates the importance of the apostle to Elaw's understanding of her life and call.

Elaw's Conversion

Elaw's autobiography begins with an account of her conversion. At the beginning of her conversion experience she suffers from an acute sense of her own sinfulness. Echoing Pauline language, she relates that she felt a "*godly sorrow* [2 Cor. 7:10] for sin in having grieved my God by a course of disobedience to His commands" (55). At the beginning of this deep sense of agony, Elaw has a dream of judgment that disturbs her so much that she discusses it with her mistress, who advises her to forget about it. After this event, she begins attending Methodist meetings, from which she "derived great satisfaction," and she also attends Quaker meetings, at which she "often found comfort from the word ministered by them" (55). She prays daily to God regarding the assurance of the forgiveness of her sins, and God responds to her prayer by bestowing upon her a vision. Elaw describes the experience in the following way:

> One evening, whilst singing one of the songs of Zion, I distinctly saw the Lord Jesus approach me with open arms, and a most divine and heavenly smile upon his countenance. As he advanced towards me, I felt that his very looks spoke, and said, "Thy prayer is accepted, I own thy name." From that day to the present I have never entertained a doubt of the manifestation of his love to my soul. Yea, I may say further than this; because, at the time when this occurrence took place, I was milking in the cow stall; and the

manifestation of his presence was so clearly apparent, that even the beast of the stall turned her head and bowed herself upon the ground. Oh, never, never shall I forget the scene. . . . I might have tried to imagine, or persuade myself, perhaps that it had been a vision presented merely to the eye of my mind; but, the beast of the stall gave forth her evidence to the reality of the heavenly appearance; for she turned her head and looked round as I did; and when she saw, she bowed her knees and cowered down upon the ground. I was overwhelmed with astonishment at the sight, but the thing was certain and beyond all doubt. I write as before God and Christ, and declare, as I shall give an account to my Judge at the great day, that every thing I have written in this little book, has been written with conscientious veracity and scrupulous adherence to truth. After this wonderful manifestation of my condescending Saviour, *the peace of God which passeth understanding* [Phil. 4:7] was communicated to my heart; and *joy in the Holy Ghost* [Rom. 14:17], to a degree, at the last, *unutterable by my tongue* [2 Cor. 12:4] and indescribable by my pen; it was beyond my comprehension; but, from that happy hour, my soul was set at *glorious liberty* [Rom. 8:21]; and, like the Ethiopic eunuch, I went on my way rejoicing in the blooming prospects of a better inheritance with the saints in light. This, my dear reader, was the manner of my soul's conversion to God. (56–57)

Elaw's dramatic conversion experience is so extraordinary that nature bears witness to her divine encounter, and the previous torment that characterized her existence lifts, resulting in an indescribable peace and joy. Paul's language enables Elaw to depict her conversion as one of divine origin, divine experience, and divine transformation. Like Paul in Acts, who has a personal encounter with Jesus on the road to Damascus, Elaw has a personal encounter with Jesus, who opens his arms and receives her as his own.[163] The experience has such a profound impact upon her that she further writes about the experience in the language of the apostle, "*The love of God being shed abroad in my heart by the Holy Spirit* [Rom. 5:5], and my soul transported with heavenly peace and joy in God, all the former hardships which pertained to my circumstances and situation vanished" (57).

For Elaw, her conversion bestows upon her peace, joy, love, liberty, and a new identity as one adopted by God, with whom she communes intimately

---

163. Elaw, like the other interpreters in this volume, does not distinguish between the Paul of Acts, the Paul of the undisputed epistles, and the Paul of the deutero-Pauline epistles, all of which are distinctions prevalent in modern biblical studies.

and habitually. This deep intimacy with God, which she describes as "habitual communion," is intricately connected to her identity as an adopted child (58): "My delights were to follow the leadings and obey the dictates of the Holy Spirit, and glorify with my body and spirit my Father who is in heaven. I enjoyed richly the *spirit of adoption* [Rom. 8:15]: knowing myself to be an adopted child of divine love, I claimed God as my Father, and his Son Jesus as my dear friend, who adhered to me more faithfully in goodness than a brother: and with my blessed Saviour, Redeemer, Intercessor, and Patron, I enjoyed a delightsome heavenly communion, such as the world has never conceived of" (60).

Paul's description of the Holy Spirit as the spirit of adoption enables Elaw to describe her new identity and to own this new identity as completely hers. Elaw is part of the divine family, for she is God's child, Jesus's friend, and with the Holy Spirit's guidance she gains access to divine realms that surpass worldly existence.

Elaw's Camp-Meeting Experience

In 1817 Elaw attends a camp meeting, where she has another profound encounter with God, which propels her into public religious life. Utilizing Pauline language, Elaw describes the encounter:

> It was at one of these meetings that God was pleased to separate my soul unto Himself, *to sanctify me as a vessel designed for honour, made meet for the master's use* [2 Tim. 2:21]. *Whether I was in the body, or whether I was out of the body, on that auspicious day, I cannot say* [2 Cor. 12:2-3]; but this I do know, that at the conclusion of a most powerful sermon delivered by one of the ministers from the platform, and while the congregation were in prayer, I became so overpowered with the presence of God, that I sank down upon the ground, and laid there for a considerable time; and while I was thus prostrate on the earth, my *spirit seemed to ascend* [2 Cor. 12:2, 4] up into the clear circle of the sun's disc; and surrounded and engulphed in the glorious effulgence of his rays, I distinctly heard a voice speak unto me, which said, "Now thou art sanctified; and I will show thee what thou must do." . . . For the space of several hours I appeared not to be on earth, but far above all earthly things. I had not at this time offered up public prayer on the camp ground; but when the prayer meeting afterwards commenced, the Lord opened my mouth in public prayer. . . . I was after this very fre-

quently requested to present my petitions to the *throne of grace* [Heb. 4:16] in the public meetings at the camp . . . and before the meeting at this camp closed, it was *revealed to me by the Holy Spirit* [1 Cor. 2:10; Eph. 3:5], that like another Phoebe [Rom. 16:1], or the matrons of the apostolic societies, I must employ myself in visiting families, and in speaking personally to the members thereof, of the salvation and eternal interests of their souls, visit the sick, and attend upon other of the errands and services of the Lord; which I afterwards cheerfully did, not confining my visits to the poor only, but extending them to the rich also, and even to those who sit in high places in the state; and the Lord was with me in the work to own and bless my labours. Like Enoch, I walked and talked with God. (66–67)

As God did with Paul, God separates Elaw and sanctifies her for divine use. In addition, her own revelatory experience echoes that of the apostle, for she too does not know whether she was in or out of the body when she had her divine encounter.[164] Similar to the apostle who ascends to the third heaven, Elaw experiences rapture into the divine sphere and receives the ability to pray publicly in such a powerful way that this first public display results in frequent invitations to pray publicly thereafter. Elaw's close communion with the Spirit appears again when she relates the Spirit's disclosure that she, like Phoebe, to whom Paul refers in Romans 16:1 as a minister, has work to do. Her subsequent ministry, she informs her readers, extends to the poor, the wealthy, and the renown. Her experience of heavenly transport facilitates her ensuing identifications with Paul, Phoebe, and Enoch. God's sanctification of her and her revelatory encounter make it possible for her to be like Phoebe and grant her the ability to see herself, not only as a Paul figure, but also as similar to Enoch, another biblical figure who experiences divine transport. This particular Pauline experience becomes an opportunity for her to identify with other biblical persons.

Significantly, the Pauline experience gives her public voice and public recognition. In a time when women were expected to follow conventional roles, and black women especially were denied public forums in which to speak, Elaw's Pauline-like experience authorizes her and empowers her with voice and witness. As a result of her first public prayer ministry, people at subsequent camp meetings approach her and ask her to pray for them, which

---

164. See also Mitzi Smith, "'Unbossed and Unbought': Zilpha Elaw and Old Elizabeth and a Political Discourse of Origins," *Black Theology: An International Journal* 9, no. 3 (2011): 298. My thanks to Emerson Powery for pointing me to this source.

demonstrates a public recognition of her new identity and status. In a society that often refused to recognize the humanity of blacks and denied that they possessed souls, Elaw becomes a disruptive figure who breaks societal rules of what is proper for women and African Americans. Thus, her ministry mirrors that of her divine encounter. As in her divine experience where she contravened the boundaries between earthly and heavenly, so too her ministry breaks boundaries, those between male and female, black and white.

Elaw's Call to Preach and Opposition to Her Preaching

Another extraordinary event Elaw describes in her narrative is her visit to her dying sister, who, on her deathbed, informs Elaw that God has called Elaw to preach the gospel. Upon hearing her ill sister's statement, Elaw is overwhelmed and confused. Even after her sister's death, Elaw struggles to accept the call, and she narrates the great trial this call to preach inflicted upon her. "Notwithstanding the plain and pointed declaration of my sister, and though the Scriptures assert that *not many wise, rich, and noble are called; but God hath chosen the foolish things of the world to confound the wise, and the weak things of the world to confound the mighty* [1 Cor. 1:27], I could not at the time imagine it possible that God should select and appoint so poor and ignorant a creature as myself to be his messenger" (75).

Finding Paul's words as a way to characterize herself as unprepared for ministry, Elaw questions God's call upon her to proclaim the gospel, since she believes herself to be unqualified for the vocation. As a result, she does not preach and becomes ill for two years. Viewing this illness as God's way of chastising her for disobedience, she enters into deep prayer. God grants her another vision, promises her healing, and informs her that she will visit another camp meeting, at which she will know God's will for her life (76–79). Elaw miraculously recovers, and during her visit to the camp meeting she is overcome by the presence of God again, but this time she begins proclaiming the gospel:

> I immediately went outside and stood at the door of the tent; and in an instant I began as it were involuntarily, or from an internal prompting, with a loud voice to exhort the people who yet were remaining near the preacher's stand; and in the presence of a more numerous assemblage of ministers than I had ever seen together before; as if God had called forth witnesses from heaven, and witnesses on earth . . . to witness on this day to my commission,

and the qualifications He bestowed on me to preach his holy Gospel. How appropriate to me was the text which had been preached from just before, *"Now, then, we are ambassadors for Christ"* [2 Cor. 5:20]. Our dear ministers stood gazing and listening with wonder and astonishment; and the tears flowed abundantly down their cheeks while they witnessed the wonderful works of God. After I had finished my exhortation, I sat down and closed my eyes; and there appeared a *light shining round about me* [Acts 9:3] as well as within me . . . and out of that light, the same identical voice which had spoken to me on the bed of sickness many months before, spoke again to me on the camp ground, and said, "Now thou knowest the will of God concerning thee; thou must preach the gospel; and must travel far and wide." This is my commission for the work of the ministry, *which I received, not from mortal man* [Gal. 1:11–12], but from the voice of an invisible and heavenly personage sent from God. (82)

Elaw's inauguration into her formal preaching ministry begins at this camp meeting, where she preaches the gospel before ministers who gaze at her in wonder and amazement. Like Paul, upon whom a light shined in his dramatic call in Acts, a light shines around Elaw, designating her as God's chosen vessel for this time and place.[165] Furthermore, similar to the apostle, who declared that his apostleship and gospel did not come from human beings but from God, she too contends the divine origin of her call and ministry. Her exhortation before these crowds demonstrates her appointment as God's ambassador for Christ.

Just as her call mirrors Paul, so does the opposition she endures. In depicting how her friends treated her once she accepted her preaching mission, Elaw writes, "Like Joseph, I was hated for my dreams; and *like Paul, none stood with me* [2 Tim. 4:16]" (83). However, despite opposition from her friends and her husband, Elaw perseveres and continues to proclaim the gospel, even traveling to the slaveholding states where at any moment she could have been captured and enslaved: "When I arrived in the slave states, Satan much worried and distressed my soul with the fear of being arrested and sold for a slave, which their laws would have warranted, on account of my complexion and features" (91). William Andrews notes the particular danger Elaw faced, for in the South it was lawful to jail and sell any "free Negro who could not prove his or her free status."[166] For example, in 1840 the

---

165. See also Pierce, *Hell without Fires*, 101.
166. Andrews, *Sisters of the Spirit*, 241n19.

Virginia Supreme Court of Appeals ruled that "In the case of a person visibly appearing to be a negro, the presumption is that he is a slave."[167] Along with such laws that had the potential to seriously hurt Elaw's ministry in the slave states, some states like Virginia had additional regulations that forbade any black person, free or slave, to conduct religious meetings.[168] Elaw could have received a public beating of thirty-nine lashes for her ministerial activity.[169] Despite her fears and the real dangers she faced, Elaw continued to preach among the enslaved Africans and the slaveholders, and her ministry was quite successful, for many people turned to God and were converted. Using Pauline language to depict her ministry in these states, Elaw declares that *just as the apostle is an earthen vessel, so too is she* (2 Cor. 4:7), and as an effectual *door was opened for Paul, God likewise opened the door for her to preach when she traveled* (1 Cor. 16:9).[170] In addition, Paul's *weakness that displays the excellency of God's power* is similar to Elaw's weakness carried in her "poor coloured" frame that allows *God's strength to prevail in her* (2 Cor. 4:7) (92).

Elaw chronicles the astonishment among whites of seeing a black woman teaching and preaching with words from 1 Corinthians 1:27: "Many of the slave holders . . . thought it surpassingly strange that a person (and a female) belonging to the same family stock with their poor debased, uneducated, coloured slaves, should come into their territories and teach the enlightened proprietors the *knowledge of God* [Rom. 11:33; 1 Cor. 15:34; 2 Cor. 10:5; Col. 1:10]. . . . *But God hath chosen the weak things of the world to confound the mighty* [1 Cor. 1:27]" (92). She recognizes that her words are not eloquent but, in the words of the apostle, are in demonstration of the Spirit (1 Cor. 2:4), for the "spirit and power of Christ" enable her to "[make] *manifest the secrets of [her audience's] hearts*" and to tell them "*all things that ever they did*" (92). Andrews insightfully observes that Elaw compares herself to Jesus in Samaria when he told the woman at the well "all the things that ever [she] did" in the

167. Andrews, *Sisters of the Spirit*, 241n19.

168. Andrews, *Sisters of the Spirit*, 241n19; Pierce, *Hell without Fires*, 93.

169. Andrews, *Sisters of the Spirit*, 241n19.

170. Elaw, *Memoirs*, 92, remarks, "A *great and effectual door of utterance opened to me by the Lord*. After laboring there for some weeks, I proceeded to the City of Washington, the capital of the United States . . . here also I laboured with much success; many souls obtaining the knowledge of salvation by the remission of their sins, with the gift of the Holy Spirit, through the instrumentality of so feeble an *earthen vessel*. I continued my travels southward into the State of Virginia. . . . I abode there two months, and was an humble agent, in the Lord's hand, of arousing many of His heritage to a great revival; and the weakness and incompetency of the poor coloured female but the more displayed the *excellency of the power to be of God*."

Gospel of John (John 4:7–30). Elaw, Andrews says, identifies herself with Christ's saving mission to the Samaritans.[171]

While this is likely, it is also likely that here, in light of her extensive use of Paul, Elaw views herself as operating in one of the gifts of the Spirit, prophecy, that Paul outlines in 1 Corinthians 14. Prophecy is one of the supernatural χάρισμα (*charisma*) Paul describes as happening in the Corinthian congregation. Paul says a person on the receiving end of this gift experiences the following: "*And thus are the secrets of his heart made manifest; and so falling down on his face, he will worship God, and report that God is in you of a truth*" (1 Cor. 14:25). Thus, Elaw, by reporting what is happening in her ministry with the language "[*make*] *manifest the secrets of their hearts*," depicts herself as a prophet who through the Spirit of God can reveal the secrets of those to whom she preaches. What is more, in the Corinthian context in which Paul writes, those who hear the prophecy will believe that the prophet comes from God, since the person can reveal someone's inner thoughts. This context also fits Elaw's situation, since as a black woman in a slave state, divine operation of the Spirit in the form of prophecy validates that "God is in [her] of a truth." Indeed, Elaw relates the triumph of her ministry in Pauline terms: "I became such a prodigy to this people that I was watched wherever I went. . . . The people became increasingly earnest in their inquiries after truth; and great was the number of those *who were translated out of the empire of darkness into the Kingdom of God's dear Son* [Col. 1:13]" (92–93). More than likely, Elaw merges the Samaritan narrative with that of the Pauline words on the gift of prophecy. Hence, she portrays herself following in the footsteps of Christ, in that just as he embarked on a salvific mission to the Samaritans, she undertakes a mission to those in the slave states.[172] Equally significant is that, like the preacher from Tarsus, the Spirit endows her with an authority and legitimacy given by the Spirit's powerful presence.

Miracles in Elaw's Ministry and Her Interpretation of Paul's Injunction on Women

Along with the Spirit-led ability to proclaim the gospel, Elaw relates that miracles occurred in her ministry. On one particular occasion, a woman named Mrs. Adams became very ill and requested to see her. Interestingly,

171. Andrews, *Sisters of the Spirit*, 241n20.
172. Andrews, *Sisters of the Spirit*, 241n20.

when Elaw goes to visit her, she herself is very sick and faints once she arrives at Mrs. Adams's home. Once Elaw recovers from her fainting spell, she enters Mrs. Adams's chamber, where all her family are gathered around her expecting her to die at any moment. Elaw prays and describes the time of prayer as one "of much power; and all the family were bathed in tears" (110). As she leaves the home, Mrs. Adams's sister asks Elaw whether her sister will live or die, and Elaw replies, "No, I think she will recover, for God showed me this in the time of prayer." Miraculously, Mrs. Adams does recover, and Elaw describes how this event strengthened the veracity of her ministry: "Mrs. Adams was vastly better. . . . This circumstance made a great impression on the inhabitants of the city, who thought it strange, indeed, that God, in answer to my prayer, should heal the sick: the intelligence flew from street to street, that Mrs. Adams was recovered; and those reverend gentleman, who had so strenuously exerted themselves to silence my ministry, were themselves completely disconcerted, and their objections silenced" (110-11). Here Elaw relates the ironic outcome of the miracle—those who attempted to silence her are now silenced.

Such miraculous events as well as her own divine encounters with God enable Elaw to resist the arguments that women should not preach and that Paul taught that women should be silent in church. In several places in her autobiography, Elaw addresses such interpretations, for she often encountered them in opposition to her ministry. She writes, "It is true that in the ordinary course of Church arrangement and order, the Apostle Paul laid it down as a rule, that *females should not speak in the church, nor be suffered to teach* [1 Cor. 14:34-35; 1 Tim. 2:12]; but the Scriptures make it evident that this rule was not intended to limit the extraordinary directions of the Holy Ghost, in reference to female Evangelists, or oracular sisters; nor to be rigidly observed in peculiar circumstances" (124). For Elaw, the Spirit's profound presence and operation in the lives of women indicated that the rule Paul enacted was not eternally binding. In fact, Elaw believes that "Scriptures make it evident" that this rule is not binding since women preachers and ministers appear throughout the New Testament. In regard to Phoebe, Elaw states, "St. Paul himself attests that Phoebe was a servant or deaconess of the Church at Cenchrea; and as such was employed by the Church to manage some of their affairs; and it was strange indeed, if she was required to receive the commissions of the church in mute silence" (124).

Elaw lists other women in ministry in Scripture, such as the four daughters of Philip who were prophets and women that Paul says labored with him in the gospel, such as Priscilla, Tryphena, sisters of Nereus, and the mother of Rufus. For Elaw, the apostle's words of silence in 1 Corinthians 14:34 were given to "a church" that, because of its "disorders and excesses," needed "stringent rules for its proper regulation" (124–25). However, those who think these regulations given to *a* church apply to *the* church are gravely mistaken, for "those brethren certainly err, who fetter all and every ecclesiastical circumstance, and even the extraordinary inspirations of the Holy Spirit with the regulations given by the apostle to a church" (124; cf. 108–10, 147–48, 155). For Elaw, ascertaining the historical context of the congregation to which Paul wrote these injunctions is significant for understanding the rule's proper place. Paul wrote these words to a particular church experiencing particular issues. Indeed, the fact that God pours out the Spirit upon women and men and that the Spirit's presence and power appear in women's preaching ministry, including hers, indicates that the apostle's words were not binding for all women, for all churches, and in all times and places.

Elaw and Spiritual Warfare

In addition to her multifaceted identification with Paul, Elaw adopts the Pauline understanding of a two-tier conflict in which a spiritual battle is taking place and strongholds need to be destroyed so that the gospel may reach many (2 Cor. 10:4).[173] This spiritual conflict manifests itself in a variety of ways in her life, but particularly in opposition to Elaw's preaching ministry. Utilizing a number of Pauline references in the following passage, Elaw embraces Paul's perspective on the spirit world:

> *The principalities and powers of evil spirits*, (Ephes. vi. 12) which Christians have to contend against, which *Christ despoiled*, (Colos. ii. 15) and which constitute the strength of the empire of darkness, the world of evil spirits, the right hand of the *prince of the power of the air*, (Ephes. ii. 2) who is the *god or deity of this world*, (2 Cor. iv. 4); these principalities occasionally obstructed me much; and, by *blinding* [2 Cor. 4:4] and infatuating the sons of men, inspired them with a hostile zeal against me. This was particularly the case at Hartford; in which city some of the most influential ministers of

---

173. She explains, "For my speech and my preaching were not with enticing words of man's wisdom, but in demonstration of the Spirit, and in power; it was mighty through God, to the pulling down of strongholds; and became the power of God to the salvation of many" (Elaw, *Memoirs*, 98).

the Presbyterian body greatly opposed me; and one of them, a Mr. House, resolutely declared that he would have my preaching stopped . . . but he . . . imagined a vain thing; for the work was of God, who made bare his arm for the salvation of men by my ministry. *Thanks be unto God who always caused me to triumph in Christ; and made manifest the savour of his knowledge by me in every place* [2 Cor. 2:14]. (104).

From Paul's perspective, all believers contend against evil spirits in the spirit world, and Elaw views herself as no exception. According to her, the god of this world blinds people and makes them hostile to her ministry. As the Holy Spirit operates in and through her, so too evil spirits work against her through other people. However, even when opponents like Mr. House try to stop her, they cannot because God makes Elaw victorious over her enemies. Like Paul, through whom God made the divine known in the midst of opposition, so too through Elaw and her ministry God manifests divine knowledge, despite the difficult reality that in "being both black and female, Elaw [was] subject to the petty and profound tyrannies of many groups: black men, white men, and even white women."[174] Although the hostility Elaw experiences comes from different quarters, she nevertheless, through the Spirit, perseveres and prevails.

Elaw's Travail for Transformation

On one particular preaching occasion, a young man in the audience, upon seeing Elaw ascend the pulpit, acted unseemly. Elaw describes his behavior as indecorous, and "as the people came in he pointed with his finger to me, tittering and laughing" (100). Yet she notes that before the meeting ended, "his laughter was turned to weeping." After the service, during a dinner conversation with her hosts, she learns that the young man is a renowned slave driver who is also a well-known drunk, and that "he had never been previously known to evince so much serious attention to a sermon as he had paid to [Elaw's] discourse . . . and that his kneeling during the concluding prayer was a matter of surprise to them" (100). Upon hearing this information, Elaw explains how she felt in Pauline terms: "My mind was greatly moved with evangelic interest for this young man: and, *like Paul for the Galatians, I travailed in birth for him* (Gal. 4:19)" (100–101). The significance of this maternal

174. Pierce, *Hell without Fires*, 107.

imagery by Paul in Galatians 4:19 has been noted, most ardently, by female biblical scholars, for Paul employs this language to signify an apocalyptic transformation, the in-breaking of God's divine invasion of liberation.[175] Paul's intense labor for the Galatians generates Elaw's own intense labor for the young man, whom she believes needs salvation. Ironically, Elaw labors for his freedom from sin although he, as a slave driver, denies freedom to her own people. Elaw's adoption of Pauline language here points to a "travail for transformation." Her life and ministry demonstrate that not only do blacks have souls, but black women have spiritual wombs with which they give birth to apocalyptic realities, such as the conversion of an oppressor whose slavery to sin enables participation in the sin of slavery. Elaw's travail for this man signals black women's significant role in bringing about physical and spiritual freedom to all in need of liberation.

Elaw as Paul and Her Pauline Resistance to Racism

That Elaw sees herself akin to Paul is evident in the numerous citations already given above as well as in the following quote where she describes the care and concern shown to her by her friend, Miss Sarah M. Coffin, during an illness: "Her affection for me was as great as that of Aquila and Priscilla for St. Paul, who would have laid down their own necks upon the block for him" (129). This comment demonstrates that Elaw sees herself as not only similar to the apostle in divine encounters, in the divine origin of her ministry, in curing the sick, in facing opposition to the gospel, and in giving birth to believers, but, like the apostle, she also participates in deep friendships formed by the bond of God's love. Elaw, therefore, portrays herself in an apostolic role, for she declares that in her ministry people are *"turned from darkness to light"* and from the *"power of Satan to the power of God,"* which are words God speaks to Paul in Acts 26:18. Elaw's ministry is affirmed because what God promised would happen through Paul's ministry is now happening through her ministry. In addition, like the apostle, who journeyed extensively to preach the gospel, Elaw travels extensively as well, proclaiming nothing but *"Christ crucified"* (1 Cor. 1:23; 2:2) in the middle Atlantic and

---

175. See, for example, Susan Eastman, "Galatians 4:19: A Labor of Divine Love," in *Recovering Paul's Mother Tongue: Language and Theology in Galatians* (Grand Rapids: Eerdmans, 2007), 89–126; Beverly Gaventa, "The Maternity of Paul," in *Our Mother Saint Paul* (Louisville: Westminster John Knox, 2007), 29–39; Mitzi Smith, "Unbossed and Unbought," 301–5.

Northeast states, including in Maryland; Washington, DC; Virginia; New York; Connecticut; and internationally in England.

Along with using Paul to characterize her call and to show that her ministry has authenticated authority, Elaw also employs the apostle's language to resist racism and to castigate the "pride of a white skin," which she says is "of great value with many in some parts of the United States, who readily sacrifice their intelligence to their prejudices" (85). Despite the value that many place upon white skin,[176] Elaw declares, "The Almighty accounts not the black races of man either in the order of nature or spiritual capacity as inferior to the white; for He bestows his Holy Spirit on, and dwells in them as readily as in persons of whiter complexion. . . . Oh! that men would outgrow their nursery prejudices and learn that *'God hath made of one blood all the nations of men that dwell upon all the face on the earth.'* Acts xvii.26" (85–86).[177] Recalling Acts, Elaw appeals to the experience of the Spirit in which the Spirit falls upon gentiles as well as Jews, indicating gentile inclusion in God's salvific plan. Similarly, Elaw proclaims that just as God's Spirit makes no distinction between whites and blacks, having been granted to both races, human beings should not employ such differences either. Furthermore, her use of Paul's speech in Acts here underscores the illegitimate claims of white supremacy, including the value placed upon white skin, and disavows that any racial difference authorizes superiority or inferiority. The outpouring of God's Spirit upon black and white and the one blood that flows through humanity indicate that God created all people as one.

In her article "Prophesying Daughters," Chanta Haywood calls Zilpha Elaw, Jarena Lee, Maria Stewart, and Julia Foote the prophesying daughters of Joel 2:28–29, who in the midst of great opposition from both women and men, black and white, continued to preach and prophesy.[178] Elaw herself cites this Joel passage to support her right to proclaim the gospel and as an indication that the times of which Joel spoke began in Acts and continue with her ministry (124). Haywood writes that when these women used their pens to record their journeys as black women preachers, they were "writing themselves into existence."[179] As illustrated in Elaw's recounting of her life,

176. See the statement by Josiah Priest regarding the superiority of white skin above.

177. This quote of Acts 17:26 appears above in one of the petitions for freedom and in the discussion of Lemuel Haynes.

178. Maria Stewart and Julia Foote are discussed in chap. 2.

179. Chanta Haywood, "Prophesying Daughters: Nineteenth-Century Black Religious Women, the Bible, and Black Literary History," in Wimbush, *African Americans and the Bible*, 356; Pierce, *Hell without Fires*, also calls Zilpha a prophesying daughter (87). Mitzi J. Smith, "'This Little Light of Mine': The Womanist Biblical Scholar as Prophetess, Icono-

she was indeed "writing herself into existence," and it is noteworthy, for our purposes, that *she utilized Pauline language to do so.* She saw her existence as intricately connected to the apostle: as he was chosen by God, so was she (2 Tim. 2:21; cf. Gal. 1:15);[180] her call was tied to his call; his mandate from God became her mandate from God; and the gospel he proclaimed became hers as well. In the act of writing herself into existence, Elaw laid claim upon the apostle's words and his experiences, and by doing so she demonstrated that these were not limited to him alone but transcended time, space, and gender. What is more, Elaw offered alternative readings of Paul that challenged and resisted the dominant oppressive interpretations of him, particularly those that promoted black and female inferiority.

David Walker (1785/1796–1830): Famous Abolitionist

Like the expositors discussed above, David Walker, a renowned abolitionist, utilized Paul in subversive ways as well. He was born free in Wilmington, North Carolina, in 1785 or 1796,[181] but as Herbert Marbury notes, "From his birth, Walker was out of place; he was a free black man in the antebellum South where slavery defined black life. Despite his legal status, the fundamental inequities and injustices of North Carolina's slave society shaped his formative environment."[182] Though free, Walker was haunted and horrified by the wrongs promoted and sustained by the slave system, as is evident in his writings. In 1825 Walker moved to Boston, a city at that time with a large politically active black citizenry deeply involved in abolition.[183] There Walker opened a clothing shop and became very active in abolitionist causes.[184] Donald Jacobs writes of Walker, "Those who knew him well said that he also 'possessed a noble and

---

clast, and Activist," in *I Found God in Me: A Womanist Biblical Hermeneutics Reader*, ed. Mitzi J. Smith (Eugene, OR: Cascade, 2015), characterizes Elaw, Lee, Stewart, Foote, and other black women interpreters during this time period as "proto-womanists interpreters" (109).

180. Elaw, *Memoirs*, 66, writes, "It was at one of these meetings that God was pleased to separate my soul unto Himself, to sanctify me as a vessel designed for honour, made meet for the master's use" (2 Tim. 2:21).

181. Donald M. Jacobs, "David Walker and William Lloyd Garrison," in Jacobs, *Courage and Conscience*, 8; Marbury, *Pillars*, 34, 214.

182. Marbury, *Pillars*, 34.

183. Jacobs, "David Walker," 8; Marbury, *Pillars*, 36.

184. This statement does not mean to suggest that Walker was not active in liberation causes before Boston. See Marbury's discussion of Walker's time in South Carolina: *Pillars*, 35–36.

courageous spirit' and that he was 'ardently attached to the cause of liberty.' . . . He was an unabashed abolitionist who, having grown up in the South, knew slavery; and knowing it, he had built up a powerful hatred of it."[185] Walker's courage, detestation of slavery, and commitment to liberation show through most vividly in the appeal he wrote.

Walker's Appeal, In Four Articles; Together with A Preamble, To The Coloured Citizens of the World, But in Particular, and Very Expressly, To Those of The United States of America, Written in Boston, State of Massachusetts, September 28, 1829, is filled with scriptural language, scriptural echoes, and detailed descriptions of slavery's atrocities.[186] Within this document Walker also refutes the racist ideology of Thomas Jefferson, Henry Clay, and other prominent figures of his time. Writing with passion and a sense of purpose to inform his fellow blacks of the tragic nature of their condition, Walker aims to inspire them to do something about it. He also writes to apprise the world of the real events occurring in slave America and the degraded conditions suffered by blacks under white Christians. He states in the beginning of his final imprint, "All I ask is, for a candid and careful perusal of this the third and last edition of my Appeal, where the world may see that we, the Blacks or Coloured People, are treated more cruel by the white Christians of America, than devils themselves ever treated a set of men, women and children on this earth."[187] In candid, forthright language bathed in scriptural vocabulary, Walker paints a graphic, multilayered portrait for his audiences. This multifaceted picture consists of the horrors of slavery, a distinction between the religion of Jesus and the Christianity practiced by white slaveholders, and impending judgment upon America. His *Appeal* is known for its anger, its bold advocacy of Christian ideals, its instructions to free blacks, and its call for an immediate response to overthrow slavery.[188] What is less known and discussed is that within this multilayered portrait Walker incorporates Pauline language.

185. Jacobs, "David Walker," 9.

186. Walker published three editions of his *Appeal* during 1829 and 1830. The quotes included here are from his third edition.

187. *Walker's Appeal, In Four Articles; Together with A Preamble, To The Coloured Citizens of the World, But in Particular, and Very Expressly, To Those of The United States of America, Written in Boston, State of Massachusetts, September 28, 1829* (Boston: Revised and published by David Walker, 1830), reprinted as *David Walker's Appeal: In Four Articles* (Mansfield Centre, CT: Martino Publishing, 2015), ix. Hereafter, page references to the reprint edition will be given in parentheses in the text.

188. James Brewer Stewart, "Boston, Abolition, and the Atlantic World, 1820–1861," in Jacobs, *Courage and Conscience,* 109.

Horrors of Slavery and the God of This Age

Walker makes it a point to demonstrate that the slavery practiced in America is worse than that practiced in Egypt, for Egyptians did not convey to Israel that they were nonhuman. He declares,

> I call upon the professing Christians, I call upon the philanthropist, I call upon the very tyrant himself, to show me a page of history, either sacred or profane, on which a verse can be found, which maintains, that the Egyptians heaped the *insupportable insult* upon the children of Israel, by telling them that they were not of the *human family*. Can the whites deny this charge? Have they not, after having reduced us to the deplorable condition of slaves under their feet, held us up as descending originally from the tribes of *Monkeys* or *Orang-Outangs*? O! my God! (10)[189]

This denial of blacks' humanity, Walker maintains, encouraged the prohibition of educating them. Several excerpts demonstrate Walker's outrage at this reality for his fellow blacks.

> It is a fact, that in our Southern and Western States, there are millions who hold us in chains or in slavery, whose greatest object and glory, is centered in keeping us sunk in the most profound ignorance and stupidity, to make us work without remunerations for our services. Many of whom if they catch a coloured person, whom they hold in unjust ignorance, slavery, and degradation, to them and their children, with a book in his hand, will beat him nearly to death . . . another law has passed the republican House of Delegates, (but not the Senate) in Virginia, to prohibit all persons of colour, (free and slave) from learning to read or write, and even to hinder them from meeting together in order to worship our Maker!!!!!! (53)

> See the inconsistency of the assertions of those wretches—they beat us inhumanely, sometimes almost to death, for attempting to inform ourselves, by reading the Word of our Maker, and at the same time tell us, that we are beings void of intellect!!!! . . . Let me cry shame upon you Americans, for such outrages upon human nature!!! If it were possible for the whites always

---

189. On page 13 he writes in reference to this same concept: "Have you not, Americans, having subjected us under you, added to these miseries, by insulting us in telling us to our face, because we are helpless, that we are not of the human family?"

to keep us ignorant and miserable, and make us work to enrich them and their children, and insult our feelings by representing us as talking Apes, what would they do? But glory, honour and praise to Heaven's King, that the sons and daughters of Africa, will, in spite of all the opposition of their enemies, stand forth in all the dignity and glory that is granted by the Lord to his creature man. (62)

In these two excerpts, one sees Walker's focus upon the prohibition of education for blacks, and in the last passage Walker highlights the irony of whites' claims that blacks are ignorant and whites' injunction regarding blacks' education.[190] Janet Duitsman Cornelius states that slaveholders had a "fear of a literate black population. Despite the protestations of the small group who would teach slaves that 'Bible literacy' would uphold the social order, the majority of white southerners knew better: they knew that knowledge was a two-edged sword which 'could defend the social fabric or cut it to shreds.'"[191] Because many whites saw black literacy as a dangerous proposition, "opposition to those who would teach slaves never ceased in the antebellum period," and for many African Americans, learning to read and write was not an option.[192] In the second excerpt above, Walker also links whites' beliefs that blacks were apes to whites' justification for withholding education from enslaved Africans. But Walker counters this depiction of blacks by claiming their African heritage and by affirming that they are human beings, God's "creature man" adorned with dignity and glory. Whites' denial of enslaved Africans' humanity resulted in not only withholding education from them but also treating them in gruesome ways. The following account by Walker details such behavior:

I will give here a very imperfect list of the cruelties inflicted on us by the enlightened Christians of America. . . . They brand us with hot iron—they cram bolts of fire down our throats—they cut us as they do horses, bulls, or hogs—they crop our ears and sometimes cut off bits of our tongues—they chain and hand-cuff us, and while in that miserable and wretched condition, beat us with cow-hides and clubs—they keep us half naked and starve us

---

190. For discussions regarding literacy among enslaved Africans, see Antonio Bly, "'Pretends He Can Read': Runaways and Literacy in Colonial America, 1730–1776," *Early American Studies* 6, no. 2 (Fall 2008): 261–94; Cornelius, *When I Can Read My Title Clear*.

191. Cornelius, *When I Can Read My Title Clear*, 6.

192. Cornelius, *When I Can Read My Title Clear*, 6.

sometimes nearly to death under their infernal whips or lashes (which some of them shall have enough of yet)—They put on us fifty-sixes and chains, and make us work in that cruel situation, and in sickness, under lashes to support them and their families.—They keep us three or four hundred feet under ground working in their mines, night and day to dig up gold and silver to enrich them and their children.—They keep us in the most death-like ignorance by keeping us from all source of information, and call us, who are free men and next to the Angels of God, their property !!!!!! . . . they tell us that we the (blacks) are an inferior race of beings! incapable of self government!!—We would be injurious to society and ourselves, if tyrants should loose their unjust hold on us!!! That if we were free we would not work, but would live on plunder or theft!!!! that we are the meanest and laziest set of beings in the world!!!!! That they are obliged to keep us in bondage to do us good!!!!!!—That we are satisfied to rest in slavery to them and their children!!!!!! . . . for we ask them for nothing but the rights of man, viz. for them to set us free, and treat us like men, and there will be no danger, for we will love and respect them, and protect our country—but cannot conscientiously do these things until they treat us like men. (65–66)

Against the backdrop of the atrocities heaped upon black bodies and the violent language amassed upon black minds, Walker echoes Psalm 8:5, declaring that African Americans are next to angels, belong to God, and thus are free.[193] Walker, therefore, asserts blacks' humanity and their rightful place in God's creation. Moreover, this language recapitulates his earlier statements that enslaved Africans "belong to the Holy Ghost" and are the "property of the Holy Ghost," which debunks white enslavers' claims to black bodies and black lives (49, 50, 71). Blacks belong to God and the Spirit, Walker argues, not to any white person who clamors after the title of "Master," for whites are made of dust and ashes and will have to appear before judgment just like everyone else. Walker asks, "What right then, have we to obey and call any other Master, but [Jesus Christ] Himself?" (16).

Into this ongoing discourse Walker inserts Pauline language to describe the condition of those who do not see the "inhuman system of slavery" for what it really is; they are *blinded by the God of this world* (2 Cor. 4:4). Paul uses the expression "god of this world" to refer to Satan, a being he describes to the Corinthian congregation as one who aims to blind the minds of peo-

193. Ps. 8:5: "For thou hast made him a little lower than the angels, and hast crowned him with glory and honour."

ple so that they cannot see and understand the truth of the gospel. Walker adopts this Pauline phrase to describe Satan's power over those who engage in racism. By contrast, those who do see the "hellish chains of slavery" are not *blinded by the God of this world* but understand that "God made man to serve Him alone and that man should have no other Lord or Lords but Himself—that God Almighty is the sole proprietor or master of the whole human family," and that blacks are "men, notwithstanding our improminent noses and woolly heads" (4–5). In addition, those who are not blinded "believe that we feel for our fathers, mothers, wives and children, as well as the whites do for theirs" (4–5). Although Walker utilizes Paul's notion of the god of this age blinding human beings to describe why some whites engage in oppressive behavior, he does not believe this alleviates them of responsibility for their actions or saves them from impending judgment. Judgment vernacular permeates Walker's treatise, and for him only repentance and change in action rescue whites and America from certain destruction. He believes that God has ears "continually open to the cries, tears, and groans of his oppressed people; and being a just and holy Being will at one day appear fully in behalf of the oppressed, and arrest the progress of the avaricious oppressors; for although the destruction of the oppressors God may not effect by the oppressed, yet the Lord our God will bring other destructions upon them" (3). Without repentance, Walker is sure that judgment will occur upon America because God does not forget the afflicted and God will judge the perverted Christianity practiced in the nation.

The Religion of Jesus, Pretenders of Christianity, and Pauline Judgment Language

Walker maintains that Americans have the Bible but do not believe it, and their unbelief appears in the way they treat African Americans since they disregard the Golden Rule. Walker particularly rails against American preachers, who have a greater responsibility to proclaim the truth but are gravely lacking in taking a stand against slavery. "An American minister, with the Bible in his hand, holds us and our children in the most abject slavery and wretchedness. Now I ask them, would they like for us to hold them and their children in abject slavery and wretchedness? . . . how far the American preachers are from preaching against slavery and oppression" (38). In fact, Walker criticizes American Christians because they constantly preach against breaking the Sabbath, infidelity, and intemperance but are silent about slavery's horrors, "compared with which, all those other evils are comparatively nothing" (40).

In article 3 of his document, Walker describes a camp meeting he attended in South Carolina where the minister, utilizing Paul's words, told the blacks in the audience that "slaves must be obedient to their masters—must do their duty to their masters or be whipped—the whip was made for the backs of fools" (39). Walker's description of his reaction to this message is invaluable: "Here I pause for a moment to give the world time to consider what was my surprise, to hear such preaching from a minister of my Master, *whose very gospel is that of peace* [Rom. 10:15; Eph. 6:15] and not of blood and whips, as this pretended preacher tried to make us believe" (39).[194] Using Paul's description of the gospel as a gospel of peace, Walker draws a distinction between the gospel of this "pretended preacher" and the true gospel of Walker's "Master," which espouses εἰρήνη (peace), not torture. In fact, early on in the treatise, Walker writes that "white Christians of America, who hold us in slavery, (or more properly speaking, pretenders to Christianity,) treat us more cruel and barbarous than any Heathen nation" (ix). He elaborates upon this idea of "pretenders to Christianity," and his camp-meeting experience becomes part of this elucidation. The cruelty white Christians inflict upon African Americans causes Walker to assert that they are not really Christians but "pretenders" and provoke him to state vehemently: "I tell you Americans! that unless you speedily alter your course, you and your Country are gone!!!!! . . . This language, perhaps is too harsh for the American's delicate ears. But Oh Americans! Americans! I warn you in the name of the Lord, (whether you will hear, or forbear,) to repent and reform, or you are ruined!!! Do you think that our blood is hidden from the Lord, because you can hide it from the rest of the world, by sending out missionaries" (39–40). Echoing Genesis, where Abel's blood cries out to God from the ground, Walker contends that, likewise, the blood of African Americans is not hidden from God despite how white Christians attempt to conceal their behavior through missionary zeal.

The fact that American Christians, including many preachers, are complicit participants in slavery who refuse to see any wrongdoing on their part is incredulous to Walker and prompts him to characterize the situation in

---

194. Note the interesting contrast between Walker's language, "the minister of my Master," and Nancy Ambrose's language, "the master's minister." The distinction is telling. Because of the message this camp-meeting preacher proffers, he is similar to Ambrose's "master's minister"; he is not, in Walker's terms, a "minister of my Master."

Romans 1 language—*"they have been nearly given up by the Lord to a hard heart and reprobate mind*, in consequence of afflicting their fellow creatures [1:28]" (41). According to Walker, whites' hard heart and reprobate mind derive from their mistreatment of blacks and will end in their destruction unless they repent. With this Pauline terminology of "giving up" and "reprobate mind," Walker depicts the dire state of America. In the final section of article 3, Walker again takes up Pauline language to describe American society and its standing before God. The eloquent passage merits full citation:

> What can the American preachers and people take God to be? Do they believe his words? If they do, do they believe that *he will be mocked* [Gal. 6:7]? Or do they believe, because they are whites and we blacks, that God will have respect to them? Did not God make us all as it seemed best to himself? What right, then, has one of us, to despise another, and to treat him cruel, on account of his colour, which none, but the God who made it can alter? Can there be a greater absurdity in nature, and particularly in a free republican country? But the Americans, having introduced slavery among them, *their hearts have become almost seared, as with an hot iron, and God has nearly given them up to believe a lie in preference to the truth!!!* [1 Tim. 4:2; Rom. 1:25]. And I am awfully afraid that pride, prejudice, avarice and blood, will, before long prove the final ruin of this happy republic, or land of *liberty!!!!* Can any thing be a greater mockery of religion than the way in which it is conducted by the Americans? ... Will the Lord suffer this people to go on much longer, taking his holy name in vain? Will he not stop them, PREACHERS and all? O Americans! Americans!! *I call God* [2 Cor. 1:23]—I call angels—I call men, to witness, that your DESTRUCTION *is at hand*, and will be speedily consummated unless you REPENT. (42-43)[195]

195. The last line of this passage echoes Isa. 13:6: "Howl ye; for the day of the LORD is at hand; it shall come as a destruction from the Almighty," and Joel 1:15: "Alas for the day! for the day of the LORD is at hand, and as a destruction from the Almighty shall it come." In this quote Walker refers to skin color and argues that this is no basis for enslavement. In another passage in his treatise he addresses the "mark of Cain" theory prevalent during this time, which stated that the mark God put on Cain was black skin. Walker writes, "And [I] have never seen a verse which testifies whether we are the seed of Cain or of Abel. Yet those men tell us that we are the seed of Cain, and that God put a dark stain on us, that we might be known as their slaves!!! Now, I ask those avaricious and ignorant wretches, who act more like the seed of Cain, by murdering the whites or the blacks? How many vessel load of human beings, have the blacks thrown into the seas? How many thousand souls have the blacks murdered in cold blood, to make them work in wretchedness and ignorance, to support them and their families?" (60-61). See also the brief discussion of the mark of Cain in n. 7, above.

In this passage and in the previous selection, Walker employs Pauline language to speak about the gross deception that has taken place among white Christians. Their concentration on matters such as Sabbath breaking while overlooking the greater evil, the enslavement of human beings, reveals the power of avarice and the extent of their deception. The context of the 1 Timothy passage quoted by Walker focuses on the last days and how many will depart from the faith in the "latter times." Such a context coheres well with Walker's contentions that white Americans are "pretenders to Christianity" who employ the gospel for their own greedy gains. Paul warns Timothy about such people who depart from the faith (1 Tim. 4:1). Walker is the Paul of his day, admonishing his readers of the dangerous characteristics embodied by white Christians and that the faith practiced by them is no faith at all. Likewise, Paul's words in Romans 1:25 enable Walker to expose the lies undergirding slavery, such as Scripture's ordination of slavery, the nonhumanness of blacks, and black inferiority. Walker censures white Americans for choosing to believe these lies rather than the truth, which is that God created all human beings as equals. Moreover, since many preachers, like the one Walker encounters at the camp meeting, utilize the gospel to sanction slavery, Walker views this practice as taking the Lord's name in vain. To use God's name to endorse enslavement of blacks is nothing short of blasphemy.

Because of this pervasive distortion of the gospel and this "mockery of religion," Walker uses Pauline language to ask his audience if they think God will allow the divine to be mocked. In addition, in typical Pauline fashion, he calls God as a witness that judgment is imminent, yet he also leaves open the possibility of its avoidance through repentance. Yet the reader notices the context of Walker's notion of repentance. It is not merely about individual salvation or inner repentance, but it is a call to a nation to repent of a societal evil that has physical, mental, and spiritual implications. Walker illustrates one of Frederick Ware's contentions about how many blacks understand sin. Sin is understood as something that is social and not just personal.[196] To call the nation to repent, then, is a major counterattack to the white Protestant theology dominant in Walker's day, which concentrated on personal sin and salvation. Sin, for Walker, is not merely something an individual does and is not only focused on destruction of individual piety, but sin is systemic in society and permeates every level of the nation's existence. For Walker, sin is a power that usurps systems, politics, and nations. Such a view of sin coheres

196. Frederick L. Ware, *African American Theology: An Introduction* (Louisville: Westminster John Knox, 2016), 141.

with Paul's own view of sin in Romans, where the apostle depicts sin as an active power whose presence controls and destroys.[197] Simply put, Walker contends that slavery is sin, and this reality means that sin's grasp through slavery affects the nation holistically by the laws it creates, the divisions it sustains, and the cruelties it perpetuates. In a sense, Walker continues the trajectory of the petitioners and of Lemuel Haynes, who asked and answered in the words of Paul, "Shall we continue in sin? God forbid!"

Although Walker calls for repentance, he posits the possibility that some whites may be destroyed because avarice's powerful hold upon them produces a refusal to repent. He writes, "For I declare to you, whether you believe it or not, that there are some on the continent of America, who will never be able to repent. God will surely destroy them, to show you his disapprobation of the murders they and you have inflicted on us" (69). Despite this probability, Walker makes a profound and powerful declaration to white Americans for their repentance.[198]

Judgment Revisited and Pauline "Body" Language:
Salvation of the Black Body

Walker's prophetic voice with which he boldly chastises white Christians for approval and participation in the slave trade also becomes an instrument to remind free blacks that they are not really free since they continue to face extreme prejudice and are not allowed to obtain vocations other than cleaning and taking care of white folks' families (29). Blacks should not be content with such "low employment" but should aspire for something greater. In addition, Walker declares that free blacks will never be free until all their

197. Scholars note that "sin" and "death" are subjects of verbs in Romans, indicating that Paul views these entities as actors on the cosmic landscape: "Sin came into the world through one man" (Rom. 5:12), "Death exercised dominion" (5:14, 17; cf. 6:9), and "Sin exercised dominion in death" (5:21; cf. 6:14) (all NRSV). For example, see Gaventa, *Our Mother Saint Paul*, 125–36; Robert Jewett, *Romans*, Hermeneia (Minneapolis: Fortress, 2007), 374–75; Ernst Käsemann, *Commentary on Romans*, trans. Geoffrey W. Bromiley (Grand Rapids: Eerdmans, 1980), 139–58.

198. Roy E. Finkenbine, "Boston's Black Churches: Institutional Centers of the Antislavery Movement," in Jacobs, *Courage and Conscience*, 185, views the appeal in this way: "The *Appeal* was first and foremost a call to repentance. Walker did not desire that slaveholders be destroyed, but rather that the institution of slavery be overthrown. Only if whites failed to repent, he warned, would God free the slaves through physical force. Yet, if compulsion was needed, Walker predicted, blacks would be God's willing instruments."

brothers and sisters are free. Utilizing Pauline language, Walker depicts coming judgment upon free blacks who join the "tyrants" in oppressing African Americans by stating that *"the Lord shall come upon you all like a thief in the night* [1 Thess. 5:2]" (29).[199] As Paul reminded his Thessalonian audience of Jesus's sudden return, Walker reminds his audiences as well that Jesus's soon reappearance will terminate oppression on all levels, that which proceeds from whites and free blacks who aid the whites in their oppression. Moreover, Walker adopts Pauline "body" language to persuade his fellow free blacks that freedom is not real freedom until *all* gain liberation:

> For I believe it is the will of the Lord that our greatest happiness shall consist in working for the *salvation of our whole body* [1 Cor. 12:13–26]. When this is accomplished a burst of glory will shine upon you, which will indeed astonish you and the world. Do any of you say this never will be done? I assure you that God will accomplish it—if nothing else will answer, he will hurl tyrants and devils into atoms and make way for his people. But O my brethren! I say unto you again, you must go to work and prepare the way of the Lord. (29–30)

Here, Walker adopts and adapts a Pauline motif, body imagery, in the phrase "the salvation of our whole body." For Walker the "whole body" refers to all blacks, and their salvation consists of their spiritual, mental, and physical freedom from slavery. Just as he did earlier in characterizing sin as not merely individualistic but social and national (where sin manifests in social and national divisions), here again Walker broadens the notion of salvation from salvation for individual souls to include physical liberation from enslavement. Free blacks cannot relish their own liberation but must also work to advance the freedom of their enslaved sisters and brothers; they, both free and enslaved, form one body. Thus, Pauline terminology underscores a unified black body, where black people stand as one collective, unified for the purpose of bringing about liberation and life for each other. Furthermore, Walker advocates divine and human agency, for although "God will accomplish it," African Americans "must go to work" and, in the language of the prophets, "prepare the way of the Lord." According to Walker, God and human beings work together for liberation and freedom; it is never only a divine project nor only a human endeavor.

199. It is possible that Walker echoes 2 Pet. 3:10 here. However, Walker's use of "body" language in this context makes the allusion to Paul more likely.

Walker's Farewell Discourse

As we have seen, at important points in his work, Walker employs Pauline language to speak about white deception, the gospel as a gospel of peace, the distorted Christianity practiced by white believers, American judgment, and unity of the black community. The last significant place Walker takes up the apostle's words occurs in reference to himself and his own impending death. Walker understood that his prophetic voice, his exposure of the hypocritical nature of white American Christianity, and his repeated calls for judgment upon America could come at the price of his life. In the final article of his treatise, article 4, Walker prognosticates about his demise with the terminology of the apostle.

> If any are anxious to ascertain who I am, know the world, that I am one of the oppressed, degraded and wretched sons of Africa, rendered so by the avaricious and unmerciful, among the whites.—If any wish to plunge me into the wretched incapacity of a slave, or murder me for the truth, know ye, that I am in the hand of God, and at your disposal. *I count my life not dear unto me* [Acts 20:24], but *I am ready to be offered* at any moment [2 Tim. 4:6]. For what is the use of living, when in fact I am dead. (71–72)

Walker uses two of Paul's most touching farewell discourses to create his own powerful farewell speech. In Acts 20:17–37, Paul says good-bye to the Ephesian church, informing them that he must go to Jerusalem and that he does not know what will await him there, but the Spirit reveals that affliction will be his lot in that city. Despite the Spirit's warnings, however, Paul declares, "None of these things move me, neither count I my life dear unto myself." That Walker would choose to echo this portion of Paul's speech in Acts speaks volumes. Like the apostle, he could not ascertain fully what was about to happen to him, but he knew that because of his missive affliction was inevitable, death even possible. Yet similar to the apostle, he could not abandon his mission, even if it cost him his life. In an analogous fashion in 2 Timothy 4:6, Paul prepares Timothy, whom he calls his "beloved son" (2 Tim. 1:2), for his death, writing that he is ready to be offered and the time of his departure is at hand. Walker, at peace with his life and with his work, declares to his audience that he too is ready to be offered up if and when the time arrives. Sadly, his prediction of his death in Pauline terms proved true. In 1830, Walker was found dead in his clothing store under conditions suggesting foul play.[200] The cause of his death remains a mystery, although some believe he died of poisoning.[201]

At pivotal moments in the *Appeal*, Walker clothes himself in the garb of the apostle Paul, depicting himself as an apostolic figure whom God calls to proclaim the "pure religion of Jesus." This "pure religion of Jesus," however, includes Pauline language to describe America's sin, its deception, and future judgment. Furthermore, Paul's image of the body is a useful one for Walker's emphasis on black unity. Additionally, the apostle's words provide Walker with the language to state that life is not dear to him, for he perceives something greater than life, the liberation of his people. Walker chooses Pauline vernacular to speak about his own death in divine terms, for he is being offered up, language that echoes sacrificial terminology and indicates a sacrifice offered to the divine on behalf of his people. Walker, then, in an evocative hermeneutical gesture, depicts his willingness to die for the cause of black salvation.[202]

Using Paul to Resist, Protest, and Be Subversive

Each of the black hermeneuts examined in this chapter engages Paul in multidimensional ways, all of which have the aim of resisting and countering slavery, racism, white supremacy, and rejection of woman ministers. In their uses of Paul, these black exegetes were no longer objects at which Scripture was directed but subjects through whom Scripture spoke to the world. The petitioners claim Paul's voice as their own to make anthropological assertions for their humanity, the importance of the black family, the Christian family's obligation to bear one another's burdens, and the unity of all human beings, since God from one blood created all the nations of the earth.

Although not always as subversive as modern readers would like, Jupiter Hammon does use Paul in some revolutionary ways for his time and place; he uses Paul in his call for repentance and in his affirmation of enslaved Africans' agency and new identity granted through the Spirit. Soteriologically speaking, Hammon argues that blacks have souls, can re-

200. Stewart, "Boston," 110; Marbury, *Pillars*, 36.
201. Marbury, *Pillars*, 36.
202. This interpretation is even more compelling in light of how Walker depicts salvation as liberation from slavery and how he encourages his fellow free blacks to work for "salvation of the whole body." Walker sees himself doing just that by giving up his life for the cause, the salvation of the black body made up of both enslaved and free.

ceive salvation, and are worthy of divine care. Like the petition writers, he maintains that blacks are rational creatures, a statement that relates to anthropology as well as epistemology and soteriology. He also takes on Paul's language to highlight enslaved Africans' moral behavior, which should surpass that of the slaveholder. In addition, Paul's demonic language describes the satanic influence over white slave owners, and his words regarding God choosing the weak instead of the rich enable Hammon to critique the white elite.

This chapter also analyzed other subversive uses of Paul by Lemuel Haynes, John Jea, Jarena Lee, Zilpha Elaw, and David Walker. Haynes employs Paul to refute directly the Ham myth and whites' use of 1 Corinthians 7:21 to justify slavery. For him, Christ becoming a curse (Gal. 3:13) removes the so-called curse of Ham, if it ever existed, and he maintains that the apostle advocated freedom, not enslavement, in 1 Corinthians 7:21. Furthermore, the notion that slavery was beneficial to Africans was not true; slavery, in fact, was sin, as identified by the apostle himself. For Jea, the miracle of literacy and Paul's language of new creation and grace through faith grants him the ability to reinterpret and renarrate his life story. Like Paul, he works with his own hands, traveling throughout the world proclaiming the gospel to the enslaved and to the free. Both Lee and Elaw view Paul as a companion in their struggle for recognition of their call. In many ways, their own mystical experiences paralleled those of Paul, demonstrating their apostolic role and call in the church. Women were not inferior to Paul or to male ministers but stood equal to them in every way.

The final African American hermeneut of this chapter, David Walker, provides a fitting end to this section as he recalls earlier themes like black agency from Hammon, judgment from Haynes, and the importance and presence of the Spirit for black existence as indicated in the writings of Hammon, Jea, Lee, and Elaw. Slavery as sin as pronounced by the petitioners and Haynes comes to heightened expression in Walker, where slavery is not only sin but deserving of harsh judgment, a theme that permeates Walker's appeal.

Each of the interpreters demonstrates that there are many ways to resist, protest, and be subversive, and all of them share the outcome of having Paul speak to and for female and black identity, not against it. Thus, these writers engage in an African American Pauline hermeneutic that is resistance and protest oriented. They engage Paul in a deep, intellectual manner. For example, as discussed above, Elaw considers the historical context of Paul's injunction against women. When interpreting Scripture, she understands that historical context matters as well as other scriptural witnesses, including Paul himself, and that if one evaluates the historical situation of the apostle's words, then one recognizes the temporal and situational mandate of Paul's statement and realizes that his words regarding women's silence do not function as an eternal mandate for all churches and for all time.

These interpreters raise another important aspect of African American Pauline hermeneutics, which will reappear in the subsequent chapters, that is, the significance of the body to this hermeneutical stance. Said differently, two of the underlying questions of these interpreters' view of Paul are how my body becomes a way to interpret Paul and whether Paul can interpret my body. Often this *body-contextual hermeneutic* is a competing one. Slave owners constantly declared to African Americans that their bodies belonged to the slaveholder. Many blacks, however, refused to believe this message, choosing instead to cling to the apostle's words in Acts 17:26: God has "made of one blood all nations of men for to dwell on all the face of the earth." While slave owners insisted to enslaved Africans that "You are my property," and whites declared black inferiority, African Americans in interpreting Paul rejected this idea and contended that their bodies belonged to God and the Spirit.

This body hermeneutic is an oppositional hermeneutic and a power move where blacks insist that the authority to determine their bodily status does not belong to whites but to God. This element, while appearing in various ways in the texts above, is seen most pointedly in Walker's declaration that enslaved Africans belong to the Holy Spirit and in Hammon's declaration of future transformation of black bodies in the eschaton. John Jea sees his spiritual deliverance as indicative of his future bodily liberation from slavery, asserting that the grace that saves him will also free him from "tyrannical power." Likewise, women hermeneuts like Jarena Lee and Zilpha Elaw allow Paul to interpret their female bodies, and they in turn utilize their female bodies to interpret Paul. Lee and Elaw find in Paul affirmation of their bodies as black women preachers whose bodies and lives belong to God and whose mystical experience, with its tangible effects upon their bodies, empowers them to stand in full authority in public spaces. The Spirit of adoption (Rom. 8:15) meant that black bodies belonged to God and the Spirit, not to the slaveholder or to the male leadership of the church hierarchy, for the Spirit's presence illustrates their worth and value and enables these interpreters to grab hold of their humanization, which is an important outcome of an African American Pauline hermeneutic. In their use of Paul, these writers were, to paraphrase Chanta Haywood, "writing their humanization into existence."[203] We will see in the next chapter, through the writings of Maria Stewart, James Pennington, Daniel Payne, Julia Foote, and Harriet Jacobs, that the black tradition of utilizing Paul to "write their humanization into existence" continues.

203. Haywood, "Prophesying Daughters," 356.

CHAPTER 2

Mid-Nineteenth Century to Late Nineteenth Century

"I'se saved. De Lord done tell me I'se saved. Now I know de Lord will show me de way. I ain't gwine to grieve no more. No matter how much you all done beat me and my chillen de Lord will show me de way. And some day we never be slaves."[1]

The previous chapter examined briefly the biblical, historical, and theological landscape during the eighteenth and early nineteenth centuries regarding slavery, racism, and the relationships and interactions between blacks and whites. It also explored the various ways in which African Americans utilized Paul to resist and protest the unjust social structures of the time and what they deemed as inappropriate readings of biblical texts. This chapter will discuss the biblical, historical, and theological landscape of the mid-nineteenth and late nineteenth century as well as examine additional African American authors who carry on the resistance and protest tradition in their use of Paul and his letters.

The Fugitive Slave Act and the Letter to Philemon

The Fugitive Slave Act, passed as part of Henry Clay's Great Compromise of 1850, reinvigorated the South's reach into free Northern states to retrieve

---

1. Norman R. Yetman, ed., *Voices from Slavery: The Life of American Slaves—in the Words of 100 Men and Women Who Lived It and Many Years Later Talked about It* (New York: Holt, Rinehart & Winston, 1970), 228.

runaway slaves.[2] This act stated that not only were law officials obligated to return slaves who absconded but also everyday citizens were mandated to assist in capturing runaway slaves. In addition, any citizen who aided slaves in running away could face fines, prosecution, and jail time. Moreover, fugitives could not testify in their own defense and were denied trial by jury.[3] In essence, this revised version of the Fugitive Slave Law of 1793 "required all American citizens to become slave catchers."[4] One of the residual effects of this law, however, was that free blacks were often taken into custody and sold into slavery, although they had gained their freedom lawfully. In addition, the amount of money the federal commissioners who oversaw the process received when returning slaves to the South encouraged many to comply with the law. These commissioners were paid five dollars if they ruled in favor of the captured black person but ten dollars if they "returned" the alleged escapee to a slave owner.[5] The passage of this law wreaked havoc upon African Americans across the country, both enslaved and free.

One of the scriptural justifications utilized by white slave owners for the Fugitive Slave Act was Paul's letter to Philemon, which they interpreted as Paul sending the runaway slave Onesimus back to Philemon. In fact, Charles Colcock Jones reports the slaves' reaction to a sermon he preached on this letter.

> I was preaching to a large congregation on the Epistle to Philemon: and when I insisted on fidelity and obedience as Christian virtues in servants, and upon the authority of Paul, condemned the practice of running away, one-half of my audience deliberately rose up and walked off with themselves; and those who remained looked anything but satisfied with the preacher or his doctrine. After dismission, there was no small stir among

2. There was an earlier version of the Fugitive Slave Act called the Fugitive Slave Law of 1793, which stipulated penalties for aiding runaway slaves and gave slave owners the right to search for and capture slaves in the free states. The 1850 legislation expanded the obligation of locating runaway slaves to citizens in the free states and also increased the penalties for assisting a slave's escape.

3. Jean Fagan Yellin, *Harriet Jacobs: A Life* (New York: Basic Civitas Books, 2004), 107; see also Laura L. Mitchell, "'Matters of Justice between Man and Man': Northern Divines, the Bible and the Fugitive Slave Act of 1850," in *Religion and the Antebellum Debate over Slavery*, ed. John R. McKivigan and Mitchell Snay (Athens: University of Georgia Press, 1998), 134–66.

4. John Ernest, introduction to *Narrative of the Life of Henry Box Brown Written by Himself*, ed. John Ernest, 1–38 (Chapel Hill: University of North Carolina Press, 2008), 13.

5. Ernest, introduction to *Narrative of the Life*, 13.

them; some solemnly declared that there was no such Epistle in the Bible; others, that it was not the Gospel; others, that I preached to please the masters; others, that they did not care if they never heard me preach again.[6]

As this scene reveals, white ministers employed Paul's letter to Philemon to justify obeying masters and to denounce running away from slavery, and blacks rejected this use of Paul in a number of ways: by walking out on the sermon, declaring the nonexistence of the letter, maintaining that this message was not the gospel, and claiming that the sermon was constructed to please the masters. African American resistance to this interpretation of this Pauline epistle rested upon an acute sense of what the gospel entailed and a recognition that what Jones proclaimed was definitely not it.[7]

In addition to revealing how white ministers preached this letter to the enslaved, this recollection by Jones also provides insight into how Paul becomes a basis for the legitimization of the Fugitive Slave Act. After all, if Paul sent Onesimus back to Philemon, then the apostle must not condone slaves running away, and so, to erect laws that forbid absconding and to punish such activities cohere with Paul's teaching.

Frederick Douglass and other abolitionists fought against this interpretation of Philemon and also, by extension, against this law. Looking at Paul's

6. Albert Raboteau, *Slave Religion: The "Invisible Institution" in the Antebellum South* (Oxford: Oxford University Press, 1982), 139.

7. The "hermeneutic of suspicion" employed by African Americans in this scene foreshadows black modern biblical scholarship discussions regarding this letter. As some black scholars have noted, the letter neither states that Onesimus ran away nor that he committed a crime, as some white interpreters had argued. Such interpretations maintained that he had stolen something from Philemon and ran away. Cain Hope Felder, "The Letter to Philemon: Introduction, Commentary, and Reflections," in *New Interpreter's Bible Commentary* 11 (Nashville: Abingdon, 2000), writes, "It is not certain that Onesimus was, in fact, a runaway at all or, if he was, that he had become one without just cause" (884). And again, "nothing in the letter provides warrant for the notion that Onesimus was a criminal fugitive who had stolen something from his master" (885). See also Allen Callahan, *Embassy of Onesimus: The Letter of Paul to Philemon*, New Testament in Context (Valley Forge, PA: Trinity Press International, 1997); J. Albert Harrill, "The Use of the New Testament in the American Slave Controversy: A Case History in the Hermeneutical Tension between Biblical Criticism and Christian Moral Debate," *Religion and American Culture: A Journal of Interpretation* 10, no. 2 (2000): 149–86; Lloyd A. Lewis, "An African American Appraisal of the Philemon-Paul-Onesimus Triangle," in *Stony the Road We Trod: African American Biblical Interpretation*, ed. Cain Hope Felder (Minneapolis: Fortress, 1991), 232–46; Mitchell, "Matters of Justice," 145–49; Abraham Smith, "Putting 'Paul' Back Together Again: William Wells Brown's *Clotel* and Black Abolitionist Approaches to Paul," *Semeia* 83–84 (1998): 256–57.

historical context and the language he uses in the letter, Douglass argues that Paul did not send Onesimus back as a slave for life, as other interpreters of the time maintained, for "there was no such thing known among the Jews as slavery for life, except it was desired on the part of the slave himself. What did the Apostle say himself? He said, he sent back Onesimus greater than a servant; and told Philemon to receive him as he would receive him, Paul; not as a slave who could be sold in the market, but as a brother beloved."[8] Douglass contends that Paul's description of Onesimus and his urging of Philemon to receive him indicate that Onesimus goes back to Philemon, but not as a servant. Elsewhere Douglass argues that Paul's language of "menstealers" in 1 Timothy 1:10 refers to the evil of slavery, and so Paul does not condone slavery but forbids it because, as 1 Timothy 1:10 states, "menstealing" is "contrary to sound doctrine."[9] Douglass, in his speeches, rails against the use of Scripture to justify slavery and the enactment of the Fugitive Slave Act:

> The constitution is pro-slavery because men have interpreted it to be pro-slavery, and practice upon it as if it were pro-slavery. The very same thing, sir, might be said of the Bible itself; for in the United States men have interpreted the Bible against liberty. They have declared that Paul's epistle to *Philemon* is a full proof for the enactment of that hell-black Fugitive Slave Bill which has desolated my people for the last ten years in that country. They have declared that the Bible sanctions slavery. What do we do in such a case? What do you do when you are told by the slaveholders of America that the Bible sanctions slavery? Do you go and throw your Bible into the fire? Do you sing out, "No union with the Bible!" Do you declare that a thing is bad because it has been misused, abused, and made bad use of? Do you throw it away on that account? No! You press it to your bosom all the more closely; you read it all the more diligently; and prove from its pages that it is on the side of liberty—and not on the side of slavery.[10]

8. Frederick Douglass, "Baptists, Congregationalists, the Free Church, and Slavery: An Address Delivered in Belfast, Ireland, on 23 December 1845," in *The Frederick Douglass Papers: Series One; Speeches, Debates, and Interviews*, vol. 1, 1841–46, ed. John Blassingame (New Haven: Yale University Press, 1979), 115–16; Abraham Smith, "Putting 'Paul' Back Together," 256–57.

9. Douglass, "Baptists," 110, 115; Abraham Smith, "Putting 'Paul' Back Together," 255. Smith also notes Douglass's use of Heb. 13:3 to encourage people to be in solidarity with slaves, to be with "those in bonds as bound with them" (255).

10. Frederick Douglass, "The American Constitution and the Slave: An Address Delivered in Glasgow, Scotland, on 26 March 1860," in *The Frederick Douglass Papers: Series One:*

As Douglass's comments demonstrate, a fierce battle was taking place for the soul of America, and this battle encompassed the Bible, including the interpretation of Philemon for justification of the Fugitive Slave Act. The struggle to save black lives was intricately linked with the struggle over sacred scriptural interpretation. Similar to the use of Ephesians 6:5–7 and Colossians 3:22 to sanction laws regarding slavocracy, Philemon becomes another instrument in slavocracy's fight to prevent slaves from leaving the South. Douglass and other abolitionists "seize hermeneutical control" of this Pauline letter to fight against such racist interpretations.[11] Thus, the Fugitive Slave Act of 1850, with part of its justification grounded in white supremacist biblical and theological interpretation, was one of the significant legislative pieces of the time period.

According to John R. McKivigan and Mitchell Snay, "the 1850s was the critical decade in the transformation of southern sectionalism into southern nationalism. From the Compromise of 1850 to the Democratic convention of 1860, southerners grew increasingly aggressive in their defense of slavery and southern rights."[12] Along with this transformation, white scriptural hermeneutics that promoted and condoned slavery based on the supposed notion of the inferiority of the black race multiplied.[13] In addition, the increased prominence of the abolitionist movement during this period and "the abolitionist contention that slaveholding was a sin forced southern clergymen to defend the morality of slavery."[14] Yet, regardless of growing antislavery sentiment in various denominations, abolitionism persisted as a minority perspective in Northern churches in 1860 and was virtually unheard of in Southern churches.[15] Virginia is a case in point. As early as 1798, Francis Asbury, bishop of the Methodist Episcopal Church, reluctantly admitted that slavery, regrettably, would continue to exist in Virginia for many years to come because "There is not a sufficient sense of religion

---

Speeches, Debates, and Interviews, vol. 3, 1855–63, ed. John Blassingame (New Haven: Yale University Press, 1985), 362–63. Also quoted in Harrill, "Use of the New Testament," 161.

11. This phrase comes from Brad Braxton, *No Longer Slaves: Galatians and African American Experience* (Collegeville, MN: Liturgical Press, 2002), 12

12. McKivigan and Snay, *Religion and the Antebellum Debate*, 17.

13. Emerson Powery and Rodney Sadler, *The Genesis of Liberation: Biblical Interpretation in the Antebellum Narratives of the Enslaved* (Louisville: Westminster John Knox, 2016), 95. See also Mark Noll, *The Civil War as a Theological Crisis* (Chapel Hill: University of North Carolina Press, 2006).

14. McKivigan and Snay, *Religion and the Antebellum Debate*, 15.

15. McKivigan and Snay, *Religion and the Antebellum Debate*, 13.

nor of liberty to destroy it" and "Methodists, Baptists, Presbyterians . . . in the highest flights of rapturous piety, still maintain and defend it."[16] Douglas Ambrose notes that Asbury and others within these denominations who tried to promote antislavery sentiments in Virginia met with severe and harsh opposition due to the deep commitment to the "peculiar institution" that prevailed among the clergy and the laypeople. Ministers and laity defended slavery on the basis of protection of property and the belief that slavery was divinely sanctioned by God. They taught and believed that the master/slave relationship was similar to the relationships between husband and wife, parent and child, because all these relationships were household configurations. Thus, the master/slave relationship spoken of in Paul's letters placed such relationships within the familial structure, of which the white male became the head. Slavery, then, became necessary for the divinely ordered family, in which it became the duty of the master to take care of his slaves as he would his children, for slaves were similar to children in their need of guidance, instruction, and correction.

This "paternalistic proslavery Christianity" that permeated Virginia is indicative of the South's view overall and resulted in the idea that "the sin of slavery lay not in the holding of slaves per se, but in the misconduct one might exercise in the holding."[17] Such views were not relegated to the South, however, but occurred in academic circles as well. Prominent biblical scholar Charles Hodge wrote in his commentary on Ephesians, "Slaves are not commanded to refuse to be slaves, to break their bonds and repudiate the authority of their masters. They are required to obey with alacrity, and with a sincere desire to do their duty to their masters, as part of their duty to Christ. Masters are not commanded, as an immediate and imperative duty to emancipate their slaves, but to treat them according to the principles of justice and equity."[18] For Hodge, if slaves obey their owners and slaveholders treat them well, such actions will eventually lead to the dissolution of the practice.[19] Being a slave

16. Douglas Ambrose, "Of Stations and Relations: Proslavery Christianity in Early National Virginia," in McKivigan and Snay, *Religion and the Antebellum Debate*, 35.

17. Ambrose, "Of Stations and Relations," 40. See the discussion, later in this chapter, of James Pennington, who vehemently denies the existence of "kind, Christian masters."

18. Charles Hodge, *A Commentary on Ephesians* (1856; reprint, Edinburgh: First Banner of Truth, 1964, 1991), 272–73. For more on Princeton Theological Seminary and its relationship to slavery, see James H. Moorhead, *Princeton Seminary in American Religion and Culture* (Grand Rapids: Eerdmans, 2012), and the Historical Slave Audit, at https://slavery.ptsem.edu/the-report/introduction/.

19. Hodge, *A Commentary on Ephesians*, 273.

owner, therefore, did not prevent one from being a good Baptist, a good Methodist, or a good Presbyterian.[20]

Consequently, central features of this "paternalistic proslavery Christianity" of the South included the Christian principles of order and duty in which slavery became fundamental to the familial structure where God ordained hierarchy and unequal membership. Members of the household—husbands, wives, children, and slaves—had specific duties attached to their roles, and how they fulfilled these roles determined their fate after death. In this view, it became easy to link the obedience to the slaveholder with the salvation of the enslaved.

For example, Henry "Box" Brown, an enslaved African who absconded through hiding in a box that was shipped to the North, describes the religion of the South as represented by a superintendent of a Sunday school, a Mr. Allen, who taught enslaved children that "they must never disobey their master, nor lie, nor steal, for if they did any of these, they would be sure to go to hell. . . . His zeal did not appear to have any higher object than that of making the children more willing slaves; for he used frequently to tell his visitors that coloured people were never converted—that they had no souls, and could not go to heaven, but it was his duty to talk to them as he did!"[21] If such people taught the slaves, Brown surmised, one can imagine how much value religious instruction had for the slaves and how they received it. Mr. Allen represents the common beliefs about blacks present during this time, and his beliefs about whites were common as well. Brown sums those up in the following statements about Allen: "His liberality to the white people, was co-extensive with his denunciation of the coloured race; he said a white man may do what he pleased, and he could not be lost; he might lie, and rob the slaves, and do anything else, provided he read the Bible and joined the church!"[22] Since slaves are taught that if they do not obey their masters they will go to hell, Brown reveals that religion becomes an instrument for keeping the slaves submissive, and so religion in the South is a "delusion."[23]

Those who espoused this type of Christian proslavery paternalism saw it as a way to strengthen slavery and reduce the possibility of slave revolts,[24] for

20. Ambrose, "Of Stations and Relations," 40.

21. *Narrative of the Life of Henry Box Brown, Written by Himself*, ed. John Ernest (Chapel Hill: University of North Carolina Press, 2008; original Manchester: Lee & Glynn, 1851), 68–69.

22. *Narrative of the Life of Henry Box Brown*, 69.

23. *Narrative of the Life of Henry Box Brown*, 69.

24. Ambrose, "Of Stations and Relations," 55.

it was believed that if slavery were taught correctly, "plots and insurrections, and all the horrid ideas, which now haunt the minds of so many misguided people, would no more be apprehended, servants would do their duty."[25] The master/slave relationship, found and ordained in Scripture, could become the "basis of a society all nations in the earth might call blessed."[26] Such attitudes as these permeated Virginia and the rest of the South, and although some Southerners may have opposed slavery, they could not lead their denominations to support antislavery efforts because of the "theologically entrenched Christian proslavery sentiment" that saturated the culture and the churches.[27] The South sought to promote the idea of an ideal Christian family where Christian slaveholders took care of the enslaved and the enslaved benefited from such care. As abolitionist attacks increased upon the institution itself, proslavery advocates redoubled their efforts to project a "Godly-ordered" household that the enslaved appreciated and loved and that ultimately worked for their benefit.

In the years before the Civil War, white Southerners intensified their efforts to portray happy enslaved Africans, the benevolence of the slave institution, and their adherence to Pauline scriptural admonitions. One of the cited evidences for happy slaves was that they often sang while they worked, which was interpreted as a sign of slaves' contentment and satisfaction with their existence under slavery. But in his narrative, Douglass debunks such thoughts:

> [These slave songs] told a tale of woe which was then altogether beyond my feeble comprehension; they were tones loud, long, and deep; they breathed the prayer and complaint of souls boiling over with the bitterest anguish. Every tone was a testimony against slavery, and a prayer to God for deliverance from chains. The hearing of those wild notes always depressed my spirit, and filled me with ineffable sadness. I have frequently found myself in tears while hearing them. . . . To those songs I trace my first glimmering conception of the dehumanizing character of slavery. I can never get rid of that conception. Those songs still follow me, to deepen my hatred of slavery, and quicken my sympathies for my brethren in bonds. . . . I have often been astonished, since I came to the north, to find persons who could speak of

25. Ambrose, "Of Stations and Relations," 56. Here Ambrose quotes a Mr. Jervas, a Virginia proslavery advocate.

26. Ambrose, "Of Stations and Relations," 56.

27. Ambrose, "Of Stations and Relations," 56–57.

the singing, among slaves, as evidence of their contentment and happiness. It is impossible to conceive of a greater mistake. Slaves sing most when they are most unhappy. The songs of the slave represent the sorrows of his heart; and he is relieved by them, only as an aching heart is relieved by its tears.[28]

In the decade leading up to the Civil War, the common picture whites painted of singing happy slaves was accompanied by increased hermeneutical activity by whites. Part of this activity involved securing the idea of a white superiority sanctioned by God.[29] If this could be securely established, then slavery of African Americans would be permanently legitimized. Two examples from enslaved narratives indicate the type of "creative exegesis" whites used to promote white supremacy. Whereas earlier in this volume we investigated the Ham story and its implications and connections with whites' readings of Paul, the following two narratives indicate additional "exegetical" accounts that served the slavery project.

The first narrative, which some white slaveholders circulated, is told by the enslaved African Henry "Box" Brown and involves a different account of human origins. In this narrative God creates four people, two soulless blacks to serve two white people. The black people, however, annoy their white masters, and so the white couple prays to God to give the blacks activities to keep them busy.

Immediately while they stood, a black cloud seemed to gather over their heads and to descend to the earth before them! While they gazed on these clouds, they saw them open and two bags of different size drop from them. They immediately ran to lay hold of the bags, and unfortunately for the black man—he being the strongest and swiftest—he arrived first at them, and laid hold of the bags, and the white man, coming up afterwards, got the smaller one. They then proceeded to untie their bags, when lo! in the large one, there was a shovel and a hoe; and in the small one, a pen, ink, and paper; to write the declaration of the intention of the Almighty; they each proceeded to employ the instruments which God had sent them, and

---

28. "Narrative of the Life of Frederick Douglass, an American Slave, Written by Himself," in *I Was Born a Slave: An Anthology of Classic Slave Narratives*, ed. Yuval Taylor, 2 vols. (Chicago: Lawrence Hill Books, 1999), 1:543.

29. Powery and Sadler, *The Genesis of Liberation*, 97. See also James O. Horton and Amanda Kleintop, eds., *Race, Slavery, and the Civil War: The Tough Stuff of American History and Memory* (Richmond, VA: Virginia Sesquicentennial of the American Civil War Commission, 2011).

ever since the colored race have had to labor with the shovel and the hoe, while the rich man works with the pen and ink![30]

As Powery and Sadler note, the story implies that the task of writing "the declaration of the intention of the Almighty" refers to whites' authorship of Scripture, and by default, to them as spokespersons for God.[31] This serves to reinforce the idea that whatever the "master's minister" proclaims as true from Scripture, such as God's ordination of black slavery, God validates. The narrative also reinforces the notion of white intellectual superiority and hard manual labor as the destiny of African Americans. In addition, the "rich man" who works with "pen and ink" is inevitably the white person, indicating that wealth belongs to whites, not African Americans. This narrative coheres with the idea of a Christian proslavery paternalism that includes an ordained master/slave relationship within the family household and the respective duties for each member of that household. The white owners had the duty and divine sanctioning, as it were, to run the business of the household, using pen, ink, and paper, whereas the slaves had their duties to fulfill by using their sanctioned tools for the manual labor for which they were designed according to this narrative. This story also shows why blacks did not need to be educated. Education belonged to whites; God did not intend for African Americans to receive it.

The second narrative is related by J. D. Green, an enslaved African who, after his mother is sold, is quite distraught and remembers a story told to him by his enslaver regarding the origins of African Americans and whites. Green's poignant reflections regarding separation from his mother begin the narrative:

Why was I born black? It would have been better had I not been born at all. Only yesterday, my mother was sold to go to, not one of us knows where, and I am left alone, and I have no hope of seeing her again. At this moment a raven alighted on a tree over my head, and I cried, "Oh, Raven! if I had wings like you. I would soon find my mother and be happy again." Before parting she advised me to be a good boy, and she would pray for me, and I must pray for her, and hoped we might meet again in heaven, and I at once commenced to pray, to the best of my knowledge, "Our Father art in

30. *Narrative of the Life of Henry Box Brown*, 92; also quoted by Powery and Sadler, *The Genesis of Liberation*, 97–98.
31. Powery and Sadler, *The Genesis of Liberation*, 98.

Heaven, be Thy name, kingdom come.—Amen." But, at this time, words of my master obtruded into my mind that God did not care for black folks, as he did not make them, but the d——l did. Then I thought of the old saying amongst us, as stated by our master, that, when God was making man, He made white man out of the best clay, as potters make china, and the d——l was watching, and he immediately took some black mud and made a black man, and called him a [n——].[32]

Again, the superiority of whiteness is the aim of such a story, and it facilitates this aim by claiming that God had no role in the creation of African Americans; instead the devil created them. Moreover, such a narrative, along with the previous one, promotes the belief that African Americans, since they are created by the devil, are soulless, and can thus be treated like animals. To sustain the credibility of such narratives and their "biblical origin," slaveholders needed to keep enslaved Africans illiterate and restrict and control access to Scripture, a practice the first narrative asserted as divinely authorized.[33]

As the debates over slavery in this country became increasingly caustic and contentious, slaveholders sought to solidify notions of black inferiority, a perspective the above narratives exemplify, and to convey life in the South as one of grandeur and Southern hospitality filled with happy, contented slaves. After all, Christian slave owners were merely following God's order for the household and carrying out their sanctioned duties. But as stories of slavery from African American escapees became increasingly known, it became clear that the pristine portrait painted by slaveholders was far from reality. This chapter discusses how escapees from slavery, such as James Pennington and Harriet Jacobs, insert Pauline language into their narratives and how these insertions enable them to tell their stories in profound ways. In addition, during this time black women preachers like Maria Stewart and Julia Foote utilize Paul to protest racism and sexism and to continue the traditions of Jarena Lee and Zilpha Elaw in employing Paul to sanction their right and call to preach. This chapter will also discuss Daniel Payne, whose autobiography and writings include Pauline Scripture to speak of his conversion and the Pauline responsibilities of African Americans during the Civil War. The discussion will also explore how these black hermeneuts' use

---

32. J. D. Green, *Narrative of the Life of J. D. Green, A Runaway Slave, Containing an Account of His Three Escapes* (Huddersfield, UK: Henry Fielding, Pack Horse Yard, 1864); reprinted in Taylor, *I Was Born a Slave*, 1:688.

33. Powery and Sadler, *The Genesis of Liberation*, 99.

of Pauline language facilitates a body hermeneutic and blacks' rejection of the two "creation" accounts discussed above.

Maria Stewart (1803–1879): First Female Public Lecturer on Political Themes

Maria Stewart is known as the first American-born woman of *any* race to lecture to men and women in public on political themes.[34] She is also known as America's first black woman political writer.[35] Stewart was born free in 1803 in Hartford, Connecticut. After being orphaned at five years old, she was "bound out" as a servant to a clergyman's family, where she lived until the age of fifteen. In Boston in 1826 she married James W. Stewart, who passed away in 1829, and she remained a widow for the rest of her life. She writes that in 1830 she "was brought to the knowledge of the truth as it is in Jesus," and in 1831 Stewart makes a "public profession" of her faith.[36] Stewart wrote a number of essays and speeches during her lifetime, and they are extraordinary because they are "both explicitly theological and explicitly political."[37] The present discussion examines her use of Pauline language in two of her writings, "Religion and the Pure Principles of Morality, The Sure Foundation on Which We Must Build. Productions From The Pen Of MRS. MARIA STEWARD [*sic*], Widow of The Late James W. Steward, Of Boston" and her farewell address entitled "Mrs. Stewart's Farewell Address to Her

34. Valerie Cooper, *Maria Stewart, the Bible, and the Rights of African Americans* (Charlottesville: University of Virginia Press, 2011), 1; Marilyn Richardson, "What If I Am a Woman? Maria Stewart's Defense of Black Women's Political Activism," in *Courage and Conscience: Black and White Abolitionists in Boston*, ed. Donald M. Jacobs (Bloomington: Indiana University Press, 1993), 191.

35. This is the title given to her by Marilyn Richardson and the title of her book, *Maria W. Stewart, America's First Black Woman Political Writer: Essays and Speeches*, ed. Marilyn Richardson (Bloomington: Indiana University Press, 1987). Cooper, *Maria Stewart*, writes, "While some characterize her speeches as political, there is frequently very little difference between them and others' sermons. Did Maria Stewart understand what she was doing as preaching? She never calls it that. Nevertheless, the line between simply giving a speech and preaching the Gospel is one that she frequently transgresses" (114). See also 119.

36. Maria Stewart, "Religion and the Pure Principles of Morality, The Sure Foundation on Which We Must Build. Productions from The Pen Of MRS. MARIA STEWARD [*sic*], Widow of The Late James W. Steward, Of Boston," in Richardson, *Maria W. Stewart*, 28–29.

37. Cooper, *Maria Stewart*, 120.

Friends in the City of Boston." The audience for both of these pieces includes free African Americans in Boston, both men and women.[38]

"Religion and the Pure Principles of Morality"

In the introduction of the first essay, "Religion and the Pure Principles of Morality," a document known as the "first political manifesto written by a black American woman," Stewart speaks of her conversion and the transformation it wrought in her life.[39] "From the moment I experienced the change, I felt a strong desire, with the help and assistance of God, to devote the remainder of my days to piety and virtue, and now possess that spirit of independence that, were I called upon, I would willingly sacrifice my life for the cause of God and my brethren."[40] Her newfound faith became the impetus by which she fought for the liberation of her fellow African Americans and became a "strong advocate for the cause of God and for the cause of freedom."[41] In this political manifesto Stewart emphasizes several important themes: a call for African Americans' pursuit of knowledge and improvement; African Americans' divine image; the special role of black women; the significance of blacks living a religious life filled with piety, morality, and virtue; and her willingness to be a martyr for the cause of justice. All these themes are dynamically interrelated in this work.

At the end of her opening paragraph, Stewart states that one of the main goals of this writing is to cause her audience to see the "great necessity of turning [their] attention to knowledge and improvement" (28). She admonishes her audience to improve their talents, to "show forth your powers of mind" (29), and to demonstrate to the world that although they are black, they are not inferior to any white person. She eloquently writes,

> Many think, because your skins are tinged with a sable hue, that you are an inferior race of beings; but God does not consider you as such. He hath

---

38. Richardson, preface to *Maria W. Stewart*, ed. Richardson, xiii. All of Stewart's essays cited in this volume appear in Richardson, *Maria W. Stewart*, and the page references are to Richardson.

39. Richardson, introduction to *Maria W. Stewart*, ed. Richardson, 8. My discussion of this essay will, of course, focus on Pauline echoes and citations. However, for other biblical passages in this speech, see Cooper, *Maria Stewart*, 42–90.

40. Stewart, "Religion and the Pure Principles," 29. Hereafter, page references from this work will be given in parentheses in the text.

41. Richardson, introduction to *Maria W. Stewart*, ed. Richardson, 8.

formed and fashioned you in his own glorious image, and hath bestowed upon you reason and strong powers of intellect. He hath made you to have dominion over the beasts of the field, the fowls of the air, and the fish of the sea [Gen. 1:26]. He hath crowned you with glory and honor; hath made you but a little lower than the angels [Ps. 8:5]; and according to the Constitution of these United States, he hath made all men free and equal. Then why should one worm say to another, "Keep you down there, while I sit up yonder; for I am better than thou?" It is not the color of the skin that makes the man, but it is the principles formed within the soul. (29)

Here Stewart vehemently rejects any notions of black inferiority and affirms African Americans' creation in the image of God. They were not created by the devil, nor were they created to serve whites, as the two narratives discussed in the introduction of this chapter suggest, but God formed them and granted them "reason and strong powers of intellect." Stewart's words that God does not consider African Americans inferior deny all the images and stories that blacks in her audience may have heard or may have internalized about themselves and their origins. Using Genesis to re-create the story of their creation, Stewart reclaims and proclaims the divine origin of African Americans. She insists that along with the Bible, the US Constitution establishes blacks' freedom and equality as well. In her statement that principles formed within the soul make a person, not the color of one's skin, she upholds the existence of African Americans' souls and simultaneously advises her audience to cultivate "the pure principles of piety, morality, and virtue" within them (30). Elsewhere in the essay, Stewart urges her audience to "prove to the world that you are neither ourang-outangs, or a species of mere animals, but that you possess the same powers of intellect as the proud-boasting American" (40). Aware of the many elements present in society and in public discourse aimed at dehumanizing African Americans, Stewart encourages her audience to resist the lies about their nature and their origin and to take charge of their destiny by proving to the world the fabrications regarding inferior black intellect and black subservience. Motivation to prove their intellectual prowess; the development of piety, morality, and virtue; and the pursuit of knowledge are all significant for Stewart's program of black uplift, including her specific focus upon black women.

Throughout the essay, Stewart urges the black women in her audience to live a life devoted to Jesus and to distinguish themselves in knowledge. "O, ye daughters of Africa, awake! Awake! Arise! No longer sleep nor slumber, but distinguish yourselves. Show forth to the world that ye are endowed with noble and exalted faculties. O, ye daughters of Africa! What have ye done to immortalize your names beyond the grave? What examples have ye set before the rising generation? What foundation have ye laid for the generations yet unborn?" (30). And again, "O woman, woman, would thou only strive to excel in merit and virtue; would thou only store thy mind with useful knowledge, great would be thine influence" (31–32). For Stewart, African American women should set themselves apart by utilizing the intellect given to them by God and by living virtuous lives. They are to live lives that leave behind a glorious legacy to future generations. To Stewart, mothers especially have an important responsibility, for they create in the minds of their children a "thirst for knowledge, the love of virtue, the abhorrence of vice, and the cultivation of a pure heart" (35). Therefore, women, particularly mothers, play a significant role in the development of children.

Religion of Jesus in Pauline Terms

Echoing Pauline language, Stewart laments the state of her fellow African Americans, how "few have been hopefully brought to the *knowledge of the truth* [1 Tim. 2:4; 2 Tim. 3:7; Heb. 10:26] as it is in Jesus" and that "few care to distinguish themselves either in religious or moral improvement" (32).[42] Yet Stewart encourages her audience to turn to the "religion of Jesus," for only in it will they find happiness and greatness. She asks, "Have you one desire to become truly great? O, then, become truly pious, and God will endow you with wisdom and knowledge from on high." Stewart demonstrates that the "knowledge of the truth" is salvation, but this salvific knowledge encompasses more than just knowledge about salvation for the soul. God will impart to them wisdom and knowledge from on high that will instruct them on how to live their lives in the present moment in such a way that they will reject the empty ways of the world and follow the "religion of Jesus," which brings happiness here on earth and comfort at the time of death (32).

Interestingly, Stewart turns to Pauline language to describe further this religion of Jesus. She eloquently writes, "Religion is pure; it is ever new; it is beautiful; it is all that is worth living for; it is worth dying for: O, could I but see the church *built up in the most holy faith* [Col. 2:7]; could I but see men *spiritually minded* [Rom. 8:6], walking in the fear of God, not given to *filthy lucre* [Titus 1:7; cf. 1 Tim. 3:3, 8], not holding religion in one hand and

---

42. See also uses of the language "brought to the knowledge of the truth" on 34.

the world in the other, but *diligent in business, fervent in spirit, serving the Lord* [Rom. 12:11]" (33). Stewart understands religion to be an integral part of the believer's life, such that it guides every part of a person's existence.

Stewart returns to Paul to depict the effect of religion upon mothers, whom she describes as "mothers in Israel," who should be *"chaste, keepers at home* [Titus 2:5], *not busy bodies, meddlers in other men's matters, whose adorning is of the inward man* [Rom. 7:22; 2 Cor. 4:16], possessing a meek and quiet spirit" (33). In a society that often denies black familial status and refuses to see black families as equal to those of whites, Stewart urges black women to take care of their households and to make them a priority, something they could not do fully under slavery, due to the constant threat of separation and the fact that blacks really had no control over their own families—white slaveholders did. Thus, Stewart encourages the free black women in her audience to exercise their freedom and focus on their home life. For Stewart, religion enables black people to be all they were created to be and to exist as full human beings in a world that consistently rejected their humanity.

She then turns to young people and, quoting Paul's words in Hebrews, equates African American youth with Moses: "Could I but see young men and maidens turning their feet from impious ways, rather *choosing to suffer affliction with the people of God rather than to enjoy the pleasures of sin for a season* [Heb. 11:25]; could I but see the rising youth blushing in artless innocence, then I could say, now, Lord let thine unworthy handmaiden depart in peace, for I have seen the desire of mine eyes, and am satisfied" (33). Hebrews 11, sometimes called the "Hall of Faith" chapter, enumerates exemplary biblical characters whose actions define what faith entails. Moses epitomizes what it means to have faith, and Stewart compares blacks with Moses, who chose to suffer with his people rather than continue to enjoy the pleasures of his royal status in Pharaoh's family. Suffering for the sake of righteousness is to be preferred over living a life of sinful pleasure that is only temporary. When people turn from their "impious" ways, they will truly understand that their call is to be part of the "people of God," not part of the world; being in solidarity with those who suffer is integral to the nomenclature "God's people." Stewart attempts to depict for her audience that they have an identity as "people of God" and that identity is primary. They belong to God, are loved by God, and called by the God that many whites at the time said did not love them or create them. Stewart affirms her people's worth to the Divine.

Furthermore, Stewart understands religion as something that transforms individuals, communities, and societies. Indeed, she prays that African

Americans may "soon become so distinguished for our moral and religious improvements, that the nations of the earth may take knowledge of us" (34). Stewart believes that the world must take note of a divine transformation of African Americans; after all, when the Divine touches human lives, nothing is ever the same. Her own life becomes an example of such a transformation. Her repeated wish that all would be brought to the knowledge of the truth echoes Pauline language. Just as Paul urged the Corinthians to "*awake to righteousness and sin not*," Stewart urges her audience to "*awake to righteousness and sin not* [1 Cor. 15:34]" (35). She takes over the Pauline imperatives to instruct her community, and by doing so demonstrates connections between who they are, what they do, and how they live. In other words, she highlights the link between the indicative and the imperative in Pauline terms.[43] Because of what God does in and for believers, God and God's Spirit empower believers to live out their divine call. Pauline imperatives serve to direct her audience to be who they already are, to live out what is already inside of them. For Stewart, who talks about the power of sin and its ability to wreak havoc upon her community right before her citation of this imperative, her employment of this Pauline imperative attempts to enable her audience to use God's power to resist sin, to repent of sin, and therefore to annihilate its consequences.

Stewart's Focus on Black Unity and Black Agency

The blatant disregard for African Americans, including widows and orphans, by the larger white society as well as the discouragement this disregard breeds are, according to Stewart, consequences of sin and its power. This disregard causes blacks to believe they cannot achieve anything, and so it generates a sense of inferiority. The vestiges of sin for Stewart are societal and systemic and simultaneously communal and individual in that sin brokers destruction in communities and upon individual people. It is all connected for her, which is why, after she cites the Pauline imperative "to awake to righteousness and sin not," she takes up another imperative from Jeremiah, admonishing her audience to "Return, O ye backsliding children [Jer. 3:22]" (35). Thus, these imperatives demonstrate her emphasis on black agency and

---

43. See J. Louis Martyn, *Galatians: A New Translation with Introduction and Commentary*, Anchor Yale Bible 33A (New York: Doubleday, 1997), 535, identifies Gal. 5:16 as an imperative in which "Paul calls on the Galatians steadily to be what they already are."

the importance of utilizing this agency to resist sin in all its manifestations, whether it manifests in the neglect of society's concern for black lives or in blacks choosing to follow impious ways rather than God. Sin is the culprit, Stewart declares, and must be resisted. When Stewart writes that she desires to see the phrase "I can't" removed from the lips of her fellow African Americans and replaced by "I will," she advocates that blacks reject the prevalent notion that they are inferior and cannot achieve anything. Her adoption of Pauline imperatives underscores black agency and becomes another way to help her audience replace "I can't" with "I will" (35).

Stewart is convinced that when African Americans unite in lifting themselves up and turning their attention toward knowledge and improvement, then the "hissing and reproach among the nations of the earth against us will cease" (37). She advocates that African American women unify by pooling their resources to save money to build their own schools and stores. Stewart's emphasis on black women seeking formal education was a political expedient, especially since laws were being passed in the South during this time that prohibited slaves from learning to read and write. Stewart's appeal, then, is the earliest record of a call to black women to become teachers, start schools, and work as pioneers in African American education.[44] Although Stewart encourages her audience to prove to the world their worth, she recognizes the possibility that any such effort may go unnoticed, and so, "if no one will promote or respect us, let us promote and respect ourselves" (37). Creating their own schools and stores would be another way for African Americans to prove to the world black value and intellect.

Although Stewart focuses a great deal on African American women, she also addresses men in the audience. For example, she urges them to rise up in behalf of liberty: "All the nations of the earth are crying out for liberty and equality. Away, away with tyranny and oppression! And shall Afric's sons be silent any longer?" (29). For her, African American men need to let their voices be heard in fighting for their freedom. They should no longer sit passively by and watch as injustice wreaks havoc upon their families and their community. They need to engage in active resistance.[45] Just as she urged women to pursue knowledge and education, she encourages the men in her audience to do the same. She exclaims, "Where is the youth who has

---

44. Richardson, introduction to *Maria W. Stewart*, ed. Richardson, 20.

45. Some scholars believe that Stewart may have been calling for armed resistance here, as did her predecessor David Walker. However, see her statements at the end of the essay, 40–41. See also Cooper, *Maria Stewart*, 176.

written upon his manly brow a thirst for knowledge; whose ambitious mind soars above trifles, and longs for the time come, when he shall redress the wrongs of his father and plead the cause of his brethren?" (31). According to Stewart, African American men play an important role in the black community in acquiring knowledge and using it in behalf of their people. In other words, their knowledge is not just for their own personal betterment but is communal in its focus and aim.

While Stewart urges her audience to lift themselves up, she recognizes that many are in despair and believe that any pursuit of betterment is worthless because of their societal status and the culture of inferiority that permeates the nation. Speaking eloquently to this pain, Stewart writes, "I am sensible, my brethren and friends, that many of you have been deprived of advantages, kept in utter ignorance, and that your *minds are now darkened* [Eph. 4:18]; and if any one of you have attempted to acquire after high and noble enterprises, you have met with so much opposition that your souls have become discouraged. . . . Oh then, turn your attention to knowledge and improvement; for knowledge is power. And *God is able to fill you with wisdom and understanding* [Col. 1:9], and to dispel your fears" (41).

Even as she recognizes their discouragement at trying to make their lives better, Stewart offers knowledge and the source of knowledge, God, as the antidote for feelings of powerlessness. She juxtaposes the "darkened minds" of her fellow African Americans that have come about through lack of educational opportunities with the God of knowledge who will bestow understanding upon them. In employing Paul, she sets up a dichotomy between the worldly system that denies blacks education and the divine system that grants understanding. Her words recall the "creation" narrative discussed at the beginning of this chapter, in which whites were deemed worthy of education while blacks were not. Instead, this "creation" story insisted that African Americans were created for manual labor. Stewart, however, rejects this racist distinction, arguing that blacks are worthy of education, so much so that the divine realm would grant it. Moreover, Stewart raises another important element that appears throughout portions of early black literature, that is, African American dependence upon God for knowledge and insight because the larger society denied them access. As one former enslaved person exclaimed, "[God] never leaves me in ignorance. Neither does he leave any that trust him in ignorance."[46] African Americans learned to trust God

---

46. Clifton Johnson, ed., *God Struck Me Dead: Religious Conversion Experiences and*

for wisdom, insight, and knowledge because they needed to depend on the Divine for assistance in all areas of their lives. Although they may have been denied access to education, they did have access to God and God had access to them, access that no law could contravene.[47] Adopting a Pauline epistemological dimension in which God is the source of all knowledge, Stewart proclaims that this God can fill them with understanding, annihilate their trepidations, and empower them in the midst of dire circumstances.

Stewart's Judgment Language

Accompanying her focus on black agency and unity, Stewart includes in her essay language of judgment on America because she understands that the plight of those in her audience derives from injustice and racism. In one of her lengthy jeremiads, which echoes the many proclamations of David Walker, who greatly influenced her, she pronounces that America will have to pay for its sins against its African American citizens.[48] She boldly declares:

> Oh, America, America, foul and indelible is thy stain! Dark and dismal is the cloud that hangs over thee, for thy cruel wrongs and injuries to the fallen sons of Africa. The blood of her murdered ones cries to heaven for vengeance against thee. Thou art almost become drunken with the blood of her slain; thou hast enriched thyself through her toils and labors; and now thou refuseth to make even a small return. And thou hast caused the daughters of Africa to commit whoredoms and fornications; but upon thee be their curse. O, ye great and mighty men of America, you rich and powerful ones, many of you will call for the rocks and mountains to fall upon you, and to hide you from the wrath of the Lamb, and from him that sitteth upon the throne, whilst many of the sable-skinned Africans you now despise, will shine in the kingdom of heaven as the stars forever and ever.

Autobiographies of Ex-Slaves (Philadelphia: Pilgrim, 1969), 156. See also the discussion of this quote in chap. 4.

47. For example, see the earlier discussion of John Jea's autobiography and his account of God granting him the ability to read the Bible.

48. Richardson, introduction to *Maria W. Stewart*, ed. Richardson, 5–6, 11–13; Christina Henderson, "Sympathetic Violence: Maria Stewart's Antebellum Vision of African American Resistance," in "New Registers for the Study of Blackness," ed. Martha J. Cutter, special issue, *MELUS* 38, no. 4 (December 2013): 52–75. See also the discussion of Stewart and Walker in Cooper, *Maria Stewart*, 133.

Charity begins at home, and *those that provide not for their own, are worse than infidels* [1 Tim. 5:8]. . . . You may kill, tyrannize, and oppress as much as you choose, until our cry shall come up before the throne of God; for I am firmly persuaded, that he will not suffer you to quell the proud, fearless and undaunted spirits of the Africans forever; for in his own time, he is able to plead our cause against you, and to pour out upon you the ten plagues of Egypt. (39–40)

Stewart's jeremiad serves two purposes: it comforts and encourages those in her audience so that they may know that God has not forgotten them, and it warns America about its impending doom.[49] Stewart believes that America will not escape harsh judgment because God hears the many cries and sees the numerous sufferings of African Americans in this country. She echoes the story of Abel in Genesis 4:10, where Abel's blood cries out from the ground, and she compares African Americans' plight to that of Israel under Egypt. God's response on behalf of American slaves will be similar to the divine response on behalf of Israeli slaves—the commencement of ten plagues. Stewart proclaims an impending divine reversal in which the rich and powerful will be brought low and the despised, enslaved Africans will be exalted by God.

Stewart's judgment language incorporates Pauline antipathy toward those who do not fulfill their obligations. Echoing Paul, who writes in 1 Timothy 5:8: "But if any provide not for his own, and specially those of his own house, he hath denied the faith, and is worse than an infidel," Stewart condemns the actions of Americans who take pride in sending aid overseas but refuse to give assistance to those African Americans within their own borders. Cooper correctly remarks about the import of this Pauline passage for Stewart's argument. "If, as Stewart has argued, blacks are in every human category equal to whites, then for whites to fail to provide for them (even the fair wages for their labor) is a sin. Stewart is here refuting the idea that the Americans are the most spiritual, most religious people on the earth, possessed of a biblical 'city upon a hill.' Instead, Stewart decries them as 'worse than' infidels, or unbelievers."[50] In Stewart's citation of this passage she opposes America's hypocrisy and its veneer of righteousness. Although

49. Richardson, introduction to *Maria W. Stewart*, ed. Richardson, 16–17; Wilson Jeremiah Moses, *Black Messiahs and Uncle Toms: Social and Literary Manipulations of a Religious Myth* (University Park: Pennsylvania State University Press, 1982), 30–49.

50. Cooper, *Maria Stewart*, 82n183.

such hypocritical actions continue in the present moment for her and her audience, she declares that they will soon end, for God will plead the African American cause. And since God will work on their behalf, she urges her audience to "Stand still, and know that the Lord he is God. *Vengeance is his, and he will repay* [Rom. 12:19]" (40). Employing the apostle's words in Romans 12:19, Stewart asserts that God will rectify all wrongs, including those committed by America.

Stewart's audacious, outspoken claims about judgment coming upon America, her forward directives toward the African American community regarding black uplift, coupled with the fact that she was an African American woman speaking in public about such issues, generate opposition from various quarters of society. She writes that "Many will suffer for pleading the cause of oppressed Africa, and I shall glory in being one of her martyrs . . . and if there is no other way for me to escape, [God] is able to take me to himself as he did the most noble, fearless, and undaunted David Walker" (30).[51] Similar to David Walker, whose mysterious death caused some to believe that he died because of his relentless pursuit of justice, Stewart recognizes that her outspokenness may cost her her life, and she prepares for that possibility. Her understanding of the price for standing up for her beliefs closes the essay, and she frames her language with Pauline terms. She writes,

> I have never taken one step, my friends, with a design to raise myself in your esteem, or to gain applause. But what I have done, has been done with an eye single to the glory of God, and to promote the good of souls. I have neither kindred nor friends. I stand alone in your midst, exposed to the *fiery darts of the devil* [Eph. 6:16], and to the assaults of wicked men. But though all the powers of earth and hell were to combine against me, though all nature should sink into decay, still I would trust in the Lord, and joy in the God of my salvation. *For I am full persuaded that he will bring me off conqueror, yea, more than conqueror* [Rom. 8:37, 38], *through him who hath loved me and given himself for me* [Gal. 2:20]. (41)

Stewart views herself as involved in a cosmic battle without human assistance from fellow warriors, for she stands alone and exposed to the fiery

51. Both Cooper and Richardson note the profound effect Walker's death had upon Stewart. As her mentor, his passing affected her greatly. As mentioned above, his death remains a mystery.

darts of the devil. The words spoken against her and the opposition to her stances become like darts from the enemy aimed at destroying her and her ministry. She exhibits a belief in both human and spiritual enemies and the intricate link between the two. As Marilyn Richardson rightfully observes, "With her conversion there came to Stewart the understanding that her new allegiance to the will of God would place her in conflict with many ways of the world, making her a 'warrior' and even a potential martyr for 'the cause of oppressed Africa.' Nonetheless, moved by 'holy indignation' she began to write and to speak out publicly against tyranny, victimization, and injustice as she felt them affecting her life, her community, and her nation."[52] Stewart's adoption of Pauline warfare imagery, then, depicts a "writer under siege."[53] Despite being alone, however, in a fight that involves the natural and supernatural realms, Stewart is confident that God makes her more than a conqueror through Jesus.

Stewart's Farewell Address

Stewart's career has involved great personal cost, and in 1833 she delivers her farewell address, entitled "Mrs. Stewart's Farewell Address to Her Friends in the City of Boston."[54] Due to the intense opposition she faces, Stewart decides to leave Boston, and this speech becomes her final formal public address.[55] In it she employs Pauline language to take her audience on a journey that includes a more detailed description of her conversion experience, her ministry, and her suffering in behalf of liberation. She also defends the presence and importance of women in the public sphere fighting against injustice and oppression in regard to race and gender.[56]

52. Richardson, introduction to *Maria W. Stewart*, ed. Richardson, 8.

53. Richardson, introduction to *Maria W. Stewart*, ed. Richardson, 17. Additional Pauline citations in this essay appear on p. 33 (Rom. 7:22; 2 Cor. 4:16, "inward man"; cf. 1 Pet. 3:3–5); p. 36 (Heb. 1:14, "heirs of salvation").

54. Richardson, introduction to *Maria W. Stewart*, ed. Richardson, 24.

55. Although this farewell speech is often referred to as Stewart's final public speaking engagement, there is some evidence that she gave lectures when she moved to New York. See Richardson, preface to *Maria W. Stewart*, ed. Richardson, xiv, xvi; Richardson, introduction to *Maria W. Stewart*, ed. Richardson, 27. After leaving Boston, she became a schoolteacher, first in New York, then in Baltimore and Washington. After the Civil War, she became a matron of a Freedmen's Hospital.

56. Milton Sernett, ed., *African American Religious History: A Documentary Witness* (Durham, NC: Duke University Press, 1999), 202.

Stewart opens the speech by echoing a passage from Acts 14:22: "*Ah no! for it is with great tribulation that any shall enter through the gates into the holy city.*"[57] This echo derives from Paul and Barnabas's speech to members of the early church, in which they encouraged the disciples regarding the suffering life of those who follow Christ. The preceding verses in Acts detail the great opposition and affliction that Paul and Barnabas endured as they traveled around spreading the gospel, including being stoned. That Stewart purposely chose this verse because it cohered with her own life experiences of opposition as she preached and spoke out publicly against injustice cannot be doubted. In addition, these words were part of the apostles' own farewell speech before they left one place and moved on to preach in another. The context of the verse and the context of Stewart's life merge, and it becomes a well-suited introduction for her own farewell discourse as she decides to move on from Boston due to the severe opposition she faces in that city.

After this introduction, Stewart briefly describes her conversion experience, how she accepted salvation as a free gift, and how she came to understand that "*we are saved by grace alone* [Eph. 2:8]" (65). This conversion experience facilitates a profound transformation in her life and sets in motion a distinctive call to suffer for the cause of Christ. She writes:

> After these convictions, in imagination I found myself sitting at the feet of Jesus, clothed in my right mind. For I before had been like a ship tossed to and fro, in a storm at sea. Then was I glad when I realized the dangers I had escaped; and then I consecrated my soul and body, and all the powers of my mind to his service, from that time, henceforth; yea, even for evermore, amen. I found that religion was full of benevolence; I found there was joy and peace in believing, and I felt as though I was commanded to *come out from the world and be separate* [2 Cor. 6:17]; to go forward and be baptized. Methought I heard a spiritual interrogation, are you able to drink of that cup that I have drank of? And to be baptized with the baptism that I have been baptized with (Matt. 20:22)? And my heart made this reply: Yea, Lord, I am able. . . . O, how bitter was that cup. Yet I drank it to its very dregs. . . . Like many, I was anxious to retain the world in one hand, and religion in the other. "Ye cannot serve God and mammon (Matt. 6:24)," sounded in my ear, and with giant-strength, I cut off my right hand, as it were, and

---

57. Maria Stewart, "Mrs. Stewart's Farewell Address to Her Friends in the City of Boston," in Richardson, *Maria W. Stewart*, 65. Hereafter, page references from this work will be given in parentheses in the text.

plucked out my right eye, and cast them from me, thinking it better to enter life halt and maimed, rather than having two hands or eyes to be cast into hell (Mark 9:43). Thus ended these mighty conflicts, and I received this heart-cheering promise, *"That neither death, nor life, nor principalities, nor powers, nor things present, nor things to come, should be able to separate me from the love of Christ Jesus, our Lord"* [Rom. 8:38, 39]. *And truly, I can say with St. Paul, that at my conversion I came to the people in the fulness of the gospel of grace* [Rom. 15:29]. (66)[58]

As this account of her conversion intimates, Stewart consecrates her life to God and God's service, and part of this consecration involves separating herself from the world and its desire to control her. This call to separate from the world consists of separation in a spiritual sense, such as living a life of holiness and godliness, and includes separating from the world's ideas of black inferiority and female subservience, including the prescribed "roles" for each. She characterizes this separation as a baptism in suffering and drinking from the same cup that Christ drinks from, for when one deviates from society's "norms," suffering inevitably follows.

The consecration of her body and mind means total surrender of her body, which she depicts as cutting off her hands and plucking out her eyes on behalf of her call, since her body belongs to God. Once she is resolved to live completely for God, the "mighty conflicts" within her cease and God speaks the reassuring words of Romans 8:38–39 to her. Her willingness to separate from the world yields the promise of never experiencing separation from Christ's love. Her conversion, then, which consists of a total surrender to God and God's purpose, facilitates her ministry, like Paul's, in the "gospel of grace." As her life merges with Paul in the experience of opposition, so too does it merge in the experience of preaching the gospel of grace. In Pauline language, she describes a life of holiness and devotion to God, a real sense of God's ongoing presence and communication with her, and she endures afflictions she would suffer for the sake of justice with the assurance that God's love would not forsake her. Stewart's use of Paul here is an act of resistance: against the common presentation of a Paul used to silence women, she declares that she, like the apostle, separates from the world and its categories, and comes in the fullness of the gospel of grace. Stewart can speak "with St. Paul," indicating that far from silencing her, the apostle speaks with her and her voice merges with his.

58. See also the discussion of this passage in Cooper, *Maria Stewart*, 145–47.

"Power of Speaking" and "Why Cannot
a Religious Spirit Animate Us Now?"

Stewart credits the Holy Spirit with guiding her ministry from its inception, for soon after she made her profession of faith in Christ, she reports that the "The Spirit of God came before me" and "A something said within my breast, *'Press forward* [Phil. 3:14], I will be with thee.' And my heart made this reply, Lord if thou wilt be with me, then I will speak for thee as long as I live. And thus far I have every reason to believe that it is the divine influence of the Holy Spirit operating upon my heart that could possibly induce me to make the feeble and unworthy efforts that I have" (67). The Spirit guides and empowers Stewart as she works to administer justice for those in her community, for "resistance to oppression was, for Stewart, the highest form of obedience to God."[59] Stewart's willingness to speak on God's behalf regarding injustice to African Americans and injustice to women garnered harsh criticism and the assassination of her character from others. She laments "the false misrepresentations" with which some characterized her (67). Despite such opposition, however, Stewart remains true to her calling and continues to speak out, even characterizing herself as a warrior. As discussed in her earlier writing "Religion and the Pure Principles of Morality," where she adopts Paul's language of "fiery darts," here, too, in her farewell speech, Stewart returns to the theme of warfare and her preparedness for battle. Interestingly, her battle language appears right before her discussion of women leaders in Scripture whom God uses to carry out divine purposes.

> I believe, that for wise and holy purposes, best known to himself, he hath unloosed my tongue, and put his word into my mouth, in order to *confound and put all those to shame* [1 Cor. 1:26] that have rose up against me. For he hath clothed my face with steel, and lined my forehead with brass. He hath put his testimony within me, and engraven his seal on my forehead. And with these weapons I have indeed set the fiends of earth and hell at defiance. What if I am a woman; is not the God of ancient times the God of these modern days? Did he not raise up Deborah, to be a mother, and a judge in Israel? Did not queen Esther save the lives of the Jews? And Mary Magdalene first declare the resurrection of Christ from the dead? Come, said the woman of Samaria, and see a man that hath told me all things that ever I

---

59. Richardson, introduction to *Maria W. Stewart*, ed. Richardson, 9.

did, is not this the Christ? *St. Paul declared that it was a shame for a woman to speak in public* [1 Cor. 14:34–35], yet our *great High Priest and Advocate* [Heb. 4:14] did not condemn the woman for a more notorious offence than this; neither will he condemn this worthless worm. The bruised reed he will not break, and the smoking flax he will not quench, till he send forth judgment unto victory. *Did St. Paul but know of our wrongs and deprivations, I presume he would make no objections to our pleading in public for our rights.* Again; holy women ministered unto Christ and the apostles; and women of refinement in all ages, more or less, have had a voice in moral, religious and political subjects. Again; why the Almighty hath imparted unto me the power of speaking thus, I cannot tell. (67–68)

In this passage, Stewart returns to the idea of a two-tier struggle in both the human and suprahuman planes, and with her weapons she defies human and spiritual enemies. Furthermore, she places her call in scriptural context and asserts the immutable nature of God. As God raised up women in the past, such as Deborah, Esther, and Mary Magdalene, why cannot God do it now? She juxtaposes the nonsilence of these women, whose voices and actions brought about defining moments in scriptural history, with the silencing of women that Paul advises in order to demonstrate the historical situatedness of Paul's words. Located within the context of Scripture, where women held prominent positions in salvation history, the apostle's words cannot be definitive for a woman's role nor negate a woman's call by God. Stewart reasons that if Jesus did not condemn the woman caught in adultery—being caught in adultery being much more grievous than speaking in public—surely he would not condemn her and other women for speaking out publicly. Equally significant is that Stewart avers that Paul himself would support the cause of women, writing that if Paul were present in her day and knew the injustice and oppression that she and other African American women suffered, he, like Jesus, would not object to them fighting for their rights in public.

After making a broad appeal to women throughout history who have contributed to the moral, religious, and political sphere of society, Stewart goes into more detail about important women in history, such as Greek women who delivered oracles, the Sibyls acknowledged by the Romans, and Egyptian women whose prophecies emperors honored. She moves from the ancient period to the fifteenth century, citing nuns who were poetesses and women who studied Hebrew and Greek and occupied chairs of philosophy and justice. Her march through history causes her to write:

If such women as are here described have once existed, be no longer astonished then, my brethren and friends, that God at this eventful period should raise up your own females to strive, by their example both in public and private, to assist those who are endeavoring to stop the strong current of prejudice that flows so profusely against us at present. . . . The religious spirit which has animated women in all ages, showed itself at this time. It has made them by turns, martyrs, apostles, warriors, and concluded in making divines and scholars. Why cannot a religious spirit animate us now? Why cannot we become divines and scholars? (69)

Stewart appeals to God's history with women to illustrate that as God operated in the past employing women in divine ministry, so God does the same now. Thus, she warns the opposition not to prohibit them, for to do so would be to go against God's power and would be "counted for sin" (69). Stewart's description of these various historical women serves to encourage the women and the men in her audience to have high aspirations and to view women as sources of social, political, and moral transformation in the public and private realms. She goes on to ask, "What if such women as are here described should rise among our sable race? And it is not impossible. For it is not the color of the skin that makes the man or the woman, but the principle formed in the soul" (70). Speaking to an audience filled with African Americans who were suffering great discrimination in Boston,[60] Stewart attempts to alert them of their potential, particularly the women in the audience, and to give them hope that, despite their circumstances, God could raise up African American women who could be apostles, warriors, and scholars. Underneath her query is the underlying question of why God cannot use women of the sable race. Her answer is, God can. She in fact embodies such a possibility and demonstrates that such a vision is possible. Hence, her inclusion of African American women, such as herself, as among those who speak for God shows that God continues to speak as well and that black women are included in the reception of the "religious spirit which has animated women in all ages." Indeed, God includes African American women in salvation history.

60. Richardson, introduction to *Maria W. Stewart*, ed. Richardson, 13–14, notes that during this time "blacks lived in segregated housing in a few crowded areas of the city. They were restricted to special sections on public transportation, in lecture halls, and in places of entertainment."

Military Language Revisited: A Woman Warrior's Labor

The military theme of her ministry returns again in the latter portion of her speech. She describes the brief time of her mission as "the short period of my *Christian warfare* [2 Cor. 10:3–5]" in which she has had "*to contend against the fiery darts of the devil* [Eph. 6:16]" because the "powers of earth and hell had combined against me, to prove my overthrow" (71). In addition to using Pauline warfare imagery to depict herself in battle, Stewart quotes Ephesians 6:14: "*Be ye clothed with the breast-plate of righteousness, having your loins girt about with truth*" to admonish her audience to fight for justice by putting on their armor as well (73). Together with military terminology, Stewart echoes Galatians 4:11 and 1 Corinthians 3:6 to portray her ministry as "*labor in vain*," resigning herself to the knowledge that "*Paul may plant, and Apollos water, but God alone giveth the increase.*" Her labor seems to her for nothing, but she trusts that God will bring something good out of it.

Stewart turns to the eschaton as a source of comfort for all that she has endured, rejoicing in the fact that in the last day, "Hatred and contention shall cease, and we shall join with redeemed millions in ascribing glory and honor, and riches, and power and blessing to the Lamb," for no "*eye hath seen, nor ear heard, neither hath it entered into the heart of man to conceive of the joys that are prepared for them that love God* [1 Cor. 2:9]" (73).[61] This vision of the eschaton contrasts greatly with Stewart's present life, about which she writes sadly in the closing lines of her speech: "Thus far has my life been almost a life of complete disappointment. God has tried me by fire. Well was I aware that if I contended boldly for his cause, I must suffer" (73). Because of great opposition and seemingly little progress made on behalf of African Americans, Stewart saw her life as filled with disappointment. Nonetheless, her suffering on behalf of women and African Americans, although causing her great pain, as evidenced by her heartrending description of her life, would bring about a reward in the future, for she believed that because of her fidelity to her divine call "a rich award awaits me, if not in this world, in the world to come" (74). Throughout the essays discussed here, Stewart describes her life as one filled with sacrifice and pain on behalf of her people, but also a life devoted to the God she loves, the one who called her to "his cause."

---

61. Additional Pauline citations that appear in this essay are Rom. 9:20–21; 1 Cor. 10:13; 1 Tim. 6:11.

Cooper describes Stewart as "fierce and tenacious," a description that fits her as well as her use of Scripture, particularly Pauline passages.[62] Stewart's bold use of Paul to describe her conversion, to depict a woman warrior, to portray the trials and loneliness of ministry, and to resist the employment of Paul to silence women indicates her belief in the relevancy of Paul for her life and for the lives of those in her audiences. Richardson notes that Stewart took up a life of public political activism at a time when it was inappropriate for women, particularly African American women, to do so.[63] Her political argumentation derives from a black resistance and black abolitionist movement that is independent of and antedates that of later white and integrated movements that promoted abolitionist ideals.[64] As the female author of a political pamphlet, Stewart moves into "unexplored territory"—the forbidden realms of male authority and province.[65] Again, Richardson aptly describes Stewart's life and calling in the following remarks: "[Stewart] was both an independent and an isolated figure in the world. Her calling was not merely reformist, it was subversive, and she herself was the first to encounter its transformative character by its challenge to her own identity."[66] This subversive call merges with her subversive uses of Pauline texts to vindicate her public speaking and preaching on behalf of women and African Americans. She conscripts Paul into the service of women, including African American women, when she writes that if Paul only knew what injustice they endured, he too would support their right to speak out and protest. In doing so, she enlists Paul in the liberation war, a move that rejects the current readings of the apostle that condone oppression and slavery. Paul was not, according to Stewart, on the side of the dominant and powerful, but like God, he was on the side of the oppressed.

James Pennington (1807–1870): The Fugitive Blacksmith

Like Maria Stewart, who employs Paul in disruptive ways, James Pennington employs Paul in revolutionary ways to delineate the evils of slavery and the slave trade, specifically the systemic nature of this evil and its erroneous

---

62. Cooper, *Maria Stewart*, 179.
63. Richardson, introduction to *Maria W. Stewart*, ed. Richardson, 19.
64. Richardson, introduction to *Maria W. Stewart*, ed. Richardson, 9-10.
65. Richardson, introduction to *Maria W. Stewart*, ed. Richardson, 25.
66. Richardson, introduction to *Maria W. Stewart*, ed. Richardson, 26.

notions of the black body.[67] He refutes the intensified efforts during this time to sanction slavery and to use Paul to do so. Pennington spends his first twenty-one years in slavery before escaping. In 1841 he published the first African American history, "A Textbook of the Origin and History of the Colored People."[68] In his riveting autobiographical narrative, *The Fugitive Blacksmith; or, Events in the History of James W. C. Pennington,* he writes about slavery's horrors and its devastating effects upon black minds, bodies, and families. By explicating the "chattel principle," he chastises Christian whites' justification for this peculiar institution.

> The sin of slavery lies in the chattel principle, or relation. Especially have I felt anxious to save professing Christians, and my brethren in the ministry, from falling into a great mistake. My feelings are always outraged when I hear them speak of "kind masters,"—"Christian masters,"—"the mildest form of slavery,"—"well fed and clothed slaves," as extenuations of slavery; I am satisfied they either mean to pervert the truth, or they do not know what they say. The being of slavery, its soul and body, lives and moves in the chattel principle, the property principle, the bill of sale principle; the cartwhip, starvation, and nakedness, are its inevitable consequences.[69]

Pennington, like Lemuel Haynes before him and so many other blacks during this time period, vehemently rejects the prevalent notion that slavery was good for African Americans and that it provides for their salvation in a Christian land. Accordingly, he refutes any idea of a "mild form of slavery." There is no such thing, Pennington declares, for in what is called the mild form, black women are still raped by slaveholders and their sons, families are still separated, and the enslaved are still beaten mercilessly. Any notion of a

67. Portions of this section on James Pennington appear by permission and are found in Lisa Bowens, "Liberating Paul: African Americans' Use of Paul in Resistance and Protest," in *Practicing with Paul: Reflections on Paul and the Practices of Ministry in Honor of Susan G. Eastman,* ed. Presian Burroughs (Eugene, OR: Wipf & Stock, 2018), 69–70, and Lisa Bowens, "God and Time: Exploring Black Notions of Prophetic and Apocalyptic Eschatology," in *T&T Clark Handbook of African American Theology,* ed. Antonia Daymond, Frederick Ware, and Eric Williams (New York: T&T Clark, 2019), 215–17.

68. Sernett, *African American Religious History,* 81.

69. James Pennington, *The Fugitive Blacksmith; or, Events in the History of James W. C. Pennington, Pastor of Presbyterian Church, New York, Formerly A Slave in the State of Maryland, United States* (London: Charles Gilpin, 1850; reprint, Westport, CT: Negro Universities Press, 1971), iv–v. Hereafter, page references from this work will be given in parentheses in the text.

"mild form of slavery" is a mistaken one. Likewise, he denies the idea that the existence of good Christian slave owners makes slavery acceptable. He queries, "Yes, sirs, many of our masters are professed Christians; and what advantage is that to us?" (xi). Since these "Christian masters" still beat, rape, and sell blacks and separate families, Pennington sees no value or benevolence in the slave system.[70]

Frederick Douglass also bears witness to the false notion of kind, Christian masters; he writes in his autobiography that Christian slaveholders were the worst of all: "I assert most unhesitatingly, that the religion of the south is a mere covering for the most horrid crimes. . . . Were I to be again reduced to the chains of slavery, next to that enslavement, I should regard being the slave of a religious master the greatest calamity that could befall me. For of all slaveholders with whom I have ever met, religious slaveholders are the worst. I have ever found them the meanest and basest, the most cruel and cowardly, of all others."[71] Like Douglass, Pennington finds the idea of kind masters that was so prevalent in the proslavery argument indefensible, and he refuses to allow the lie of kind masters to prevail in public opinion. Pennington bears witness to the oppression and degradation of a system that strips blacks of their dignity and their human worth, and in such a system kind masters cannot exist. He writes poignantly of this obloquy in the following citation:

> It is the chattel relation that robs [the slave] of his manhood, and transfers his ownership of himself to another. It is this that transfers the proprietorship of his wife and children to another. . . . On looking at the family record of his old, kind, Christian, master, there he finds his name on a catalogue with the horses, cows, hogs, and dogs. However humiliating and degrading it may be to his feelings to find his name written down among the beasts of the field, that is just the place, and the only place assigned to it by the chattel relation. I beg our Anglo-Saxon brethren to accustom themselves to think that we need something more than mere kindness. We ask for justice, truth, and honour as other men do. (xii)

For Pennington, the practice of listing the enslaved along with animals owned by Christian enslavers portrays in its most tangible terms the denial

---

70. Pennington, therefore, argues against the idea discussed above of a paternalistic proslavery Christianity.

71. "Narrative of the Life of Frederick Douglass," 572.

of enslaved Africans' humanity and intrinsic value, illustrating the evil of slavocracy.

The Great Moral Dilemma

After his repudiation of the institution in the preface of his narrative, Pennington tells about his difficult life in slavery and the awful event of his enslaver beating Pennington's father, an incident that helped him decide to escape. After inflicting his father with fifteen or twenty lashes, the slave owner arrogantly declared, "I will make you know that I am master of your tongue as well as of your time!" This tragic episode affects Pennington in a profound way, causing him to write, "Let me ask any one of Anglo-Saxon blood and spirit, how would you expect a *son* to feel at such a sight?" and "Although it was some time after this event before I took the decisive step, yet in my mind and spirit, I never was a *Slave* after it" (7). After highlighting many of the degradations of slavery, Pennington, in the section of his autobiography entitled "The Great Moral Dilemma," highlights another aspect of the effect of slavery upon African Americans by presenting a contextual ethic in which the slave must choose whether to submit to whites or to be subject to a higher power, which is God, who grants all people the right to be free (20–31).[72]

During his escape from slavery, Pennington is chased and captured by white men, who ask him two questions that become the focal point of this section of his story: "Who do you belong to, and where did you come from?" (21). Pennington immediately realizes that he has three options:

> I knew according to the law of slavery, who I belonged to and where I came from, and I must now do one of three things—I must refuse to speak at all, or I must communicate the fact, or I must tell an untruth. . . . The first point decided was, the facts in this case are my private property. These men have no more right to them than a highway robber has to my purse. What will be the consequence if I put them in possession of the facts. In forty-eight hours, I shall have received perhaps one hundred lashes, and be on my way to the Louisiana cotton fields. Of what service will it be to them. They will get a paltry sum of two hundred dollars. Is not my liberty worth more to me than two hundred dollars are to them? I resolved, therefore, to insist that I was free. (22)

---

72. See Sernett's introduction to this essay (*African American Religious History*, 81).

At the end of this harrowing section of his narrative, Pennington relates that he was taught by his slave parents to tell the truth always, but at this moment in his life he could see no other way to escape than by telling an untruth. For to tell the truth would mean that he would be returned to certain torture, possibly death. The "moral dilemma" of that day inspired him "with a deeper hatred of slavery" (30). Slavery, he laments, not only takes one's freedom, one's body, and one's life, but it also places the enslaved in moral conundrums that may cause him to die "with a lie upon his lips." Pennington, then, is not proud of the fact that he lied. In his final remarks in this part of the narrative, he emphasizes that the system of slavery causes blacks to do things they do not want to do and to engage in acts that are contrary to their belief system. Using Paul's words from Romans 7:21, "*I find then a law, that, when I would do good, evil is present with me,*" Pennington characterizes the plight of the enslaved African: "*How, when he [the slave] would do good, evil is thrust upon him*" (30). Pennington broadens this text, transforming it from one in which evil is present within the self to one in which evil comes from outside the self. One could argue that in this verse the apostle depicts the struggle of a person wrestling with inner evil. But for the enslaved, the text speaks to evil being thrust upon them, making them engage in behavior in which they would not normally participate. The evil is not within, Pennington insists, but without. That evil, the white's slavery system, has inherent in it an antimoral, antiethical impetus. When blacks desire to do what is good, such as seek freedom, and to live a good moral life, white slaveholders and the larger white society will not allow them to do so. Pennington calls upon the readers of his escape story to "See how human bloodhounds gratuitously chase, catch, and tempt him to shed blood and lie" (30). Evil is forced upon the enslaved, giving them no choice but to act in ways contrary to what they desire.

This episode vividly displays that one of the evils thrust upon Pennington and other enslaved Africans is a distortion of their identity. For Pennington writes, "I knew according to the law of slavery, who I belonged to and where I came from." The law of slavery bestowed upon him an enslaved identity contrary to God's law, and Pennington illustrates what it means to embody this distorted identity, for to insist that he is free becomes a lie when in fact in God's divine economy it is the truth; God created him as a free human being. The evil thrust upon Pennington, "the law of slavery," attempts to usurp his identity and his human existence. As Pennington so brilliantly depicts in this escape narrative, evil perverts the truth by turning the truth into a lie and a lie into the truth.

Pennington's use of Paul in resistance and protest in this instance occurs in what I label reformulation. This reformulation takes place in light of the enslaved's continual existential crisis. In this reformulation Pennington resists the white definition of evil as his body, his origin, or his skin color and declares that slavery itself is what is evil and generates evil; it is the system that is wicked, not him. Such a statement undercuts the notion during this time that blacks—as indicated by their skin color—were malevolent beings. Pennington resists such views and denounces the system for its intrinsic immorality. Slavery is the culprit, Pennington announces to his audience, not my black body.

Gospel as Antisin and Antislavery

In two other places in his autobiography Pennington inserts Pauline language at critical junctures. The fact that the gospel becomes an instrument for justifying slaveholding compels him to speak out against this misuse of the gospel. In a poignant letter written to his parents, which he includes in the appendix, Pennington advises them not to be "prejudiced against the gospel because it may be seemingly twisted into a support of slavery" (76). He understands that the distorted version of the gospel proclaimed by many whites is no gospel at all. What he writes next to his parents is worth quoting at length:

> The gospel rightly understood, taught, received, felt and practised, is antislavery as it is anti-sin. . . . There is not a solitary decree of the immaculate God that has been concerned in the ordination of slavery, nor does any possible development of his holy will sanctify it. He has permitted us to be enslaved according to the invention of wicked men, instigated by the devil, with intention to *bring good out of the evil* [Rom. 8:28], but He does not, He cannot approve of it. He has no need to approve of it, even on account of the good which He will bring out of it, for He could have brought about that very good in some other way. God is never straitened; He is never at a loss for means to work. Could He not have made this a great and wealthy nation without making its riches to consist in our blood, bones, and souls? And could He not also have given the gospel to us without making us slaves? (76–77)

Several significant motifs appear in this evocative excerpt: (1) the gospel is antislavery and antisin; (2) God does not ordain or sanctify slavery even though God may bring good out of it; (3) evil men invented slavery; and (4) slavery originates from the devil. As we can see, this powerful passage revisits several themes addressed by interpreters in chapter 1, above, but develops them in a more robust fashion.

First, similar to Jupiter Hammon, Pennington refuses to utilize ordination language when it comes to slavery, the language employed by such people as Josiah Priest, who stated that blacks' slavery was ordained for all time. Second, like Hammon, Pennington applies permission language to the institution but goes a step further than Hammon in arguing against God's ordination of slavery. Not only was slavery not ordained by God, but Pennington contends that it originates with Satan and is carried out by the hands of wicked men. Such an origin indicates that God cannot approve or sanction such a practice, for the gospel is antisin and antislavery. Indeed, Pennington reveals a deep caesura between the divine will and human motivation. Third, Pennington takes up Lemuel Haynes's disputation of the belief that good derives from the slave trade and expands the line of reasoning. That good may transpire from the slave trade does not mean that God approves of it. God can bring good out of something without approving of it, Pennington maintains. He insists that the "good" that God brings about in the slave trade could have been brought about in some other way. The idea that Africans receive the gospel through slavery and, therefore, slavery is good for them is, for Pennington, a misrepresentation of God's character, since "God is never straitened" and "never at a loss for a means to work." Pennington asserts that God could have provided Africans with the gospel without making them slaves. In this eloquent passage, Pennington debunks common proslavery views of the time by illustrating that use is not the same as authorization. In other words, just because God can use something to bring about good does not mean God authorizes it or approves of it. The distinction between use and approval is significant to Pennington's argumentation and his refutation of slavocracy.

After this powerful passage, Pennington inserts Pauline language to define the true gospel, which is the *"fullness of God"* (Eph. 3:19). He, like the apostle, asks, *"Nay, is Christ divided?"* (1 Cor. 1:13) (77). The true gospel, which is antislavery and antisin, is also antidivision, countering societal polarities of black and white, slave and free. The antidivision impetus of the gospel appears in Paul's letter to Titus, several verses of which Pennington quotes next: *"The grace of God that bringeth salvation hath appeared to (for) all men, teaching us that denying ungodliness and worldly lust, we should live soberly, righteously, and godly in this present world, looking for that blessed hope and glorious appearing of the great God and our Saviour Jesus Christ, who gave himself for us that he might redeem us from all iniquity, and purify unto himself a peculiar people zealous of good works"* (Titus 2:11–14) (77). In light of its context, this passage serves as a critique of the slave trade and the "twisted" gospel that supports it. God's salvation comes to all people, which underscores the depravity of slavery in its delineation of white superiority and black inferiority. In addition, Pennington employs these verses to launch a critique upon the slaveholders, since the ungodliness and worldly lust that Paul speaks of in this passage lead to the wealth and riches of this nation being founded upon black "blood, bones, and souls." In his narrative that precedes this quote, Pennington exposes the fallacy of a mild form of slavery, of kind Christian masters, and here, with the apostle's words, he paints a drastic counterportrait of the slaveholders and reveals that although they think they live by the gospel, the apostle's words indicate that they live antithetically to it. To live sober, righteous, and godly lives serves as a censure to white slave owners as well as a call to blacks to live in a way that counters the moral failure of their enslavers. Such a life results in redemption from "all iniquity," Pennington proclaims, which, in light of all that has come before this passage, includes slavery.

Letter to the Slaveholder

Pennington's rejection of slavery, his refutation of its justification by whites, and his own life story provide significant context for the final part of his narrative, the letter he sends years later to his former owner, whom he knows is old and will soon die. He reminds his former slaveholder of the owner's evil deeds and urges him to repent before he dies so that he may be saved. Two citations demonstrate Pennington's aim:

> I would, to convince you of my perfect good will towards you, in the most kind and respectful terms, remind you of your coming destiny. You are now over seventy years of age, pressing on to eternity with the weight of these seventy years upon you. Is not this enough without the blood of some half-score of souls? (81)

> If the Bible affords no sanction to slavery, (and I claim that it cannot,), then it must be a sin of the deepest dye; and can you, sir, think to go to God in hope with a sin of such magnitude upon your soul? (81)

Pennington's admonition to his former slave owner that he will "go to God" reveals his eschatological framework, a framework that consists of justice, retribution, and judgment after death. He urges his former owner to review his life and to remember that "at the awful bar of the impartial *Judge of all* [Heb. 12:23] who doeth right," he will meet all the enslaved Africans he abused in the past, including the persons he presently owned. Pennington goes on to list the names of the enslaved that the slaveholder will meet in judgment and concludes this enumeration with the statement, "Sir, I shall meet you there" (82). This graphic depiction of the "last things," where oppressor and oppressed meet face-to-face, is for Pennington God's ultimate act of reckoning and making right what is wrong.

Pennington also depicts this time of justice and retribution as a time for the enslaved to speak and to be heard, for he describes this event at the "bar of God" to his former enslaver as one where Pennington will be able to make a "complaint in my mouth against you" (83). Whereas in the past, the slave owner would not listen to him or to the other enslaved persons, the slaveholder would now have to listen, and this time in God's presence. This future depiction of making a complaint against his former enslaver with his mouth signifies a profound reversal of his former owner's statement to Pennington's father: "I am master of your tongue as well as of your time!" At the bar of God, Pennington will speak and the slaveholder will not be able to prohibit him. This turnaround demonstrates the erroneous nature of the slave owner's claim to control the speech and time of the enslaved. The tongue the slaveholder mistakenly asserted he owned, Pennington reclaims and uses to speak against him at judgment. Moreover, the true arbiter of time, God, will bring the enslaver before "the bar" and arbitrate justice for the oppressed slaves, indicating that all time, past, present, and future, ultimately belongs to the "Eternal One."

Pennington asks his former enslaver to review not only his past actions with the enslaved but also all the privileges the slave owner enjoyed, such as the fine education and his continued exposure to the "gospel of love" throughout his life. These benefits, Pennington argues, bestow upon his previous enslaver no excuse for his adherence to slavery. He had all the benefits of knowledge, both secular and religious, and yet did not utilize it for truth and justice. He will face these facts at the judgment unless he changes before he dies (83).

In the final paragraphs of his appeal to his former enslaver, Pennington writes that he wishes he could address him as an elder brother in Christ or a father in Israel but realizes that he cannot because of the slaveholder's behavior. Yet he recognizes that Jesus's blood can remove all stains, implying that this includes the stain of slaveholding. Echoing Ephesians 2:14 and 2 Corinthians 5:20–21, he asserts that this same blood can *"break down the middle wall of partition and reconcile us not only to God but to each other*, then the word of his mouth, the sentence will set us at one." For Pennington, reconciliation happens through Jesus's blood, but it is absent without judgment and repentance, which he calls for throughout the letter. For reconciliation to occur there must be justice, an admission of sin, and an accounting for past wrongs. That judgment, repentance, and reconciliation go hand in hand for Pennington is seen in what he says next: "As for myself, I am quite ready to meet you face to face at the bar of God. I have done you no wrong; I have nothing to fear when we both *fall into the hands* [Heb. 10:31] of the just God" (83–84). Pennington's Pauline echoes of Ephesians 2:14 and 2 Corinthians 5:20–21 function in a trifold manner: (1) to contest the human-made division of black and white, slave and free (Eph. 2:14), (2) to speak of the reality of reconciliation through Jesus's blood (2 Cor. 5:20–21), and (3) to speak of a spiritual reconciliation (to God) and an earthly reconciliation (to each other) (2 Cor. 5:20–21). At the same time, this Pauline language undergirds Pennington's belief in the intricate links between repentance, judgment, and reconciliation; for him, these three are deeply intertwined.

Pennington's depiction of judgment describes the ramifications of his former enslaver's past and present conduct.[73] One of his main goals in this letter is to persuade his previous enslaver to change his behavior, and so he provides a fitting example of eschatology's ability to impact anthropology. Frederick Ware insightfully observes this aspect of eschatology: "Eschatology is vision not only of a certain end but also of a people's true humanity. This vision inspires people to moral and ethical action."[74] In Pennington's case, the eschatological vision he casts for his former owner serves to call him to do what is right as well as to demonstrate that justice will prevail, whether or not his past enslaver heeds his admonitions. Pennington's desire for the enslaver's salvation is quite extraordinary and demonstrates a sad irony that the amazing care and concern he exhibits toward the slaveholder's soul are more than the care and concern the slave owner gave to Pennington's body and mind.

---

73. See also James H. Cone, "Calling the Oppressors to Account: Justice, Love, and Hope in Black Religion," in *The Courage to Hope: From Black Suffering to Human Redemption*, ed. Quinton Dixie and Cornel West (Boston: Beacon, 1999), 74–85.

74. Frederick L. Ware, *African American Theology: An Introduction* (Louisville: Westminster John Knox, 2016), 171.

Pennington employs Paul in a number of ways to resist and protest slavery and white supremacy. Through reformulation he uses the apostle to denote the existence of systemic evil and not just an inner struggle with evil. Accordingly, his identification of systemic evil allows him to argue against the notion of evil as endemic to African American bodies but to view evil as incarnate in systems that pervert and distort justice. In addition, Pennington believes that the true gospel, which the apostle preached, is antislavery and antisin. It is also not divided, nor does it promote a gospel of division, just as Christ is not divided. Pennington employs Paul to describe both judgment and justice. Christ's death brings about the annihilation of the wall of partition and the possibility of reconciliation between the enslaver and the enslaved, a reconciliation founded upon the slaveholder's repentance and God's judgment.

Daniel Payne (1811–1893): America's First African American College President

Daniel Payne, born in 1811 in the slaveholding state of South Carolina to free Christian parents who instilled in him a love for God and Scripture, had an extraordinary life that he believed was directed by the providence of God. Similar to Pennington, Payne had a deep faith in God and in the Word of God. He writes in his autobiography, *Recollections of Seventy Years*, that he "was the child of many prayers" and that his father dedicated him to the service of God before he was born, telling God that "if the Lord would give him a son that son should be consecrated to him, and named after the prophet Daniel."[75] Payne explains that after his birth he was taken to the house of God and "consecrated to his service in the holy ordinance of baptism." Even at a young age, Payne describes God's dealings with him, remarking that "Many a time, when the people of God were telling their experience in the divine life, in the class meeting, I have felt the Spirit of God moving my childish heart" (16). Orphaned by the age of nine due to the death of both parents, Payne's grandaunt raised him and continued to instill in him love for God, the Scriptures, and education.

75. Daniel Alexander Payne, *Recollections of Seventy Years* (Nashville: Publishing House of the AME Sunday School Union, 1888), 16. The designation "first African American college president," included in the heading, occurs in the opening of this book. Hereafter, page references from this work will be given in parentheses in the text.

Words from the Spirit World

At age eighteen, Payne experiences conversion, which he describes in the words of Philippians 4:7 and 1 Peter 1:8: "Here I too gave him my whole heart, and instantly felt that *peace which passeth all understanding and that joy which is unspeakable and full of glory*" (17). A few weeks after this experience, Payne enters into prayer and receives a divine word from the Lord. "Several weeks after this event, between twelve and one o'clock one day, I was in my humble chamber, pouring out my prayers into the listening ears of the Saviour, when I felt as if the hands of a man were pressing my two shoulders and a voice speaking within my soul saying: 'I have set thee apart to educate thyself in order that thou mayest be an educator to thy people.' The impression was irresistible and divine; it gave a new direction to my thoughts and efforts" (17).

The divine call to educate his people coheres with Payne's own love of learning and his passion to pursue education, despite the limited opportunities afforded him. Prior to this event Payne had been an avid learner, reading every book he could find, even resolving to learn Latin, Greek, and Hebrew upon reading the Self-Interpreting Bible by Rev. John Brown of Haddington, Scotland (15). After this divine word to him regarding God's purpose for his life, he relates how his pursuit of education intensified.

> After this circumstance I resolved to devote every moment of leisure to the study of books, and every cent to the purchase of them. I raised money by making tables, benches, clothes horses, and "corset-bones." . . . During my apprenticeship I would eat my meals in a few minutes and spend the remainder of the hour allowed me at breakfast and dinner in reading. After the day's work was done I perused my books till nearly twelve o'clock; and then, keeping a tinder-box, flint, steel, and candle at my bedside, I would awake at four, strike a light, and study till six, when my daily labors began. Thus I went on reading book after book, drawing pictures with crayon, and now and then composing verses. In my nineteenth year I forsook the carpenter's trade for the life of an educator. (18)

At the age of nineteen, in 1829, Payne opens a school in Charleston for free African Americans that begins with six students, each paying fifty cents a month. Because of the low pay, however, he could not afford to live, so he closes the school, only to reopen it in 1830 because he believes it is God's call for him and he could not abandon it. His school increases to about sixty pupils, but in 1835 state law forces the school to close. In December 1834 South Carolina's General Assembly hears a proposed bill and passes a law to take effect in April 1835 that prohibits education of slaves or free people of color. This action by the legislature profoundly impacts Payne physically, emotionally, and spiritually. He loses sleep and eventually begins to question God, which results in a crisis of faith:

> Sometimes it seemed as though some wild beast had plunged his fangs into my heart, and was squeezing out its life-blood. Then I began to question the existence of God, and to say: "If he does exist, is he just? If so, why does he suffer one race to oppress and enslave another, to rob them by unrighteous enactments of rights, which they hold most dear and sacred?" . . . Again said I: "Is there no God?" But then there came into my mind those solemn words: "With God one day is as a thousand years and a thousand years as one day. Trust in him, and he will bring slavery and all its outrages to an end." These words from the spirit world acted on my troubled soul like water on a burning fire, and my aching heart was soothed and relieved from its burden of woes. (28)

These comforting words from God, a prophetic dream, and some encouraging admonitions from both white and black friends enable Payne to persevere and to decide to go north to teach. When Payne arrives in the North to become a teacher, he ends up studying at the Lutheran Theological Seminary in Gettysburg, and while in seminary he opens a school teaching all the "colored children in the neighborhood" (59). Along with teaching, he holds religious meetings and organizes societies. Yet even during his time at the seminary, he remembers the closing of the Charleston school with lament and regret, which indicates the acute effect this event continues to have upon him. He writes,

> O the parting scene in that school-room, those interesting children. . . . But what made my thought almost agonizing was the recollection of the fact that this separation was the bitter product of unjust, cruel, and blasphemous laws—cruel and unjust to a defenseless race, blasphemous of that *God who of one blood did make all the nations of the earth, all its races, all its families, every individual man* [Acts 17:26]. Every night for many years after I left Charleston did I dream about it—wandering over its streets, bathing in its rivers, worshiping in its chapels, or teaching in my school-room, and sometimes I was sailing into it and sometimes flying out of it. (57)

The memory of the mandated school closing haunts Payne because of its unjust nature and because the law that precipitated such action contradicts the God who from one blood made all nations of the earth. The unity that exists in God's creation of humanity racism takes apart and denies, a view fully expressed in the law that causes Payne's school to close. Such laws, according to Payne, are blasphemous and cruel because they oppose God's intended purpose of unity for humanity. This particular Pauline text, Acts 17:26, persists among African American writers during this time period, for in it they see a refutation of unjust laws, racism, slavery, and white supremacy. An appeal to God's creative act in behalf of humanity indicates a fundamental truth about that humanity and its divine existence and purpose. Payne's assertion here of Acts 17:26, like that of so many other black hermeneuts before him, affirms African American humanity and African American equality with other races.

While in seminary, Payne receives the call to preach, describing the experience as a "pressure from on high that constrained me to say with the *Apostle Paul: 'Woe is me if I preach not the gospel!'* [1 Cor. 9:16]" (62). Payne, like Paul, realizes that he cannot ignore this call to proclaim the gospel and so accepts God's vocation. Yet in 1837 Payne becomes extremely ill and confined to his home for a lengthy period of time. During this illness he experiences a visitation from God: "During my sickness my religious experience was deep and sweet. Then it was that I felt that to *'die was gain, but to live was the Lord's'* [Phil. 1:21]. On one occasion it seemed to me that a band of holy angels had made a descent into my lonely chamber to cheer and comfort me in my affliction" (69). Using Paul's language of Philippians, Payne describes his own sense of his life at that moment in time. Death means not only freedom from affliction and illness but also the opportunity to be with Christ in a more intimate way. At the same time, "to live was the Lord's" means that Payne's life belongs completely to God and that he would continue to experience Christ's presence and guidance in all that he did, if and when he recovers.

Payne does recover, and in 1841 he joins the African Methodist Episcopal (AME) Church, believing that God guided him to this denomination. One of his endeavors upon joining this body includes advocating strongly for an educated clergy, which he believes is necessary to insure equipping preachers to lead and minister effectively to the people within their care. Although Payne meets with severe opposition, some calling him a devil and others believing that such actions are unnecessary, other leaders support Payne's efforts, and the church adopts such measures (74–77, 64).[76]

---

76. To give a picture of the opposition he faced to advocating ministerial education,

Election to Bishop and College President

In 1852, Payne reluctantly becomes a bishop in the AME Church. Four years prior he had been approached for the bishopric but refused to have his name considered. In 1851 Payne senses that his name will be resubmitted, and this realization causes him great consternation. "I saw and felt that my brethren were determined to elect me, and therefore I prayed earnestly up to that time that God would take away my life rather than allow me to be put into an office for which I felt myself so utterly unfit" (110). Upon learning of his election as bishop, Payne eloquently describes his state of mind. "I trembled from head to foot, and wept. I knew that I was unworthy the office, because I had neither the physical strength, the learning, nor the sanctity which makes one fit for such a high, holy, and responsible position. . . . The announcement fell like the weight of a mountain upon me. . . . I now felt that to resist this manifest will of the Great *Head of the Church* [Eph. 5:23; Col. 1:18], so clearly and emphatically expressed, would bring upon me his displeasure. I yielded because I felt that the omnipotent Arm that had thrust me into the position would hold me in it" (109–10). Ironically, at this same conference Payne is asked to give the opening sermon but has only two hours to prepare it. He chooses as his text a passage from Paul, 2 Corinthians 2:16: *"Who is sufficient for these things?"* A message that perhaps encourages him upon his own assumption of the bishopric, it also outlines to his fellow ministers their duties and responsibilities before God and their respective congregations.

He preaches that Christian ministers are to imitate Christ, to proclaim humanity's need for salvation, to train their flock in the Word, to discipline and govern the church, and to live a life of holiness, prayer, and faith. Payne also emphasizes that ministers need to cultivate their minds by learning science, literature, and philosophy. He closes the sermon with a round of queries that summarize his message and energize his listeners to perform their God-given duties:

> But to return to the text, I ask *who is sufficient* to preach the Gospel of Christ, and govern the Church which he has purchased with his own blood?

Payne relates information from a friend of his father's on how preachers in this denomination often began their sermons: "It was a common thing for the preachers of that Church to introduce their sermons by declaring that they had 'not rubbed their heads against college-walls,' at which the people would cry, 'Amen!' they had 'never studied Latin or Greek,' at which the people would exclaim, 'Glory to God!' they had 'never studied Hebrew,' at which all would 'shout'" (64).

Who is sufficient to train this host of the Lord, and lead it on from earth to heaven? *Who is sufficient* to guide it through this war against *principalities and powers, against spiritual wickedness in high places* [Eph 6:12], against all the hosts of earth and hell, and place it triumphant upon the shining plains of glory? *Who is sufficient?* I answer, the man who makes Christ the model of his own Christian and ministerial character. This man, and he alone, is *sufficient for these things.*[77]

Identifying the spiritual conflict that resides within ministerial duty, Payne asserts that only those who follow Christ's life and example will prevail and be able to preach, govern, and train the church in the way that God designed. Opposition will come from different quarters—spiritual and earthly—but the sufficiency to meet these challenges comes from following Christ wholeheartedly.

Payne was not only a bishop, he was also a member of the trustees board and executive board of Wilberforce University, which had opened in 1856. However, because of the Civil War, the university closed from 1862 to 1863. But Payne reports that "On the 10th of March, 1863 I was called to attend a meeting of its Board of Trustees in Cincinnati, O. It had been decided to sell the property, and between the hours of nine and ten P.M. I agreed with them to purchase the property, 'in the name of God, for the A.M.E. Church.' The sun [*sic*] required was ten thousand dollars. When I made the bid for the property, I had not a ten-dollar bill at my command, but I had faith in God" (152–53). Amazingly, Payne raises the money to acquire the school for the AME Church, and a new board of trustees is set in place. He is elected president of the school and writes, "In this manner I began my connection with Wilberforce University as its President—a connection that lasted for thirteen years, and in which I assumed the double duties of head of an infant institution and one of the heads of the whole Church. My work henceforth was to lie in two channels, and my whole heart, soul, and body were to need strength from on high to wisely perform it" (154). The dream that Payne had many years before in which he was told that he would be an educator takes on new dimensions in his role as college president. Charles Killian states that this "first venture in higher education for blacks stands as his greatest legacy."[78] Indeed, the sermon he gives during the conference in which he is

77. Daniel Payne, "General Conference of 1852," in *Sermons and Addresses, 1853–1891: Bishop Daniel A. Payne*, ed. Charles Killian (New York: Arno, 1972), 271.

78. Charles Killian, introduction to Payne, "General Conference of 1852."

elected bishop anticipates the divine sufficiency needed for the bishopric as well as the presidency.

Welcome to the Ransomed

In another significant address he delivers ten years later in Washington, DC, "Welcome to the Ransomed; or, Duties of the Colored Inhabitants of the District of Columbia," Payne brings to the fore some of the same themes present in the sermon he gives when he assumes the role of bishop. On April 11, 1862, Congress passes a bill to abolish slavery in the District of Columbia, at which time Payne presides as bishop of the Second Episcopal District of the AME Church, whose headquarters are in Washington and Georgetown (146).[79] After Congress passes the bill, Payne meets with President Lincoln to encourage him to sign it. His description of the meeting merits full citation:

> I will now state the substance of our conversation. I said: "I am here to learn whether or not you intend to sign the bill of emancipation?" He answered and said: "There was a company of gentlemen here to-day requesting me by no means to sign it." To which Senator Schurz replied: "But, Mr. President, there will be a committee to beg that you fail not to sign it; for all Europe is looking to see that you fail not." Then said I: "Mr. President, you will re-member that on the eve of your departure from Springfield, Ill., you begged the citizens of the republic to pray for you." He said, "Yes." Said I: "From that moment we, the colored citizens of the republic, have been praying: 'O, Lord just as thou didst cause the throne of David to wax stronger and stron-ger, while that of Saul should wax weaker and weaker, so we beseech thee cause the power at Washington to grow stronger and stronger, while that at Richmond shall grow weaker and weaker.'" Slightly bending his head, the President said: 'Well, I must believe that God has led me thus far, for I am conscious that I never would have accomplished what has been done if he had not been with me to counsel and to shield." But neither Carl Schurz nor I could induce him to say "Yes" or "No" to our direct question.... There was nothing stiff or formal in the air and manner of His Excellency—nothing egotistic.... President Lincoln received and conversed with me as though I had been one of his intimate acquaintances or one of his friendly neighbors.

79. Milton Sernett, "Daniel Alexander Payne: 'Welcome to the Ransomed,'" in Sernett, *African American Religious History*, 232.

I left him with a profound sense of his real greatness and of his fitness to rule a nation composed of almost all the races on the face of the globe. (146–48)

On April 16, 1862, Lincoln signs the bill, and Payne's address, "Welcome to the Ransomed," targets the enslaved who are newly free. Payne takes as his text another Pauline Scripture, 1 Timothy 2:1–8, to underscore the duties of the African Americans in DC who have just experienced liberation.

St. Paul addressed the Epistles to Timothy, the young Bishop of Ephesus, for the purpose of giving him instructions touching the false doctrines inculcated by certain false teachers, as well as instructions respecting the qualifications of the Christian ministry, their duties to themselves, to God, and the flock committed by the Holy Spirit to their special guidance. But the foremost of all the duties which he enjoined upon the Ephesian ministry and laity were those of making "Supplications, prayers, intercessions, and giving of thanks for all men." For men in general, embracing the whole family of Adam, in all their varieties as nations, tribes, communities, peoples. This is God-like, because the Eternal loves all, and manifests the infinity of his nature, by his universal care for all mankind. In this, He also demonstrates His universal Fatherhood, and thereby establishes the brotherhood of man.[80]

Payne utilizes Paul to speak of blacks' foremost duties, which are to offer supplications, prayers, intercessions, and giving of thanks for all men, for to do so is the "peculiar privilege of the Colored People in the United States" (238). He elaborates upon Paul's last phrase, "all men," and emphasizes that the expression means the "whole family of Adam, in all their varieties as nations, tribes, communities, peoples" (233). Here, Payne utilizes Paul as a basis for family language; there is one ancestor, Adam, albeit differences exist inside the family. Payne asserts one ancestor for all people and invokes also the universal Fatherhood of God, who loves all and cares for all, thereby establishing the brotherhood of man. Similar to his understanding of Acts 17:26, another Pauline text he employs in his autobiography, Payne sees here in Paul's universal language a universal family of Adam in which no inferiority, superiority, or racial division exists in God's world.

Payne goes on to welcome the liberated slaves to the churches, the homestead, and the social circles of the AME Church. He also admonishes

---

80. Sernett, "Welcome to the Ransomed," 232–33. Hereafter, page references from this work will be given in parentheses in the text.

them that their physical freedom, although important and celebrated, is no substitute for spiritual freedom, so they should also seek liberation from sin. "As certain as the American Congress has ransomed you, so certain, yea, more certainly has Jesus redeemed you from the guilt and power of sin by his own precious blood. As you are now free in body, so now seek to be free in soul and spirit, from sin and Satan. The noblest freeman is he whom Christ makes free" (234). In these statements, Payne highlights the double meaning of his title. The American Congress ransomed the enslaved, but the enslaved have also been redeemed by Jesus's blood, as Paul writes in 1 Timothy 2:6 that Jesus *"gave himself a ransom for all."* Payne's welcome to the ransomed signifies embracing the physically and spiritually liberated, both realities made possible by God's divine power. As Cleophus LaRue remarks, "Payne had a profound sense of the omnipotence of God and God's determination to set things right."[81] Payne urges his audience, in response to this God who has begun to set things right, to seek salvation and to live godly lives filled with work and pursuit of knowledge.

Payne encourages his audience to "Work, work, work!" and to learn to read, especially the Bible. He also urges them to pool their money for community building so that they can build schools and churches. For Payne, God is the architect behind the slaves' freedom: "Now, if we ask, who has sent us this great deliverance? The answer shall be, the Lord; the Lord God Almighty, the God of Abraham and Isaac and Jacob . . . the angels of mercy, justice, and liberty, hovering over the towering Capitol, inspired the heads and hearts of the noble men who have plead the cause of the poor, the needy and enslaved, in the Senate and House of Representatives. . . . Thou, O Lord, and thou alone couldst have moved the heart of the Nation to have done so great a deed for this weak, despised and needy people!" (237). These selections reveal Payne's perspective behind the emancipation of the DC enslaved. God intervenes and brings it to pass, and so, consequently, African Americans need to use their freedom in a productive manner by living godly lives, by uniting to build and sustain community resources, and by doing what the apostle Paul commands, praying for all men, including all those in authority.

Payne advises his audience that when Paul tells Timothy to pray for all those in authority, he means the government, which parallels Payne's own audience's call to pray for the president and the Congress. He recounts the

81. Cleophus LaRue, *The Heart of Black Preaching* (Louisville: Westminster John Knox, 2000), 56.

history behind the letter writing: Paul lived under the reign of Nero, an evil emperor known for setting Rome on fire, blaming Christians for that act, and killing many Christians for the crime that he himself committed.[82] Payne contends that "If it was the duty of the ancient Christians to pray for such monsters of wickedness, by how much more is it our duty to pray for a Christian Government. . . . We shall beseech the God of nations to send the spirit of wisdom, justice, liberty—of wisdom seeing the end from the beginning—of justice incorruptible—of liberty governed by righteous law. . . . The service of prayer which is required from us, contemplates the most difficult as well as the noblest objects. It contemplates the end of the war. It contemplates legislation before and after the end" (238). Payne applies Paul's words of praying for those in power to the current situation of praying for the American government and all those involved in the war, including soldiers, so that the combat may end successfully with the liberation of the enslaved. He also urges his audience to pray that legislation during and after the war will be such that justice and equality prevails. In addition to praying for the public office and activities of government officials, Payne advocates praying for government officials' personal salvation as well, because, as the apostle says, God "*will have all men to be saved, and to come to the knowledge of the truth*" (240). Payne views prayer as a weapon, one just as powerful or more powerful than the physical weapons of war, and urges his hearers to take up this supernatural arsenal because prayers are, in the words of Paul, "*not carnal, but mighty through God, to the pulling down of strongholds* [2 Cor. 10:4]; even the *casting down of principalities and powers* [Eph. 3:10; 6:12; Col. 1:16; 2:15; Titus 3:1]—the moving of heaven and earth" (239). From Payne's use of Paul's words, prayer is a form of resistance where humans meet the divine in a contest against evil, injustice, and oppression, and join forces to defeat that which tries to enslave and devour humanity. Payne views prayer as a supernatural agent that can bring about the liberation of the enslaved as well as guide the legislature in its deliberations on bills and laws that promote equality. Payne understands that to bring about justice requires more than human power and agency.

In the closing paragraphs of this address, as he does in his General Conference sermon, Payne lifts up Jesus as an example of all that he has said before and as an example of Paul's words to pray for all men. Jesus himself engaged in such actions and still continues to do so, since he is the "*Mediator between God and Man, who ever liveth to make intercession* [Heb. 7:25] for his foes as well as

---

82. Payne, like the other black hermeneuts in this volume, assumes that Paul wrote 1 Timothy. Among modern biblical scholars, the identity of the writer is debated.

his friends, and with whom there is no respect of persons. Black men, red men, white men, are all alike before Him" (241). Payne ends the speech as he began it, focusing on the idea that all people are alike before God; there is a common humanity that binds all people together since there is a common ancestor, Adam, a universal Father, God, and one mediator for all people, Jesus. If one sees the commonality, then one can pray even for those deemed enemies because they too are part of the human family in need of God's divine aid and salvation.

Payne concludes the address with a conditional blessing upon America. "But God will bless [this nation] if it will do right, administering justice to each and to all, protecting the weak as well as the strong, and throwing the broad wings of its power equally over the men of every color. This is God-like, and God will bless his own image, be it in a nation or in a man" (241). Payne believes that the blessing upon the nation is tied to actions of protecting the weak and treating all people equally. America is not simply blessed because of its origins or because it claims to be Christian. Payne understands that to secure divine favor, the nation has to do right by all of its citizens, regardless of race. LaRue appositely comments that "An over-riding understanding of the power of God informs this entire sermon. It is an understanding of God who acts mightily on behalf of the marginalized and powerless."[83] God's power is central to Payne's sermon, and he utilizes Paul to indicate that prayer becomes a way to participate in the power of this God who moves and acts on behalf of the marginalized. Divine and human cooperation make possible African Americans' liberation.

Payne utilizes Paul in a number of ways in his autobiography and in his speeches. He uses the words of the apostle to describe his conversion and call to preach, his illness, the unity of humanity, the duties of ministers, and spiritual warfare. In addition, the words of the apostle are essential to his advocacy for prayer for the government. African Americans' movement into freedom gives rise to an understanding of the possibility of God using the government to carry out God's divine will of liberation. Earlier in David Walker's and Maria Stewart's work, the presence of judgment language and destruction upon America was prevalent. To be sure, some African Americans as well as some white abolitionists saw the Civil War as God's judgment upon the United States for engaging in slavery and the slave trade. Others saw it as liberation, for "they had witnessed God's liberating action in their lives when, as they interpreted it, God used President Abraham Lincoln and

83. LaRue, *Heart of Black Preaching*, 56–57n61.

the Union soldiers to destroy the yoke of slavery."[84] And still others saw it as both judgment and liberation. In this vein, the freedom of the enslaved in the District of Columbia enables a view that Paul could be used to encourage prayer for the president, the Congress, and the entire governmental structure so that they may enact just laws and freedom for all those in bondage.

Whereas earlier Paul was used by whites to proclaim, "Slaves, obey your master," Payne shifts the use of Paul. The apostle becomes justification to pray that the enslavers will now have to obey the government, which is under the direction of the God to whom the enslaved pray. As one enslaved African put it, "We prayed a lot to be free and the Lord done heered us."[85]

Thus, Paul is used to depict a radical reversal of obedience brought about by the prayers of the enslaved.

Julia Foote (1823–1900): Ordained Female Deacon

Like the other black hermeneuts in this chapter, Julia Foote had a deep personal relationship with God and with Scripture. Foote, a daughter of former slaves who were devout Christians, was born in 1823 in Schenectady, New York. At the age of fifteen, Foote became converted and shortly thereafter sought and received the gift of sanctification.[86] Despite much opposition, Foote accepted the call to preach and proclaimed the gospel in various places, including New England, Ohio, and Canada. She was the first woman ordained a deacon in the AME Zion Church, and she was ordained an elder in the same denomination, making her only the second woman to hold such an office in her church.[87]

Foote's Conversion, Sanctification, and Call to Preach

As demonstrated throughout her autobiography, *A Brand Plucked from the Fire: An Autobiographical Sketch by Mrs. Julia A. J. Foote*, the Bible, notably

---

84. Raynard D. Smith, "Seeking the Just Society: Charles Harrison Mason's Quest for Social Equality," in *With Signs Following: The Life and Ministry of Charles Harrison*, ed. Raynard Smith (St. Louis: Christian Board Publication, 2015), 100.

85. Raboteau, *Slave Religion*, 218.

86. William L. Andrews, introduction to *Sisters of the Spirit: Three Black Women's Autobiographies of the Nineteenth Century*, ed. William L. Andrews (Bloomington: Indiana University Press, 1986), 9.

87. Andrews, introduction to *Sisters of the Spirit*, 10.

Paul, is central to Foote's understanding of the conversion experience and her commission to proclaim the gospel. As she states in her preface, Foote believes in salvation from all sin in this life and that the words of Paul in Galatians 2:20 sanction such a view: *"I am crucified with Christ: nevertheless, I live; yet not I, but Christ liveth in me; and the life which I now live in the flesh I live by faith of the Son of God, who loved me, and gave himself for me."*[88] According to Foote, Jesus's blood destroys "the very root of sin that is in the heart" and does not just remove the guilt of sin (163). Although she did not believe in and teach absolute perfection, she upholds Christian perfection, which for her means an "extinction of every temper contrary to love" and that one cannot commit sin and remain a Christian (232). The *sanctification of spirit, soul, and body* advocated by Paul (1 Thess. 5:23)[89] is a present reality for the believer, since *God's faithfulness* compels *divine completion* (1 Thess. 5:24) and *God has set forth Jesus to be a propitiation for sin through faith in his blood* (Rom. 3:25). For Foote, since Paul says that *God is able to do exceeding abundantly above all that we ask or think* (Eph. 3:20) and since *believers have access by faith to this grace in which they stand* (Rom. 5:2), Christian perfection is an attainable gift from God (232).

Foote comes to this belief through her own conversion and subsequent experience of sanctification. Her conversion experience takes place at a quarterly meeting on a Sunday evening. The minister's text, Revelation 14:3, impacts her tremendously: "And they sung as it were a new song before the throne, and before the four beasts and the elders: and no man could learn that song but the hundred and forty and four thousand, which were redeemed from earth." The sermon affects her in such a profound way that she describes her reaction to it in the following manner:

> I beheld my lost condition as I never had before. Something within me kept saying, "Such a sinner as you are can never sing that new song." No tongue can tell the agony I suffered. I fell to the floor, unconscious, and was carried home. Several remained with me all night, singing and praying. I did not recognize any one, but seemed to be walking in the dark, followed by some one who kept saying, "Such a sinner as you are can never sing that new

88. Julia Foote, *A Brand Plucked from the Fire: An Autobiographical Sketch by Mrs. Julia A. J. Foote* (Cleveland, OH: Printed for the author by W. F. Schneider, 1879), reprinted in Andrews, *Sisters of the Spirit*, 163. Hereafter, page references from the reprint edition will be given in parentheses in the text.

89. Although Foote cites this verse as 2 Thess. 5:23, it is actually 1 Thess. 5:23. See Andrews, *Sisters of the Spirit*, 245.

song." . . . In great terror I cried: "Lord, have mercy on me, a poor sinner!" The voice which had been crying in my ears ceased at once, and a ray of light flashed across my eyes, accompanied by a sound of far distant singing; the light grew brighter and brighter, and the singing more distinct, and soon I caught the words: "This is the new song—redeemed, redeemed!" I at once sprang from the bed where I had been lying for twenty hours, without meat or drink, and commenced singing: "Redeemed! redeemed! glory! glory!" Such joy and peace as filled my heart, when I felt that I was redeemed and could sing the new song. (180)

After Foote's conversion, she experiences peace and joy for about six months, then suffers a terrible accident in which her brother inadvertently hits her in the eye, causing her to lose sight in it. Along with the physical pain that this accident causes, an inner turmoil ensues that heaps upon her deep troubles and anguish. She describes her inner struggle with the words of Paul, "I knew what was right, and tried to do right, but *when I would do good, evil was present with me* [Rom. 7:21]" (183).[90] Her inner wrestling with feelings of anger, pride, impatience, and "other signs of carnality" (182) causes her to seek counsel from her preacher, parents, and others, who inform her that "all Christians had these inward troubles to contend with, and were never free from them until death" (183). Refusing to accept these answers, Foote learns about the gift of sanctification from an old couple who visit her church and tell of their own struggle against pride, anger, and other sins, from which the Lord through sanctification delivered them. Upon hearing this news, Foote decides to seek this gift for her own life, and one day she receives it:

While waiting on the Lord, my large desire was granted, through faith in my precious Saviour. The glory of God seemed almost to prostrate me to the floor. There was, indeed, a weight of glory resting upon me. . . . Glory to the Father! Glory to the Son! And glory to the Holy Ghost! Who hath plucked me as a brand from the burning, and sealed me unto eternal life. I no longer hoped for glory, but I had the full assurance of it. *Praise the Lord for Paul-like faith! "I am crucified with Christ: nevertheless, I live; yet not I, but Christ liveth in me"* [Gal. 2:20]. This, my constant prayer, was answered, that *I might be strengthened with might by his Spirit in the inner man; that being rooted and grounded in love, I might be able to comprehend with all*

90. See a different interpretation of this verse offered by James Pennington above.

saints what is the length, and breadth, and height, and depth, and to know the love of Christ which passeth knowledge, and be filled with all the fullness of God [Eph. 3:16–19]. I had been afraid to tell my mother I was praying for sanctification, but when the "*old man*" [Rom. 6:6] was cast out of my heart, and perfect love took possession, I lost all fear. (186–87)

"Paul-like faith" enables Foote to receive the gift of sanctification, and the apostle's prayer for the Ephesians becomes her own prayer for her life, that God will strengthen her through the Spirit, ground her in love, grant her the ability to understand the divine dimensions of Christ's love and to experience God's fullness. The glory of God fills her body, and the weight of this כבוד (glory) causes her to become prostrate on the floor. This gift of sanctification enables her to resist fear and reveal to her mother her divine experience. Once Foote informs her mother and other people regarding her sanctification, she faces opposition from them and others, who state that it is impossible to live without committing sin, just as it is impossible to live without eating (193). Yet Foote refuses to be dissuaded about her new divine awakening, declaring that Jesus frees "me from the guilt of sin, and *sin hath no longer dominion over me* [Rom. 6:14]" (188). Along with describing her freedom from sin in Pauline language, Foote expresses her peace with Paul-like simplicity: "From this time, many, who had been my warmest friends, and seemed to think me a Christian, turned against me, saying I did not know what I was talking about—that there was no such thing as sanctification and holiness in this life—and that the devil had deluded me into self-righteousness. Many of them fought holiness with more zeal and vigor than they did sin. Amid all this, I had that sweet *peace that passeth all understanding* [Phil. 4:7] springing up within my soul like a perennial fountain—glory to the precious blood of Jesus!" (187).

The opposition that Foote experiences for receiving sanctification foreshadows to some extent the opposition she faces when she accepts her call to preach. The first round of opposition she faces, however, comes from herself. Foote views herself as an unworthy vessel to proclaim God's Word. Her detailed call to preach, sprinkled with Pauline language, is worth examining at length: "When called of God, on a particular occasion, to a definite work, I said, 'No, Lord, not me.' Day by day I was more impressed that God would have me to work in his vineyard. I thought it could not be that I was called to preach—I, so weak and ignorant. Still, I knew all things were possible with God, even to *confounding the wise by the foolish things of this earth* [1 Cor. 1:27]. Yet in me there was a shrinking" (200).

Foote believes that because she is not well educated she cannot proclaim God's Word, even though she acknowledges that God often chooses the foolish to confound the wise. Her sense of calling leads her to pray for direction: "I took all my doubts and fears to the Lord in prayer, when, what seemed to be an angel, made his appearance. In his hand was a scroll, on which were these words: 'Thee have I chosen to preach my Gospel without delay.' The moment my eyes saw it, it appeared to be printed on my heart. The angel was gone in an instant, and I, in agony, cried out, 'Lord, I cannot do it!'" (200).

Foote wrestles with her call from God, loses sleep and her appetite, and finally discloses one of the main reasons for her struggle to accept God's call. "I had always been opposed to the preaching of women, and had spoken against it, though, I acknowledge, without foundation. This rose before me like a mountain, and when I thought of the difficulties they had to encounter, both from professors and non-professors, I shrank back and cried, 'Lord, I cannot go!'" (201). Foote's previous opposition to women preachers causes her reluctance to become what she had always disparaged. Since she was a former opponent of women preachers, she knew firsthand what kind of opposition she would have to endure. To comfort herself she repeatedly reads Hebrews 6, a Pauline writing, and two months later she receives two angelic visitations, the second of which causes her to consent totally to God's call upon her life.

> The angel led me to a place where there was a large tree, the branches of which seemed to extend either way beyond sight. Beneath it sat, as I thought, God the Father, the Son, and the Holy Spirit, besides many others, whom I thought were angels. . . . [The Father] then pointed my hand in different directions, and asked if I would go there. I replied, "Yes, Lord." He then lead me, all the others following, till we came to a place where there was a great quantity of water, which looked like silver, where we made a halt. My hand was given to Christ, who led me into the water and stripped me of my clothing, which at once vanished from sight. Christ then appeared to wash me, the water feeling quite warm. . . . When the washing was ended, the sweetest music I had ever heard greeted my ears. We walked to the shore, where an angel stood with a clean, white robe, which the Father at once put on me. In an instant I appeared to be changed into an angel.[91] The

91. Foote's experience of being transformed into an angel bears similarities to some seers in Jewish texts who have divine encounters with God. For example, in 2 Enoch ("2 [Slavonic Apocalypse of] Enoch," trans. F. I. Andersen, in *Old Testament Pseude-*

whole company looked at me with delight, and began to make a noise which I called shouting. We all marched back with music. When we reached the tree to which the angel first led me, it hung full of fruit . . . the Holy Ghost plucked some and gave me, and the rest helped themselves. . . . Then God the Father said to me: "You are now prepared, and must go where I have commanded you." I replied, "If I go, they will not believe me." Christ then appeared to write something with a golden pen and golden ink upon golden paper. Then he rolled it up, and said to me, "Put this in your bosom, and, wherever you go, show it, and they will know that I have sent you to proclaim salvation to all." He then put it into my bosom, and they all went with me to a bright, shining gate, singing and shouting. Here they embraced me, and I found myself once more on earth. (202–3)

Foote's divine encounter in which she meets the Father, Son, and Holy Ghost precipitates her acceptance of the call to preach. She experiences a divine transformation represented by Christ's washing her, which is similar to baptism. Her exchanging her old attire for a new robe illustrates a change in status; the feelings of unworthiness have been stripped away and replaced with a divine endorsement. Interestingly, Christ bestows this divine authorization with pen, paper, and ink, the very utensils denied to blacks in the narrative slaveholders related to Henry "Box" Brown, where God grants only whites these materials. Contrary to this narrative, the Divine utilizes instruments "given" to whites alone to bestow authority upon Foote, a black woman, who because of race had limited opportunities for education. The reversal that this bestowal highlights both underscores the falsehood of the slaveholding narrative and invalidates the notion of white superiority. Moreover, this signals a bestowal of power upon Foote, a power backed up by the Divine. Paper, pen, and ink, which represent

---

pigrapha: Apocalyptic Literature and Testaments, ed. James Charlesworth [New York: Doubleday, 1983]), the writer describes his experience in the following manner: "And the Lord said to Michael, 'Go, and extract Enoch from [his] earthly clothing. And anoint him with my delightful oil, and put him into the clothes of my glory.' And so Michael did, just as the Lord had said to him. He anointed me and he clothed me. And the appearance of that oil is greater than the greatest light. . . . And I looked at myself, and I had become like one of his glorious ones, and there was no observable difference" (22:8–10 manuscript J; see also the shorter recension, manuscript A). The parallels between this text and Foote's vision are interesting. Like Enoch, she experiences a change in clothing and becomes like an angel. See also the Apocalypse of Zephaniah 8:2–4; Martyrdom and Ascension of Isaiah 7:25.

education, and all that education signifies such as worth, intellect, prestige, and power, do not belong exclusively to the white race but ultimately with God, and God grants these gifts to all people regardless of race and gender. The description of the paper, pen, and ink as golden serves to denote the heavenly origin of Foote's authorization, which trumps any earthly authority. The fact that God instructs Foote to place these heavenly papers in her bosom and to show them wherever she goes illustrates permanence and that God's authorization travels with her wherever her feet may tread. Along with directly opposing the story that blacks were not worthy of education, this vision serves to encourage and affirm Foote despite her lack of education credentials. God provides her with all the credentials she will ever need.

Excommunication and a Pauline Response

As a result of Foote accepting God's call to preach, her local church excommunicates her and her pastor spreads false rumors about her among the congregation. Foote appeals in a letter to her church's National Conference, but to no avail, writing sadly that her letter was "slightingly noticed, and then thrown under the table. Why should they notice it? It was only the grievance of a woman, and there was no justice meted out to women in those days. Even ministers of Christ did not feel that women had any rights which they were bound to respect" (207).

Foote laments the treatment women preachers receive from the church and decries the double standard applied to women who, according to some in the church, must produce supernatural evidence to signify their call to preach. "We are sometimes told that if a woman pretends to a Divine call and thereon grounds the right to plead the cause of a crucified Redeemer in public, she will be believed when she shows credentials from heaven; that is, when she works a miracle. If it be necessary to prove one's right to preach the Gospel, I ask of my brethren to show me their credentials, or I can not believe in the propriety of their ministry" (208–9). That women need to work a miracle to receive recognition of their call seems outrageous to Foote, who demands that the same requirement be applied to male preachers. Two different standards for credentials are not necessary, since God calls both women and men. In fact, after this passage, in which she critiques this double standard, Foote cites Paul to indicate the absurdity of such distinctions.

The Bible puts an end to this strife when it says: "There is neither male nor female in Christ Jesus" [Gal. 3:28]. Philip had four daughters that prophesied, or preached. Paul called Priscilla, as well as Aquila, his "helper," or, as in the Greek, his "fellow-laborer." Rom. xv.3; 2 Cor. viii.23; Phil. ii.5; 1 Thess. iii.2.[92] The same word, which in our common translation, is now rendered a "servant of the church," in speaking of Phebe (Rom. xix.1), is rendered "minister" when applied to Tychicus. Eph. vi.21. When Paul said, "Help those women who labor with me in the Gospel [Phil. 4:3]," he certainly meant that they did more than to pour out tea. In the eleventh chapter of First Corinthians Paul gives directions, to men and women, how they should appear when they prophesy or pray in public assemblies; and he defines prophesying to be speaking to edification, exhortation and comfort. (209)[93]

Foote views Paul's words in Galatians 3:28 as the *Auflösung* (resolution) for gender discrimination and as the *wesentlich* (essential) passage for understanding the equal status of women and men in ministry. In addition to the apostle's words, his references to women as fellow laborers and ministers indicate that he viewed women as integral to the preaching vocation. They were not just in charge of hospitality and pouring tea, an idea that Foote rejects in her comments about Paul's references to women laboring with him. As Foote notes, Paul uses the same word, διάκονος, to describe Phoebe and Tychicus, but translators unfortunately translate the words differently, "servant of the church" for Phoebe and "minister" for Tychicus. Yet the differing translations have no basis. In fact, Paul employs this same term a number of times to speak of himself (e.g., 1 Cor. 3:5; 2 Cor. 3:6; 6:4; 11:23), a fact probably unknown to Foote, who more than likely would have cited it had she known it. As indicated by the above passage, Foote marshals scriptural evidence to validate her call from God. She uses these and other scriptural examples of women preachers to encourage other women who believe God called them to ministry as well.

92. Foote is correct that Paul uses the same term, συνεργός, for Priscilla, Aquila, Titus, Euodia, Syntyche, and Timothy. In 2 Cor. 8:23 and Phil. 4:3, Paul also employs two other terms, κοινωνός and σύζυγος, respectively. In addition, several of her scriptural citations are incorrect. Rom. 15:3 should read Rom. 16:3, Phil. 2:5 should be Phil. 4:3, and Rom. 19:1 should be Rom. 16:1.

93. See also the brief discussion of this passage in Cooper, *Maria Stewart*, 136–37.

A Word to My Christian Sisters

Toward the end of her autobiography, in a chapter entitled "A Word to My Christian Sisters," Foote explicitly encourages women preachers who face opposition to their call to preach. She writes to them, saying, "Sisters, shall not you and I unite with the heavenly host in the grand chorus? If so, you will not let what man may say or do, keep you from doing the will of the Lord or using the gifts you have for the good of others. . . . Be not kept in bondage by those who say, '*We suffer not a woman to teach*,' thus quoting Paul's words [1 Cor. 14:34], but not rightly applying them" (227). Foote directly takes on the use of Paul's words to silence female preachers. She vehemently opposes this use, arguing that those who employ Paul to deny women the use of their preaching gifts do not apply his words correctly. They simply misappropriate him, especially in light of how he speaks about women ministers in other places. Significantly, Foote likens the use of Paul's words in this manner to bondage, indicating her belief that the oppression of women ministers bears some resemblance to the bondage of African Americans in that both are rooted in a supremacist attitude, whether it be white or male. Foote, then, admonishes her female audience to do God's will despite what others, especially men, may say or do.

Foote ends her autobiography just as she began it, with a focus on holiness and sanctification. Utilizing Paul's words in Romans 12:1–2; 1 Timothy 2:9–10; 1 Thessalonians 1:13; 4:7; Hebrews 12:14; Romans 6:19; 1 Corinthians 3:16, 17; and 2 Corinthians 6:16–17, Foote exhorts her audience to live holy lives and to separate their lives from the world. They are to remember that they are the temple of the Lord and thus to live lives worthy of such a call. For those in her audience who may not have experienced sanctification, she encourages them to "believe, and be sanctified now—now, while reading? '*Now is the day of salvation*' [2 Cor. 6:2]" (234). Foote advocates seeking sanctification immediately and not waiting to receive this divine gift. For her, sanctification comes from God and means that "the root, the inbeing of sin, is destroyed" (231). Foote acknowledges that one of the purposes of her book is to "promote the cause of holiness in the Church," a cause she deeply believed in and a manner of life to which she adhered (234). She closes her autobiography with the Pauline doxology of Ephesians 3:20–21: "*Now, unto Him who is able to do exceeding abundantly, above all that we ask or think, according to the power that worketh in us; unto Him be glory in the church by Christ Jesus throughout all ages, world without end. Amen*" (234).

Foote's focus on sanctification becomes a central theme of her life and her call to preach. She believes that when Paul writes that sin no longer has dominion over believers, this is a lived reality, not futuristic thinking. In addition, when the apostle proclaims the sanctification of body, soul, and spirit, this too denotes cleansing of every part of a human being. Believers have been crucified with Christ and so are called to live a new life in which the Holy Spirit leads and guides in every area of their existence. Though Foote faces opposition because of her belief and preaching regarding holiness, she does not give up or give in to her detractors. Instead she is assured through divine visions and experiences that God calls her to proclaim this message.

First Corinthians 1:27 and Galatians 3:28 become significant texts for her, affirming that God confounds the wise by using the foolish and that social distinctions, such as male and female, do not determine one's ability to preach. Such distinctions in the divine economy have been made null and void. Foote finds the truth of Galatians 3:28 throughout Scripture, in which Paul uses the same term to denote Priscilla as he does to denote Aquila and the same term to describe Phoebe and Tychicus. To those who dared to proclaim Paul's silencing of women, Foote asserts that they were not using Paul's words correctly, for a true reading of Paul affirmed women preachers and did not condone silencing them.

Harriet Jacobs (1813–1897):
First Enslaved African American Woman to Write an Autobiography

Unlike Foote, who was born free to formerly enslaved parents who purchased their freedom, Harriet Jacobs was born in slavery in 1813 in Edenton, Chowan County, North Carolina, and is the first female enslaved African to pen an autobiography. She writes a very personal and gripping narrative, *Incidents in the Life of A Slave Girl*, which details her life as an African American woman in slavery.[94] According to her, she lived in slavery twenty-

94. Harriet Jacobs, *Incidents in the Life of A Slave Girl*, ed. L. Maria Child (Boston: Published for the author, 1861), 540, reprinted in "Harriet Jacobs," in Taylor, *I Was Born a Slave*, 2:534. All of Jacobs's autobiographical quotes cited in this volume appear in Taylor, *I Was Born a Slave*, and the page references are to Taylor. Yellin, *Harriet Jacobs*, 3; Emerson Powery, "'Rise Up, Ye Women': Harriet Jacobs and the Bible," *Postscripts* 5, no. 2 (2009): 171–84. See also the discussion of Harriet Jacobs's narrative in Joanne Braxton, *Black Women Writing Autobiography: A Tradition within a Tradition* (Philadelphia: Temple University Press, 1989), 18–38.

seven years before escaping.[95] Her narrative is the first first-person written account to depict the horrors of slavery specifically for African American women.[96] Encouraged by others to write her story, she does so after she escapes, secretly, because she believes the husband of the couple she works for, Nathaniel Parker Willis, is an advocate of slavery.[97] One of her friends who encourages her to share her story is Amy Post, a Quaker and abolitionist, with whom she stays for a time after she absconds. In 1854 she shares the circumstances of her writing progress with Post: "As yet I have not written a single page by daylight . . . with the care of the little baby the big Babies and at the household calls I have but a little time to think or write." And again, "the poor Book is in its Chrysalis state and though I can never make it a butterfly I am satisfied to have it creep meekly among some of the humbler bugs."[98]

Jacobs publishes her narrative herself in 1861, and in the preface she reveals the ultimate purpose of her work.

> I have not written my experiences in order to attract attention to myself; on the contrary, it would have been more pleasant to me to have been silent about my own history. Neither do I care to excite sympathy for my own sufferings. But I do earnestly desire to arouse the women of the North to a realizing sense of the condition of two millions of women at the South, still in bondage, suffering what I suffered, and most of them far worse. I want to add my testimony to that of abler pens to convince the people of the Free States what Slavery really is. Only by experience can any one realize how deep, and dark, and foul is that pit of abominations.[99]

Jacobs aims to reveal to women of the North the reality of slave life for African Americans overall, but African American women in particu-

95. Jacobs, *Incidents*, 2:540.

96. There was a narrative by Mary Prince (1831), and another by Sojourner Truth (1850), but these were dictated, oral accounts. My thanks to Emerson Powery for calling these sources to my attention.

97. Jean Fagan Yellin, introduction to *Incidents in the Life of A Slave Girl Written by Herself*, by Harriet A. Jacobs, ed. L. Maria Child (Cambridge, MA: Harvard University Press, 1987), xviii. See also *The Harriet Jacobs Family Papers*, ed. Jean Fagan Yellin et al., vols. 1–2 (Chapel Hill: University of North Carolina Press, 2008).

98. Yellin, *Harriet Jacobs*, 129; "Harriet Jacobs," in Taylor, *I Was Born a Slave*, 2:534.

99. Jacobs, *Incidents*, 2:540.

lar.[100] The sexual abuse suffered by them was generally not acknowledged or discussed, for the subject was considered too delicate to broach. One can see that Jacobs desires to instill a sense of solidarity in Northern white women with their African American counterparts in the South. Lydia Maria Child, a prominent female writer and abolitionist, who aided Jacobs by editing the work, also endorsed the writing by providing an introduction to it. Child realized that the details of Jacobs's narrative, which spoke candidly and openly about the sexual abuse of female slaves by slaveholders, may be viewed as inappropriate and too forward. Yet, in her introduction to Jacobs's book, Child acknowledges the expediency and necessity of such exposure to truth and her role in making Jacobs's story available.

> I am well aware that many will accuse me of indecorum for presenting these pages to the public; for the experiences of this intelligent and much-injured woman belong to a class which some call delicate subjects, and others indelicate. This peculiar phase of Slavery has generally been kept veiled; but the public ought to be made acquainted with its monstrous features, and I willingly take the responsibility of presenting them with the veil withdrawn. I do this for the sake of my sisters in bondage, who are suffering wrongs so foul, that our ears are too delicate to listen to them. I do it with the hope of arousing conscientious and reflecting women at the North to a sense of their duty in the exertion of moral influence on the question of Slavery, on all possible occasions. I do it with the hope that every man who reads this narrative will swear solemnly before God that, so far as he has power to prevent it, no fugitive from Slavery shall ever be sent back to suffer in that loathsome den of corruption and cruelty.[101]

As Child indicates, she, like Jacobs, believes that sharing Jacobs's story is essential to rallying Northern women to assist their African American sisters in the South and in succoring support for rejecting compliance to the Fugitive Slave Act.

---

100. For further information as to what life for enslaved women was like, see Deborah Gray White, *Ar'n't I a Woman? Female Slaves in the Plantation South* (New York: Norton, 1985).

101. L. Maria Child, "Introduction by the Editor," in *Incidents in the Life of A Slave Girl*, ed. L. Maria Child (Boston: Published for the author, 1861), reprinted in Taylor, *I Was Born a Slave*, 2:541.

Jacobs and the Cult of True Womanhood

Jacobs, like all the African American women we have discussed so far, writes during a time when the "cult of true womanhood" was upheld as the standard for women.[102] Women were to be submissive, pious, pure, and to remain at home, while men were to work outside the home and fulfill their roles as protectors and heads of households.[103] Cooper notes that "Men were to be the protectors; women were to be protected." Yet Cooper correctly observes that for black women the home was not a safe haven, and black men could not protect their daughters, wives, or mothers.[104]

This inability to provide protection is described poignantly by Jacobs's brother in his description of their father. "To be a man, and not to be a man—a father without authority—a husband and no protector—is the darkest of fates. My father," he testifies, "taught me to hate slavery, but forgot to teach me how to conceal my hatred. I could frequently perceive the pent-up agony of his soul, although he tried hard to conceal it in his own breast. The knowledge that he was a slave himself, and that his children were also slaves, embittered his life, but made him love us the more."[105] The powerlessness slavery enacted upon black men created both agony and anger and simultaneously tried to reinforce the white supremacist notion of their nonbeing. Not only did the cult of true womanhood not apply to black women, but the underlying assumptions of maleness integral to this ideal—including roles and responsibilities such as provider and protector—did not apply to black men either, because they were seen as less than human.

Moreover, the cult of true womanhood placed the white woman as the epitome of womanhood and the black woman at the bottom of this hierarchy. Two quotes from Cooper help to accentuate the dynamics of this ideal for black women during this time:

> The Cult of True Womanhood was just one part of a larger system of romanticized racial, gender, and class hierarchies that were intended to offer explanations for Western economic and social domination of slaves, local populations, and far-flung colonial holdings. This Victorian reasoning argued that whites were superior to other races, that women ought to be

102. See also the discussion of the cult of true womanhood in chap. 1.
103. Cooper, *Maria Stewart*, 115.
104. Cooper, *Maria Stewart*, 115.
105. Yellin, *Harriet Jacobs*, 7.

submissive to men, and that the West, by virtue of its moral, intellectual, and technological superiority, ought, by (divine) right, to rule the world.[106]

That the Cult of True Womanhood excluded black women is not surprising, given the prevailing racial and social hierarchies of the nineteenth century. African American women were at the time barely considered to be human and were never to be treated as ladies. Terms like *lady* and even *woman* were so encumbered by the prevailing racial hierarchies of the day that they were not regarded as applicable to African American women.[107]

These quotes capture the romantic ideals and the white supremacist notions that formed the basis for this view of womanhood. They also highlight that black women were, for the most part, excluded from the category of women. Against this backdrop, Jacobs dares to speak out about the reality for black women in slave households, and in doing so exposes the hypocritical underpinnings of the cult of true womanhood.

"One Great Wrong"

In the beginning of her narrative, Jacobs speaks about how kind her first mistress treated her and how, because of this great kindness, she had great hopes that her mistress would free her upon her death. However, when the mistress's will is read, Jacobs finds out that her owner did not free her but bequeathed her to her sister's child. Upon this profound disappointment, Jacobs makes some keen observations:

> My mistress had taught me the precepts of God's Word: "Thou shalt love thy neighbor as thyself." "Whatsoever you would that men should do unto you, do ye even so unto them." But I was her slave, and I suppose she did not recognize me as her neighbor. I would give much to blot out from memory that one great wrong. As a child, I loved my mistress; and, looking back on the happy days I spent with her, I try to think with less bitterness of this act of injustice. While I was with her, she taught me to read and spell; and for this privilege, which so rarely falls to the lot of a slave, I bless her memory.[108]

106. Cooper, *Maria Stewart*, 116.
107. Cooper, *Maria Stewart*, 117.
108. Jacobs, *Incidents*, 2:546.

These insightful comments by Jacobs underline one of the evils of slavery. The enslaved are taught the precepts of God orally from Scripture and at the same time are taught through actions of slaveholders that some precepts do not apply to them. As Jacobs states, even though her mistress was kind to her, teaching her to read and write, she nevertheless did not conceive of Jacobs as a neighbor, a fellow human being worthy of freedom. As Hazel Carby insightfully observes, "Having taught her slave to read and spell, this mistress had contributed to the ability of Jacobs to tell her tale, but the story Jacobs told condemned the mistress."[109] This "one great wrong" by Jacobs's mistress became the life-changing event for Jacobs. As an enslaved woman now bequeathed to her mistress's niece, Jacobs meets Dr. Flint, the father of the mistress's niece, who constantly torments Jacobs with sexual oppression.

This act of injustice precipitates the events of Jacobs's narrative that allow readers to catch a glimpse of the hell endured by enslaved women from white slaveholders. Jacobs candidly reveals the trials of an "enchained woman of color."[110]

I now entered on my fifteenth year—a sad epoch in the life of a slave girl. My master began to whisper foul words in my ear. Young as I was, I could not remain ignorant of their import. I tried to treat them with indifference or contempt. . . . He tried his utmost to corrupt the pure principles my grandmother had instilled. He peopled my young mind with unclean images, such as only a vile monster could think of. I turned from him with disgust and hatred. But he was my master. . . . He told me I was his property; that I must be subject to his will in all things. My soul revolted against the mean tyranny. But where could I turn for protection? No matter where the slave girl be as black as ebony or as fair as her mistress. In either case, there is no shadow of law to protect her from insult, from violence, or even from death; all these are inflicted by fiends who bear the shape of men. The mistress, who ought to protect the helpless victim, has no other feelings towards her but those of jealousy and rage. The degradation, the wrongs, the vices, that grow out of slavery, are more than I can describe.[111]

109. Hazel V. Carby, "'Hear My Voice, Ye Careless Daughters': Narratives of Slave and Free Women before Emancipation," in *African American Autobiography: A Collection of Critical Essays*, ed. William Andrews (Englewood Cliffs, NJ: Prentice Hall, 1993), 69.

110. This phrase comes from C. Michelle Venable-Ridley, "Paul and the African American Community," in *Embracing the Spirit: Womanist Perspectives on Hope, Salvation, and Transformation*, ed. Emilie M. Townes (Maryknoll, NY: Orbis, 1997), 213.

111. Jacobs, *Incidents*, 2:559.

When an enslaved girl reaches a certain age, she begins to experience unwanted sexual advances from her enslaver. Therefore, when she wants to retain her virginity, she is not allowed to do so. Jacobs writes in another part of her autobiography, "[An enslaved African woman] is not allowed to have any pride of character. It is deemed a crime in her to wish to be virtuous."[112] As Jacobs relates, slaveholders continually repeat to the enslaved women that because they owned them the women could not resist or refuse them, and as Jacobs admits in the above citation, enslaved women had no protection under the law. Even their mistresses did not provide them with protection but often created additional distress due to jealousy and blaming the enslaved women for their husbands' actions. Jacobs's narrative reveals the torment endured by enslaved women from their slaveholders as well as the hatred endured by them from their slaveholders' wives.[113]

Jacobs constantly runs away from Dr. Flint and rejects his many advances toward her. Yet he is relentless.

My master met me at every turn, reminding me that I belonged to him, and swearing by heaven and earth that he would compel me to submit to him. If I went out for a breath of fresh air, after a day of unwearied toil, his footsteps dogged me. If I knelt by my mother's grave, his dark shadow fell on me even there. The light heart which nature had given me became heavy with sad forebodings. The other slaves in my master's house noticed

112. Jacobs, *Incidents*, 2:561.

113. Jacobs, *Incidents*, writes, "[My mistress] felt that her marriage vows were desecrated, her dignity insulted; but she had no compassion for the poor victim of her husband's perfidy. She pitied herself a martyr; but she was incapable of feeling for the condition of shame and misery in which her unfortunate, helpless slave was placed" (2:563). In her book *White Women's Christ and Black Women's Jesus: Feminist Christology and Womanist Response* (Atlanta: Scholars Press, 1989), Jacquelyn Grant writes about the huge chasm that existed between black women and white women during slavery. She states, "The biographies, autobiographies, and narratives [of the enslaved] . . . reveal how Black women experienced White women. White women in slave and ex-slave narratives are always identified as members of the oppressor race. The terms 'misus' and 'mistress' implied for White women a status which Black women did not have. Black women, as a part of the servicing class, were not awarded the protection of White patriarchy. Apparently, from the point of view of the mistresses, Black women's purpose in life was to serve their domestic needs. No special and very little different treatment was accorded slave women because they were women. The Victorian concept of ladyhood was not applied to slave women. They were treated like slave men as a lower species of animals. Brutality was administered not only by masters and foremen but also by mistresses, reflecting the fact that White women were just as much participants in this system of slavery as were White men" (196–97).

the change. Many of them pitied me; but none dared to ask the cause. They had no need to inquire. They knew too well the guilty practices under that roof; and they were aware that to speak of them was an offence that never went unpunished.[114]

Jacobs describes the horrible dilemma of the enslaved woman who wants to keep herself pure and is not allowed to do so in a "Christian environment," "Christian household," and "Christian nation." In addition, her autobiography details the powerlessness of African American women and their inability to control what happens to their bodies. Even their mouths are controlled by slavery, for to speak of this "offence" was to incur punishment.

The case of *State of Missouri v. Celia* exemplifies the lack of power black enslaved women had over their bodies during slavery. Celia, an enslaved woman, murdered her master during an attempted rape; he had often forced her to have sex with him before and had made her pregnant. The case involved whether or not the Missouri law that prohibited rape of any woman included Celia. Thus, the case hinged upon whether Celia was considered a woman. Her defense lawyer tried to show that the slaveholder's murder was one of self-defense, since he did not have the right to rape Celia under the law. Yet Celia was convicted and executed in 1855, for the court maintained the slaveholder's right to his property, which included the right to perpetrate sexual violence. The law did not deem enslaved black women as women but as property, and so the legal system afforded them no protection.[115] Cases such as this underscore the horrible daily reality that Harriet Jacobs depicts in her own autobiography, a reality all too familiar for enslaved African American women.

Peter Randolph, in his autobiography, *Sketches of Slave Life*, notes the danger black women experienced when they did not submit to the slaveholders. Randolph describes L. Hobbs, an overseer, who "was very cruel to the people, especially to all women who would not submit to him. He used to bind women hand and foot, and whip them until the blood run down to the earth, and then wash them down in salt and water, and keep them tied all day. . . . He used to take my cousin, and tie her up and whip her so she could not lie down to rest at night until her back got well. All this was done

114. Jacobs, *Incidents*, 2:560.
115. See discussion of this case in Evelyn Brooks Higginbotham, "African-American Women's History and the Metalanguage of Race," in *"We Specialize in the Wholly Impossible": A Reader in Black Women's History*, ed. Darlene Clark Hine, Wilma King, and Linda Reed (Brooklyn, NY: Carlson Publishing, 1995), 7; Cooper, *Maria Stewart*, 117–18.

on Edloe's plantation, the good slaveholder who owned me; and the other slaveholders used to say to him that he 'spoiled his [n——];'—but this was the way he spoiled them."[116] Randolph, sarcastically calling the enslaver "the good slaveholder," paints a disturbing picture of life on the plantation for black women. He captures the cruel reality of slavery for African American women, including the atmosphere of powerlessness that permeated their situation. In her own narrative, Jacobs depicts this powerlessness firsthand.

Jacobs's enslaver's words, that he rules her body and soul, represent the thoughts of white slaveholders in general, and she highlights the prevalence of this view and the sanction of it even by the church. She writes with biting sarcasm, "There is a great difference between Christianity and religion at the south. . . . If a pastor has offspring by a woman not his wife, the church dismiss him, if she is a white woman; but if she is colored, it does not hinder his continuing to be their good shepherd."[117] This hypocrisy displayed and permitted by the church enabled slaveholders to continue such practices without threat of reprisal from the church. As property, enslaved women had no recourse, not even in the community of faith. Due to such tolerance of these atrocities, Jacobs highlights the recognition by the enslaved that the church the slaveholders attend and to which the enslaved are sometimes allowed to go is not in reality God's church; they perceive satanic influence in the white man's church. Such recognition by the enslaved is their rejection of the common idea that blacks are devils and demonic in nature; the enslaved believed that slaveholders were under the influence of Satan, not them.

Jacobs's Pauline Critique of Sexual Violence

Into the various layers of her portrait of slavery's degradations Jacobs inserts the words of Paul in Acts 17:26, which, as discussed above, is an important text for many black hermeneuts. Jacobs writes that when Northerners move to the South and become slaveholders, "They seem to satisfy their consciences with the doctrine that God created the Africans to be slaves. What a libel upon the heavenly Father, *who 'made of one blood all nations of*

---

116. Peter Randolph, *Sketches of Slave Life: or, Illustrations of The "Peculiar Institution"* (Boston: Published for the author, 1855), 54. Randolph, *"Sketches of Slave Life" and "From Slave Cabin to the Pulpit,"* ed. Katherine Clay Bassard (Morgantown: West Virginia University Press, 2016), 54.

117. Jacobs, *Incidents*, 2:592.

men!' And then who are Africans? Who can measure the amount of Anglo-Saxon blood coursing in the veins of American slaves?"[118] Jacobs attests to the prevalent belief that blacks were created to be slaves and proclaims how this belief slanders God, who made humanity of one blood. The oneness of blood highlighted in this Pauline text, also known as the one-blood doctrine, rejects the idea of black inferiority and the resulting justified captivity of blacks.[119] Accordingly, it renounces the treatment black women receive under slavery and the corresponding belief system that justifies such treatment. If God has made all one blood, then Africans are not animals or inhuman but have the same status as whites and are human beings made in the image of God.

Yet, significantly, in her narrative, Jacobs adds another interpretative layer to this Pauline citation that other hermeneuts, such as Zilpha Elaw, Lemuel Haynes, and Daniel Payne, do not mention. Because of what she endures as an enslaved woman at the hand of her enslaver and because of what she sees other enslaved women endure, she asks, "Who are Africans? Who can measure the amount of Anglo-Saxon blood coursing in the veins of American slaves?" Paul's words in Acts 17:26 become a way for Jacobs to wage a two-pronged attack upon the belief that Africans were created for slavery. First, the apostle's declaration provides scriptural evidence that blacks and whites are one, and so are equal in nature and status. His words form a basis to reject the myth that blacks are not human like whites.

And second, at the same time, Jacobs, in citing Paul in this particular place in her narrative, also identifies a perverse inversion of Acts 17:26, that is, the actions of white men who through rape and sexual violence mingle their blood with that of African women. Jacobs's queries, then, become a stinging critique of white enslavers' behavior and simultaneously an ironic recognition that the sexually predatory behaviors of slaveholders, which have resulted in children of mixed races, literally have made one blood between Africans and Anglo-Saxons. Although God has already made humanity one blood, slaveholders do the same, but in a perverse manner. Jacobs's use of Pauline Scripture at this point is ingenious. The apostle's words refute the notion of blacks as created slaves because of the one-blood doctrine. Con-

---

118. Jacobs, *Incidents*, 2:571.

119. Allen Callahan, *The Talking Book: African Americans and the Bible* (New Haven: Yale University Press, 2006), 115–16; Powery, "Rise Up," 176; Demetrius Williams, "The Acts of the Apostles," in *True to Our Native Land: An African American New Testament Commentary*, ed. Brian Blount et al. (Minneapolis: Fortress, 2007), 236–38.

comitantly, since slavery produces mixed children, one can no longer argue that Africans are created slaves since many Africans now have white blood coursing through their veins. Jacobs's use of this Pauline passage serves as a basis to reject slave ideology *and* to critique derisively slaveholders' sexually predatory behavior. Their behavior is an additional libel upon the heavenly Father, because he has already made humanity one blood, but through sexual violence the slave owners perpetrate a heinous usurpation of the Divine's unity of humanity.

Paul's words also appear in Jacobs's description of a church service she attends. She writes of a minister, Rev. Pike, preaching to the slaves the apostle's words in Ephesians 6:5, that they should obey their masters as unto Christ.[120] He tells the slaves that God sees them and hears them, and that if they disobey their earthly master, they offend their heavenly master. After hearing him preach a second time, in which he took the same text and sermon topic, Jacobs determines that she "had heard the Reverend Pike for the last time" and therefore did not go to hear "sanctimonious Mr. Pike" after that.[121]

Through assistance from family and friends, Jacobs eventually escapes slavery after hiding from her enslaver for about seven years in a hole "almost deprived of light and air, and with no space to move [her] limbs."[122] The physical effects of this extended period in hiding affected her for the rest of her life, but after many years and heartaches, including being continually hunted by her former enslaver once she escaped to the North, she eventually gains freedom for herself, her children, and her brother. She becomes an antislavery activist and during the Civil War returns to the South to help black refugees and to report to the Northern press the stories of black refugees' realities.[123]

Remarkably, Jacobs is able to distinguish between the Paul proclaimed by Rev. Pike and the Paul of Acts 17:26. For her the Christianity of the Bible and that practiced in the South were mutually exclusive. Due to her use of the Bible throughout her narrative, Emerson Powery calls Jacobs "a fore-

120. Jacobs, *Incidents*, 2:587. See the discussion of similar sermons to slaves in previous chapters.

121. Jacobs, *Incidents*, 2:588.

122. Jacobs, *Incidents*, 2:640.

123. Yellin, *Harriet Jacobs*, xv, 3. See also Jean Fagan Yellin, "Harriet Jacobs in the Refugee Camps," in *Race, Slavery, and the Civil War: The Tough Stuff of American History and Memory*, ed. James O. Horton and Amanda Kleintop (Richmond: Virginia Sesquicentennial of the American Civil War Commission, 2011), 92–98.

runner of black hermeneutics" and "an early proto-Womanist interpreter."[124] For Jacobs, the one-blood doctrine trumped the "Slaves, obey your masters" text because she instinctively knew the Bible could not and did not sanction the atrocities presently taking place. Throughout her autobiography Jacobs repeatedly calls slavery a demon and her master a devil, illustrating her recognition of the true source of this "peculiar institution."

Jacobs eloquently writes about the difficult details of her life, and in one of her many insightful passages she describes slavery's effect upon all involved.

> I can testify from my own experience and observation that slavery is a curse to the whites as well as to the blacks. It makes the white fathers cruel and sensual; the sons violent and licentious; it contaminates the daughters, and makes the wives wretched. And as for the colored race, it needs an abler pen than mine to describe the extremity of their sufferings, the depth of their degradation. . . . If you want to be fully convinced of the abominations of slavery, go on a southern plantation, and call yourself a negro trader. Then there will be no concealment; and you will see and hear things that will seem to you impossible among human beings with immortal souls.[125]

Jacobs's depiction of slavery and its devastating effects upon both blacks and whites coheres with her designation of slavery as a demon and exemplifies its insidious touch upon all that live in its clutches. Her autobiography provides a firsthand account of the painful realities of African American women in the grip of American slavocracy.

Using Paul to Challenge the Status Quo

The black interpreters explored in this chapter utilize Paul and his letters in numerous ways. Maria Stewart adopts Pauline imperatives to affirm black agency and power over their own lives and over their own destiny. Stewart refuses to allow society's verdict over black life to stand and take precedence, but calls upon the apostle to assist her in articulating the possibility of black uplift. Similarly, the apostle becomes instrumental in depicting the importance of a life of purity and spiritual renewal, a life that follows God

124. Powery, "Rise Up," 181.
125. Jacobs, *Incidents*, 2:576.

completely. Because of such lives, African Americans could be assured that the God of knowledge would supply them with insight and wisdom in the midst of a society that deemed them inferior. In addition, Stewart employs Paul's warfare imagery to depict herself in battle, fighting for the equality of her people, including African American women. In fact, she takes on the passage of Paul silencing women and argues that if Paul knew how women were suffering in slavery, he himself would support women's rights. In this exegetical move, Stewart implicitly understands the apostle's words of silence as contextually oriented and that, in her context, the apostle would advocate *for* women and not against women. Furthermore, she uses the apostle's words to critique America's propensity to send aid abroad while neglecting the African Americans within its own borders.

James Pennington takes up Paul's words to speak about systemic evil, thereby broadening the understanding of Romans 7:21 as not just about personal sin or sin within the self but also denoting systems of evil outside of the self that oppress and dehumanize. In his use of Paul, Pennington argues against the common notions during this time that black bodies were evil but rather contends that the systems of slavery and racism were evil. Moreover, Pennington maintains that the Pauline gospel is antisin and, since slavery is sin, the gospel is also antislavery. Pennington believes that just as repentance, reconciliation, and judgment form a tridimensional nexus for Paul, this tridimensional nexus also applies to Pennington's current context. Judgment will come upon his former slaveholder and all of America unless repentance takes place. Only when repentance comes forth can reconciliation be a reality.

Pennington also echoes the Pauline Scripture of Romans 8:28: "And we know that all things work together for good to them that love God, to them who are the called according to his purpose" in order to make a marked distinction between divine use and divine approval. Slavery, Pennington contends, is not approved by God but derives from Satan and is practiced by wicked people. Pennington argues that if any good comes from the slave trade, it is a good that God could have achieved in another way. The claim that slavery is beneficial is an erroneous notion to Pennington, as it was to so many of his black contemporaries. God's character does not sanction enslaving people to give them the gospel, and to say otherwise is to misrepresent the nature of God.

Similar to Stewart, Daniel Payne utilizes Paul to describe conversion and to advocate for living holy, clean lives before God and the world. Living according to Pauline admonitions is central to what it means to follow a Christian way of life. The apostle's words regarding one humanity and God's unification of all the races in Christ are also important for Payne. Likewise, the apostle's admonitions to pray for the government are for Payne essential to African Americans' duty toward the nation. Through prayer they can ask God to guide the government during and after the Civil War in creating just laws that do not discriminate or oppress. For Payne prayer is a form of resistance. At the same time, Payne asserts that, along with prayer, the nation must do right by the weak and powerless within its borders, in order to incur God's blessings. These blessings are not automatically a result of prayer, but the government must also act in godly ways toward those in need.

Julia Foote employs Paul to speak of Christian perfection, complete sanctification of body, mind, and soul.[126] She believes that Christians can live pure, holy lives in which sin no longer has dominion or power over the individual. The apostle's language of crucifixion is important to her because it denotes a death to the old self and the resurrection of a new self through faith in Christ. Like Stewart, who spoke out on behalf of the equality of women, Foote enlists Paul in the fight for women preachers. Since Paul wrote Galatians 3:28, which says there is neither male nor female, and since he uses similar terms to denote women in ministry, Paul cannot be used to prohibit women ministers. If interpreters use Paul to disallow women preachers, Foote argues, his words are not being used correctly. Moreover, the divine bestowal in a vision from God of instruments of pen, paper, and ink directly contradicts the prevailing norms of society in which blacks were consistently denied education and access to information. This vision, in which God grants Foote divine authorization for her ministry, simultaneously undercuts any notion of black inferiority, for she is given all the tools needed to carry out her God-given mandate.

Likewise, the body hermeneutic, which we saw in chapter 1, appears again in Foote's vision of her baptism, in which Christ washes her with warm water that looks like silver. This body hermeneutic is an oppositional hermeneutic and a power move where blacks insist that the authority to determine their bodily status does not belong to whites but to God. Foote's baptismal

---

126. Borrowing the language of William Andrews's designation of Zilpha Elaw, Jarena Lee, and Julia Foote as "Sisters in the Spirit," Sue E. Houchins, introduction to *Spiritual Narratives* (New York: Oxford University Press, 1988), writes that "the piety of all of the sisters of the spirit (medieval and revivalist) was not only Pentecostal but also 'Christocentric, a theology of love that found its supreme expression in the incarnation'" (xxxv). Houchins's comments touch upon the fact that the Spirit plays an important role in these women's narratives. In a sense, then, they could be designated as proto-Pentecostal. Houchins also links these black female autobiographies with "the first philosophical black writer: Saint Augustine" and other mystic writers such as Julian of Norwich and Teresa of Ávila (xxxi).

cleansing signifies the importance of her female body and the importance of her black body. In a time when black bodies were devalued, especially black female bodies, the washing of her body by Christ and the robe with which the Father clothes her after her baptism highlight African American significance. Paul's emphasis on baptism that appears throughout his letters becomes a means for Foote to denote the value of black bodies in general, and African American female bodies in particular.

The focus on the value of black bodies comes to the forefront again in Harriet Jacobs's autobiography, in which she lays out for the reader the daily degradations enslaved African American women faced. Their bodies, considered property, had no protection from the slaveholder's sexual oppression and violence. Jacobs takes a prevalent passage found in black writings, Acts 17:26, and uses it as a stinging critique of the sexual abuse black women experienced under slavery. The blood coursing through the veins of black people is already, by God's design, the same as that found in their white counterparts, but white slaveholders were making humanity "of one blood" in a perverse way by raping and impregnating enslaved African women. Jacobs takes a Pauline passage often used in a positive way to depict one humanity and uses it to censure slaveholders' illicit behavior.

Sue E. Houchins observes that one of the aims of black autobiography was to enter into dialogue with those who believed that African Americans had no souls and who doubted the possibility of their redemption.[127] All these narratives, as well as the ones in the previous chapter, take on such beliefs and demonstrate their absurdity. These autobiographies indicate that not only do blacks have souls but they experience real divine encounters that transform their lives and cause them to advocate for a corresponding transformation of their society, their communities, and their nation. Pauline language is central to their formulations of these experiences and to their call for justice and equality. Accordingly, the apostle's words are also central to the denouncement of sexual violence perpetrated upon enslaved African American women. The black tradition of enlisting Paul in the struggle for justice and in order to resist and protest dehumanization continues in the work of these black hermeneuts. As will be seen in the next chapter, the twentieth century brings on new challenges for African Americans, but Paul continues to be used primarily by them in subversive ways. Yet we will also encounter some black rejection of Paul in this next chapter, a stance heretofore not demonstrated by black interpreters.

127. Houchins, introduction to *Spiritual Narratives*, xxix.

CHAPTER 3

Late Nineteenth Century
to Mid-Twentieth Century

"O Prejudice! thou cruel monster! wilt thou ever cease to exist?"[1]

At the close of the nineteenth century and the beginning of the twentieth, African Americans experienced grave losses of the civil and political rights gained after the Civil War and the Reconstruction period. The Compromise of 1877, in which the Republican Party agreed to remove the last federal troops from the South, troops whose job was to protect the rights of the freed slaves, especially their voting rights, became a harbinger of further withdrawals of the government in regard to protecting the newly won rights of African Americans.[2] As Jacquelyn Grant writes of this time, "For many Black people, emancipation meant slavery without chains."[3] By the late 1890s and first decade of the new century, blacks had virtually lost the right to vote because of numerous regulations imposed upon voting such as the poll tax, literacy tests, and the grandfather clause.[4]

Furthermore, several important Supreme Court decisions served to reverse and annihilate any political or social gains African Americans had made. In 1883 the Court invalidated the Civil Rights Act of 1875, and in 1896 its

1. Julia Foote, *A Brand Plucked from the Fire: An Autobiographical Sketch by Mrs. Julia A. J. Foote* (Cleveland, OH: Printed for the author by W. F. Schneider, 1879), reprinted in *Sisters of the Spirit: Three Black Women's Autobiographies of the Nineteenth Century*, ed. William Andrews (Bloomington: Indiana University Press, 1986), 218.

2. Calvin S. Morris, *Reverdy C. Ransom: Black Advocate of the Social Gospel* (Lanham, MD: University Press of America, 1990), 130.

3. Jacquelyn Grant, *White Women's Christ and Black Women's Jesus: Feminist Christology and Womanist Response* (Atlanta: Scholars Press, 1989), 197.

4. Morris, *Reverdy C. Ransom*, 130.

separate but equal ruling in the *Plessy v. Ferguson* case condoned segregation legally. At the dawn of the twentieth century, then, African Americans "found themselves abandoned by former friends and allies and subject to segregation, intimidation and violence. Lynching was commonplace in the South and anti-black riots occurred in cities throughout the country."[5] Under Woodrow Wilson's administration, segregation in the federal government started by President Taft continued and became the norm. Blacks in the government were segregated, including in areas such as offices, restrooms, and restaurants. In addition, voting rights in the South were destroyed under Wilson's administration, and African Americans experienced total disenfranchisement.[6] The Taft and Wilson administrations gave in to Southern pressure and facilitated the advancement of segregation legislation.[7] The Civil War and its aftermath ruptured the South economically, politically, and socially, and African Americans became the "scapegoat" for the white community.[8] Anthony Pinn observes how this reality affected Southern whites: "Even destitute white Americans could compare themselves to the 'scapegoat' community (even middle-class blacks) and perceive the advantages resulting from whiteness. If not politically and economically, these poor white Americans were psychologically comforted by their 'status' in the 'New' South."[9]

This "new South" prohibited black participation in civic and commercial life by implementing separation in schools, parks, buses, restaurants, clubs, and taxis. Ordinances were enacted that restricted African Americans to "negro blocks" and prohibited them from walking through white neighborhoods unless they worked for one of the residents. In addition, such laws often required blacks to live in poor housing owned by white landlords who often took advantage of them without fear of reprisal.[10] This new South was really the old South dressed in Jim Crow garb, in which the plantation mentality still governed racial existence and racial interactions.

Along with these realities, economic hardships added additional tensions. Due to the abandonment of Reconstruction, segregation, and the de-

5. Morris, *Reverdy C. Ransom*, 130.

6. Morris, *Reverdy C. Ransom*, 152.

7. *Making the Gospel Plain: The Writings of Bishop Reverdy C. Ransom*, ed. Anthony Pinn (Harrisburg, PA: Trinity Press International, 1999), 44. Hereafter, cited as Ransom, *Making the Gospel Plain*.

8. Ransom, *Making the Gospel Plain*, 44.

9. Ransom, *Making the Gospel Plain*, 44–45.

10. Herbert Marbury, *Pillars of Cloud and Fire: The Politics of Exodus in African American Biblical Interpretation* (New York: New York University Press, 2015), 139.

struction of the cotton crop by the boll weevil insect, many black families migrated to the North in what is known as the Great Migration, which took place from 1914 to 1930.[11] Blacks obtained employment in industrial jobs, but the number of people migrating to the North outnumbered the available jobs, and Northerners resented the presence of Southern blacks whom they believed took jobs away from them. Employer racism, housing discrimination, and the Great Depression formed a potent mixture that contributed to black exploitation and suffering.[12]

For those blacks who remained in the South, the sharecropping system replaced the plantation structure after the Civil War. African Americans worked under oppressive circumstances, with planters exacting astronomical interest rates on crops. The rules that bound these workers to the fields were, as Calvin White Jr. notes, another form of enslavement. To be sure, this system affected poor whites as well, but coupled with the existence of Jim Crow laws that further served to dehumanize African Americans, the sharecropping system became another way to reinforce the view of black subservience and to restrict their economic progress.[13]

Grant describes further the plight of African Americans postslavery, post–Civil War, and post-Reconstruction: "The end of slavery as a formal, legal institution brought neither change in the image of, nor significant change in the condition of Black people in the United States. The image that Blacks were inferior and that they were intended to service white America remained intact. Consequently, when freed blacks, sought work they were relegated in the labor market to the same service jobs and menial work which had been forced upon them during slavery."[14]

11. Jennifer T. Kaalund, *Reading Hebrews and 1 Peter with the African American Great Migration: Diaspora, Place, and Identity* (London: T&T Clark, 2019) 26; Ransom, *Making the Gospel Plain*, 45. See also Marbury, *Pillars*, 136–40.

12. Ransom, *Making the Gospel Plain*, 45. See also Marbury, *Pillars*, 136–40.

13. Calvin White Jr., *The Rise to Respectability: Race, Religion, and the Church of God in Christ* (Fayetteville: University of Arkansas Press, 2012), 12; James Brewer Stewart, "Abolitionists, the Bible, and the Challenge of Slavery," in *The Bible and Social Reform*, ed. Ernest Sandeen (Philadelphia: Fortress, 1982), writes of the failure of the abolitionist movement to ensure equality of freed slaves: "Emancipation came as a result of military necessity, not moral suasion, and throughout North and South long established patterns of white supremacy were to endure. Despite the best abolitionist efforts, the former slave was destined not to become an equal citizen but a segregated sharecropper, intimidated and coerced by vengeful whites. By the early 1870s, as abolitionism lost all coherence as a movement, whites in both sections found increasing areas of agreement concerning the subjugated position of the black race" (53).

14. Grant, *White Women's Christ*, 197.

Even while the injustices described by Grant existed, concerted efforts by white Americans to depict black inferiority intensified in American society through the release of a book called *Clansmen* by Thomas Dixon and the racist movie *Birth of a Nation* in 1915, based upon Dixon's book. Dixon depicts African Americans as animals and savages and continues the lies of black inhumanity promulgated during slavery. In addition, scientists argued for black inferiority based upon "studies" that claimed to reveal such inferiority due to biological and physiological differences. Thus, some circles within the academic community sanctioned views of black intellectual and physical subservience to whites.[15] The permeation of such ideas and beliefs made it easier for Southerners to engage in lynching, an ugly practice that became commonplace during this period. C. Eric Lincoln provides statistics on this horrendous practice:

> In the South the total abrogation of the black man's rights was symbolized by the common practice of the savage custom of lynching, and by the social acceptance of the practice as a desirable methodology for "keeping the [n——] in his place," and by the indisposition of any government, local, state, or federal, to do anything effective about it. In the last sixteen years of the nineteenth century, 2,500 human beings were sacrificed to the rope and faggot. Thereafter, from 1900 to the outbreak of World War I in 1914, the pace of the killing was more leisurely; an annual average of seventy-eight black men and women graced the magnolias, or popped and sputtered in the bonfires before the altar of white supremacy.[16]

The prevalence of lynching and the reemergence of the Ku Klux Klan during this period "served as a constant reminder of the expendability of black bodies and the pervasiveness of the danger living in America posed to African Americans."[17] The ubiquitous ideas of black inferiority and blacks as nonhumans along with beliefs of preserving the purity of the white race contributed to the custom of lynching and to the silence emanating from both Northerners and Southerners regarding the practice. In addition, the

---

15. Ransom, *Making the Gospel Plain*, 45.

16. C. Eric Lincoln, *Sounds of the Struggle: Persons and Perspectives in Civil Rights* (New York: Friendship, 1968), 229. Also quoted in William C. Turner Jr., *The United Holy Church of America: A Study in Black Holiness-Pentecostalism* (Piscataway, NJ: Gorgias, 2006), 8. See also James Cone, *The Cross and the Lynching Tree* (Maryknoll, NY: Orbis, 2011), who denotes 1880–1940 as the "lynching era" (3).

17. Kaalund, *Reading Hebrews*, 27.

racist views promoted by Dixon and others influenced the depictions of black men as hypersexualized rapists of white women and black women as loose and immoral people whose aims were to seduce white men.[18]

In light of the racist mores and conditions of the nineteenth century, a major concern of the black church was to remove the stigma of inferiority from black consciousness. Thus, the mission of the church was to impart the concept that individual worth was not ultimately promulgated by white society, but rather, given by God. The underlying premise for this belief was that God had not created blacks as inferior beings to the rest of creation.[19] As the nineteenth century closed and the twentieth began, the black church still needed to address the issue of inferiority and individual worth, but it also faced a myriad of problems, not least of which was dealing with the issues outlined above. The Great Migration meant that many Northern black churches needed to address the vast influx of African Americans from the South into their communities and congregations. As will be seen below, these issues weighed heavily upon Reverdy Ransom. Similarly, the institution and enforcement of Jim Crow laws meant that Southern black churches had to address the loss of civil rights gains and the legacy of slavery that appeared in segregationist attitudes and policies. The church was the center of African American life in public and private realms, for pastors were expected to speak to black spiritual life as well as to protest and challenge segregation. They were counted upon to use the pulpit to "better the race."[20]

While many black churches and pastors during this period continued the legacies of prophetic preaching and speaking out against racism and injustice bequeathed to the black church by people such as David Walker, Maria Stewart, Julia Foote, and James Pennington, some black churches "tended to turn inward and address spiritual issues."[21] It is possible that the tumultuous experiences of gaining freedom, gaining rights, and then having them taken away by Jim Crow laws contributed to this inward turn by some. However, black churches continued to thrive during this period, in spite of white supremacy, segregation, and other dehumanizing tactics, and part of this flourishing came from the pivotal place churches occupied in black life. The church was the place black people came to receive education and to

18. Ransom, *Making the Gospel Plain*, 45–46.
19. Morris, *Reverdy C. Ransom*, 74, citing Timothy L. Smith, "Slavery and Theology: The Emergence of Black Christian Consciousness in Nineteenth Century America," *Church History* 41 (December 1972): 504.
20. White, *The Rise to Respectability*, 14.
21. Ransom, *Making the Gospel Plain*, 48.

learn to read. It was also the place that recognized and acknowledged their humanity and worth. Moreover, it was where blacks encountered a God who loved them and sustained them, providing them with a hope and peace that, unlike legislation, could not be revoked or vetoed. It was also the place where they could interpret Scriptures for themselves, seizing hermeneutical control of the Bible and denying white supremacist interpretations.

As will be seen, Paul continues to play a major role in black scriptural interpretation during this period. This chapter will focus on Reverdy Ransom, William Seymour, Charles Harrison Mason, Ida B. Robinson, and Martin Luther King Jr., all of whom use Paul in revolutionary ways. This chapter will also discuss Howard Thurman and Albert Cleage, two prominent African American theologians and preachers whose rejection of Paul derives from the slaveholders' use of the apostle. Thurman and Cleage believed that Jesus and Jesus's teachings trump Paul. All these interpreters and their use or nonuse of Paul provide important glimpses into the ongoing struggle of blacks in America's racialized environment with its "twentieth-century incarnations."[22]

Reverdy Ransom (1861–1959): "Inspirer of Men and Movements"

Reverdy Cassius Ransom, born in Flushing, Ohio, in 1861, was a graduate of Wilberforce University and was called an "inspirer of men and movements."[23] Ransom was an African Methodist Episcopal pastor who led congregations in Ohio, Pennsylvania, Illinois, Massachusetts, and New York. In 1912 he became the editor of the *A.M.E. Review*, and in 1924 he became bishop in the AME Church, although he "had no strong aspiration, or desire to become a Bishop."[24] He was a social political activist who inaugurated the idea of an Institutional Church and Social Settlement House in Chicago, which he modeled after Jane Addams's Hull House and Richard Wright Jr.'s reformulated social gospel principles.[25] He implemented the Institutional

22. Ransom, *Making the Gospel Plain*, 48.

23. A phrase used to describe him by President R. R. Wright of Wilberforce University. See the preface of Ransom's book *The Negro: The Hope or the Despair of Christianity* (Boston: Ruth Hill, 1935).

24. Bishop Reverdy C. Ransom, *The Pilgrimage of Harriet Ransom's Son* (Nashville: Sunday School Union, 1949), 261. See also Milton C. Sernett, *African American Religious History: A Documentary Witness* (Durham, NC: Duke University Press, 1999), 337–46.

25. Kenyatta Gilbert, *A Pursued Justice: Black Preaching from the Great Migration to Civil Rights* (Waco, TX: Baylor University Press, 2017), 43.

Church and Social Settlement House during his time in Chicago, but the seeds for it were planted early on in his ministry.

He describes the conditions of blacks during an early pastorate in Pittsburgh. "There were hundreds of my people there [North Pittsburgh], living in wretched tenements in the alleys, and in shanty boats along the river front."[26] He goes on to say, "My first vision of the need of social service came to me as my wife and I almost daily, went through the alleys and climbed the dark stairways of the wretched tenements, or walked out on the planks to the shanty boats where our people lived on the river. My wife gathered a considerable Sunday School from these sources. We were also able to turn many to aspire in changing their material condition as well as in things of the spirit."[27] The conditions and needs he recognized in Pittsburgh among African Americans played a role in his pastorate in Chicago, albeit in a somewhat different form. When Ransom first moved to Chicago to pastor Bethel Church, he noticed that the congregation was filled every Sunday.

> I preached to standing room, morning and evening the entire time I remained at Bethel. I flattered myself that the crowds of people were drawn hither by my preaching but chief contributing cause was not my preaching but the fact that Chicago's filling up with Negroes from the South, brought there to work chiefly at the stock-yards and other industrial establishments. The number of these people increased so rapidly that the colored clergymen of the city were bewildered. They were unprepared by training, experience and vision, to cope with the moral, social and economic conditions so suddenly thrust upon them. I soon realized that the old stereotype form of church services practiced in all Negro churches fell far short of meeting the religious, moral, and social conditions that confronted them.[28]

To meet the growing needs of the congregation, Ransom spearheaded the development of the Men's Sunday Club, which was the "first organization of the kind under the patronage of a Negro church." Although primarily for men, women could also attend its monthly meetings, and it "drew no lines in regard to religion or church affiliation. All were welcome who were willing to join us to whom our moral, social, and cultural objectives appealed. The very best men and women that Chicago had to offer in the lines of religion, social,

---

26. Ransom, *Harriet Ransom's Son*, 47.
27. Ransom, *Harriet Ransom's Son*, 49.
28. Ransom, *Harriet Ransom's Son*, 82.

industrial, intellectual and business lines were drawn upon from Sunday to Sunday."[29] The Men's Sunday Club provides a glimpse into what Ransom did later as the tremendous need for churches to provide services continued. He left Bethel AME Church to create the Chicago Institutional and Social Settlement Church, which was revolutionary for its time by offering a nursery; a kindergarten; cooking and sewing classes; an employment agency; manual training classes; a boys' and girls' club; a gym; a Men's Forum, which discussed educational, industrial, and philosophical topics; and a Women's Club, in which papers written by its members were read and discussed along with news from around the world. In addition, the church supplied food, clothes, and assistance to those in need, both black and white. It also stressed and provided the opportunity for black girls to read, study, and discuss black literature. Alongside such social services, the church also offered religious activities: sermons, prayers, and praise songs.[30] The Institutional Church faced great opposition, however; it faced accusations that it "was not really a church."[31] Eventually Ransom left the Institutional Church and went to pastor churches elsewhere, but the Institutional Church in Chicago stands as an important monument to his belief that black pastors and the black church ought to be about "political and social justice."[32]

"The Race Problem in a Christian State"

As subversive and revolutionary as his approach to the possibilities and programs of the black church were for his time, so also were Ransom's utilization of Pauline texts in two addresses, "The Race Problem in a Christian

---

29. Ransom, *Harriet Ransom's Son*, 83.

30. Ransom, *Harriet Ransom's Son*, 105–10. Gilbert, *A Pursued Justice*, 43. A number of scholars note the impact of the Social Gospel movement upon Ransom. Gilbert states that Ransom was an example of how "in the hands of certain Black preachers, the Social Gospel was refashioned to become something of a tertium quid [a third something]" (42). In other words, Ransom may have been influenced by the Social Gospel but in the end converted it into a theological and social approach that met the social, spiritual, moral, and industrial needs of African Americans. See Gilbert's discussion, *A Pursued Justice*, 39–45; Susan Lindley, "'Neglected Voices' and Praxis in the Social Gospel," *Journal of Religious Ethics* 18, no. 1 (1990): 75–102; Ralph Luker, *The Social Gospel in Black and White: American Racial Reform, 1885–1912* (Chapel Hill: University of North Carolina Press, 1991); Ransom, *Making the Gospel Plain*, 49–56.

31. Ransom, *Harriet Ransom's Son*, 112.

32. Ransom, *Harriet Ransom's Son*, 85.

State" and "The Negro, the Hope or the Despair of Christianity." Ransom begins the former essay with a depiction of Pentecost, where people from all backgrounds and nationalities were filled with the Holy Spirit. He moves from the opening chapters of Acts to Acts 17:26, where Paul, he says, stands upon Areopagus and declares to the Athenians, "[*God*] *hath made of one blood all nations of men for to dwell on all the face of the earth.*"[33] For Ransom, this declaration by Paul coheres with the teachings of Jesus, the originator of Christianity, who started the religion in the "midst of the most bitter and intense antagonisms of race and class. Yet he ignored them all, dealing alike with Jew, Samaritan, Syro-Phoenician, Greek and Roman" (64). For Ransom, Jews become the ideal race, for "God, through the Jew, was educating the world, and laying a moral and spiritual foundation. The foundation was the establishment of the one God idea" (65). The monotheistic faith of the Jews revealed not only that there was one God but also that there was one humanity. Jesus built upon this foundation the "super-structure of the Fatherhood of God and its corollary, the brotherhood of man." Echoing the language of Ephesians 2:14–15, Ransom writes next, "The crowning object at which Jesus Christ aimed was to *break down the middle wall of partition, between man and man, and to take away all the Old Testament laws and ordinances that prevented Jew and Gentile from approaching God on an equal plane. And this he did, 'that He might reconcile both unto God in one body by the cross, having slain the enmity thereby, so making peace'* " (65). According to Ransom, the "one God idea" that was the heart of the Jewish faith in Scripture manifests itself completely in Jesus, who is able to abolish totally the divisions between Jews and gentiles; Jesus makes both groups equal before God.

For Ransom, this elimination of divisions between Jews and gentiles becomes the living paradigm for eradication of divisions between blacks and whites in America. As Paul answered the Macedonians' cry for help in Acts 16:9–12, America needs to answer the call of living up to its self-proclaimed name of a "Christian nation" (66).[34] America needs to hear the cries for help from its black citizens. To do this, America must address what Ransom calls "the Race Problem," for if the nation is to follow Christianity properly, it can-

33. Reverdy Ransom, "The Race Problem in a Christian State," in *The Negro: The Hope or the Despair of Christianity* (Boston: Ruth Hill, 1935), 64. Hereafter, page references from this work will be given in parentheses in the text.

34. Acts 16:9: "And a vision appeared to Paul in the night; There stood a man of Macedonia, and prayed him, saying, Come over into Macedonia, and help us."

not avoid the race issue.[35] He declares, "American Christianity will un-Christ itself if it refuses to strive on, until this Race Problem is not only settled, but settled right; and until this is done, however much men may temporize and seek to compromise, and cry 'peace! peace!' there will be no peace until this is done" (66). Since Ransom gives this address in the early 1900s, addressing the race problem "right" entails a number of issues that relate to the topics of his day, which include providing job training and opportunities for blacks, and not just training in farming and working as domestics. They should be trained as bankers, manufacturers, and business owners. The following quote sums up Ransom's view on the topic of equal opportunity:

> This nation is not rich enough in trained minds, skilled hands and cultured brains to put a discount upon the ability and aspiration of any class of its citizens, nor will it act in the *spirit of Christ* [Rom. 8:9; cf. Phil. 1:19] toward the black toilers of this land, until Negroes are as freely permitted to run locomotive engines as they are elevators; to work in a national bank, as they are a coal bank; to sell dry goods over the counters of the store as they are to wash them in the laundry; to work in a cotton mill, as they are in a cotton field . . . this and nothing less than this, is the justice which a Christian nation should be willing to give. . . . It would add to the nation's strength by making so many more millions of her citizens prosperous; by permitting them to contribute to the upbuilding of the nation along with all the lines of its defense, protection, development, and growth. (70–71)

Ransom contends that African Americans should have the same job opportunities as their white counterparts, and if they do, the nation itself would benefit from a stronger economy and a stronger workforce. Citing Romans 8:9, Ransom demonstrates how the nation is to act in the *"spirit of Christ"* by providing equal employment. In Romans 8:9 Paul writes that *"if any man have not the Spirit of Christ, he is none of his."* Thus, Ransom provides another basis for how America will "un-Christ itself," for if it does not treat its black citizens fairly, then it demonstrates that it really is not a Christian nation but a nation devoid of the spirit of Christ. In his use of this Pauline text, Ransom brings together the Spirit and the economical realm, thereby declaring an intricate connection between the two.

Along with advocating for equal job opportunities, Ransom decries the disenfranchisement of blacks in which they are denied the right to vote and

35. Ransom, *Making the Gospel Plain*, 51.

are told to give it up and to forget getting involved in politics. The South's suppression of the Negro vote is an egregious offense to Ransom, and he urges the "true supporters of the Christian State" to "resist in the name of God and of human liberty" (74). Working for equality was to Ransom a divine work of God with which believers participate, because in doing so they bear witness to a God who creates all people in the divine image and desires justice for every human being.

The last two issues that Ransom addresses in this speech are the brutalization and murder of African American people and the segregation sweeping the South. Ransom discusses the "rationale" given for black murder, that it is "justified by the plea that it is necessary in order to protect the homes of white men and the chastity of their women. The highest ambition of the Negro, it is claimed, is to achieve social equality with the whites, therefore, he may be beaten, hung, shot, and burned at the stake, in the name of the preservation of social purity" (74–75).[36] Ransom points out America's hypocrisy in that it projects to the world a nation that sympathizes with the oppressed in other lands, even granting asylum to those who flee persecution in their home countries. Yet within its own borders,

a Negro may be beaten with more brutality than one would dare treat a horse or even a dog, for an alleged crime against a white person, and in many instances no crime at all. He may be tortured and put to death with all the shocking horrors of savage ferocity. These things are done within the borders of this nation and have become so common that if the public conscience is not dead, it is at least asleep for the time. The perpetrators of mob violence have ceased to mask themselves, not even shielding themselves with the veil of darkness. They stalk abroad in the open light of day, quite frequently that Day, the holy Sabbath. It is made a gala day, the railroads run excursions to the scene of burning at the stake, children, reared in our Sunday Schools and Christian homes are witnesses to these scenes, while men contend with each other for ghastly trophies of the incinerated bodies of the victims. Against all these there is no united voice of protest from the American pulpit. (75–76)

In this quote Ransom refers to the common practice of lynching African American people, which had become during this period a "festive" event on Sundays. Parishioners would gather outside and have picnics as

36. See the statistics on lynching earlier in this chapter.

they watched black bodies being tortured, hung, and burned. It was considered a family event, as parents and children took in these scenes on Sunday afternoons. Afterward people would vie for "souvenirs," which consisted of something from the victim, so that they might have an item to commemorate the event.[37]

The lack of outcry from the pulpit against these murderous practices as well as the silence of the president, the Congress, and the press cause Ransom to ask if this Christian nation has simply acquiesced to such behavior as normal. In addition to this vicious violence experienced by African Americans, Ransom highlights the crime of segregation, which further inflicts African American bodies, minds, souls, and spirits. He describes this as another way for the "public sentiment of this nation to humiliate and to degrade the Negro" (76). Ransom characterizes the broad reach of the segregation arm, for it extends to every area and facet of societal life. "[The Negro] has been rigorously segregated by being generally refused admission to places of public resort, entertainment and amusement, and upon equal terms upon the common carriers. In the South upon the railroads he is forced to ride in a separate car, with inferior accommodations, though paying first-class fare; forced to ride there no matter what his education, wealth, character or culture. He is excluded from parks, libraries, museums, and even Young Men's Christian Associations. If this be *the spirit of Jesus* [Phil. 1:19], then give us Mohammed or any other redeemer!" (76).

The reality of segregation demonstrated that the spirit of Jesus was not operating in these policies and that the Christianity of this nation was potentially "un-Christing" itself. The solution for Ransom was the one God idea with which he began his address. He writes, "As God is above man, so man is above race" (77). God's transcendence of humanity becomes the basis for humanity's ability to reject racism in all its forms. God creates human beings above the divisive tendencies around race and in Christ destroys the divisions that human beings erect. Ransom wants his audience to know that every human being is connected to every other human being, whether or not he or she realizes it. "The white millions of this nation can never lift themselves up in Christianity and civilization by beating back and trampling under foot the simple rights and aspirations of ten million blacks" (76). Ransom knew that true Christianity was not about the suppression and oppression of one group at the expense of another, for this was not God's design for humanity and not what Christ's death accomplished. Returning

---

37. See Cone, *The Cross and the Lynching Tree*, 9.

to Pauline language (Eph. 2:14), Ransom writes, "There is nothing to fear by forever demolishing every wall, religious, political, industrial, social, that separates man from his brotherman" (77). Ransom expands Paul's idea of the demolition of the wall between Jews and gentiles to include every religious, political, industrial, and social division. The gospel is not about destroying divisions only between races but also any other division that arises from human identity markers, which serve to separate and disconnect people from the common bond of humanity in each other. Just as God taught the world the one God idea through the Jewish race, God will use both white and black to teach the world about the unity of humanity, for they will become "school masters of all the world, teaching by example the doctrines of the brotherhood of man" (77).

"The Negro, the Hope or the Despair of Christianity"

Ransom also incorporates Pauline language at important junctures in his speech "The Negro, the Hope or the Despair of Christianity."[38] Ransom begins the speech with recognition that the world itself is changing, economically, religiously, and socially. Yet he avers that although change is rampant, fundamental and basic truths remain throughout time.[39] Christianity, he declares, bases its authority upon Jesus's teachings and the writings of the New Testament, and he argues that America's democracy itself finds its basis in the teachings of Jesus. Jesus teaches that "God is the father of all mankind; all people of every race are brothers and sisters, and are therefore equals" (2). Jesus's teaching emphasizes love of God and love of neighbor, and so characterizes the heart of the gospel. Ransom interprets America as the new Babel, and the human race that was scattered long ago across the earth has now met again on American soil, offering all people a "common meeting place." At this "common meeting place," "representatives of every family of the human race here under one flag, speaking one language, dominated by a common religious faith," ought to be able to live out the brotherhood that Jesus taught. If they cannot do so, then the "case for Christianity

---

38. Ransom gave this speech at the World Fellowship of Faiths (Second Parliament of Religions) in Chicago in 1933.

39. Reverdy Ransom, "The Negro, the Hope or the Despair of Christianity," in *The Negro: The Hope or the Despair of Christianity*, 1. Hereafter, page references from this work will be given in parentheses in the text.

is hopeless" (3). For Ransom, Christianity, because of its basis in love, has the power to unite all people across ethnic, social, and economic divides. In fact, Ransom believes that such divisions disappear if and when the gospel is preached correctly and embraced completely.

Ransom moves on to discuss Epicureanism and Stoicism, which existed during the time of early Christianity, and he argues that these philosophies, although offering valuable insights into the world and the human condition, were nevertheless focused on individual existence. They "failed to give a concrete program for the realization of practical social values" (4). The Christian faith, however, offers such a program and thereby addresses the failure of these philosophies. "Under the teachings of the Christian faith all followers of Jesus are committed to a concrete program of social salvation growing out of their relationship to God through Jesus Christ. While the *weapons of its warfare are not carnal* [2 Cor. 10:4], the Christian faith has its arsenal filled with an inexhaustible store of moral and *spiritual weapons* [2 Cor. 10:4; Eph. 6:13-18]. The cross of Christ is the symbol under which it goes forth in the way of life taught by Jesus, for the reconstruction of society by moral and spiritual conquest" (4). The Christian faith, in Ransom's view, integrally links the individual and the social. Out of one's personal relationship to God through Christ comes the person's new relationship to the social sphere. In other words, a person's individual experience of salvation will have societal implications, which include the changing of power structures and systems that do not embrace Jesus's love ethic and ethic of equality. For Ransom, salvation is not just about saving the individual but is also about liberating the social—the community, the society, the nation—for society suffers from contamination of social sin such as prejudice and oppression.

Moreover, Paul's emphasis on the cross as the center of the gospel becomes for Ransom the basis for the reconstruction of society, that is, the concrete program of social salvation. The cross enables transformation of society, morally and spiritually. In another essay, entitled "The Coming Vision," Ransom again emphasizes the cross as the place of unity and brotherhood, stating so eloquently:

> But our highest goal is not a unified church, but a unified humanity in the bonds of brotherhood. The wise men from the East were guided by a star, but wiser men of our unfolding, coming from the four corners of the earth, are guided by a higher vision. They seek not a manger but a cross where all men stand with equal footing on common ground. It is the final stand of humanity's last retreat. All other meeting places have failed. For all ages men

have tried the decisions of the battlefield, the prerogatives of kings, the decisions of courts, the enactments of parliaments, and union of great power seeking to underwrite the peace of the world. All these have left in their trail misery and chaos, division, and strife. But at the cross one man is lifted up so high above all the causes that divide, and his arms are extended so wide that they enfold in their loving embrace every tribe, kindred, tongue, and nation, to bind them together with his wounded hands in the everlasting bonds of brotherhood and love.[40]

Just as the cross was central to Paul's proclamation, so too with Ransom the cross is the heart of the gospel's call to unity. At the cross all people stand equally before God, and this equality at the cross should transfer to human social relationships. On the cross Jesus is lifted high above all divisions, and his outstretched arms embrace every person, no matter their race or their language. To see the cross in this light is to understand God's vision for humanity.

Such a view of the cross coheres with what one finds in his essay "The Negro, the Hope or the Despair of Christianity." Ransom links social salvation with the Pauline language of 2 Corinthians 10:4, where the apostle contends that the weapons he utilizes are not physical weapons but weapons that God empowers, and so they are effective in carrying out God's divine purposes for social transformation. Like the apostle, Ransom characterizes the weapons of the faith as spiritual and moral in nature. Although at this point in the speech Ransom does not delineate what these weapons entail, earlier in the address he speaks of the "Supreme Law of Love," loving one's neighbor as oneself and doing unto each other what each person would want done to him or her. These are likely the weapons he envisions at this moment in his lecture. Interestingly, Ransom does not understand these weapons as destructive in nature or intent but rather as contributing to the "reconstruction of society" ("The Negro," 4). Rather than seeing warfare as something evil or inappropriate, Ransom perceives the positive outcome of this spiritual battle. Society's reconstruction, desperately needed because of the invasive power of sin, can only come about through employment of the inexhaustible arsenal of the spiritual weapons of love, justice, and truth. Paul's language becomes a way to express what social salvation means—the reconstruction of a society, in which racism, oppression, and injustice no longer exist and where God's highest ideals of human sisterhood and brotherhood flourish. In addition to functioning as a clarion call for social

---

40. Reverdy Ransom, "The Coming Vision," in *Making the Gospel Plain*, 222.

salvation and transformation, the apostle's words also function for Ransom as an indictment upon current American society, for the way things are is not the way things should be.

The real test of Christianity is the presence of the American Negro, declares Ransom, for it is in the treatment of African Americans that one sees how Christian this nation really is. The Negro stands as a "challenge to the earnestness of its [the nation's] faith, the strength of its courage, and the depth and sincerity of its love" (4). Ransom merges the nation and the church, calling America a "*household of faith*" [Gal. 6:10; cf. Eph. 2:19] in his critique of the nation's inability and unwillingness to repent or confess any guilt over its treatment of black Americans. In Galatians 6:10, where Paul utilizes this phrase, he admonishes the Galatians to do good to all people, but especially to those of the household of faith. By echoing this verse and invoking this phrase, Ransom draws a distinct contrast between what Paul admonishes and what white American Christians do to their fellow black Christian sisters and brothers.

Although all are one through Christ and live together in one household of faith, injustice and oppression by white Christians upon black Americans dominate. Whites are not "doing good" to their fellow believers, Ransom laments; rather, "at this very moment our Negro population stands politically, socially, and economically, ruthlessly disinherited by their white fellow Christians. . . . For three hundred years, our Negro population has been a *stone of stumbling and rock of offense* [Rom. 9:33; 1 Cor. 1:23] to American Christianity. Has the Gospel of Jesus Christ the power to transform men and bring them into brotherhood and love across the differences of color and race? America faces that test" (5). In Romans 9:33, the stumbling stone is Jesus, and in 1 Corinthians 1:23 the gospel becomes a stumbling block. Yet Ransom substitutes the American Negro for both Jesus and the gospel. By echoing Paul's language and applying it to African Americans, Ransom underscores the grave division present in American culture over the plight of blacks. As the gospel was not understood or accepted by many Jews and Greeks in the apostle's day, and was a stumbling block and offense to them, so too are blacks not accepted and understood in Ransom's time. Unlike Paul's day, however, where the gospel was relatively new on the scene, Ransom emphasizes the time dimension of the African Americans' situation. For three centuries this Christian nation has not accepted its black citizens, but instead has treated them as less than human beings.

Therefore, the disillusionment of blacks is great, Ransom proclaims, because at one time blacks believed that Christianity, along with hard work, morality, and education, would enable them to achieve equal rights, but they have unfortunately begun to realize that Jesus "has not been able to break the American color line" (5–6).[41] Although the government eliminated slavery, the nation through its laws and policies strategically stops and blocks any political, social, or economic progress African Americans make. The following quote by Ransom sums up the African Americans' plight: "Before the doors of every church and school, before every court of justice and hall of legislation, at all the places of public necessity and amusement, public convenience and recreation, and in all the avenues of labor, business, commerce, and trade, the Negro stands rejected" (6). The amount of resistance and opposition blacks face in every arena of life leads to many feeling disappointed and skeptical about the future.

Despite the presence of great discouragement in the current state of affairs, Ransom remains hopeful regarding blacks' future and, as a result, America's future. Like Jesus and the gospel, the proclamation of which saves humanity, African Americans will rise as salvation and healing to the nations who are in desperate need of divine deliverance. Ransom believes that a Negro prophet will arise in the spirit of Ezekiel and prophesy to the "dry bones of our civilization until they are united, clothed with flesh that knows no distinction of race, pulsate with the warm blood of our common human brotherhood and be made alive by the *spirit of God dwelling in their hearts* [1 Cor. 3:16; 15:22]" (7). Along with Ezekiel, Ransom employs Paul to describe the prophetic role of African Americans and the salvific function that blacks will have in the nation. Here Ransom upholds the black prophetic tradition in which African Americans speak out against injustice and oppression and proclaim God's purpose of sisterhood and brotherhood for humanity. Through their prophetic voice, blacks will bring to life a new people whose identity is shaped by the true gospel and formed by the Spirit. Just as Jesus, the stumbling block, becomes the chief cornerstone (1 Cor. 1:23; Eph. 2:20), here African Americans, who are a stumbling block and rock of offense, become the chief cornerstone for society's reconstruction, the foundation for the building of the household of faith through their prophetic gift. African Americans, then, become central to Ransom's idea of social salvation.

Reverdy Ransom's speeches epitomize what Frederick Ware raises as an important aspect of black theology: "Black theology understands sin

---

41. The phrase the "color line" reappears later in this chapter, in Frank Bartleman's observations about the Azusa Street revival.

as something that is social and not just personal only."[42] Ransom's pointed designation of social salvation indicates that he extends the idea of salvation beyond an individual accepting Christ as Savior. Salvation for him is holistic, transforming the individual but also reconfiguring society. "The inordinate focus on individual acts leads to an oversight of the social practices, maintained by a complex web of individual actions that are oppressive to certain groups of persons in society. African American theologians contend that the matter of sin cannot be limited to a discussion or corrective of personal conduct. Sin must be dealt with in its social manifestation. Since sin is manifested socially, it needs to be addressed in a social manner. . . . Salvation is personal but it is not individualistic; it is a possibility for the entire human society."[43] Ware's comments represent the core of Ransom's theological trajectory: salvation is comprehensive, changing individual people and simultaneously converting systems, communities, governments, and nations.

William J. Seymour (1870–1922): Bringer of Hope

William Seymour, born to former slaves, was the pastor of the Apostolic Faith Gospel Mission at 312 Azusa Street, Los Angeles, California.[44] The Pentecostal revival that took place in this mission spread throughout the world, and its monumental impact exists to the present day. Larry Martin characterizes the significance of Seymour for American religious history: "If Seymour was not a black man, his rise from poverty to become pastor of one of America's greatest revivals would be remarkable. Because he was a black man in an era charged with racial hatred his accomplishments go beyond remarkable; they are truly supernatural."[45] Although Seymour had come to Los Angeles to be an associate pastor of an African American Holiness congregation, theological disagreement caused Seymour to leave the church and to begin a home Bible study. During this time, he and several of the attendees experienced the phenomenon of speaking in tongues, or glossolalia,

---

42. Frederick L. Ware, *African American Theology: An Introduction* (Louisville: Westminster John Knox, 2016), 141.

43. Ware, *African American Theology*, 142.

44. Larry Martin, preface to *Azusa Street Sermons by William J. Seymour*, ed. Larry Martin (Joplin, MO: Christian Life Books, 1999), 17. The phrase "bringer of hope," in the section heading, is a paraphrase of Calvin White's comments regarding Seymour bringing hope to a racially divided nation (*The Rise to Respectability*, 33).

45. Martin, preface to *Azusa Street Sermons*, 17.

and news of this event spread. Attendance grew, and eventually the group, led by Seymour, rented the building at 312 Azusa Street. The events taking place at the Azusa Street mission caught the attention of the media, and numerous news reports were written about the activities occurring there.[46]

Calvin White emphasizes the social significance of the Azusa Street event and its coverage in the media. He writes, "Working-class blacks especially enjoyed hearing the news that a black man of their class standing had gained national attention. Moreover, newspapers reported that interracial crowds assembled to hear Seymour, standing in direct contradiction to the Jim Crow laws that blacks despised. During a time when black men possessed little to no authority over whites and the widely held assumption of black inferiority permeated throughout society, no matter how insignificant, Seymour brought hope. As he stood before the interracial crowds and commanded their attention, Seymour channeled the dreams of equality of thousands of blacks."[47] The overturning of racial division and segregation, evidenced by Seymour's leadership and made possible through the outpouring of the Spirit, could be seen in the worship services at the Azusa Street revival. Frank Bartleman, a participant and eyewitness of the events, writes that at Azusa Street "the 'color line' was washed away in the blood"[48] and "no subjects or sermons were announced ahead of time, and no special speakers for such an hour. No one knew what might be coming, what God would do. . . . We had no 'respect of persons.' The rich and educated were the same as the poor and ignorant. . . . We only recognized God. All were equal. No flesh might glory in His presence."[49] Estrelda Alexander captures the essence of these services in the following descriptions: "Camp meeting style worship services were held daily, generally lasting for several hours and running from ten in the morning until midnight. These ecstatic services included, along with speaking in tongues, impromptu sermons, prophesying, singing in tongues, interpretation of tongues, conversions, divine healing, and exorcisms. . . . Another prominent feature of these meetings was their radically egalitarian nature. People of different races came together in an unprecedented manner to experience this 'new religion.' Blacks, whites, His-

---

46. Estrelda Alexander, *Limited Liberty: The Legacy of Four Pentecostal Women Pioneers* (Cleveland, OH: Pilgrim, 2008), 7–8.

47. White, *The Rise to Respectability*, 33.

48. Frank Bartleman, *Azusa Street: The Roots of Modern-Day Pentecost*, introduction by Vinson Synan (Gainesville, FL: Bridge-Logos, 1980), 61.

49. Bartleman, *Azusa Street*, 65.

panics, and Asians worshiped side by side."[50] Seymour himself describes the international and interracial dimensions of the revival: "People from all nations came and got their cup full. Some came from Africa, some came from India, China, Japan, and England."[51]

Along with racial harmony, class and gender equality occurred in the services at Azusa Street. Again, Frank Bartleman: "In honor we 'preferred one another.' The Lord was liable to burst through any one. We prayed for this continually. Someone would finally get up anointed for the message. All seemed to recognize this and gave way. It might be a child, a woman, or a man. It might be from the back seat, or from the front. It made no difference. We rejoiced that God was working."[52] Alexander, noting the eyewitness accounts of Bartleman and others, writes, "Though most worshipers were from lower and working classes, there was no stratification by class, race, gender, or age in participation or leadership in the services. Women, as well as men, enjoyed freedom to minister within the services as they felt God leading them. Even children who felt inspired by God had a voice in the worship."[53] Early on, the services at Azusa Street exhibited a racial and gender egalitarianism that was not common in those days. To paraphrase Albert Raboteau, the outpouring of the Spirit during this revival demonstrated the Spirit's potential of bending the seemingly inflexible positions of racial segregation and gender hierarchy.[54]

According to Alexander, the revival lasted eight years (1906–1914), and by the time it ended, more than twenty Pentecostal denominations and hundreds of Pentecostal congregations had come into existence.[55] Twenty years after the revival, more Pentecostal denominations had been formed

50. Alexander, *Limited Liberty*, 8–9.

51. William J. Seymour, *The Doctrines and Discipline of the Azusa Street Apostolic Faith Mission of Los Angeles, California by William J. Seymour Its Founder and General Overseer*, Complete Azusa Street Library, vol. 7, ed. Larry Martin (Joplin, MO: Christian Life Books, 2000), 30; William Seymour, "Apostolic Address," in *A Reader in Pentecostal Theology: Voices from the First Generation*, ed. Douglas Jacobsen (Bloomington: Indiana University Press, 2006), 53.

52. Bartleman, *Azusa Street*, 66.

53. Alexander, *Limited Liberty*, 9.

54. Albert Raboteau, *Slave Religion: The "Invisible Institution" in the Antebellum South* (New York: Oxford University Press, 1978), 148.

55. Alexander, *Limited Liberty*, 10. But according to Jacobsen, the revival lasted from 1906 to 1908 (introduction to *A Reader in Pentecostal Theology*, 10). Others, such as Ronald Minor, foreword to *Azusa Street Sermons by William J. Seymour*, 9, claim it lasted three years, 1906–1909.

and thousands of Pentecostal congregations had been founded. In addition, hundreds of existing churches became Pentecostal.[56] The message of Spirit baptism resounded from Azusa Street throughout the world and remains a significant part of Christianity in America and globally, as evidenced by the statistics.[57]

In the introduction to his book *A Reader in Pentecostal Theology: Voices from the First Generation*, Douglas Jacobsen asks the following two questions: "What is it that distinguishes [Pentecostals] from the wide variety of other Christian traditions that exist in the world? What sets pentecostalism apart?"[58] His answers are instructive for our ensuing examinations of William Seymour, Charles Mason, and Ida B. Robinson. He writes, "Pentecostalism is Spirit-centered faith. It is the belief in the present-day power of the Holy Spirit to work miracles and supernaturally change lives. . . . In terms of religious practices, the Spirit-inspired ability to speak in 'tongues' (also known as 'glossolalia') is what makes pentecostalism different." This "Spirit-centered faith" is central in the sermons and writings of Seymour, Mason, and Robinson. These Pentecostal hermeneuts emphasize Paul's language regarding the Spirit and the Spirit's power to speak and transform racial relations, economics, and society at large.

Jacobsen describes the importance of glossolalia for Pentecostal believers. They are "convinced that speaking in tongues is a special form of communication inspired by God, and they derive profound meaning from the experience. Even if speaking in tongues is not a language in any usual sense of the term, something significant occurs when people engage in it." Glossolalia is also described by some Pentecostals as receiving the "baptism of the Holy Spirit" and is the sign that one has undergone this type of baptism. Integral to the baptism of the Holy Spirit is the transformation wrought by the Spirit's presence to the believer's character, faith, and ministry.[59] Important also to

---

56. Alexander, *Limited Liberty*, 10.

57. The Pew Forum states that by "all accounts, pentecostalism and related charismatic movements represent one of the fastest-growing segments of global Christianity. According to the World Christian Database, at least a quarter of the world's 2 billion Christians are thought to be members." "Spirit and Power—a 10-Country Survey of Pentecostals," Pew Research Center, October 5, 2006, http://www.pewforum.org/2006/10/05/spirit-and-power/.

58. Jacobsen, introduction to *A Reader in Pentecostal Theology*, 3.

59. Jacobsen, introduction to *A Reader in Pentecostal Theology*, 4; David D. Daniels III, "'Doing All the Good We Can': The Political Witness of African American Holiness and Pentecostal Churches in the Post–Civil Rights Era," in *New Day Begun: African American*

Pentecostal belief and tradition is the serious role that religious experience has for doing Christian theology.[60] Pentecostals' pneumatological emphasis on "experienced presence" is a vital voice in African American religious history.[61]

William Seymour's Employment of Paul's Spirit Language

Although the story of Acts 2 plays a prominent role in Seymour's understanding of the baptism of the Holy Spirit, so too do the letters of Paul, particularly 1 Thessalonians, 1 and 2 Corinthians, Romans, Ephesians, and Hebrews. Seymour's sermons "Receive Ye the Holy Ghost" and "Gifts of the Spirit" utilize texts from all these letters. In "Receive Ye the Holy Ghost," Seymour outlines his view of the different steps of the salvation experience. Citing Romans 5:1, Seymour contends that when one repents and receives forgiveness of sins, the "pardoned sinner becomes a child of God in justification."[62] This is what he calls the "first work of grace."[63] The second work of grace is sanctification, which comes about by the power of Jesus's blood and the Holy Ghost. Citing Hebrews 10:14-15 and Hebrews 2:11, Seymour contends that the gift of sanctification prepares the believer for the baptism of the Holy Spirit. Although many believers are consecrated, sanctified, and cleansed from sin, many have not had a "real personal Pentecost," which God promises in 2 Corinthians 1:21-22: *"Now he which stablisheth us with you in Christ, and hath anointed us, is God, who hath also sealed us, and given the earnest of the Spirit in our hearts."*[64] The present baptism of the Spirit is, according to Seymour, the third step and God's sealing of the believer until the eschaton. Thus, the experience of the Spirit has present and future implications.

In his sermon "Gifts of the Spirit," he employs 1 Corinthians 12:1 as the foundational text: *"Now concerning spiritual gifts, brethren, I would not have*

Churches and Civic Culture in Post–Civil Rights America (Durham, NC: Duke University Press, 2003), 167.

60. Eric Lewis Williams, "'Mad with Supernatural Joy': On Representations of Pentecostalism in the Black Religious Imagination," *Journal of the Interdenominational Theological Center* 44 (Fall–Spring 2016): 81–97 (here 93).

61. Williams, "Mad with Supernatural Joy," 94–95.

62. William Seymour, "Receive Ye the Holy Ghost," in Martin, *Azusa Street Sermons by William J. Seymour,* 49.

63. Seymour, "Receive Ye the Holy Ghost," 49.

64. Seymour, "Receive Ye the Holy Ghost," 50.

you ignorant." Seymour cites this passage at the beginning of the sermon and then proceeds to describe the Corinthian community to which Paul wrote. They did not know their "privileges in this blessed gospel" and so did not know that the gospel of Christ is the "*power of God unto salvation to everyone that believeth* [Rom. 1:16]."[65] For him the Corinthians' ignorance corresponds to that of believers in Seymour's own context. For Seymour, the baptism of the Spirit is important because it is the Spirit that empowers the believer to live a holy and sanctified life before God and others. Just as important as the Spirit's power is the fruit of the Spirit, which should characterize every believer's life. The cure for believers' ignorance regarding all that God wills for their lives is to search and study the Scriptures and to follow the Spirit's leading.[66]

Seymour also addresses those who criticize the gift of speaking in tongues and ask what good it does when you do not know what you are talking about. Seymour answers that Paul instructs us to desire spiritual gifts (1 Cor. 14) and that every gift God gives is good. Thus, the gift of speaking in tongues is not to be worshiped, but it is not to be rejected or despised either. The gift is for God's glory and not for self-aggrandizement.[67] For Seymour, as for other Pentecostals, gifts of the Spirit are a present reality, and all the gifts and miracles that took place in the New Testament are available to believers if only they would ask for them.[68]

Paul's words on sanctification in 1 Thessalonians were also instrumental to Seymour's teaching about the Holy Spirit: "*For this is the will of God, even your sanctification*" (4:3). In his sermon "Sanctified on the Cross," Seymour interprets this passage to his audience along with Romans 6:6-7: "*Knowing this, that our old man is crucified with him, that the body of sin might be destroyed, that henceforth we should not serve sin. For he that is dead is freed from sin*": "So it is His will for every soul to be saved from all sin, actual and original. . . . So it takes the death of the old man in order that Christ might be sanctified in us. . . . God is calling His people to true holiness in these days."[69]

---

65. William Seymour, "Gifts of the Spirit," in Martin, *Azusa Street Sermons by William J. Seymour*, 53.

66. Seymour, "Gifts of the Spirit," 53–54.

67. Seymour, "Gifts of the Spirit," 55. Seymour writes, "May we all use our gift to the glory of God and not worship the gift. The Lord gives us power to use it to His own glory and honor."

68. Jacobsen, introduction to *A Reader in Pentecostal Theology*, 4.

69. William Seymour, "Sanctified on the Cross," in Martin, *Azusa Street Sermons by William J. Seymour*, 103–4.

Sanctification "makes us holy and destroys the breed of sin, the love of sin and carnality."[70] Seymour proclaims the need for sanctification because it creates purity of heart, purity of body and soul. The Spirit desires to lead believers out of sin and to help them live clean lives before the world. Once one is sanctified, one is prepared to "get into one accord for the gift or power of the Holy Ghost, and God will come in like a rushing mighty wind and fill every heart with the power of the Holy Spirit."[71] Thus, human beings become the Spirit's "instruments," and the display of the Spirit's power causes people to see the reality of Jesus Christ.[72] Important to Seymour's understanding of the Spirit's presence in the believer's life is the following statement: "When you have the Holy Ghost, you have an empire, a power within yourself. . . . So when we get the power of the Holy Ghost, we will see the heavens open and the Holy Ghost power falling on earth, power over sickness, diseases and death."[73] In light of Seymour's social location and the social location of many in his audience, one cannot help but think about the power of these words. In the midst of what may be happening throughout the country, such as segregation and lynchings, Paul's words enable Seymour to ask the question, "Where is true power located?" It is located in the Holy Ghost. William Turner describes this sense of power: "Such empowerment from above enabled one to stand over against the world. Despite calamity, suffering, and hostile culture, there is access to power from this spiritual realm, which provides toughness, resilience, inner fortitude, and endurance to defy odds of every sort. This sense of interpenetration between the spiritual and the objective realms provided for a posture in which life, destiny, and fortunes were not dictated finally by the surrounding culture."[74] Turner's words help to underscore the significance of the Spirit's power for Seymour and others at Azusa Street. Seymour takes Paul's depiction of the Spirit and the Spirit's gifts as power to mean that, despite the awful realities of everyday life that he and his audience may face, the Spirit provides them with "a toughness," a "resilience," to use Turner's words, that enables them not only to endure but to overcome. So the Spirit as a power, as an empire, as Seymour states, is an empire that is more powerful than the American empire or the nation's

---

70. Seymour, "Sanctified on the Cross," 104.

71. William Seymour, "The Baptism of the Holy Ghost," in Martin, *Azusa Street Sermons by William J. Seymour*, 108.

72. Seymour, "The Baptism of the Holy Ghost," 108-9.

73. Seymour, "The Baptism of the Holy Ghost," 109.

74. Turner, *The United Holy Church of America*, 124.

laws. Seymour preaches Paul in a way that reveals the authority and power of God and God's Spirit over against societal discrimination and realities.

God's Spirit is depicted as an empowering entity, but this empowerment not only benefits the believer but also enables the believer to help those in need, such as those suffering illnesses and near death.[75] Whereas Seymour does speak of a personal Pentecost, he says it is for the "enduement of power for service and work."[76] Baptism of the Spirit has an outward focus, empowering believers for service in the world.

Part of this outward focus includes providing financial assistance to those in need. In his sermon "Money Matters," Seymour rejects what appears to be misunderstandings by those in the congregation about not needing to work since they have the baptism of the Spirit. These people have been listening to false teachers who tell them to "sell out," give away all their money, and leave their families. Apparently some were in fact leaving their families to go out and preach the gospel and neglecting their jobs. Seymour rejects these false teachings, proclaiming that "We let the Spirit lead people and tell them what they ought to give. . . . God does not tell you to forsake your family. *He says if you do not provide for your own you are worse than an infidel* [1 Tim. 5:8]."[77] To counter these erroneous notions, Seymour cites Paul's words in 1 Timothy 5:8, in which the apostle advises Timothy that "*if any provide not for his own, and specially for those of his own house, he hath denied the faith, and is worse than an infidel.*" Seymour thus rebukes those in the congregation who utilize faith as a way to deny their family responsibilities; they are to take care of their own households. If they do not take care of their families, they betray their faith; they do not exhibit it.

Furthermore, Seymour quotes Paul's admonition in Ephesians 4:28: "*Let him labour, working with his hands the thing which is good, that he may have to give to him that needeth,*" and 1 Corinthians 16:1–2: "*Now concerning the collection for the saints, . . . upon the first day of the week let everyone of you lay by him in store, as God hath prospered him.*"[78] Seymour focuses on the apostle's admonition to give to those who need. To be able to help those in financial straits, believers need to work and have finances themselves. In addition, Seymour maintains that leaders should not tell people

---

75. The Pentecostal belief in supernatural miracles is evident in this statement by Seymour.

76. Seymour, "Receive Ye the Holy Ghost," 50.

77. William Seymour, "Money Matters," in Martin, *Azusa Street Sermons by William J. Seymour*, 35.

78. Seymour, "Money Matters," 36.

what to give because that "would not be the Spirit of the Lord." Instead, "We let the Spirit lead people and tell them what they ought to give."[79] As the church in Corinth contributed to Paul's collection for the Jerusalem saints, Seymour lifts them up as examples of how believers in his time need to work so that they can utilize their income in a similar manner to assist those in need. Moreover, the Spirit will lead them as to how much to give and to whom to give. Contrary to those who believed that Spirit baptism negated work, Seymour maintained, "We must know our calling. We can work when baptized with the Holy Ghost."[80] The apostle's words in Ephesians 4:28 and 1 Corinthians 16:1-2 enable Seymour to emphasize the Spirit's role in giving and the divine expectation that believers work and contribute to the needy. Consequently, Seymour underscores practical application of Spirit baptism.

Paul's Spirit Language and Racism

Along with utilizing Paul to speak of the Spirit's significance and the Spirit's power to heal, to help the believer live a holy life, and to lead in giving, Seymour also employs Paul to address racism in his congregation. While early on the Azusa Street congregation consisted of different races worshiping together, racial tension arose later because of whites' prejudice against blacks. Seymour describes the situation in his "Apostolic Address," and his description exhibits his use of Paul to attempt to rectify it:

> Very soon division arose through some of our brethren, and the *Holy Spirit was grieved* [Eph. 4:30]. We want all of our white brethren and white sisters to feel free in our churches and missions, in spite of all the trouble we have had with some of our white brethren in causing diversion, and spreading wild fire and fanaticism. Some of our colored brethren caught the disease of this spirit of division also. *We find according to God's word [that we are] to be one in the Holy Spirit, not in the flesh; but in the Holy Spirit, for we are one body.* 1 Cor. 12:12-14. If some of our white brethren have prejudices and discrimination (Gal. 2:11-20), we can't do it, because God calls us to follow the Bible. . . . *We must love all men as Christ commands.* (Heb. 12:14)[81]

79. Seymour, "Money Matters," 35.
80. Seymour, "Money Matters," 37.
81. Seymour, *Doctrines and Discipline*, 30; Seymour, "Apostolic Address," 53.

Several interesting Pauline elements appear in Seymour's description of the divisions taking place at Azusa Street. First of all, he echoes Ephesians 4:30, where Paul writes that believers should *"grieve not the holy Spirit of God, whereby ye are sealed unto the day of redemption."* Seymour views the occurrence of divisions as actions that cause the Spirit pain and grief, and the apostle's language enables him to depict the gravity of the situation not only from a human standpoint but also from a divine perspective. God's Spirit laments when racism takes place. Similarly, Paul's language of unity in 1 Corinthians 12 with which he addresses the divisions in Corinth becomes the apostle's words through Seymour to address the racial tensions at Azusa Street. Just as the Corinthians did not understand their call to unity in the Spirit, so too some of the white and black people at Azusa Street did not understand their call to be one body regardless of race.

In 1 Corinthians 12:12–14, Paul writes, *"For as the body is one, and hath many members, and all the members of that one body, being many, are one body: so also is Christ. For by one Spirit are we all baptized into one body, whether we be Jews or Gentiles, whether we be bond or free; and have been all made to drink into one Spirit. For the body is not one member, but many."* Seymour's statements that in the Holy Spirit believers are one body echo Paul's language in these verses and indicate that Seymour believes the baptism of the Holy Spirit is not just an individual experience but is a communal one as well, for the experience of the Spirit has social consequences. The bodily manifestations of Spirit baptism, such as glossolalia, divine healings, and ecstatic behavior, have communal body implications for the larger body of Christ as well, and one of those ramifications is racial unity. The Spirit makes racial unity possible and obliterates racial hierarchy. The social repercussions of a Spirit experience come to the fore again in the next statements Seymour makes.

When Seymour writes that "If some of our white brethren have prejudices and discrimination," he cites Galatians 2:11–20, the episode in Antioch where Peter withdraws from the gentiles while eating. Paul writes, *"But when Peter was come to Antioch, I withstood him to the face, because he was to be blamed. For before that certain came from James, he did eat with the Gentiles: but when they were come, he withdrew and separated himself, fearing them which were of the circumcision. And the other Jews dissembled likewise with him; insomuch that Barnabas also was carried away with their dissimulation"* (2:11–13). By selecting this passage, Seymour is in effect interpreting Peter's decision to separate from the gentiles during meals as an instance of prejudice. In doing so, Seymour aligns the actions of the whites in his congregation with that of Peter. Just as Peter's actions were deemed by Paul as not *"according to the truth of the gospel"* (2:14), Seymour views whites' racism as not in line with the gospel by which they claim to live. Interesting also is how Seymour characterizes the behavior of some of the blacks in the congregation, who follow their white peers by catching the "disease of this spirit of division." This too corresponds with Paul's description of what happened when Peter separated himself from the gentiles. Other Jews followed his example: *"And the other Jews dissembled likewise with him; insomuch that Barnabas also was carried away with their dissimulation."* In an incisive move, Seymour compares what happened in Paul's day to what is happening in his day. Just as some Jews followed Peter's erroneous example by separating themselves from gentiles, some blacks were following the wrong example of their white counterparts by advocating division.

Whereas Seymour aligns the whites in his congregation with Peter, he implicitly aligns himself with Paul. As Paul took it upon himself to rebuke Peter openly and to charge him with hypocrisy, Seymour, like Paul, publicly rebukes the whites in his midst in this "Apostolic Address" and names their actions as wrong.[82] He also admonishes the blacks in his congregation not to follow the behavior of the whites. He states that although *they* (the whites) may be prejudiced, *we* cannot do that because we are called to follow the biblical command to love everyone. Here blacks are called upon to act in a way that is true to biblical faith and to distinguish themselves from their white counterparts.[83]

The analysis of Seymour demonstrates that early on in Pentecostalism, Pentecostals were thinking seriously about their "Spirit-centered faith" and how the Spirit experience guides one's engagement with the world.[84] Jacobsen notes a common caricature of Pentecostalism, that its emphasis on experience

82. Paul says in Gal. 2:14: "But when I saw that they walked not uprightly according to the truth of the gospel, I said unto Peter *before them all*, If thou, being a Jew, livest after the manner of Gentiles, and not as do the Jews, why compellest thou the Gentiles to live as do the Jews?" (emphasis added).

83. Interestingly, this response to racial divisions occurred in 1915, the same year the film *Birth of a Nation* was released (see above in this chapter). It is also important to note that not all whites at Azusa exhibited prejudiced behavior. In this same "Apostolic Address," Seymour acknowledges that "Some of our white brethren and sisters have never left us in all the division; they have stuck to us. We love our white brethren and sisters and welcome them. Jesus Christ takes in all people in his Salvation" (*Doctrines and Discipline*, 30).

84. According to Ithiel C. Clemmons, *Bishop C. H. Mason and the Roots of the Church of God in Christ* (Bakersfield, CA: Pneuma Life Publishing, 1996), "Pentecostalism is the only denomination of the Christian faith in the United States founded by African-American people" (31).

of the Spirit negates an intellectual aspect. Jacobsen rightly critiques such a stereotype, writing that the "truth is that pentecostal Christians do think about their faith. They always have. They have engaged in theological reflection since the very beginning of the movement, and they continue to do so today. The popular stereotype is wrong."[85] Our analysis of Seymour illustrates the assertions of Jacobsen that Pentecostals have always thought about their faith, and at the center of their intellectual and theological engagement is Paul.

In this volume we have seen instances in which instead of the common framework of white ministers having Paul preach to blacks, blacks utilize Paul to preach to whites about their racism. Here, too, a black pastor, William Seymour, employs Paul to articulate the implications of Spirit baptism for everyday life and the practical theology that flows out of a Spirit experience. A Spirit-empowered life affects every aspect of that life: relationships with others, societal structures, handling of finances and family care. Indeed, to live by the Spirit means to live by a power that promotes compassion and equality and that abolishes racism and injustice. Like so many of the black hermeneuts before him, Seymour utilizes Paul to censure whites who act contrary to the liberating power of the gospel and the Spirit. The way Seymour characterizes Azusa Street also emphasizes the social focus and implications of Spirit baptism from his perspective. His words echo the universality of Paul's words in Acts 17:26 and Galatians 3:28. The unity of believers and the abolishment of societal barriers through the outpouring of the Spirit at Azusa Street are well known, and here we see through Seymour's sermons and writings that Paul's words play a significant role in the characterization of this social transformation. Racial unity is evidence of the Spirit's presence and orchestrated by the divine will.

Accordingly, Seymour takes up the apostle's rebuke of Peter in Galatians and makes it his own reproof of the whites and blacks within his congregation that are sowing seeds of discord. Seymour puts on the Pauline mantle to proclaim the gospel's eradicating nature of racial division.

Charles Harrison Mason (1864–1961):
Founder of Largest Pentecostal Denomination in the United States

Charles Harrison Mason was born to freed slaves in 1864 near Shelby County, Tennessee. In 1878, the family fled the area because of a yellow fever epidemic and moved to Plumersville, Arkansas. Mason became seriously ill

---

85. Jacobsen, introduction to *A Reader in Pentecostal Theology*, 5.

with tuberculosis and was miraculously healed of the disease. After that experience he consecrated his life to God and at fourteen years of age was baptized, ordained, and licensed to preach in the black Baptist church by his half brother, Israel Nelson.[86]

Pauline Origin of a Denomination

In his preaching, Mason focused on holiness and sanctification, emphasizing a Spirit-led life and personal holiness, and because of this teaching he and another minister, Charles Price Jones, who taught the same beliefs, were ordered to leave the Baptist church. The two men then started the Church of God in Christ Fellowship of churches.[87] Mason recounts how this name, a Pauline phrase, came to him through divine revelation. As he was walking down the street in Little Rock, Arkansas, the Lord revealed to him the name Church of God in Christ, and to confirm the name, God placed upon his heart the Scripture 1 Thessalonians 2:14, in which Paul reminds the Thessalonians of when they began to follow the faith of Christ: *"For ye, brethren, became followers of the churches of God which in Judaea are in Christ Jesus."*[88] This Pauline phrase became the name of the new African American denomination, and in 1897 Mason and Jones registered the denomination with the state and began ordaining ministers.[89] Today the Church of God in Christ (COGIC) is the largest Pentecostal denomination in the United States.[90]

86. "Charles Harrison Mason," in *Preaching with Sacred Fire: An Anthology of African American Sermons, 1750 to the Present*, ed. Martha Simmons and Frank E. Thomas (New York: Norton, 2010), 434.

87. "Charles Harrison Mason," in Simmons and Thomas, *Preaching with Sacred Fire*, 434.

88. E. W. Mason, *The Man . . . Charles Harrison Mason: Sermons of His Early Ministry (1915–1929) and a Biographical Sketch of His Life* (Memphis, TN: Church of God in Christ Publishing House, 1979), 13. See also Sherry Sherrod DuPree, *A Compendium: Bishop C. H. Mason Founder of the Church of God in Christ* (Gainesville: Sherry Sherrod DuPree, 2017), 12.

89. Jacobsen, *A Reader in Pentecostal Theology*, 214. Ithiel C. Clemmons maintains that the "roots of the Church of God in Christ go back at least thirty years before the Emancipation Proclamation of 1863. Slave narratives, with their heartwrenching descriptions of conversion experiences, provide a rich resource for exploring the beginnings of the Church of God in Christ tradition" (*Bishop C. H. Mason*, 20). See chap. 4 for some of these conversion experiences.

90. Jacobsen, *A Reader in Pentecostal Theology*, 214. For information on women in the COGIC, see Anthea Butler, *Women in the Church of God in Christ: Making a Sanctified*

Mason's use of Pauline language here is subversive, for Paul's words, which had historically been used by whites to subjugate and dehumanize African Americans, are now employed by Mason to designate a black-led denomination. This move signifies blacks' continued practice of interpreting Paul and utilizing his writings on their own terms.

Baptism of the Spirit

Mason went to Los Angeles in 1907 to be part of the Azusa Street revival and received the baptism of the Holy Spirit.[91] He describes the experience with the language of Paul and the language of Acts:

> The sound of a mighty wind was in me and my soul cried, "Jesus, only, one like you." My soul cried and soon I began to die. It seemed that I heard the groaning of Christ on the cross dying for me. All of the work was in me until I died out of *the old man* [Rom. 6:6; cf. Eph. 4:22; Col. 3:9]. The sound stopped for a little while. My soul cried, "Oh, God, *finish your work in me*" [Phil. 1:6].... So there came a wave of glory into me, and all of my being was filled with the glory of the Lord.... When I opened my mouth to say glory, a flame touched my tongue which ran down to me. My language changed and no word could I speak in my own tongue.... And from that day until now there has been an overflowing joy of the glory of the Lord in my heart.[92]

Mason's description of his baptism of the Holy Spirit as a death to his old man echoes Paul's repeated use of old man language in his letters. In Romans 6:6 Paul writes that *"our old man is crucified with him [i.e., Christ], that the body of sin might be destroyed, that henceforth we should not serve sin."* Mason, then, views his baptism as a distinct phase in his salvific journey, in which the old man dies and a new transformation happens. Similarly, his prayer to God that God will complete the divine work recounts Paul's promise in Philippians 1:6 that God will finish the good work begun in believers' lives.

World (Chapel Hill: University of North Carolina Press, 2007). For a more general overview of women in the sanctified church as a whole, see Cheryl Townsend Gilkes, "The Role of Women in the Sanctified Church," in *If It Wasn't for the Women ... : Black Women's Experience and Womanist Culture in Church and Community* (Maryknoll, NY: Orbis, 2001).

91. Jacobsen, *A Reader in Pentecostal Theology*, 214; "Charles Harrison Mason," in Simmons and Thomas, 434–35.

92. E. W. Mason, *The Man*, 19.

Mason remains at Azusa Street for five weeks under the teaching of Seymour, and when he returns home, he shares his experiences with Jones, who rejects the idea of speaking in tongues. As a result, the two men separate, with Jones organizing a separate denomination, Church of Christ (Holiness), and Mason keeping the name Church of God in Christ; all the churches in the fellowship that accepted the teaching of baptism in the Holy Spirit remained in the group.[93] Mason's experience at Azusa Street deeply affected him; he relates how when he returned to his church he prayed and asked God to give him the gift of interpretation of the tongues he spoke.

> The third day after reaching Memphis I asked Him to give me the *interpretation of what was spoken in tongues* [1 Cor. 12:10], for I did not fully understand the operation of the Spirit. I wanted the church to understand what the Spirit was saying through me, *so that they might be edified* [1 Cor. 14:5]. *My prayers were not in vain* [1 Cor. 14:13]. The Lord stood me up and began to speak in tongues and interpret the same. He soon gave me the gift of interpretation [1 Cor. 12:10]—that is, He would interpret sounds, groans and any kind of spiritual utterance.[94]

Mason's description of his deep desire to interpret his divinely inspired language reverberates with the language of 1 Corinthians and Paul's discussion of spiritual gifts, including tongues and interpretation of tongues. In 1 Corinthians 12:10 Paul writes that one of the gifts of the Spirit is the ability to speak in tongues and another is the ability to interpret those tongues. He goes on to say in 1 Corinthians 14:5 that interpretation of tongues edifies the church because the church can now understand what the person's language means. Mason prays for interpretation so that what he says may build up the church and edify it. Moreover, Paul instructs those in the Corinthian congregation who speak in tongues to pray that they may interpret them. Mason, following the apostle's admonition, does so and reports that God hears his prayers, for he is granted the gift to interpret his glossolalia, for he can interpret "sounds, groans, and any kind of spiritual utterance."[95]

---

93. Jacobsen, *A Reader in Pentecostal Theology*, 214; "Charles Harrison Mason," in Simmons and Thomas, 435.

94. E. W. Mason, *The Man*, 20.

95. See also Mason's words regarding the Spirit, Spirit baptism, glossolalia, and interpretation in Mary C. Mason, ed. and comp., *The History and Life Work of Bishop C. H. Mason* (1924; reprint, Memphis, TN: Church of God in Christ, 1987), 57-59.

Paul and Racism

As is the case for Seymour, Paul's letters play an important role in Mason's understanding of the Spirit and spiritual gifts. Additionally, for Mason, the apostle's words become the appellation of his denomination, and his teachings shape and characterize the denomination's Pentecostal identity. Also, like Seymour, Mason led an interracial organization, as the COGIC welcomed white ministers into the denomination. White Pentecostal ministers were part of the church's ecclesiastical powers, and, as licensed COGIC ministers under Mason, they had access to the COGIC charter so that they could perform marriage ceremonies, grant preaching licenses, carry out baptisms, and ride trains at a discount, as other COGIC ministers did. According to Ithiel Clemmons, Mason ordained more than 350 white Pentecostals.[96] Mason himself states, "The Spirit through me has saved, sanctified and baptized thousands of souls of all colors and nations."[97] Clemmons observes the interracial thrust of these early COGIC congregations, writing, "where local congregations of the Church of God in Christ were founded, black and white Saints worked, worshiped, and evangelized together in an inter-racial, egalitarian fellowship modeled after the interracial fellowship of Azusa Street. This occurred throughout the South, including in Mississippi, Tennessee, Arkansas, Florida, Louisiana, Alabama, and Georgia at a most racially tense time in the United States."[98] Yet, due to this "racially tense time," these interracial congregations would not last. In 1914 the white members of the COGIC separated and formed a white denomination, Assemblies of God.[99] But Mason continued to preach and to proclaim the gospel that

96. Clemmons, *Bishop C. H. Mason*, 70; "Charles Harrison Mason," in Simmons and Thomas, 435.

97. Mary C. Mason, *The History and Life Work of Bishop C. H. Mason*, 31.

98. Clemmons, *Bishop C. H. Mason*, 27.

99. Clemmons, *Bishop C. H. Mason*, 71; "Charles Harrison Mason," in Simmons and Thomas, 435. Albert Raboteau, *American Prophets: Seven Religious Radicals and Their Struggle for Social and Political Justice* (Princeton: Princeton University Press, 2016), eloquently writes about the interracial origins and possibilities of the Pentecostal movement and the movement's subsequent capitulation to societal racism: "The Holiness-Pentecostal movement seemed poised to develop a truly interracial Christianity. The great three-year-long Azusa Street revival, begun in Los Angeles in 1906, involved interracial leadership, and included the participation of Asian and Mexican as well as European and African Americans. Early Pentecostals understood the interracial character of their movement as a sign of its authenticity—a new Pentecostal outpouring of the Holy Spirit on diverse races as well as diverse tongues. For a time, black Pentecostal leaders ordained whites to

"God's church is made one, of every nation, tongue and people that are upon the face of the earth," that *"the church is the body of Christ"* (Eph. 1:22), that *"Christ is the head of the body, 'the one church'"* (Eph. 4:4–5), and that *"God rules in one faith and in one Lord and in one baptism."*[100] For Mason, the unity proclaimed in these Pauline epistles was God's vision for the church, and no matter the earthly realities, they could not negate the truth of the gospel. To speak the language of unity in the midst of a nation filled with racial division was, in a sense, to speak another language, a type of glossolalia, speech that contradicted the prevalent separatist discourse of the time.[101]

Paul and War

The last significant subversive use of Paul by Mason occurs in his sermon "The Kaiser in the Light of the Scriptures," given on June 23, 1918. During 1917–1918 the Federal Bureau of Investigation investigated Mason because of his pacifist teaching and because the COGIC charter stated that the church did not believe in shedding blood: "We believe that the shedding of human blood or the taking of human life to be contrary to the teachings of our Lord and Savior Jesus Christ and as a body we are averse to war in all its forms."[102] This belief was demonstrated in Mason's letter to President Wilson

---

the ministry and involved themselves in interracial revivals. But once again, race emerged to constrain the movement's flow and turn it aside into the old well-worn paths of discrimination" (97).

100. Jacobsen, *A Reader in Pentecostal Theology*, 218.

101. According to DuPree, *A Compendium*, "On the first week of April 1914, Elder C. H. Mason traveled to the Hot Springs convention to invoke God's blessings on the General Council of the Assemblies of God. He preached to more than four hundred white preachers. Elder C. H. Mason never showed racist or hostile intent after the whites dropped his church's name, which resulted in the formation of the Assemblies of God in 1914. [He] viewed his lifelong task as one of preserving the 'Holy Ghost spiritual essence' and the 'prayer tradition' of the Pentecostal religious experience" (40).

102. Juanita Williams Faulkner and Raynard D. Smith, eds., *It Is Written: Minutes of the General Assembly Church of God in Christ Held at Memphis Tennessee, 1919–1932* (Memphis, TN: COGIC Publishing House, 2017), 47; see 61–62 for a similar but extended statement; also quoted in Raynard D. Smith, "Seeking the Just Society: Charles Harrison Mason's Quest for Social Equality," on *With Signs Following: The Life and Ministry of Charles Harrison Mason*, ed. Raynard Smith (St. Louis: Christian Board Publication, 2015), 107. See also the FBI documents regarding the surveillance of Mason in Sherry Sherrod DuPree and Herbert DuPree, *Exposed!!! Federal Bureau of Investigation Unclassified Reports on Churches and Church Leaders* (Washington, DC: Middle Atlantic Regional Press, 1993), 9–11, 15, 31–32.

explaining why he and other members objected to participation in World War I on religious grounds.[103] David Daniels notes that this pacifist campaign by Mason "was the first major political activity of Pentecostal African Americans."[104]

Along with his scriptural beliefs regarding war, Mason also objected to blacks participating in the fighting because "he witnessed how Whites were vehemently opposed to African Americans wearing their military uniforms in America," and he "questioned the legitimacy of African Americans fighting for democracy abroad when they had no democracy at home."[105] Because of these views, the Bureau alleged that Mason subverted the draft and advised black men not to fight in the war.[106] On July 16, 1918, a short time after he preached this sermon, Mason and two other men, William B. Holt and Henry Kirvin, were arrested and charged with committing offenses against the government.[107] One of the FBI documents regarding the matter reads as follows: "The activities of the Church of God in Christ have recently been called to our attention because of religious literature which is spreading among the Southern Negroes. Its general headquarters are in Memphis, Tennessee. The literature of this organization states that 'the shedding of blood or the taking of human life is contrary to the teaching of the Savior, and that since 1895 its members have been forbidden to take up arms or to shed human blood in any form.' [Bureau Deletion] The chief overseer of this organization is Elder C. H. Mason, now in custody at Jackson, Miss."[108]

In the end, because of no solid evidence, the grand jury did not indict Mason, Holt, or Kirvin, and the charges were dropped.[109] Mason describes his victory over the situation in Pauline terms: "The enemy (the devil) tried

---

My thanks to Sherry Sherrod DuPree for alerting me to this source. See also DuPree, *A Compendium*, 44–52.

103. White, *The Rise to Respectability*, 65. See White's chapter, "Mason Told Us Not to Fight," which provides detailed information about the hardships Mason and others faced in objecting to the war.

104. Daniels, "Doing All the Good We Can,"168.

105. Raynard D. Smith, "Seeking the Just Society," 107.

106. Raynard D. Smith, "Seeking the Just Society," notes that Mason's preaching and teaching were quite persuasive, for, although the black population was nearly 80 percent in Holmes County, Mississippi, where Mason's church was located, more than half of those eligible for the draft did not sign up (107–8).

107. DuPree and DuPree, *Exposed!!!*, 9; White, *The Rise to Respectability*, 74.

108. DuPree and DuPree, *Exposed!!!*, 32.

109. White, *The Rise to Respectability*, 75.

to hinder me and bound me over in jail for several days. I thank God for the persecution. *'For all that will live Godly must suffer persecution'* [2 Tim. 3:12]."[110] Like Paul, Mason understood that to embody the gospel and to proclaim what is right inevitably leads to suffering. In Mason's case, to speak out against war and to fight to protect black lives meant speaking out against the nation and its laws. With his use of 2 Timothy 3:12, Mason demonstrates that he understands such activity as part of what it means to "live godly." Godly living involves utilizing the same mouth that engages in glossolalia to protest racial injustice, oppression, and war.

Mason begins the sermon by quoting Habakkuk 2:2 and then moves to a discussion about the German kaiser. "They tell me the Kaiser went into prayer and came out and lifted up his hands and prayed; and afterwards declared war. Let us see, what did he pray and for what reason did he pray? Surely he did not pray Thy kingdom come, because the *kingdom of God is righteousness, peace and joy in the Holy Ghost* [Rom. 14:17]. If he had been praying for peace, he would not have declared war."[111] Here Mason employs Paul to critique the German kaiser, asserting that the kingdom of God is peace and the kaiser's declaration of war is antithetical to peace, to God's kingdom, and to the Spirit. Mason continues to critique the kaiser by employing 1 Timothy 2:1-2, 8, in which "supplications, prayers, intercessions" are to be made for all people so that "we may lead a quiet and peaceful life" and that people should "pray everywhere lifting up holy hands, without wrath and doubting." The German leader, according to Mason, does not have the spirit of prayer because he is not endeavoring to live a peaceful life but rather prays in wrath "with the purpose to work wrath," thereby doing the opposite of what the apostle advises.[112]

In addition, Mason proclaims that the kaiser is not of God and does not have the *Spirit of Christ* (Rom. 8:9).[113] Rather, the kaiser's actions demonstrate that he is under a "devilish spirit" because he "causes women to be ravished, infants to be dashed to pieces, and prisoners of war to be tortured."[114] Depicting the kaiser as the war beast of Revelation 13 and the antichrist, Mason declares that the German ruler will have to answer to God for his actions and for the destruction of human life.[115] Although Mason supports

110. Raynard D. Smith, "Seeking the Just Society," 108.
111. E. W. Mason, *The Man*, 36.
112. E. W. Mason, *The Man*, 36.
113. E. W. Mason, *The Man*, 36, 38.
114. Mary C. Mason, *The History and Life Work of Bishop C. H. Mason*, 39.
115. E. W. Mason, *The Man*, 37, 39.

the purchase of liberty bonds to help the American government, he prays that "peace will be restored to a war-torn world."[116] What is new and subversive in Mason's utilization of Paul in this sermon is that Paul is no longer only used to critique America, its racist policies and government action or inaction, but now blacks appropriate the apostle to critique foreign governments and their violation of scriptural admonitions. In public space Mason openly declares that Paul advocates for life and peace and his letters serve as a means to protest war. As we have seen throughout this volume, African Americans employ Paul in various ways to protest racism, injustice, oppression, and men's refusal to ordain women. Here, Mason expands the sphere of African American Pauline protest literature to include black resistance to war, a resistance that extends from America's participation in the war and all the way to Germany.

Mason's use of Paul's words to name his denomination speaks to the ability of black preachers and black interpreters to refuse to relegate Paul to white surpremacist interpretations. It could be argued that the divine revelation Mason receives for naming his church is in some sense a divine refutation of a white supremacist reading of the apostle. Mason continues the long historical trajectory of black hermeneuts appropriating Paul in a liberating manner. Like the conversion narratives and the divine encounters that appear in this volume, Mason's account of his baptism of the Spirit and his subsequent prayer regarding the gift of interpretation are replete with Pauline echoes and citations. He adopts and adapts Pauline language, and in so doing depicts a significant link with the apostle and his own understanding of God's present continued activity in the church. Although societal pressure prevented Mason's "racially inclusive" vision for his denomination from coming to pass, "it was C. H. Mason . . . who grasped and stood with Seymour in the revival that united glossolalia with the Pauline vision of an all-inclusive egalitarian fellowship in which there is '. . . neither Jew nor Greek, bond nor free, . . . male nor female . . .' (Galatians 3:28, Colossians 3:11)."[117] Mason believes that what God began in Acts continues with the present-day church, for the present church is part of the same people of God upon which God poured the divine Spirit. Significantly, Mason also employs Paul's words to critique the German kaiser and therefore gives the protest dimension of African American Pauline hermeneutics an international lens.

116. E. W. Mason, *The Man*, 39.
117. Raynard D. Smith, "Seeking the Just Society," 104.

Ida B. Robinson (1891–1946): Denominational Founder

Ida B. Robinson founded the largest African American Pentecostal denomination established by a woman, and she also has the honor of starting the largest denomination led by an African American woman. Mount Sinai Holy Church of America, Inc., from its inception in 1924, has been a church body that has upheld and fostered women leadership and equality in ministry, and until recently has had women bishops leading the organization.[118] Robinson was born in 1891 in Hazelhurst, Georgia, and moved to Florida with her family while she was still a child, and she associated early on with the Church of God (Cleveland, Tennessee). In 1917, during the Great Migration, she and her husband moved to Philadelphia, and she became a part of the Mount Olive Holy Church, where Elder Henry Fisher ordained her to the ministry. When the pastor of the church passed away, Robinson became the pastor. The church was one of the originating congregations of the Northern District of the United Holy Church of America.[119] Robinson was a powerful pastor renowned for her speaking, singing, and preaching abilities, and as an evangelist she traveled around the country proclaiming the gospel. Male leaders of the United Holy Church recognized her gifts and often called upon her to assist them in church services.[120]

Due to her powerful ministry, other women within the denomination began to seek ordination and leadership roles. In response, the male leadership decided in 1924 to no longer "'publicly' ordain women to the ministry." Robinson reacted to this decision by fasting and praying for ten days in order to seek God's guidance as to what to do, after which she contended that God had told her to leave the United Holy Church and to start a new denomination, which she immediately did, calling it the Mount Sinai Holy Church of America. In her protest of the United Holy Church's decision regarding women ordination, she argued, "If Mary the mother of Jesus could carry the word of God in her womb, why can't women carry the word of God in

118. Alexander, *Limited Liberty*, 119. According to the 100th anniversary edition of the *Mount Olive Times* (vol. 2, issue 1), the bishops that succeeded Robinson after her death were Bishop Elmira Jeffries (1946–1964), Bishop Agnes Ziegler (1964–1969), Bishop Mary Jackson (1969–1980), Bishop Sylvester Webb (1980–1991), and Bishop Amy Stevens (1991–2000). The first male leader of the church was Bishop Sylvester Webb, and as of this writing, the pastor is Bishop Thomas Martin, who began the pastorate in 2001.

119. Alexander, *Limited Liberty*, 121.

120. Alexander, *Limited Liberty*, 122.

their mouth?"[121] Another version of her departure from the United Holy Church appears in Rosalie S. Owens's recent biography, in which Robinson's decision to leave after her ten-day fast was not precipitated by the decision of the United Holy Church but came about because "God told her to do so," commissioning her to start a new work.[122] At any rate, Robinson's new ministry focused on elevation of women preachers and leaders, and like Zilpha Elaw, Jarena Lee, and Julia Foote before her, she affirmed God's call upon women to preach and maintained that this call cannot and should not be proscribed by men.

Led by Robinson, who became the denomination's first bishop, the Mount Sinai denomination grew, reaching as far as Cuba and Guyana. Robinson ordained women across America, and although male ministers and officers were present in the organization, the leadership of the church consisted mainly of women.[123] Estrelda Alexander insightfully observes the impact of Robinson's decision: "Even though her own future in the United Holy Church would probably have been secure, Robinson's intention in starting her movement was specifically to establish an organization in which every woman minister would have full freedom to participate in every level of ministry, and in which women would have full clergy rights—including the right to ordination as bishop. Accordingly, every action she took as head of the newly formed denomination reflected this commitment and intention."[124] Robinson's unswerving belief that God called women just as God called men compelled her to create spaces for women so that they could fulfill their divine mandates without human-made restrictions.

Like the other hermeneuts examined in this chapter, Robinson believed the church should minister to the whole person. Therefore, she started a soup kitchen, began a school for elementary through high school students, and purchased a farm. And, like Charles Harrison Mason, she had pacifist leanings.[125] Because of this stance and because her congregations were ra-

---

121. Alexander, *Limited Liberty*, 123.

122. Rosalie S. Owens, *Bishop Ida Bell Robinson: The Authoritarian Servant Leader* (Middletown, DE: Rosalie Owens, 2019), 39. According to Alexander, *Limited Liberty*, although Robinson left the United Holy Church, she remained friends with its leaders and continued to fellowship with them in services (125). See also Owens, 39–40.

123. Bettye Collier-Thomas, *Daughters of Thunder: Black Women Preachers and Their Sermons, 1850–1979* (San Francisco: Jossey-Bass, 1998), 194.

124. Alexander, *Limited Liberty*, 125.

125. Alexander, *Limited Liberty*, 130–31. Alexander notes that many African American Pentecostals were pacifists during this period.

cially mixed, Robinson came under FBI surveillance during World War II. Alexander notes that she used her radio broadcast to speak out against the war, and since her secretary was a German woman whose husband was Italian, Robinson and her congregation became "suspected of sympathizing with the enemy."[126] One of her FBI files states that she was "placed on a list of agitators in Philadelphia for statements she made."[127] Later, however, the FBI dropped her name from their list.[128]

As indicated, Robinson was a trailblazer in a number of ways. Her intrepid spirit is also manifest in the way she utilizes Paul in her sermons to emphasize holiness and separation from the world and to speak out against the horrendous practice of lynching in this country. In her sermon "Economic Persecution," Robinson describes the plight of the early church: "In the early days of Christianity, under the old order of things, everyone who openly called on the name of the Lord Jesus was persecuted indescribably. Many of them died calling on the name of the Lord to the very end."[129] She speaks about the martyrs of the early church and how the gospel, in spite of persecution, continued to spread. In response to the Christians' prayers regarding the severe persecution they were experiencing, God touched the heart of Constantine, who became a converted "witness of Jesus Christ, and a powerful friend of the church."[130] As a result of his conversion to Christianity, persecution of believers ceased and the gospel continued to expand.

After providing this historical backdrop, Robinson proceeds to compare blacks' situation in the South with that of the early Christian believers. "At present the same conditions [prevail] in substance. Our people in certain southern states, are killed, their bodies dismembered and thrown to vultures. This, of course, is a common occurrence, and unfortunately, [occurs] where 'Christianity' is more prevalent than any other part of our Union. For in this section of the country laws are made to uphold 'Christianity' in their states, and to prevent any teachings in their institutions of learning that tend to distort, minimize or otherwise change the principle of

126. Alexander, *Limited Liberty*, 132.

127. DuPree and DuPree, *Exposed!!!*, 37. See also 38, 48, 53.

128. Alexander, *Limited Liberty*, 132.

129. Collier-Thomas, *Daughters of Thunder*, 203. Parts of this sermon are also quoted in Alexander, *Limited Liberty*, 133–34. Collier-Thomas calls this text a sermon, whereas Alexander refers to it as an article that Robinson wrote for her organization's newsletter, the *Latter Day Messenger*.

130. Collier-Thomas, *Daughters of Thunder*, 203.

the doctrine of Christianity as taught in the Bible."[131] Robinson denounces Christianity as practiced in the South, arguing that the South's Christian religiosity condones and permits blacks to be murdered, thereby indicating that its Christianity is no Christianity at all. Southerners actually "ignore the words of the sacred 'Book' they pretend to love so dearly." Since they ignore those words, Robinson declares that she will, in stark contrast, appeal to the Bible's "wisdom and justice." She then quotes Ephesians 4:5–6, where Paul emphasizes Christian unity. Robinson writes, "There is but *'One Lord one faith and one baptism'* [Eph. 4:5] so that, if *God is the Father of all* [Eph. 4:6], the relationship that [exists] between Gentile and Jew, as well as Ethiopians, is [inseparable] and unquestionably established. So let us saints, pray that the Constantine of our day (if there be one) sends a letter to the modern pagans in the [polluted] southland in the form of 'Anti-lynch' legislation that is now pending in Congress."[132] Robinson draws upon the apostle's language of unity and God's fatherhood of all people to point out that the lynchings occurring in the South directly oppose God's vision of a united humanity.

Robinson's use of Paul at this point is a perfect example of what Peter Paris calls the ability of black Americans to extricate "the gospel from its racist entanglements. In the Bible, blacks found a perspective on humanity that was wholly different from that which they experienced in the teachings and practices of white Americans. The universal parenthood of God implied a universal kinship of humankind. This is the basic proposition of the hermeneutic designated as the black Christian tradition."[133] For Robinson, Paul's words affirm that God established a bond between gentiles, Jews, and Ethiopians, a divinely created human bond between the races that confirms the humanity of all people, including black people. Thus, the fact that people do not speak out against the lynchings of African Americans is antithetical to God's divine decree.

Robinson likens blacks with early Christians and Southern whites with pagans in the time of the early church. As pagans back then persecuted believers, so too are some white Christians persecuting African Americans.

---

131. Collier-Thomas, *Daughters of Thunder*, 204.

132. Collier-Thomas, *Daughters of Thunder*, 204. The full citation is as follows: "One Lord, one faith, one baptism, One God and Father of all, who is above all, and through all, and in you all" (Eph. 4:5–6). See also the discussion of this sermon in Collier-Thomas, 197–99, and Alexander, *Limited Liberty*, 133–34.

133. Peter Paris, "The Bible and the Black Churches," in Sandeen, *The Bible and Social Reform*, 135.

Courageously, Robinson avers that although white believers in the South maintain that they are Christians enacting laws to "uphold Christianity," they are in fact "modern pagans" who defy the gospel they proclaim to love. Robinson urges those in her congregation to pray like the early believers did, so that, like in the time of old, God may raise up a modern-day Constantine who, like the Constantine in the past, will put an end to the killing of innocent people. In addition, Robinson employs Paul's reference to Satan in 2 Corinthians 4:4, in which Paul calls Satan the "god of this world," to indicate the satanic element of the spiritual dimension behind the false Christianity prevalent in the South.[134] This reality comes to the fore through the actions of those who claim to be righteous but whose behavior reveals that they are really "enemies of Jesus Christ."[135] As someone who led a denomination that had churches and congregations in the South, which she often visited, it is no doubt that the practice of lynching was a disturbing reality for her.

Robinson draws upon Paul's writings to assert blacks' humanity and the value of black lives in a time when lynching had become the norm. God as the Father of all affirms that black people are made in the image of God, and so they deserve to live and not die. Bettye Collier-Thomas says Robinson "has not received adequate recognition and is still virtually unknown to scholars and the general public" but that "her legacy survives through the denomination she founded and the church she established in Philadelphia."[136] As has been demonstrated throughout this volume, many white interpreters utilized Paul's words to dehumanize blacks, yet an important part of Robinson's legacy is her use of Paul to argue for black personhood and the value of black lives. She follows in the footsteps of so many courageous black women preachers before her, some of whom are discussed in this volume, such as Jarena Lee, Zilpha Elaw, and Julia Foote, who dared to preach and refused to be silenced by male leadership. Although she follows in their footsteps, she does what they could not do in their own time and place historically, which is to begin a denomination run by women. Along with championing women's rights to preach, she champions the right of black people to live and employs Paul in the articulation of that right.

134. Collier-Thomas, *Daughters of Thunder*, 198; 2 Cor. 4:4 reads: "In whom the god of this world hath blinded the minds of them which believe not, lest the light of the glorious gospel of Christ, who is the image of God, should shine unto them."

135. Collier-Thomas, *Daughters of Thunder*, 204.

136. Collier-Thomas, *Daughters of Thunder*, 195–96.

Howard Thurman (1899–1981):
Twentieth-Century Pastor, Activist, Mystic, and Theologian

Howard Thurman has been called one of the most important theologians of the twentieth century.[137] He attended Morehouse College and Rochester Theological Seminary (now Colgate Rochester Crozer Divinity School) and graduated from both as valedictorian of his class. Later he became professor of religion and director of religious life at Morehouse and Spelman, and after that, he pastored the Church for the Fellowship of All Peoples in San Francisco, a multiracial congregation. After almost ten years there (1944–1953), he became the first African American dean of Marsh Chapel at Boston University and professor of spiritual disciplines and resources (1953–1965).[138] After retiring from this position, he continued his work for racial justice and interracial community through his charitable and education foundation, the Howard Thurman Educational Trust, which he led until his passing in 1981.[139] Albert Raboteau remarks that Thurman "was a mesmerizing preacher whose voice and presence articulated with power his vision of interracial religious community"[140] and that he believed that "true social change needed to be grounded in spiritual experience."[141] His work on racial reconciliation, his efforts for justice for the oppressed, and his spiritual insight into Christian Scripture forged interpretive pathways for many subsequent explicators of these sacred texts.

As indicated in the opening chapter of this volume, Thurman's story regarding his grandmother, Nancy Ambrose, and her aversion to many of the Pauline texts because of her experience of these Scriptures in slavery, has become quite well known. In some circles, her story has become the Ur-text to advocate African American rejection of Paul. However, Ambrose's powerful story is only a part of the narrative regarding African Americans'

137. See the insightful analysis of Howard Thurman and his life by Raboteau, *American Prophets*, 95–117, who writes, "In looking at the life and thought of this mystic, poet, ecumenist, and preacher, Howard Thurman, perhaps we may gain a measure of hope and wisdom for our own situation, if we, like him, are truly committed to the search for common ground" (98).

138. Walter Earl Fluker and Catherine Tumber, eds., *A Strange Freedom: The Best of Howard Thurman on Religious Experience and Public Life* (Boston: Beacon, 1998), 3–6; Raboteau, *American Prophets*, 101–8.

139. Raboteau, *American Prophets*, 108.

140. Raboteau, *American Prophets*, 108.

141. Raboteau, *American Prophets*, 110.

relationship with Paul. Most African Americans, by and large, despite how Paul was used against them, adopted and adapted him to their own lives and contexts, and in many instances they heard his voice as one that denounced the oppression he was used to legitimize.

Not only has Ambrose's experience with Paul become an avenue for some to dismiss Paul's relevance for African Americans, but her experience also profoundly shaped Howard Thurman's view of Paul. After relating his grandmother's words to him, he writes of how her account deeply affected him: "Since that fateful day on the front porch in Florida I have been work-ing on the problem her words presented."[142] In *Jesus and the Disinherited*, we find the most comprehensive articulation of Thurman's view of Jesus and Paul. Thurman begins the book by raising the question of what Je-sus's teaching and life mean for those who have "their backs against the wall" (11), which are the majority of the people in the world, because most of the human population consists of "the poor, the disinherited, and the dispossessed. What does our religion say to them?" (13). This critical ques-tion leads Thurman to assess the current state of Christianity as woefully inadequate in relation to its founding, since it originated in suffering and persecuted communities but now is in the hands of the wealthy and the powerful and so becomes another instrument with which to oppress the weak and the dispossessed.

According to Thurman, several reasons exist for this co-optation of the Christian religion. First, the "missionary impulse" that is so much a part of Christian thought is problematic, because although it encourages people to share with others, this impulse can facilitate pride and arrogance. Christians are encouraged to see their role in helping the poor and the needy, but this same role may cause them to view themselves as superior to those they help, which fosters within them a sense of self-righteousness and racial superior-ity. Thurman understands that such views have caused many Christians to divorce mission from humanity. "For decades we have studied the various peoples of the world and those who live as our neighbors as objects of mis-sionary endeavor and enterprise without being at all willing to treat them either as brothers or as human beings" (13). Echoing the sentiments of black

---

142. Howard Thurman, *Jesus and the Disinherited* (Richmond, IN: Friends United, 1981), 31. Hereafter, page references from this work will be given in parentheses in the text. For collections of additional writings by Thurman, see Fluker and Tumber, *A Strange Free-dom*; *The Papers of Howard Washington Thurman*, ed. Walter Fluker (Columbia: University of South Carolina Press, 2009–2017).

hermeneuts before him, such as Harriet Jacobs, Thurman laments American Christianity's emphasis on mission to other countries while at the same time refusing to see the African Americans in their own country and the people to whom they minister in other countries as human beings.

The second reason for the co-optation of the Christian religion by the powerful, according to Thurman, is the disconnection in Christian thought and teaching between Jesus and his Jewish heritage. Jesus's Jewish heritage is central to understanding Jesus's identity, for when one examines his history, one sees that Jesus was a poor Jew and a member of a minority group dominated by Roman imperial rule. His economic position in society means that he can identify with the "mass of men on the earth," since the "masses of the people are poor" (17). Understanding Jesus's background is important because if one's faith derives from a people who suffered, who were poor and under oppression by the Romans, then one does not want to inflict suffering upon others or justify it. Moreover, how could one argue that their religion is to dominate the world if their own faith came about in the midst of domination where oppression remained rampant?

Thurman views Jesus's situation as similar to the Negro's plight in America. Both Jesus and blacks are minorities, experiencing oppression by the dominant and the powerful. In proclaiming this parallel, Thurman argues that Jesus provided a technique of survival for the oppressed in his own day and so also offered a technique of survival for blacks and all who experience oppression in the modern world.

> The basic fact is that Christianity as it was born in the mind of this Jewish teacher and thinker appears as a technique of survival for the oppressed. That it became, through the intervening years, a religion of the powerful and the dominant, used sometimes as an instrument of oppression, must not tempt us into believing that it was thus in the mind and life of Jesus. "In him was life; and the life was the light of men." Wherever his spirit appears, the oppressed gather fresh courage; for he announced the good news that fear, hypocrisy, and hatred, the three hounds of hell that track the trail of the disinherited, need have no dominion over them. (29)

That Christianity later became the religion the dominant used as an instrument of oppression means that many people find little or no relevance in the church's teaching regarding Jesus and Scripture for their everyday lives. They see Christianity as a largely otherworldly religion fixated on heaven and not eradicating the injustices of the present. Indeed, Thurman observes that for many Christianity seems to be a "betrayal of the Negro into the hands of his enemies by focusing his attention upon heaven, forgiveness, love, and the like" (29). Thurman admits that although these elements are part of Jesus's teaching, one must look at the entire context of Jesus's life before injudiciously espousing such attributes. He maintains that if one focuses on retrieving the "religion of Jesus," then it is possible even in the midst of the church's "betrayal of his faith" to recover a Christianity that speaks to those whose backs are against the wall. Thurman asserts that if we can understand the religion of Jesus, we can embrace Christianity even though it has been used to victimize and oppress.

The third reason for the co-optation of Christianity by the powerful rests upon Paul, who has been given undue weight in the course of Christian history and thought. Although Paul, like Jesus, was a Jew and a minority, in contradistinction to Jesus, he was a Roman citizen, which afforded him a great amount of privilege, privilege not shared by Jesus. As a result, Thurman describes Paul as "a minority but with majority privileges" (32). Since Paul enjoyed such privileges of Roman citizenship, he could appeal to Caesar when in trouble (Acts 25:11), write that slaves should obey their masters (Eph. 6:5; Col. 3:22), and write that all government is ordained by God (Rom. 13:1). His privileged position deeply affected how he viewed the world and how he wrote about it in his letters. Thurman acknowledges that there are places within the Pauline correspondence in which the apostle proclaims that the gospel transcends race, class, and other conditions, but the fact that there is another side to Paul that has been used throughout history to subjugate and afflict others cannot be ignored. For Thurman, then, Paul's citizenship creates a chasm between the world of Jesus and the world of Paul. He eloquently writes, "Now Jesus was not a Roman citizen. He was not protected by the normal guarantees of citizenship—that quiet sense of security which comes from knowing that you belong and the general climate of confidence which it inspires. If a Roman soldier pushed Jesus into a ditch, he could not appeal to Caesar; he would be just another Jew in the ditch. . . . Unless one actually lives day by day without a sense of security, he cannot understand what worlds separated Jesus from Paul at this point" (33–34).

The danger and the lack of protection that derive from noncitizenship, which describes Jesus's life and blacks' lives, are what make Jesus's life and faith relevant for African Americans and Paul irrelevant to a great extent and in some ways harmful. Thurman asserts that

The striking similarity between the social position of Jesus in Palestine and that of the vast majority of American Negroes is obvious to anyone who tarries long over the facts. . . . It is the similarity of a social climate at the point of a denial of full citizenship which creates the problem for creative survival. For the most part, Negroes assume that there are no basic citizenship rights, no fundamental protection, guaranteed to them by the state, because their status as citizens has never been clearly defined. There has been for them little protection from the dominant controllers of society and even less protection from the unrestrained elements within their group. (34)

When one recalls that Thurman writes at a time when lynchings, police brutality, lack of voting rights, and segregation reign supreme, one sees clearly the analogues he makes at this point in his argument. Unlike Paul, who had a sense of belonging and a sense of status, Jesus and the Negro have no status, no protection from violence from the state or elsewhere, and no recognition of their worth to the body politic.[143]

Unlike other interpreters examined above, Thurman explicitly and purposefully juxtaposes Paul with Jesus and determines that Jesus trumps Paul because Jesus's life was not one of privilege. For Thurman, Paul's words are in many ways relativized by his privileged status and can only be of limited relevance for the everyday lives of the oppressed and disinherited. Paul's Roman citizenship hampers his vision and causes him to espouse views that throughout history have been harmful to the weak and the dispossessed.[144] Jesus's *Sitz im leben* (situation in life), however, is more similar to the Negro's plight than to the apostle's. His life, teaching, and faith intersect with the African American liminal space of citizenship and the accompanying suffering and injustices that inhabit that space.

---

143. In this work Thurman does not deal with the *peristasis catalogues* that appear frequently in Paul's letters and list the sufferings that he undergoes, including violence at the hand of the Roman authorities (e.g., 2 Cor. 4:8–12; 6:4–10; 11:23–29). See my brief discussion of Paul and the violence of the Roman state in Lisa Bowens, "Painting Hope: Formational Hues of Paul's Spiritual Warfare Language in 2 Corinthians 10–13," in *Practicing with Paul: Reflections on Paul and the Practices of Ministry in Honor of Susan G. Eastman*, ed. Presian Burroughs (Eugene, OR: Wipf & Stock, 2018), particularly 117–20.

144. Thurman, like all the black hermeneuts discussed in this monograph, does not distinguish between the Paul of Acts and the Paul of the letters. Modern critical biblical scholarship does make the distinction, however, and so there is current debate as to whether Paul really was a Roman citizen, since he does not mention this fact in his letters.

Albert Cleage Jr. (1911–2000):
Advocate and Activist for the Black Nation

Albert Cleage was born in 1911 in Indianapolis but grew up in Detroit. He enrolled at Wayne State University, majoring in psychology, and in 1936 became a social worker. He then went on to study with Charles Johnson, a premiere sociologist at Fisk University. In 1938 he decided to pursue ministry and earned his MDiv degree at Oberlin. In his studies, he rejected the social gospel because of its nonrealistic stance and leaned more toward Reinhold Niebuhr, whose realism he found to be a more adequate depiction of society.[145]

After ordination in the Congregational Church in 1943, Cleage became an interim pastor at a newly established integrated church, San Francisco Church for the Fellowship of All Peoples, among whose founding members was Howard Thurman. Cleage was copastor of the church until Thurman arrived and took on the position. The church had one black pastor, Cleage, and one white pastor, Albert Fisk, a white Presbyterian, to model integration and interracial leadership. But Cleage protested that his copastor, while well intentioned, preached an optimistic social gospel that "avoided crises such as the Japanese interment and the treatment of black soldiers."[146] For Cleage, Fisk's refusal to engage such pressing faith matters indicated "white Christianity's utter inability to address systemic moral evil" and that "black and white theological interests were fundamentally oppositional."[147] In 1953, he started his own church that was devoted to providing programs for the poor, advocating for better education for blacks, and promoting black empowerment. As D. Kimathi Nelson notes, "the first tenet of his newly founded church was that, 'No area of Black life was too controversial for our church to be involved,'"[148] and that "his integrity as a champion of black people was beyond reproach. When people had problems that reflected racism or injustice, they knew to call Reverend Cleage."[149]

---

145. Marbury, *Pillars*, 174, 176, 177. See also the important analysis of Albert Cleage in Paris, "The Bible," 148–51.

146. Marbury, *Pillars*, 177.

147. Marbury, *Pillars*, 177, 178.

148. D. Kimathi Nelson, "The Theological Journey of Albert B. Cleage, Jr.: Reflections from Jaramogi's Protégé and Successor," in *Albert Cleage Jr. and the Black Madonna and Child*, ed. Jawanza Eric Clark (New York: Palgrave Macmillan, 2016), 23.

149. Nelson, "The Theological Journey," 24.

Cleage was an outspoken advocate of the civil rights movement but disagreed with Martin Luther King Jr.'s methods. His approach aligned more with Malcolm X's sense of direct action. Cleage rejected the idea that American society could be just toward blacks; history and the present circumstances taught him otherwise.[150] The nation's constant declaration of black inferiority through its policies and laws indicated to him that the full integration advocated by the civil rights movement could not be realized.[151] Cleage was deeply concerned that black people internalized this idea of black inferiority, causing a black person to "hate everything about his community, everything about his culture, everything about his imitation institutions which he has patterned after white institutions, believing that all of these things are inferior because he is inferior."[152] Cleage believed that one of the significant roles of the black church was to combat and destroy the myth of black inferiority.

To fulfill this mission of destroying the notion of black inferiority, he launched the Black Christian Nationalist movement and the Pan African Orthodox Christian Church.[153] And in 1967, on Easter Sunday, Cleage revealed an eighteen-foot painting of a black Madonna and renamed Central Congregational the Shrine of the Black Madonna. For Cleage, this unveiling symbolized black freedom from a distorted Christianity that taught that black was evil and unworthy of divine salvation.[154] He writes of the meaning of this black Madonna:

It wasn't so long ago that such a conception [black Madonna] would have been impossible for us. Our self-image was so distorted that we didn't believe that even the Almighty God could use us for his purpose because we were so low and despised. Now we have come to the place where we not only can conceive of the possibility, but we are convinced, upon the basis of our knowledge and historic study of all the facts that Jesus was born to

150. Marbury, *Pillars*, 178–79; William C. Turner Jr., "Preaching the Spirit: The Liberation of Preaching," *Journal of Pentecostal Theology* 14, no. 1. (2005): 4.

151. Marbury, *Pillars*, 179. Marbury's insightful analysis of Cleage's views and his relationship to King and the civil rights movement is invaluable. See 174–200.

152. As quoted in Marbury, *Pillars*, 178.

153. Jawanza Eric Clark, "Introduction: Why a White Christ Continues to Be Racist: The Legacy of Albert B. Cleage Jr.," in Clark, *Albert Cleage Jr. and the Black Madonna and Child*, 1–2; Nelson, "The Theological Journey," 22.

154. For example, see the discussion in chap. 2 regarding narratives told about black people's origins.

a black Mary, that Jesus, the Messiah was a black man who came to save a Black nation. . . . Our unveiling of the Black Madonna is a statement of faith. . . . It is an unfolding conception, tremendous in its meanings, as we begin to think through this knowledge which has been kept from us for so long, and which we are only now beginning to understand. To reclaim our own history, our own faith, our own religion, our own Black Messiah, and to begin to conceive again of the resurrection of a black nation is a wonderful thing.[155]

According to Cleage, Jesus was a black revolutionary Messiah who came to resurrect the black nation of Israel; historically, the nation of Israel during Jesus's time was black, since all the people in that part of the world during this period were black (99). Jesus proclaimed a message of liberation and revolution to his people, who were oppressed by white Rome. Integral to the resurrection message for African Americans in the present day is a refutation of a distorted Christianity based on white supremacy, which portrays Jesus and God as white. African Americans, therefore, must recover the true message and identity of Jesus. To facilitate this process, one must reject Paul and his teachings, since he is the reason for the loss and perversion of Jesus's original message. On this point Cleage's view is worth quoting at length:

> During this early period when people were trying to determine the meaning of the life and death of Jesus, the Apostle Paul came on the scene with an entirely new interpretation. He had never seen Jesus in the flesh, but his interpretation dominated the early Church and greatly influenced the Gospels when they were written. So in the Book of Galatians and in the Acts of the Apostles, you have a whole lot of arguing going on between the Disciples and the Apostle Paul. . . . Why were the followers of Jesus critical of the Apostle Paul? Because the Apostle Paul was leaning over backward to convert the Gentiles. "Apostle to the gentiles" meant Apostle to the white people. Paul was taking the religion of a Black Nation to white people who had no background in religion. But to make it acceptable to them he had to change it. (88–89)

Since Jesus was black, he preached to a black Jewish nation. However, Paul takes Jesus's message and changes it in order to make it suitable for

155. Albert B. Cleage Jr., *The Black Messiah* (Kansas City, MO: Sheed & Ward, 1968), 85–86. Hereafter, page references from this work will be given in parentheses in the text.

gentiles, who, in Cleage's formulation, consist of white people. Thus, because of Paul, "the historic Jesus is completely lost. Paul's distortion of Jesus could even be taken into Europe where there were nothing but heathens, pagans and barbarians who lived in caves and ate raw meat. They accepted violence as a way of life. These were the white barbaric European Gentiles who now dominate the world. The Apostle Paul kept trying to change the religion of Jesus to meet their needs and so he lost the concept of the Black Nation which gave the teachings of Jesus meaning" (89–90).

For Cleage, the Gospels provide glimpses of Jesus's revolutionary character as indicated by the charges brought against him, such as stirring up trouble and forbidding people to give tribute to Caesar. Such accusations were "political charges" that reveal Jesus was a revolutionary leader engaging in nation building and guiding his people into conflict with their oppressors (91). Paul, on the other hand, takes the nation-oriented message of Jesus, which urges the Jewish people to resist their oppressors, and turns it into an individual-oriented proclamation, which emphasizes individual faith in Christ and individual salvation (92–93). And so, the "Resurrection of the Nation" to which Jesus's own resurrection points is lost due to the apostle Paul. Yet, it can be recovered, according to Cleage, if one goes to the Bible, searches for the religion of Jesus, and separates the black Messiah's religion from that of Paul (98).

Cleage's interpretation of Paul resonates with that of Howard Thurman in that both view Paul as largely dispensable to the articulation of black Christian faith. In other words, unlike the majority of interpreters discussed in this monograph, both explicitly reject Paul. In addition, both set Jesus and Paul in opposition to each other, giving Jesus and Jesus's message precedence over the apostle. Cleage, however, is arguably more radical in this sense than Thurman. Whereas Thurman acknowledged some of the egalitarian elements of Pauline Scripture, Cleage does not. In fact, Cleage "deletes the writings of St. Paul from the canon."[156] As William Turner observes, both Thurman and Cleage "credit Paul with planting the seeds of slaveholding Christianity."[157] These two Pauline interpreters, although not representing the dominant perspective of the apostle Paul present in African American writings, nevertheless exemplify the complicated relationship of African Americans with the apostle

156. Paris, "The Bible," 149. See also the recent collection of essays on Cleage entitled *Albert Cleage Jr. and the Black Madonna and Child.*

157. Turner, "Preaching the Spirit," 4. The phrase "slaveholding Christianity" comes from Frederick Douglass. See chap. 2.

and his letters. In their dismissal of Paul, they seek to demonstrate Scripture's relevancy to black lives and the everyday conditions faced by black people, such as police brutality, poverty, racism, and injustice. Whereas other black interpreters utilized Paul to combat these issues, for them, Paul was part of the problem and a central source of black oppression. Their rejection of Paul, then, is also an African American Pauline hermeneutic because it is another attempt by blacks to interpret Paul on their own terms, and in their cases to reject him, just as blacks historically experienced rejection because of him. Significantly, as had many of the black hermeneuts before them, their hermeneutic approaches to Paul sought to analyze the apostle's historical context (i.e., Thurman's analysis of Paul's Roman citizenship), to analyze the larger biblical history (i.e., Thurman's and Cleage's recognition of Jewish oppression by Rome), and to place these contexts in conversation with the African American plight. The complexity of the relationship of African Americans with Paul reflects Paul's own complex history.

Martin Luther King Jr. (1929–1968): Theologian of Resistance

Martin Luther King Jr. has been deemed a prophet,[158] "God's trombone,"[159] "a drum major for justice,"[160] and a "theologian of resistance"[161]—all deserved appellations that attempt to capture the profound impact he has made as the quintessential leader of the civil rights movement. Born in January

158. Paris, "The Bible," 141. Paris places King in the prophetic strand of the black church, and he defines this strand as "that of criticism, subjecting the prevailing institutions, beliefs, and practices to scrutiny in order to uncover their racist bias. This strand assumes that the nation has the will to correct its practices and beliefs when its errors are pointed out. Hence its style of criticism is constructive . . . it neither affirms nor celebrates the past uncritically but subjects all events, deeds, and actions to rigorous evaluation in accordance with the principles of the black Christian tradition. It diligently seeks to reveal the contradictions inherent in the life of the nation and to clarify the moral dimensions of those contradictions and to urge their resolution" (140–41). See also Obery M. Hendricks Jr., "An MLK Birthday Sermon," in *The Universe Bends toward Justice: Radical Reflections on the Bible, the Church, and the Body Politic* (Maryknoll, NY: Orbis, 2011), 195–206.

159. Richard Lischer, *The Preacher King: Martin Luther King, Jr. and the Word That Moved America* (New York: Oxford University Press, 1995), 12.

160. Lewis Baldwin, *Behind the Public Veil: The Humanness of Martin Luther King, Jr.* (Minneapolis: Fortress, 2016), 5.

161. Rufus Burrow Jr., *Martin Luther King, Jr., and the Theology of Resistance* (Jefferson, NC: McFarland, 2015), 5.

1929, King grew up in Atlanta, Georgia, in a household where his mother, Alberta King, was a teacher and his father, Martin Luther King Sr., was the pastor of Ebenezer Baptist Church. He graduated from high school at the age of fifteen and in 1948 received his bachelor's degree from Morehouse College. After graduating from Crozer Theological Seminary, King went on to receive his PhD from Boston University in 1955.[162]

In 1954, a year before receiving his doctorate, King became the pastor of Dexter Avenue Baptist Church in Montgomery, Alabama, where he helped lead a bus boycott in protest of the racial injustice against African Americans in which blacks were relegated to the back of the bus due to Jim Crow laws. The boycott, which began when Rosa Parks courageously refused to give up her seat on a bus, lasted over a year. During this protest, people bombed King's home and threatened his life, and he and other protestors endured physical brutality and intimidation by police and other government officials. The endurance of King and other African Americans during this boycott resulted in a victory for racial equality.[163]

The Montgomery boycott thrust King into the national spotlight and solidified his leadership in the civil rights movement. King's life as a Baptist preacher's kid, his training in seminary, and his doctoral studies enabled him to fuse his love for God, for the church, and for God's people with a gospel that spoke to individual and social concerns, particularly the racial prejudice and discrimination that permeated the Jim Crow South. King merged this liberative gospel with the nonviolence ideas of Mahatma Gandhi and became a champion for political, economic, and social equality. The following quote captures his view of the connection between being a minister and being an advocate for justice:

> Before I was a civil rights leader, I was a preacher of the gospel. This was my first calling and it still remains my greatest commitment. You know, actually all that I do in civil rights I do because I consider it a part of my ministry. I have no other ambitions in life but to achieve excellence in the Christian ministry. I don't plan to run for any political office. I don't plan to do anything but remain a preacher. And what I'm doing in this struggle, along with many others, grows out of my feeling that the preacher must be concerned about the whole man. Not merely his soul, but his body.[164]

162. Simmons and Thomas, *Preaching with Sacred Fire*, 514–15.
163. Simmons and Thomas, *Preaching with Sacred Fire*, 515.
164. Martin Luther King Jr., "'Why Jesus Called a Man a Fool,' Sermon Delivered at Mount

King understands a preacher's role to involve caring for people's souls as well their everyday issues. Being concerned about the whole man involves fighting oppression and advocating for equality. King does not compartmentalize social justice, ministry, and preaching. For him, each of these areas is deeply connected, and in fact, civil rights work derives from understanding what true ministry entails. To achieve excellence in the Christian ministry means to be concerned for the whole person. In this regard, King follows in the footsteps of others like Reverdy Ransom, who understood the preacher's job as to combine the spiritual and the physical and to see that these two realms are ultimately related.[165]

In 1957 King became the leader of the Southern Christian Leadership Conference, a group that formed to help lead the revived civil rights movement, and in 1963 he led another huge protest against racial injustice in Alabama, which led to his writing the now classic work "Letter from Birmingham City Jail," which will be discussed below. The protests, which occurred via sit-ins and marches, captured the nation's attention, especially the violent responses from the police department, which used hoses and dogs against the protestors. As was the case with the Montgomery boycott, these protests resulted in a victory as well.

In August of that same year, King led the famous March on Washington for Jobs and Freedom, at which over a quarter million attended, where he gave his renowned "I Have a Dream" speech. And in 1965, he was instrumental in the passage of the Voting Rights Act, which occurred after he, John Lewis, and Hosea Williams led several marches with the Student Nonviolent Coordinating Committee (SNCC) demanding an end to discrimination in voter registration. The marchers experienced violence and abuse from police officers, who beat them with clubs and terrorized them with tear gas. National television coverage of these events outraged the nation, and President Lyndon Johnson signed the Voting Rights Act in response to these events.[166]

Pisgah Missionary Baptist Church," August 27, 1967?, Stanford University Martin Luther King, Jr., Research and Education Institute, https://kinginstitute.stanford.edu/king-papers/docu ments/why-jesus-called-man-fool-sermon-delivered-mount-pisgah-missionary-baptist.

165. King stands in a long line of black ministers whose concern for the whole person permeates their work. This idea that the gospel transforms the entire individual was in direct opposition to some whites' theology in which the gospel affected the soul but not the body. Thus, slaves could be free spiritually but not physically. Blacks could be Christian, but they still needed to sit in the back of the bus. See additional analysis in the section on King's "Letter from Birmingham City Jail."

166. Simmons and Thomas, *Preaching with Sacred Fire*, 515.

King employs Paul and his letters extensively in his essays and speeches. We will discuss only four of his works, "Paul's Letter to American Christians," "The Letter from Birmingham City Jail," "Transformed Non-Conformist," and "Shattered Dreams." In each King employs Paul in subversive ways, developing an African American Pauline hermeneutic that counters the bigotry prevalent in American society.

"Paul's Letter to American Christians"

In King's essay "Paul's Letter to American Christians," he takes on the persona of the apostle to pen a letter to Christian believers in the United States. The assumptions undergirding this essay are that Paul would have something to say to America and that Paul is respected by the intended audiences. As discussed throughout this monograph, both white Christians and black Christians have used Paul and cited Paul for their respective causes. Here in this letter purported to be from the apostle himself, the historical veneration of Paul by white Americans and black Americans comes together in a heightened way. It is important to note that King does not write Jesus's letter to America but instead chooses to recognize the sacred place the apostle holds in both black and white Christian traditions. Thus, in this essay, the three hundred plus years in American history of using Paul to argue against injustice and oppression regarding race issues come to a head. It is because Paul has been and is still so venerated by both blacks and whites that King can pen a letter in his name and assume that his audiences would be willing to hear it.

The letter opens with a typical Pauline epistolary greeting: "Paul, called to be an apostle of Jesus Christ by the will of God, to you who are in America, grace be unto you, and peace, from God our Father, through our Lord and Savior, Jesus Christ."[167] As the historical Paul longed to see the Roman and Philippian believers, so too he has longed to see believers in America because he has heard so much about America's scientific and technological achievements. "Paul"[168] extols these advancements, noting America's supe-

167. Martin Luther King Jr., "Paul's Letter to American Christians," in *Strength to Love* (New York: Harper & Row, 1968), 127. Hereafter, page references from this work will be given in parentheses in the text. Letter greetings usually consist of sender, addressees, and wish of grace and peace from the sender to the recipients. See, for example, Rom. 1:1–7; Phil. 1:1–2.

168. Throughout the discussion of this essay, I place Paul in quotation marks to denote King taking on Paul's persona in this correspondence.

riority in these areas compared to other nations: "Through your scientific genius you have dwarfed distance and placed time in chains. You have made it possible to eat breakfast in Paris, France, and lunch in New York City" (127). At the same time, however, he chastises America because its moral progress and spiritual progress have not developed in the same way that its technological accomplishments have. "Paul" censures Americans: "Through your scientific genius you have made of the world a neighborhood, but you have failed to employ your moral and spiritual genius to make of it a brotherhood" (128). This ability to make distant places easily accessible coupled with a failure to improve morally and spiritually in loving each other leads to a devastation of the most painful kind, the destruction of the heart.

"Paul" reminds his audience that the ethical principles of Christianity are important to follow, and one cannot just be a Christian in name only but a Christian lifestyle must accompany that name. Just as he represented these ethical principles in his day, even though they were not popular, so, too, must American believers. They cannot allow themselves to follow societal "mores" that contradict scriptural admonitions. He cites Romans 12:1–2, declaring, "American Christians, I must say to you what I wrote to the Roman Christians years ago '*Be not conformed to this world: but be ye transformed by the renewing of your mind*'" (128). "Paul" admonishes his hearers to "Be who you say you are"; your actions must cohere with your Christian profession. King through Paul's voice contends that white Christians cannot be conformed to the world around them, which promotes and accepts segregation as the norm, but they must have a higher loyalty to God than to their Southern heritage. Paul's language enables King to challenge white Christians to allow God to renew their minds toward justice and equality.

Through the Romans 12 passage "Paul" espouses an apocalyptic notion of dual citizenship. Because God has broken into the present through the Christ event, this divine in-breaking creates for believers a dual citizenship in which they live in both time and eternity, in both the new age and the old age simultaneously (128). Although believers have an earthly citizenship and a heavenly citizenship, the heavenly citizenship should affect how they live out their earthly citizenship. "You must never allow the transitory, evanescent demands of manmade institutions to take precedence over the eternal demands of the Almighty God. In a time when men are surrendering the high values of the faith you must cling to them, and despite the pressure of an alien generation preserve them for children yet unborn. You must be willing to challenge unjust mores, to champion unpopular causes, and to buck the status quo" (128–29). When believers allow their heavenly citizenship to take precedence over their earthly citizenship, they will not conform to racist ide-ologies, white supremacy, segregation, or any forms of injustice. This notion of dual citizenship brings together spiritual and earthly realities and demon-strates how each reality is intricately linked with the other. Spiritual transfor-mation leads to earthly transformation, as demonstrated in one's behavior, beliefs, and social practices. Like the many black interpreters before him, such as David Walker and Reverdy Ransom, King proclaims an inextricable connection between the spiritual and the earthly; that is, salvation for him is comprehensive, transforming the individual but also reconfiguring society.

"Paul" also critiques the exploitative tendencies of capitalism, citing the unfairness of his time, that "one-tenth of 1 per cent of the population controls more than 40 per cent of the wealth." "America," he decries, "how often have you taken the necessities from the masses and given luxuries to the classes. If you are to be a truly Christian nation, you must solve this problem," and not by turning to communism, which is "based on ethical relativism, a meta-physical materialism, a crippling totalitarianism, and a withdrawal of basic freedom that no Christian can accept" (129). Instead, the country can utilize its democratic ideals to make sure that all have enough and that there is a better distribution of wealth.

Utilizing his body of Christ imagery (1 Cor. 12), "Paul" criticizes denom-inational divisions and divisions between races, where white churches and black churches worship separately. The imagery of the body functions as a way to emphasize God's plan of unity (129–30). Adopting a Pauline tone of indignation, King exclaims, "Another thing that disturbs me about the Amer-ican church is that you have a white church and a Negro church. How can segregation exist in the *body of Christ*? . . . How appalling this is!" Applying Paul's voice as found in Galatians 3:28 and Acts 17:26, King goes on to write,

> I understand that there are Christians among you who try to find biblical bases to justify segregation and argue that the Negro is inferior by nature. Oh, my friends, this is blasphemy and against everything that the Christian religion stands for. I must repeat what I have said to many Christians before, that in Christ *"there is neither Jew nor Greek, there is neither bond nor free, there is neither male nor female: for ye are all one in Christ Jesus"* [Gal. 3:28]. Moreover, I must reiterate the words I uttered on Mars Hill: "God that made the world and all things therein . . . *hath made of one blood all nations of men for to dwell on all the face of the earth"* [Acts 17:26]. So, Americans, I must urge you to be rid of every aspect of segregation. Segregation is a blatant denial of the unity which we have in Christ. (130)

King's appeal to Galatians 3:28 stresses further that in Christ all divisions are eradicated despite what some may say. Like his predecessors before him, King also holds up Acts 17:26 as a passage that excoriates racial division and white supremacy by demonstrating the unity God intends for all humanity. Segregation, then, opposes the unity believers have in Christ, and so to oppose desegregation is to oppose God's eternal will (131).[169]

"Paul" then calls upon the churches of America to resist segregation through social action, and he speaks directly to the victims of this horror by encouraging them to fight and protest injustice. Their overlap of citizenship (both earthly and heavenly) and the overlap of ages (new age and old age) in which they live mean that they wrestle against evil powers exhibited in the intransigence of racism and white supremacy. Therefore, they must fight with "*Christian weapons*" (2 Cor. 10:3–6) and "Christian methods" to defeat such entities (131). For King, these Christian weapons include nonviolent protest and the enduring power of love (132).

"Paul" knows, however, that when one stands up against evil, suffering and persecution inevitably result:

> Do not worry about persecution, American Christians; you must accept this when you stand up for a great principle. I speak with some authority, for my life was a continual round of persecutions. After my conversion I was rejected by the disciples at Jerusalem. Later I was tried for heresy at Jerusalem. I was jailed at Philippi, beaten at Thessalonica, mobbed at Ephesus, and depressed at Athens. I came away from each of these experiences more persuaded than ever that "*neither death, nor life, nor angels, nor principalities, nor things present, nor things to come . . . shall . . . separate us from the love of God, which is in Christ Jesus our Lord*" [Rom. 8:38–39]. The end of life is not to be happy nor to achieve pleasure and avoid pain, but to do the will of God, come what may. I have nothing but praise for those of you who have already stood unflinchingly before threats and intimidation, inconvenience and unpopularity, arrest and physical violence, to declare the doctrine of the Fatherhood of God and the brotherhood of man. (132)

In this essay King merges his voice and Paul's voice, but in this selection we see an extension of this merging. The sufferings that Paul undergoes

---

169. King's bold declaration that segregationists oppose God echoes Lemuel Haynes's provocative statement back in the 1700s that "Slavery is sin!" See the discussion of Lemuel Haynes in chap. 1.

for the gospel in his day become intertwined with the sufferings that King experiences in the civil rights struggle, and by extension the apostle's afflictions become interweaved with the hardships of all who suffer in the civil rights movement for the causes of justice and equality, ideals that are also, as King demonstrates in the essay, part of the gospel message. King succeeds in linking Paul to himself, but also to everyone, black and white, who endure enormous persecution because they protest segregation policies and laws. Paul's life becomes an example of what it means to suffer for righteousness and for those who struggle for justice; he becomes a fellow companion in the suffering. In addition, his words offer comfort and hope that no matter what happens in the fires of persecution, nothing can separate a person from God's love.

King closes the letter with a paraphrase of Paul's love chapter to the Corinthians (1 Cor. 13), a paraphrase shaped by what he sees as the issues endemic to the American church. The following excerpt from part of this final section of the correspondence illustrates the brilliant eloquence of the writer:

> [American Christians,] you may have the gift of scientific prediction and understand the behavior of molecules, you may break into the storehouse of nature and bring forth many new insights, you may ascend to the heights of academic achievement, so that you have all knowledge, and you may boast of your great institutions of learning and the boundless extent of your degrees; but, devoid of love, all of these mean absolutely nothing. But even more, Americans, you may give your goods to feed the poor, you may bestow great gifts to charity, and you may tower high in philanthropy, but if you have not love, your charity means nothing [1 Cor. 13]. (133)

As the Corinthians chose to overlook the value of love and focus on other gifts, such as prophecy and speaking in tongues, Paul reminds them that these gifts, while important, do not replace the gift of love. In fact, love should operate in tandem with these gifts because in the end love is the greatest gift of all (1 Cor. 13:13). Likewise, King here admonishes the American believers that their focus on such things as technology, science, philanthropy, and education does not negate the need for love either, because "love is the most durable power in the world" (133). King here discerns the reasoning behind the apostle's focus on love in the letter to the Corinthians and to the Americans, for Paul's focus on love is theological, christological, soteriological, and ecclesiological in that it is God-centered and cross-centered at the same time, an important nexus that shapes the community of faith. Since love is the essence of who God is, love then should characterize believers' own lives and practices. "Calvary," King writes, "is a telescope through which we look into the long vista of eternity and see the love of God breaking into time." God's love that breaks into time creates an overlapping of ages for believers who live in both the old and new age simultaneously, and yet through the power of divine love can bear witness to this divine in-breaking of God. Once he finishes his paraphrase of 1 Corinthians 13, "Paul" reiterates the words he spoke to the Corinthians at the end of another letter to them, in 2 Corinthians 13:11, and urges American believers to "Be of good comfort; be of one mind; and live in peace" (134). As the apostle closes his letter with exhortations of peace and unity, so too, King ends his correspondence with the same appeals.

"Letter from Birmingham City Jail"

King's essay "Letter from Birmingham City Jail" is, as Milton Sernett describes, "a classic in protest literature."[170] Arrested on Good Friday 1963 for his participation in a protest march, King remained in jail for eight days. While there he decides to respond to eight white religious leaders who have written a letter in opposition to the civil rights movement, asking its leaders and supporters to cease and desist. King responds to each of their accusations against the movement, and in doing so employs Pauline language and Scripture to repudiate their contentions and to present an alternative vision to the segregationist present.

King's writing of the letter itself presents similarities to Paul's prison epistles, such as Philippians, which the apostle wrote from jail after being incarcerated for the sake of the gospel. Like Paul, who suffered for proclaiming the truth of the gospel, King also undergoes imprisonment for his proclamation of the gospel. As Paul used the occasion of his imprisonment to address believers, so too does King utilize his incarceration to address the white clergymen and all believers, both black and white. Just as Paul's imprisonment epistles were aimed at believing communities to instruct, encourage, and exhort them to some type of godly action and deeper commitment to the faith, so too is King's letter written to communities of faith, particularly the white communities, to instruct them regarding the biblical

170. Sernett, *African American Religious History*, 519.

and theological bases of the civil rights movement as well as to encourage those black sisters and brothers already in the struggle.

The eight white religious leaders objected to the presence of the civil rights activists in Birmingham because they were "outside agitators" who had no right interfering in the local issues of the city. After rehearsing for his audience his organizational ties to the city, that is, the presence of the Southern Christian Leadership Conference, King justifies his being there from a biblical point of view. As the Old Testament prophets were often led by God to go out of their native cities to proclaim the divine word of the Lord, so he and other civil rights leaders are led to Birmingham. King then expands from Old Testament paradigms to the New Testament figure of Paul: "Just as the eighth century prophets left their villages and carried their 'thus saith the Lord' far beyond the boundaries of their hometowns; *and just as the Apostle Paul left his village of Tarsus and carried the gospel of Jesus Christ to practically every hamlet and city of the Graeco-Roman world, I too am compelled to carry the gospel of freedom beyond my particular hometown. Like Paul, I must constantly respond to the Macedonian call for aid.*"[171] The phrase "Thus saith the Lord" indicates a prophetic mantle, a prophetic voice, and a prophetic charge by God, all of which King uses to describe his own calling. Along with a prophetic mandate, King casts himself as a modern-day Paul who carries the gospel around the world. As Paul took the gospel throughout the Roman Empire, so King must also carry the gospel of freedom throughout the United States.

King's reference to the "Macedonian call for aid" recalls the story in Acts 16:9–12 in which Paul receives a summons for help in a dream:

> And a vision appeared to Paul in the night; There stood a man of Macedonia, and prayed him, saying, Come over into Macedonia, and help us. And after he had seen the vision, immediately we endeavoured to go into Macedonia, assuredly gathering that the Lord had called us for to preach the gospel unto them. Therefore loosing from Troas, we came with a straight course to Samothracia, and the next day to Neapolis; And from thence to Philippi,

---

171. Martin Luther King Jr., "Letter from Birmingham City Jail," in *A Testament of Hope: The Essential Writings of Martin Luther King, Jr.*, ed. James Melvin Washington (San Francisco: HarperSanFrancisco, 1986), 290. Hereafter, page references from this work will be given in parentheses in the text. See also my discussion of this essay in "God and Time: Exploring Black Notions of Prophetic and Apocalyptic Eschatology," in *T&T Clark Handbook of African American Theology*, ed. Antonia Daymond, Frederick Ware, and Eric Williams (New York: T&T Clark, 2019), 219–21.

which is the chief city of that part of Macedonia, and a colony: and we were in that city abiding certain days. (Acts 16:9–12)

As the apostle Paul heard the Macedonian call for aid and responded, King, a modern-day Paul, hears and heeds the call of the Birmingham residents who summoned him and asked for his help.[172] Birmingham is a present-day Macedonia that needs apostolic and prophetic assistance. King frames the letter and the situation in Birmingham with Scripture: prophetic, apostolic, and Pauline. Moreover, King answers his detractors who decry his presence in their city by stating that all of humanity is interrelated and that just because he lives in Atlanta does not mean he should not be concerned about what is happening in Birmingham. After all, he writes, "Injustice anywhere is a threat to justice everywhere. We are caught in an inescapable network of mutuality, tied in a single garment of destiny. Whatever affects one directly, affects all indirectly. Never again can we afford to live with the narrow, provincial 'outside agitator' idea. Anyone who lives inside the United States can never be considered an outsider anywhere in this country" (290).

King cites the reasons why he and other civil rights advocates are in Birmingham as well as why demonstrations are needed: Birmingham has the most unsolved cases of Negro home and church bombings; it is one of the most segregated cities in the United States; its brutality regarding black lives is well known; and it refuses to negotiate in "good faith" with black leaders. For example, city business owners had agreed to remove racial signs in the stores in exchange for the cessation of demonstrations. Yet the signs remained, and those that were temporarily removed reappeared (290–91). As a result of the city's consistent refusal to honor its promises, King echoes Romans 12:1 in depicting the African American community's response: "We had no alternative except that of preparing for direct action, whereby *we would present our very bodies* [Rom. 12:1] as a means of laying our case before the conscience of the local and the national community. . . . We started having workshops on nonviolence, and repeatedly asked ourselves the questions: 'Are you able to accept blows without retaliating? Are you able to endure the ordeals of jail?'" (291). Here King's echo of Romans 12:1, *"I beseech you therefore, brethren, by the mercies of God, that ye present your bodies a living sacrifice, holy, acceptable unto God, which is your reasonable service,"* takes on concrete, tangible form in which black bodies literally suffer physical violence and trauma in their struggle for justice. King sees the

172. See the discussion of this passage in the section on Reverdy Ransom.

suffering that he and those working with him endure as a bodily sacrifice that will bring awareness to the national community regarding the gross injustices taking place in Birmingham. The result of this sacrificial suffering is that peoples' consciences will be affected, and they will hopefully advocate for justice around the country. These demonstrators sacrifice their bodies on behalf of the larger black population, so that all may experience freedom from discrimination and racism.

King's use of Paul to frame this direct action of nonviolence indicates that he views nonviolence as suffering on behalf of fellow black sisters and brothers, which also means that this suffering is simultaneously an offering of their bodies to God, for God is the author of the "gospel of freedom," and it is on behalf of this "gospel of freedom" that he and others endure affliction. Paul's words of "living sacrifice" take on added meaning in light of King's context, in which demonstrators were often beaten, attacked, and killed by vicious mobs. King's use of Paul also serves as another riposte to the white clergymen who do not want him in Birmingham. The work he engages in is holy, acceptable to God, and is the reasonable service God expects from those called by the Divine. God is a God of justice, and so one must live a life that promotes and advocates justice, which is what he and the other civil rights workers are doing.

The white clergymen accuse King and his coworkers of breaking laws and not waiting for a more opportune time to protest. King responds to the first accusation by citing Saint Augustine, who states that "an unjust law is no law at all" (293). He also cites Saint Thomas Aquinas, who believes that an unjust law does not originate in eternal or natural law. King eloquently writes, "Any law that uplifts human personality is just. Any law that degrades human personality is unjust. All segregation statutes are unjust because segregation distorts the soul and damages the personality. It gives the segregator a false sense of superiority and the segregated a false sense of inferiority. . . . So segregation is not only politically, economically and sociologically unsound, but it is morally wrong and sinful" (293). Like the African American petition writers and Lemuel Haynes before him who dared to call slavery and the slave trade sin, King declares that segregation, slavery's descendant, is sin and morally reprehensible.

King responds to the white clergy's demand that blacks should wait with a litany of reasons why they can no longer wait: the prevalence of lynchings and drownings of black people; the astronomical poverty rates among blacks; the nonexistence of voting rights for African Americans; the daily reminders of racial injustice such as being called "[n———]," "boy"; signs that say "white" and "colored"; the nonexistence of school buses for black children; the practice of giving textbooks to black schools with pages missing; and the inability to stay in hotels or take black children to amusement parks because they refuse to serve blacks. King concludes that the time for waiting is over, for "we have waited for more than 340 years for our constitutional and God-given rights" (292).

In addition, King rejects the idea advocated by some whites that all things will be made well for blacks in America if they just wait and allow time to run its course. One advocate of this view wrote this to King: "All Christians know that the colored people will receive equal rights eventually, but it is possible that you are in too great of a religious hurry. . . . The teachings of Christ take time to come to earth" (296). King calls this idea of time a myth and echoes Pauline language to refute it:

> All that is said here grows out of a tragic misconception of time. It is the strangely irrational notion that there is something in the very flow of time that will inevitably cure all ills. Actually, time is neutral. It can be used either destructively or constructively. . . . Human progress never rolls in on wheels of inevitability. It comes through the tireless efforts and persistent work of *men willing to be co-workers with God* [2 Cor. 6:1], and without this hard work, time itself becomes an ally of the forces of social stagnation. We must use time creatively, and forever realize that the time is always ripe to do right. (296)

The neutrality of time means that people utilize the time they have been given for good or evil. Even for their silence will good people need to repent. King asserts that human progress takes work, and it takes working with God, a divine-human partnership, if you will, in which both God and human beings work together to bring about God's will on earth. Time itself does not take care of injustice, but people must use time to act in concert with God to do so.

In this letter King also depicts himself as caught between two groups of Negroes, those who have grown complacent in large part because of systemic oppression that has generated a loss of self-respect and those who have become violent, like the black nationalist groups who have lost faith in America and in Christianity. King sees himself standing between these two factions, writing that "we need not follow the 'do-nothingism' of the complacent or the hatred and despair of the black nationalist. *There is the more excellent way of love* [1 Cor. 13:1] and nonviolent protest. I am grateful to God that, through the Negro church, the dimension of nonviolence entered our struggle" (297). King utilizes Paul to point to a third way, the more excellent way of love from the apostle's "love" chapter. Significantly, King expands Paul's view of the more excellent way to include nonviolent protest, signifying that the Pauline conception of love encompasses action and resistance, which in this case means embracing the philosophy of nonviolence.

King also utilizes Paul to answer the charge that he is an extremist, a charge that at first King finds ludicrous, considering his nonviolent stance. Then, upon second thought, he realizes that the label extremist puts him in good company.

> I must admit that I was initially disappointed in being so categorized. But as I continued to think about the matter I gradually gained a bit of satisfaction from being considered an extremist. Was not Jesus an extremist in love—"Love your enemies, bless them that curse you, pray for them that despitefully use you." Was not Amos an extremist for justice—"Let justice roll down like waters and righteousness like a mighty stream." Was not Paul an extremist for the gospel of Jesus Christ—: "*I bear in my body the marks of the Lord Jesus*" [Gal. 6:17]. . . . So the question is not whether we will be extremist, but what kind of extremist will we be. Will we be extremists for hate or will we be extremists for love? (297–98)

In this excerpt King sets forth a scriptural lineage of those who follow God's ways in a radical manner to such an extent that they proclaim God's will in a world filled with violence and hate. Jesus's words address a people oppressed by the Romans and represent extreme love of the enemy; Amos's words speak to a time of great injustice in Israel and call upon God's justice to come forth; and Paul's bearing of Jesus's marks upon his body demonstrates the radicality of the gospel, for he suffers for its proclamation, carrying in his body the marks he receives from all the hardships he endures for preaching Christ crucified. King sets himself in the company of these extremist followers of the Divine, and his reference to Paul's marks recalls his earlier depiction in the essay of himself and others as people who present their bodies as living sacrifices, suffering blows for the cause of justice and not retaliating in their nonviolent struggle. It follows that those who engage in this nonviolent practice will, like the apostle, also bear in their own bodies the marks of Jesus, the incarnation of extreme love. Here, then, one finds a link between Jesus's body, King's body, the bodies of those in the civil rights movement, and Paul's body—all suffer for the sake of gospel extremism.

The theme of the body reappears in King's lament regarding the leadership of the white church. Although he had hoped that white clergy would support the cause of desegregation and rally behind the nonviolent protests, he found that for the most part they were staunch opponents of the movement and encouraged their congregations to oppose it as well. With great disappointment King writes, "In the midst of blatant injustices inflicted upon the Negro, I have watched white churches stand on the sideline and merely mouth pious irrelevancies and sanctimonious trivialities. In the midst of a mighty struggle to rid our nation of racial and economic injustice, I have heard so many ministers say: 'Those are social issues with which the gospel has no real concern,' and I have watched so many churches commit themselves to a completely otherworldly religion which made a strange distinction between body and soul, the sacred and the secular" (299).

In this passage, King underscores the distinction often made by white interpreters of Scripture that spiritual salvation has no earthly implications, for salvation only matters for the soul and results in no elements of social transformation. Such a distinction goes as far back as slavery, when laws were passed to make sure that slaves who underwent baptism understood that their baptism did not become a basis for their freedom. Their salvation and baptism affected only their soul and spirit, but not the transference of their physical body from slavery to freedom. Such perspectives of slave owners persisted in the civil rights era, with whites maintaining the same distinction. For them, the gospel had nothing to do with transformation of society or elimination of segregation; its chief concern related to the soul. King's phrase the "strange distinction between body and soul" highlights the absence of such a division in black interpretation of Scripture where God's invasion through the Christ event transforms body and soul and erases the demarcation between secular and sacred.

King goes on to lift up Paul's body-of-Christ imagery to depict the church and to emphasize the egregious nature of the behavior of white clergy: "Yes, I see the church as the *body of Christ* [1 Cor. 12:12–27]. But, oh! How we have blemished and scarred that body through social neglect and fear of being nonconformists" (299–300). He views the entire church as the body of Christ, which is why he admits that he weeps over the church, for this body of Christ includes blacks and whites together as sisters and brothers in the faith. The scarring of the body takes place because of the white church's refusal to see its black sisters and brothers as humans worthy of justice and equality and its refusal to stop racial injustice. For King, when whites refuse to help African Americans in their struggle for freedom, they demonstrate that they do not see their connection with their sisters and brothers of color and that what happens to blacks affects them as well, for they are part of the body. Thus, the whole body experiences blemishes and scars—not just black churches, but the entire body of Christ. King, then, lifts up Paul's words: "*And whether one member suffer, all the members suffer with it*" (1 Cor. 12:26). As part of Christ's body, when African Americans suffer, the white members of Christ's body suffer also.

"Transformed Nonconformist"

King's essay "Transformed Nonconformist" begins with a citation of Romans 12:2, which shapes the structure of the entire treatise: "*Be not conformed to this world: but be ye transformed by the renewing of your mind*." King commences the exposition by recognizing that Paul's advice is hard to follow in the modern world, given the emphasis placed on conformity and following the status quo. Despite the pressures to conform, however, King maintains that Christians have been given a mandate from the apostle to be nonconformists. Believers are "called to be people of conviction, not conformity; of moral nobility, not social respectability. We are commanded to live differently and according to a higher loyalty."[173] This mandate to live by a different set of ideals originates from the believer's dual existence, in which she lives in both time and eternity simultaneously. Although believers live in the present time, they are to remember the apostle's words to the Philippians that "*we are a colony of heaven*," which means that heavenly citizenship shapes one's earthly existence and commitments (9).

Regrettably, King argues, the church, albeit called to nonconformity, often capitulates to the majority opinion, especially in issues of race and class.

The erstwhile sanction by the church of slavery, racial segregation, war, and economic exploitation is testimony to the fact that the church has hearkened more to the authority of the world than to the authority of God. Called to be the moral guardian of the community, the church at times has preserved that which is immoral and unethical. Called to combat social evils, it has remained silent behind stained-glass windows. Called to lead men on the highway of brotherhood and to summon them to rise above

---

173. Martin Luther King Jr., "Transformed Nonconformist," in *Strength to Love*, 8–9. Hereafter, page references from this work will be given in parentheses in the text.

the narrow confines of race and class, it has enunciated and practiced racial exclusiveness. (11)

This capitulation to racial exclusiveness and class division arises from a preoccupation with money and prestige by the church's leadership, who are more concerned about the size of their parsonage and not offending their members than they are about preaching sermons that align with the true tenets of the gospel (12). Quoting Emerson, who wrote in his essay "Self-Reliance" that "Whoso would be a man must be a nonconformist," King asserts that Paul likewise reminds us that "whoso would be a Christian must also be a nonconformist. Any Christian who blindly accepts the opinions of the majority and in fear and timidity follows a path of expediency and social approval is a mental and spiritual slave" (12). Yet believers are not called to be mental and spiritual slaves to the larger society but are called to "imbue an unchristian world with the ideals of a higher and more noble order" (9). As people who have tasted eternity, Christians are called to impart that eternal reality into the present social order, which does not yet exemplify the kingdom of God.

At the same time that King recognizes the importance of nonconformity, he also realizes that nonconformity by itself does not automatically engender transformation, for people could choose to be nonconformists for various reasons, such as exhibitionism and self-interest. Paul, he contends, offers a way to engage in "constructive nonconformity" in the latter part of Romans 12:2: "*Be ye transformed by the renewing of your mind*" (13). This transformation of the inner self, which encompasses a new mental trajectory, is central to the nonconformity sensibility. King writes, "By opening our lives to God in Christ we become *new creatures* [2 Cor. 5:17; Gal. 6:15]. This experience, which Jesus spoke of as the new birth, is essential if we are to be transformed nonconformists. . . . Only through an inner spiritual transformation do we gain the strength to fight vigorously the evils of the world in a humble and loving spirit" (13). King links Paul's new-creature language with Jesus's language of new birth found in John 3, and by connecting these two themes he underscores the need for divine transformation in order to engage in social justice work. The evils of this world are so powerful that people who dare to fight against them cannot do so in their own strength, lest they become cold, hardhearted, and self-righteous, "speaking irresponsible words which estrange without reconciling" and making "hasty judgments which are blind to the necessity of social process." An inner spiritual transformation enables believers to avoid the aforementioned pitfalls of exhibitionism, self-interest, self-righteousness, and coldheartedness.

King ends the essay with an acknowledgment that transformed non-conformity is costly and often leads to suffering, which is inevitably part of the Christian life.

> But we are gravely mistaken to think that Christianity protects us from the pain and agony of mortal existence. Christianity has always insisted that the cross we bear precedes the crown we wear. To be a Christian, one must take up his cross, with all of its difficulties and agonizing and tragedy-packed content, and carry it until that very cross leaves *its marks upon us* [Gal. 6:17] and redeems us to that *more excellent way* [1 Cor. 12:31] which comes only through suffering. In these days of worldwide confusion, there is a dire need for men and women who will courageously do battle for truth. (14–15)

In this statement King draws upon two Pauline citations he uses in the "Letter from Birmingham City Jail." The Galatians passage, which refers to marks upon the body, becomes a vivid description of the suffering civil rights workers undergo, since they are trained to receive blows upon their bodies without retaliating. Here again, King affirms that those who fight for justice and equality, and embrace a transformed nonconformist lifestyle, will also live a life characterized by physical trauma and violence. In addition, although in its original context Paul speaks of a more excellent way of love in his discussion of spiritual gifts, King makes the interpretative move of putting the reference in the context of suffering, which demonstrates that he views the way of love as filled with suffering, since love often means acting against the majority and not conforming to the prevalent misguided discourse and standards of society. When one acts for the sake of love, justice, and truth, all ideals that run counter to the world and its ways, this more excellent way of love often results in suffering at the hands of a world that refuses to embrace nonconformity.

"Shattered Dreams"

The final King essay under examination in this volume is entitled "Shattered Dreams" and begins with the Pauline citation from Romans 15:24: "*Whensover I take my journey into Spain, I will come to you.*"[174] King employs

---

174. Martin Luther King Jr., "Shattered Dreams," in *Strength to Love*, 78. Hereafter, page references from this work will be given in parentheses in the text.

this passage from Paul to discuss the topic of unfulfilled hopes and dreams. Evocatively he writes,

> In Paul's letter to the Roman Christians we find a potent illustration of this vexing problem of disappointed hopes. . . . One of his ardent hopes was to travel to Spain where, at the edge of the then known world, he might further proclaim the Christian gospel. On his return he wished to have personal fellowship with that valiant group of Roman Christians. . . . What a glowing hope stirred within Paul's heart! But he never got to Rome according to the pattern of his hopes. Because of his daring faith in Jesus Christ, he was indeed taken there but as a prisoner and was held captive in a little prison cell. Nor did he ever walk the dusty roads of Spain, nor look upon its curvacious slopes, nor watch its busy coastal life. He was put to death, we presume, as a martyr for Christ in Rome. Paul's life is a tragic story of a shattered dream. (78–79)

As indicated by this excerpt, Paul's life becomes an exemplar for King of what it means to have a deep desire or wish and to not have it fulfilled. In fact, this reality touches all human beings, prompting King to ask, "Who has not set out toward some distant Spain, some momentous goal, or some glorious realization, only to learn at last that he must settle for much less?" (79). After citing several historical and biblical examples of people who did not live to see their dreams fulfilled, King links this reality with African American experiences in this country before returning to Paul: "Many Negro slaves in America, having longed passionately for freedom, died before emancipation. . . . And the Apostle Paul repeatedly and fervently prayed that *the 'thorn' might be removed from his flesh* [2 Cor. 12:7], but the pain and annoyance continued to the end of his days. Shattered dreams are a hallmark of our mortal life" (79). King realistically depicts a life of faith as one in which a person does not always receive what she prays for and does not always experience a pain-free life. He links the reality that many blacks died in slavery, although desiring freedom, with Paul's unanswered prayer for deliverance from the thorn in the flesh. Although occurring in different times in human history, both cases nevertheless show a continuity of mortal experience in which human existence is often fraught with disappointment and unrealized hopes and dreams.

In light of this inevitable fact, how does one live in such a world? King outlines three common responses: (1) people become bitter, mean, and resentful; (2) people become introverts and withdraw into themselves; or

(3) people adopt fatalism and believe external forces control all things, and so they believe there is no need to try to change their circumstances. While rejecting all these options, King singles out fatalism, saying it rests upon an inappropriate conception of God.

> For everything, whether good or evil, is considered to represent the will of God. A healthy religion rises above the idea that God wills evil. Although God permits evil in order to preserve the freedom of man, he does not cause evil. That which is willed is intended, and the thought that God intends for a child to be born blind or for a man to suffer the ravages of insanity is sheer heresy that pictures God as a devil rather than as a loving Father. The embracing of fatalism is as tragic and dangerous a way to meet the problem of unfulfilled dreams as are bitterness and withdrawal. (81–82)

King's answer to the reality that people may experience unfulfilled dreams is to confront the shattered dream and not to pretend that the disappointment does not exist. He promotes a living in tension, as it were, accepting "finite disappointment even as we adhere to infinite hope." One of the questions King suggests that a person asks is, "How may I transform this liability into an asset?" He links this question with the apostle Paul's experience of not reaching Spain and uses the verse in Romans to formulate an additional question: "How may I, confined in some narrow Roman cell and unable to reach life's Spain, transmute this dungeon of shame into a haven of redemptive suffering?" King contends that one must not settle for being held captive in the Roman prison but should seek to utilize the prison captivity as a way to serve God's purpose.

King holds up African American experience as an example of living in this tensive hope. Recalling the options people often choose when facing disappointment, King encourages his audience to cling to hope. This section is worth quoting at length:

> We Negroes have long dreamed of freedom, but still we are confined in an oppressive prison of segregation and discrimination. Must we respond with bitterness and cynicism? Certainly not, for this will destroy and poison our personalities. Must we, by concluding that segregation is within the will of God, resign ourselves to oppression? Of course not, for this blasphemously attributes to God that which is of the devil. To co-operate passively with an unjust system makes the oppressed as evil as the oppressor. Our most fruitful course is to stand firm with courageous determination, move for-

ward nonviolently amid obstacles and setbacks, accept disappointments, and cling to hope. . . . While still in the prison of segregation, we must ask, "How may we turn this liability into an asset?" By recognizing the necessity of suffering in a righteous cause, we may possibly achieve our humanity's full stature. To guard ourselves from bitterness, we need the vision to see in this generation's ordeals the opportunity to transfigure both ourselves and American society. Our present suffering and our nonviolent struggle to be free may well offer to Western civilization the kind of spiritual dynamic so desperately needed for survival. (83)

African Americans, despite the difficulties and harsh realities of their present existence, have to cling to hope and refuse to succumb to hate. Like Reverdy Ransom before him, King believes that African Americans have the opportunity to salvage America, albeit from King's perspective this rescue will take place through nonviolent demonstration and suffering for the righteous cause of racial equality. This suffering has the power to transform not only the social location of blacks as a people group but society as a whole, for black suffering can lead to achievement of "humanity's full stature." African Americans have the chance to save Western civilization from itself, from its destructive tendencies, and to help it find spiritual life through the black struggle for justice. The redemption of the nation and indeed Western civilization is how blacks can turn the liability of segregation into an asset.

A person's refusal to be defeated and her determination to cleave to hope despite circumstances is what King calls the "courage to be" (84). This "courage to be" is evidence that the divine image resides within every person. For King, Paul becomes the exemplar of this type of courage due to the constant oppositions he faced and the prevalence of disappointing circumstances in his life. In part of the following quote from King, the reader will see that King takes up Paul's own words in describing his frequent challenges.

> [Paul's] life was a continual round of disappointments. On every side were broken plans and shattered dreams. Planning to visit Spain, he was consigned to a Roman prison. Hoping to go to Bithynia, he was sidetracked to Troas. His gallant mission for Christ was measured *"in journeyings often, in perils of waters, in perils of robbers, in perils by mine own countrymen, in perils by the heathen, in perils in the city, in perils in the wilderness, in perils in the sea, in perils among false brethren"* [2 Cor. 11:26]. Did he permit these conditions to master him? *"I have learned,"* he testified, *"in whatsoever state I am, therewith to be content"* [Phil. 4:11]. Not that Paul had learned to be

complacent, for nothing in his life characterizes him as a complacent individual. . . . By discovering the distinction between spiritual tranquility and the outward accidents of circumstance, Paul learned to stand tall and without despairing amid the disappointments of life. Each of us who makes this magnificent discovery will, like Paul, be a recipient of that true peace *"which passeth all understanding . . ."* [Phil. 4:7]. . . . The peace of which Paul spoke is a calmness of soul amid terrors of trouble, inner tranquility amid the howl and rage of outer storm, the serene quiet at the center of a hurricane amid the howling and jostling winds. We readily understand the meaning of peace when everything is going right and when one is "up and in," but we are baffled when Paul speaks of that true peace which comes when a man is "down and out," when burdens lie heavy upon his shoulders, when pain throbs annoyingly in his body, when he is confined by the stone walls of a prison cell, and when disappointment is inescapably real. True peace, a calm that exceeds all description and all explanation, is peace amid storm and tranquillity amid disaster. (84–85)

King connects the peace that Jesus declares as a divine gift in John 14:27 ("Peace I leave with you, my peace I give unto you") with the peace that Paul speaks of in Philippians. This legacy of peace sustained Paul, the early Christians, and the slaves during slavery, and it is this peace that will be present with African Americans as they engage in the struggle for civil rights and equality. King writes the following in regard to this legacy of peace.

Through faith we may inherit Jesus' legacy, "Peace I leave with you, my peace I give unto you." Paul at Philippi, incarcerated in a dark and desolate dungeon, his body beaten and bloody, his feet chained, and his spirit tired, joyously sang the songs of Zion at midnight. The early Christians, facing hungry lions in the arena and the excruciating pain of the chopping block, rejoiced that they had been deemed worthy to suffer for the sake of Christ. Negro slaves, bone weary in the sizzling heat and the marks of whip lashes freshly etched on their backs, sang triumphantly, "By and by I'm gwin to lay down this heavy load." These are living examples of *peace that passeth all understanding* [Phil. 4:7]. (85)

King makes significant parallels in this selection. First, in each case Paul, the early Christians, and the slaves have beaten and bloody bodies due to persecution. Second, each example contains an element of singing in the midst of suffering, whether it was Paul singing in a jail cell while bearing the marks of Jesus on his back or the slaves singing sorrowful songs in the fields with slavery's marks upon their bodies. And third, peace in the midst of suffering connects these historical figures with each other. With these linkages King places black suffering in the context of Christian history and inserts black suffering into the Christian narrative. Like Paul and the early believers before them, slaves endured much hardship, and in doing so become exemplars themselves for the legacy of peace as described in Scripture. Once again, as he did in the "Letter from Birmingham City Jail," King merges the suffering of African Americans with that of Paul and the early church, demonstrating in this convergence a shared reality of Christian existence, that is, black lives become part of Christian salvific history. Black suffering is a symptom of living in a hostile world that rejects God and God's people. Against the backdrop of a nation that repeatedly denied black significance, King locates black lives within sacred history, thereby demonstrating the worth and sanctity of black life.

King closes the essay by appealing to faith in God as the ultimate antidote for shattered dreams. Even if a person dies without seeing her dream realized, she must trust that in death as in life she belongs to God and that "*God through Christ has taken the sting from death* [1 Cor. 15:56] *by freeing us from its dominion* [Rom. 6:9]" (86). Death, then, for King is not the end but the beginning of a mysterious, glorious new existence in which God "ultimately join[s] virtue and fulfillment." This is the type of faith, King declares, that Paul writes about in Romans 8:28 when he states "*that all things work together for good to them that love God, to them who are the called according to his purpose*," signifying that God works out all things for the believer's good, for even those disappointments and shattered dreams somehow through divine machination become part of God's overarching plan and purpose.

In summary, King employs Paul in a number of ways in his sermons and speeches. He uses Paul to critique segregation and its underlying notion of black inferiority. He utilizes the apostle to proclaim that segregation is sin and those who sanction it are not following the Word of God, despite their claim to be Christian. In fact, King declares that condoning segregationist policies is conforming to the ways of the world, not to the ways of God. One's heavenly citizenship transforms how one thinks about earthly life and compels one to see and participate in God's justice and love for all humanity.

Moreover, Paul's "body" imagery enables King to highlight the importance and value of black bodies and thereby to focus upon significant aspects of his body hermeneutic. Because the body of Christ consists of black and white believers together, when black believers suffer, as they do under Jim

Crow, the entire body suffers. With this body imagery, King seeks to affirm the connectedness of every human being to each other. Whites cannot harm blacks without at the same time doing harm to themselves.

The Pauline body imagery also allows King to talk about the suffering of black bodies as they present themselves as sacrifices for the black struggle of liberation. They endure beatings and imprisonment for the sake of black freedom, and so Paul's sacrificial language of the body coheres with the lived experiences of King and other civil rights activists.[175] In addition, like Paul, who bore the marks of Jesus on his body, King and the civil rights workers bear the marks of Jesus, the extremist for love, on their bodies as well. When King talks about the suffering of the early church and the persecution those Christians endured, he merges the sufferings of the civil rights movement with this history and underscores his view that black suffering is part of sacred history. By doing this, King affirms the sacredness of black bodies in a time when black bodies were considered nothing and expendable. King fuses the two histories into one proclaiming that just as the martyrs of the early church underwent persecution, so too are black Americans undergoing persecution for Jesus's gospel of liberation.

Furthermore, along with understanding "that the gospel of Christianity is one that seeks social change religiously and morally,"[176] King also understands that people are coworkers with God and partner with God to bring about the manifestation of these changes on earth, so that justice and liberation are never only a human enterprise nor solely a divine endeavor. Quoting Pauline language of being coworkers with God, King believes that the Divine and human work in concert to bring about change, for when one becomes a new creature, this transformation of the inner self leads to transformation of the outer world. The need for divine and human collaboration becomes extremely clear in King's narration of one of the most difficult moments in his life, the moments after he receives a phone call from someone who threatens his life:

> It seemed that all of my fears had come down on me at once. I had reached the saturation point. . . . In this state of exhaustion, when my courage had almost gone, I determined to take my problem to God. My head in my

---

175. This language of sacrifice echoes Walker's use of Paul to characterize his own death in divine terms as a sacrifice on behalf of his fellow African Americans. See the discussion of Walker in chap. 1.

176. King, "Shattered Dreams," 116.

hands, I bowed over the kitchen table and prayed aloud. The words I spoke to God that midnight are still vivid in my memory. "I am here taking a stand for what I believe is right. But now I am afraid. The people are looking to me for leadership, and if I stand before them without strength and courage, they too will falter. I am at the end of my powers. I have nothing left. I've come to the point where I can't face it alone." At that moment I experienced the presence of the Divine as I had never before experienced him. It seemed as though I could hear the quiet assurance of an inner voice, saying, "Stand up for righteousness, stand up for truth. God will be at your side forever." . . . My uncertainty disappeared. I was ready to face anything. The outer situation remained the same, but God had given me inner calm.[177]

In this account, King highlights the centrality of God in the struggle for justice, for human strength, wisdom, and knowledge are finite. Yet the Infinite One can renew strength and provide courage and hope, as well as peace in the midst of chaos and in the face of death. When King cites and echoes Paul's words of Philippians 4:7 regarding a peace that surpasses understanding, he knows from real-life experience what the apostle means in that verse, and he attempts to convey to his audience that they too can experience this peace in the midst of all that they undergo to bring about God's liberative will upon the earth.

Like so many of the black hermeneuts before him, King adopted and adapted Pauline language and demonstrated that the apostle could be employed in the fight against racism, specifically Jim Crow and segregation. Yet compared to earlier interpreters, King broadens the use of Paul by taking on the persona of Paul and writing a letter to America in the apostle's name. Similarly, the fact that he pens a letter from the Birmingham jail makes him even more similar to Paul, who writes epistles during his imprisonment. Both were jailed because of what they proclaimed: a gospel of liberation. Paul is not just someone King quotes and cites; King takes on his mantle and sees himself as a modern-day Paul answering the Macedonians' cry for help, writing letters of encouragement and exhortation from prison, traveling around preaching the gospel, and bearing in his body the marks of Jesus.

177. King, *Strength to Love*, 107; Peter Paris, *Black Religious Leaders: Conflict in Unity* (Louisville: Westminster John Knox, 1991), 104. Paris's comments regarding King's view of God are apropos: "In all of King's thought, speeches, and writings no other theme is more pervasive than that of God. I contend that all other important concepts pervading his works—for example, nonviolence, love, justice, human dignity, reconciliation, freedom, morality—are either explicitly or implicitly related to his understanding of God" (100).

Pauline Hermeneutics in Twentieth-Century Black Discourse

Into the twentieth century, black hermeneuts continue to discuss the figure of Paul in their speeches, sermons, and writings, illustrating that the apostle remains an important figure during this time for black discourse. Reverdy Ransom employs Paul in a number of ways, one of the most important being his use of Paul's language to speak of Christ abolishing the wall of partition between Jews and gentiles, which becomes for Ransom a paradigm for the destruction of the division between black and white. In regard to the theme of a body hermeneutic, a theme we have traced in previous chapters, Ransom takes on Paul's "Spirit of Christ" language to critique the United States and to state that America's actions against African Americans, including the silence around the lynching of black bodies, demonstrate that as a nation, it does not contain the Spirit of Christ, despite its claims. Moreover, for Ransom, black bodies and lives are salvific for the nation, rescuing it from itself by transforming society from one filled with hate to one filled with love.

William Seymour adopts Paul's language regarding the Jerusalem collection to emphasize that the baptism of the Spirit has practical implications. As Paul encourages his congregations to give to the poor in Jerusalem, Seymour sees the collection as a model for Spirit-empowered believers to try to help those in financial need. In regard to racism, Seymour takes up the apostle's image of a grieving Holy Spirit to depict divine lamentation over racial division. He also employs the body of Christ motif to declare that the church is one and consists of black and white believers together. Also, part of Seymour's body hermeneutic is that Spirit manifestations upon the body, such as glossolalia and divine healings, have transformative implications for society. Equally important for Seymour is that black bodies experience God's power, an experience that challenges the notions of black inferiority and black rejection by the divine. Moreover, just as Paul spoke out against Peter when Peter separated himself from the gentiles, Seymour speaks out against racial divisions taking place in the Azusa Street congregation. Although the racial unity Seymour desires does not last, one of his lasting legacies is that "[Azusa Street] was an egalitarian, ecumenical, interracial, interclass revival that for about three years defied the prevailing patterns of American life."[178]

Like Seymour, Charles Harrison Mason emphasizes racial unity through Pauline language, maintaining that despite the divisions taking place in society, God wills unity between black and white people. In addition, Mason

---

178. Clemmons, *Bishop C. H. Mason*, 58.

adopts a Pauline passage to designate the black-led denomination he starts, which is an important glimpse into black resistance to oppressive uses of Paul and blacks' positive appropriation of the apostle. Mason also expands the subversive use of Paul to include advocating peace and protesting war. Part of Mason's body hermeneutic includes rejecting the call of enlisting black bodies to fight in a war for a country that denied their humanity. Additionally, he calls upon Pauline Scripture to form his critique of the German kaiser, and by doing so he gives African American Pauline hermeneutics an international dimension to its protest tradition.

The theme of a body hermeneutic appears in Ida B. Robinson's adoption of Paul's words to denounce the nation's refusal to stop the lynching of African Americans. The language of God's Fatherhood and the bond that God creates between people of different races demonstrate that black lives are just as important as white lives. The universality of God's Fatherhood means that humanity is one family. This reality makes whites' murdering of their black brothers and sisters especially egregious, for they slaughter their own kin. To Robinson, such atrocities indicate that the Christianity of the South is really no faith at all.

Both Howard Thurman and Albert Cleage Jr. reject Paul because of the oppressive ways in which many white people utilized him to tyrannize and dehumanize black people. For them, Paul lends himself to such interpretations because of his privilege. According to Thurman, the apostle's Roman citizenship enables him to write such passages as "Slaves, obey your masters" and makes him irrelevant to blacks and others whose backs are against the wall. Cleage believes that Paul is responsible for Christianity's distortion because the apostle takes away the important black nation-building element of the gospel and turns the gospel into an individual phenomenon for white gentiles. To Thurman and Cleage, Jesus and Jesus's life are more akin to the African American experience.

The last interpreter examined in this chapter is Martin Luther King Jr., who employs Paul extensively in his speeches and sermons. In "Paul's Letter to American Christians," King brings to a climactic point Paul's place in the nation's discourse regarding black and white relationships. It is because the apostle has been such a central figure historically that King sees the importance of penning a letter in his name to an audience that consists of black and white citizens. In addition, for King the apostle's sufferings reflect the afflictions of the civil rights activists. In his body hermeneutic, King merges these sufferings with those of Paul, and by doing so asserts the fusion of black history with sacred history, indicating that despite white historical claims to the contrary, black lives are important to God and to God's history with the world.

CHAPTER 4

Pauline Language in Enslaved Conversion Experiences and Call Narratives

I knew very well, if God was able to deliver me from the corrupt influence of the world and the power of Satan, that he was able to deliver me from this slave-holder. Yet I was like so many others, I did not see by what method he would secure my deliverance. Still with childlike simplicity I trusted him.[1]

This chapter explores the reception of Pauline language in conversion stories of enslaved Africans. These narratives demonstrate that African Americans received, adopted, and adapted the apostle's writings regarding their view of the world and their own supernatural conversion experiences with God, including their call stories.

One way to begin to understand the reception of Paul in these conversion stories is to examine briefly the impact of the Great Awakening upon enslaved Africans. The Awakening's emphasis on evangelism, salvation, and conversion experiences for all people influenced the Bible's reception among the enslaved. The evangelists of this movement noted the huge presence and the large number of conversions of enslaved Africans in their meetings.[2] Importantly, during the Great Awakening, conversion was linked with the ability to read the Bible for oneself and, thus, compelled the need for liter-

---

1. A quote from David Smith, an enslaved person, in Albert Raboteau, *Slave Religion: The "Invisible Institution" in the Antebellum South* (New York: Oxford University Press, 1978), 311.
2. Janet Duitsman Cornelius, *When I Can Read My Title Clear: Literacy, Slavery, and Religion in the Antebellum South* (Columbia: University of South Carolina Press, 1991), 19; Raboteau, *Slave Religion*, 128–29, 132–33.

acy among the enslaved.[3] The idea of granting the enslaved literacy, however, met with great resistance among slaveholders.[4] In addition, the Great Awakening tended to proclaim personal salvation, which allowed blacks and whites to believe that Christ had died personally for them. Such an emphasis de-stressed a person's social status.[5] Important for the present discussion is the fact that as time went on the emphasis on personal relationship with God became even more important.

Significantly, the Bible became the primary source for religious instruction and education among the enslaved. It shaped the way they thought about themselves, their enslavers, and the world around them. It formed their view of their situation and, for many, became a source of life in the midst of oppression. As Janet Cornelius states, "By the last decades of slavery, with only a few exceptions, black people had fashioned a religious faith which embraced Christianity as a system of morals, a promise for a future life, and 'spiritual release from anxieties, frustrations, and animosities,' but they rejected Christianity as practiced by white slaveholders."[6] She also observes that for the enslaved, "knowledge of the Bible, the sacred text, was a tool for attaining salvation and for living in a personal relationship with God."[7] Enslaved Africans did not merely convert to Christianity, but they shaped the Christian tradition to fit their own situation of enslavement. They engaged in a "dual process," accepting the gospel and at the same time making the gospel their own.[8]

Part of this dual process involved a deep reverence of Scripture. This reverence created a desire to read Scripture for themselves, which many pursued after freedom.[9] Until then, slaves learned many of the biblical stories through oral tradition and committed these stories to memory. C. Michelle Venable-Ridley writes, "Meaning and significance were found in the telling

---

3. Cornelius, *When I Can Read My Title Clear*, 19.

4. For more information on this subject, see Cornelius, *When I Can Read My Title Clear*, especially 32–58. As Kenneth Stampp, *The Peculiar Institution: Slavery in the Ante-Bellum South* (New York: Knopf, 1978), observes, "The master class understood, of course, that only a carefully censored version of Christianity could have this desired effect. Inappropriate biblical passages had to be deleted; sermons that might be proper for freemen were not necessarily proper for slaves" (159–60). See chapters above regarding slaveholders limiting access to Scripture.

5. Raboteau, *Slave Religion*, 148. See also the discussion on 132–47.

6. Cornelius, *When I Can Read My Title Clear*, 86.

7. Cornelius, *When I Can Read My Title Clear*, 87.

8. Raboteau, *Slave Religion*, 209.

9. Raboteau, *Slave Religion*, 240.

and retelling, the hearing and rehearing of biblical stories—stories of perseverance, of strength in weakness and under oppressive burdens, of hope in hopeless situations."[10] Furthermore, some enslaved Africans, because they could not read the Bible, believed God gave them revelation in their hearts. As Albert Raboteau writes, "Several ex-slaves claimed that they recognized verses read to them from the Bible because they had heard them before in visions they had experienced during slavery."[11] Their reverence for Scripture and their belief in God's power to deal directly with them allowed many enslaved Africans to apply and shape scriptural teaching to their own life and circumstances. Thus, these conversion experiences highlight God's transformative presence with the enslaved, and these divine encounters reaffirm the God-given dignity already within them, the dignity that refused to allow them to believe the distorted gospel of their slaveholders.

Conversion

The African American conversion narratives discussed below often follow a similar pattern. They commence with the convert suffering from a feeling of extreme guilt of sin and a sense of heaviness or being weighed down. Often the initiate cannot eat or sleep and undergoes great anxiety. Next, the person receives a vision, which may consist of potential damnation or divine rescue from damnation or both. In many instances, the person sees hell, heaven, angels, Satan, God, or Jesus. As a result of such divine encounters, the convert prays for forgiveness, mercy, or salvation, and in response to this posture of surrender, experiences acceptance by God and a new birth, often with the outcome of receiving a call to preach.[12] This is roughly the pattern these experiences follow, although the order may vary.[13] For ex-

10. C. Michelle Venable-Ridley, "Paul and the African American Community," in *Embracing the Spirit: Womanist Perspectives on Hope, Salvation, and Transformation*, ed. Emilie M. Townes (Maryknoll, NY: Orbis, 1997), 212. Here she credits Vincent Wimbush.

11. Raboteau, *Slave Religion*, 242.

12. William L. Andrews, introduction to *Sisters of the Spirit: Three Black Women's Autobiographies of the Nineteenth Century*, ed. William L. Andrews (Bloomington: Indiana University Press, 1986), 11; Raboteau, *Slave Religion*, 266-75.

13. James Craig Holte, *The Conversion Experience in America: A Sourcebook on Religious Conversion Autobiography* (New York: Greenwood, 1992), writes that "most conversion narratives follow a predictable three-part structure—early sinful life, the conversion experience, life and works after conversion—each writer adapts that pattern to the particular circumstances of his or her own experience" (vii).

ample, in some cases, prayer may precede the vision, and some converts may pray and fast in order to receive salvation, whereas in other instances no sense of guilt precedes conversion, God comes to them unexpectedly. Nonetheless, these visionary conversion experiences lead the converts to view themselves afterward as completely different people transformed into new creations.

William Andrews touches upon the major themes of these conversion narratives, which are freedom from sin and Satan and a call to a new way of being in the world. As the subsequent conversion accounts demonstrate, the converts often describe themselves in two ways, a preconversion self that existed in sin and engaged in sinful activities and a postconversion self in which they live renewed lives aimed at following God and doing what God called them to do. In many cases, their conversions allow them to view their preconversion selves in light of God's mercy and grace in that they see that God cared for them and watched over them even before they began to follow God. In other words, their postconversion selves view their past in light of God's grace.

In the foreword to *God Struck Me Dead: Religious Conversion Experiences and Autobiographies of Ex-Slaves*, a collection of enslaved African American conversion narratives from which the excerpts in this chapter derive, Paul Radin argues that although these enslaved conversions may exhibit patterns and terminology similar to those of white models, "they are not mere imitations or an inert continuation of a white tradition."[14] For an enslaved African American, conversion meant "Christ had recognized him and that he had recognized Christ. In fact, it was not so much the Negro who sought God as God who sought the Negro."[15] Conversions of enslaved Africans brought about a disruption and a transformation of their total selves, for conversion signified a disruption of a distorted identity hoisted upon them by the exterior white society in which their black bodies equaled sin and evil. Conversion meant the rejection and cancellation of such an identity and a transformed recognition in which the enslaved saw herself as loved by God and created in the divine image. These conversion experiences point to a distinction between sin as intrinsic to blackness and black people and sin as an outside power that affects them. This distinction refutes the theology of many white believers during this time, in which blacks and sin were

14. Paul Radin, foreword to *God Struck Me Dead: Religious Conversion Experiences and Autobiographies of Ex-Slaves*, ed. Clifton H. Johnson (Philadelphia: Pilgrim, 1969), x.
15. Radin, foreword to *God Struck Me Dead*, xi.

synonymous. To the contrary, sin was a power from which both whites and blacks needed liberation.

Correspondingly, although similar patterns may exist between African American conversions and white conversions, the meanings behind the patterns are significantly different because of the social locations of the groups. For blacks, these divine encounters affirmed their equality to whites, their possession of a soul, and their humanity; whites who underwent conversion experiences did not need such affirmations. Because they were white, society assumed they possessed souls, were superior to blacks, and were human. Accordingly, then, conversion experiences for blacks were much more than religious experiences; they were social and political experiences as well, for they enabled them to resist the racist social and political structures built upon white supremacy that sought to reify black inferiority and inculcate black dehumanization.

The belief of the enslaved that God loved them and worked in their lives despite their social status becomes apparent when examining their conversion accounts and divine commissions to preach. Remarkably, despite slaveholders' attempts to dehumanize African Americans with Scripture, many slaves remained largely "convinced that God is for them."[16] They believed in a "God of infinite power who could be trusted to act on their behalf."[17] The following ex-slave accounts demonstrate this belief in divine power and in God's ability to overcome any opposition. Moreover, these narratives indicate that this view of divine power derives in part from Pauline language, for these slaves adopt and adapt the apostle's cosmology and view of the world in relation to God, Satan, deliverance, salvation, and visions. Accordingly, they adhere to the belief in God to overcome satanic power.

The voices of the ex-slaves who tell of their supernatural encounters with God and Satan in *God Struck Me Dead* display a genuine belief in the supernatural world, that is, that "human and spiritual beings share social space."[18] To share social space means that the realms of the human and the supernatural interpenetrate and intermingle in such a way that the two are

---

16. Cleophus J. LaRue, *I Believe I'll Testify: The Art of African American Preaching* (Louisville: Westminster John Knox, 2011), 59.

17. LaRue, *I Believe I'll Testify*, 60.

18. Loren T. Stuckenbruck, "Prayers of Deliverance from the Demonic in the Dead Sea Scrolls and Related Early Jewish Literature," in *The Changing Face of Judaism, Christianity, and Other Greco-Roman Religions in Antiquity*, ed. Ian H. Henderson and Gerbern S. Oegema, Studien zu den Jüdischen Schriften aus hellenistisch-römischer Zeit 2 (Gütersloh: Gütersloher Verlagshaus, 2006), 163.

intimately connected; events in the supernatural realm affect the human arena, and humanity's activities impact the supernatural.[19] These conversion stories illustrate that the cosmic conflict between God and Satan affects humanity and that humanity's salvation depends upon God's power of deliverance. Accordingly, the seers in these narratives express a faith in a God who hears and acts on behalf of human beings, particularly those experiencing oppression.

Story of Morte

In the story "I Am Blessed but You Are Damned," an enslaved African called Morte plows a field and, while doing this chore, encounters God.

> One day while in the field plowing I heard a voice. I jumped because I thought it was my master coming to scold and whip me for plowing up some more corn. I looked but saw no one. Again the voice called, "Morte! Morte!" With this I stopped, dropped the plow, and started running, but the voice kept on speaking to me saying, "Fear not, my little one, for behold! I come to bring you a message of truth." . . . I looked up and saw that I was in a new world. . . . As I prayed an angel came and touched me, and I looked new. I looked at my hands and they were new; I looked at my feet and they were new. I looked and saw my old body suspended over a burning pit by a small web like a spider web. I again prayed, and there came a soft voice saying, "My little one, I have loved you with an everlasting love. You are this day made alive and freed from hell. *You are a chosen vessel unto the Lord* [Acts 9:15—God's description of Paul to Ananias]. Be upright before me, and I will guide you unto all truth. *My grace is sufficient for you* [2 Cor. 12:9]. Go, and I am with you. Preach the gospel, and I will preach with you. You are henceforth the salt of the earth."[20]

The beginning of Morte's account is rich with scriptural language and is indicative of the scriptural language that permeates the rest of his narrative. Echoes of prophetic call stories ("Fear not") exist as well as echoes of the

---

19. Lisa Bowens, *An Apostle in Battle: Paul and Spiritual Warfare in 2 Corinthians 12:1–10*, Wissenschaftliche Untersuchungern zum Neuen Testament 2.433 (Tübingen: Mohr Siebeck, 2017), 30, 35–36.

20. Johnson, *God Struck Me Dead*, 15.

Gospels, such as "salt of the earth." Interspersed with this scriptural language is language that indicates transport into another world, which leads to: (1) an identification with Paul's Damascus road experience and God's subsequent speech to Ananias concerning Paul: he is a chosen vessel unto the Lord, and (2) a linkage to the apostle's *Himmelsreise* (ascent) to the third heaven: "my grace is sufficient for you." These particular references to Paul's experiences shape Morte's own supernatural encounter and suggest a connection between himself and the apostle; they become motifs developed further in the account. God's speech about Paul to Ananias becomes direct divine speech to Morte: "You are my chosen vessel," and God's word to Morte about the sufficiency of grace, the same words God gives to Paul regarding his *Himmelsreise* (ascent), underscores the supernatural element of Morte's own encounter and signals Morte's foray into the suprahuman realm, where conflict between God and Satan exists. The sufficiency of grace becomes evident in God's deliverance of Morte later in the narrative. As this inclusion of Pauline language shows, the divine encounters Paul experiences are now renarrated in the life of this enslaved African.

After this part of the narrative, Morte relates a vision of the heavenly throne in which he sees God and, upon seeing him, falls upon his face. He receives another commissioning directive from God instructing him to preach, and then finally he comes to himself. At that point he realizes that most of the corn has been plowed up since the horse had run off with the plow during Morte's experience. When the slave owner comes and is visibly upset with Morte about what has happened, Morte relates the next unexpected event of his story. "I told him that I had been talking with God Almighty, and that it was God who had plowed up the corn. He looked at me very strangely, and suddenly I fell for shouting, and I shouted and began to preach. The words seemed to flow from my lips. When I had finished I had a deep feeling of satisfaction and no longer dreaded the whipping I knew I would get. My master looked at me and seemed to tremble. He told me to catch the horse and come on with him to the barn."[21]

As Morte attempts to carry out the slaveholder's orders, he receives another supernatural encounter.

> I went to get the horse, stumbling down the corn rows. Here again I became weak and began to be afraid for the whipping. After I had gone some distance down the rows, I became dazed and again fell to the ground. In a

21. Johnson, *God Struck Me Dead*, 16.

vision I saw a great mound and, beside it or at the base of it, stood the angel Gabriel. And a voice said to me, "Behold your sins as a great mountain. But they shall be rolled away. Go in peace, fearing no man, for lo! I have cut loose your stammering tongue and unstopped your deaf ears. A witness shalt thou be, and thou shalt speak to multitudes, and they shall hear. My word has gone forth, and it is power. Be strong, and lo! I am with you even until the world shall end. Amen." I looked, and the angel Gabriel lifted his hand, and my sins, that had stood as a mountain, began to roll away. I saw them as they rolled over into a great pit. They fell to the bottom, and there was a great noise. I saw old Satan with a host of his angels hop from the pit, and . . . I cried out, "Save me! Save me, Lord!" And like a flash there gathered around me a host of angels. . . . Then stepped one in the direction of the pit. Old Satan and his angels, growling with anger and trembling with fear, hopped back into the pit. Finally again there came a voice unto me saying, "Go in peace and fear not . . . rejoice and be exceedingly glad, *for I have saved you through grace by faith, not of yourself but as a gift of God*" [Eph. 2:8]. . . . I must have been in this trance for more than an hour. I went on to the barn and found my master there waiting for me. Again I began to tell him of my experience . . . my master sat watching and listening to me, and then he began to cry. He turned from me and said in a broken voice, "Morte, I believe you are a preacher. From now on you can preach to the people here on my place in the old shed by the creek. But tomorrow morning, Sunday, I want you to preach to my family and neighbors." . . . The next morning at the time appointed I stood up on two planks in front of the porch of the big house and, without a Bible or anything, I began to preach to my master and the people. . . . Ever since that day I have been preaching the gospel and am not a bit tired. I can tell anyone about God in the darkest hour of midnight, for it is written on my heart.[22]

Morte's story illustrates what Albert Raboteau insightfully observes as the potential for religion to "bend the seemingly inflexible positions of master and slave."[23] Morte's supernatural encounter allows him to experience divine revelations and to experience a divine interruption of the master/slave hierarchy, thereby illustrating that true divine encounters can destabilize an oppressive status quo. Just as Paul's Damascus road encounter changed the trajectory of his life, Morte's conversion experience alters his life too. Morte's

22. Johnson, *God Struck Me Dead*, 16–18.
23. Raboteau, *Slave Religion*, 148.

second supernatural encounter that comes about as he attempts to "catch the horse" develops the Pauline language present in the opening part of the narrative. During Morte's otherworldly experience, Satan and Satan's angels interfere and attempt to grab him, but he prays for deliverance, and God's angels come to the rescue. The similarity with Paul's own *Himmelsreise* in 2 Corinthians 12:1–10 is striking. In these verses, Paul receives a revelatory experience in his ascent, faces opposition from Satan and Satan's angels to this experience, and formulates a prayer of deliverance from this satanic opposition.[24] Morte's divine encounter follows this same pattern: revelation, satanic opposition, and a prayer for deliverance.

Yet, although Morte's supernatural episode follows the same pattern as Paul's *Himmelsreise*, Morte's social location as an enslaved African adds another dimension. The idea that a supernatural battle rages between God and Satan makes sense to Morte as part of a people whose own lives are filled with hardship and struggle. For them, the conflict in the supernatural realm merely reflects what occurs in their lives on a daily basis. To ascend to heaven and experience opposition on the way mirrors the trials and opposition in life they face every day. Thus, the apostle's ascent experience both coheres with their view of the world and shapes their view of the world.

Furthermore, just as Paul becomes a mediator of divine knowledge to the Corinthians in which he reveals to them through his ascent the existence of a cosmic conflict, Morte's experience sanctions him as a mediator of divine knowledge too, a minister of God's Word who reveals God's "matchless love," the need for all to "be born again" and "freed from the shackles of hell."[25] The slaveholder even acknowledges Morte's experience and invites him to proclaim the gospel to him, his family, and his friends. That Paul's experience shapes this narrative is evident in the way his supernatural episodes and terminology permeate the account as well as bracket it. At the beginning and the end of the experience, references to Paul occur. In the opening of the narration, God's words regarding Paul appear as words to Morte, "You are a chosen vessel" and "My grace is sufficient for you." At the closing of the narrative, God speaks to Morte with Paul's words regarding salvation as a gift through grace (Eph. 2:8).

For Morte, this experience is both his conversion and commissioning story. God saves him from his sins and from the attack of Satan and Satan's angels and commissions him to preach the gospel. His vision of the heavenly

---

24. Bowens, *An Apostle in Battle*, 123–204.
25. Johnson, *God Struck Me Dead*, 18.

throne and his reception of divine revelations demonstrate the adoption and adaptation of Paul's cosmology, including his language of an ascent. In both Paul's and Morte's narratives, the visionary becomes a means of revelation, but in Morte's particular case, the vision allows the visionary to transcend social status, at least to a certain extent. For Morte this experience leads to an unprecedented event in his life, preaching to the slave owner, and precipitates an event that stands as a counternarrative to those many instances of the white slaveholder and the white minister constantly preaching to the slaves, "Slaves, obey your master." A vision of the heavenly has earthly implications, for here Morte, an enslaved African, proclaims the gospel to the slaveholder and in his own person becomes a tangible symbol of a divine interruption of the oppressive status quo.

Story of Charlie

In another narrative entitled "The Slave Who Joined the Yanks," an enslaved African named Charlie provides detailed information about his life under slavery. Several important episodes in the earlier part of his narrative shed light on his use of Paul later in the story. As a house slave, Charlie's tasks include taking care of the family and doing chores around the house. "I had to get up in the morning, around four o'clock—I guessed the time by the stars—and blow the horn for the hands to get up and go feed. Then I would make fires, bring the water, milk the cows, get the horses ready for school, sweep, and help clean up the house. Along about six o'clock I would have to go in and waken Mars' Bill, Ole Missey, and Little Mistress."[26] He tells of one particular episode in which his mistress orders him to wake up her daughter and make her bed.

> One Saturday morning Little Missey was sleeping late. She did not have to go to school. Ole Missey told me to go and make up her bed. I went in, and she didn't want to get up so that I could make the bed. I told her then that it was late, and that Ole Missey said for her to get up. Then she got mad, jumped up in the bed, and said, "You black dog, get out of here. I'll get up when I get ready." With that she slapped me as hard as she could, right in my face. I saw stars. As soon as I got back to myself I swung at her, and if she hadn't been so quick I would have almost killed her, for I hit at her with my fist and with all the force I had. I was just about ready to jump

26. Johnson, *God Struck Me Dead*, 24.

up on the bed and choke the life out of her when Ole Missey happened in. She told Ole Missey that I had snatched the cover off the bed and sassed her. Ole Missey turned on me and said, "What do you mean, you black devil? I'll strap your back good for this." I was too worked up and full to say anything. She tied my crossed hands to the bedposts and gave me a lashing with a buggy whip.[27]

Among other things, this episode highlights the complexity of the enslaved life, for enslaved Africans were subject not only to the whims of their male slaveholders but also to those of their slaveholders' wives and children. And as this episode underscores, white children often took advantage of their status over the enslaved by lying about them. Their word was believed over any enslaved person's point of view, which often resulted in enslaved people suffering punishment for something they did not do.

After narrating the harshness of his life as a slave and several more whippings he receives for "offenses," Charlie provides details about another incident in which his enslaver sneaks up on him and his brother Jeff while the two are talking.

My brother had an awful heavy voice and couldn't talk low, so while we were talking our master came up and listened to what we were saying. I remember so well how I swore and said, "I'll be damned if I want to run away and be brought back here and whipped and then have to have my back greased in castor oil. When I run away I am going for good." About this time our master stepped around the corner of the crib and said, "You two damn rascals are plotting to run away, are you? Come right around here and I will teach you how to run away. I will tear your —— and backs to pieces."[28]

Charlie does receive a severe whipping, and although his brother runs away, he is caught and brutally whipped also. Eventually, however, both Charlie and his brother Jeff run away to join the Yankees and help them fight during the war. Years later, after the war, Charlie sees his former enslaver, and the encounter is worth narrating at length.

One day, while I was down on the public square, I met my old master. I had not seen him for nearly thirty years. He said to me, "Charlie, do you remem-

---

27. Johnson, *God Struck Me Dead*, 24–25.
28. Johnson, *God Struck Me Dead*, 29.

ber me lacerating your back?" I said, "Yes, Mars'." "Have you forgiven me?" he asked. I said, "Yes, I have forgiven you." There were a lot of people gathering around because we were a little distance apart and talking loud. I was never scared of nobody, so when he asked me the next question, "How can you forgive me, Charlie?" I said, "Mars', when we whip dogs, we do it just because we own them. It is not because they done anything to be whipped for, but we do it just because we can. That is why you whipped me. I used to serve you, work for you, almost nurse you, and if anything had happened to you I would have fought for you, for I am a man among men. What is in me, though, is not in you. I used to drive you to church and peep through the door to see you all worship, but you ain't right yet, Marster. I love you as though you never hit me a lick, for the God I serve is a God of love, and I can't go to his kingdom with hate in my heart." He held out his hand to me and almost cried and said, "Charlie, come to see me and I will treat you nice. I am sorry for what I did." I said, "That's all right, Marster. I done left the past behind me." I had felt the power of God and tasted his love, and this had killed all the spirit of hate in my heart years before this happened. *Whenever a man has been killed dead and made alive in Christ Jesus* [1 Cor. 15:22; Gal. 2:19–20], he no longer feels like he did when he was a servant of the devil. *Sin kills dead* [Rom. 6:15, 23; 7:11] *but the spirit of God makes alive* [Rom. 6:2–11].[29]

This powerful account of Charlie's exchange with his former enslaver underscores several important elements endemic to slavocracy. As Charlie points out, the slave owner's cruel treatment of him stemmed from his position of absolute power over Charlie. He whipped Charlie because he could, not because Charlie had done anything wrong. Slave owners' absolute power over the enslaved facilitated their harsh treatment and torturous habits. This notion of the slaveholders' unbridled power appears in Julia Foote's autobiography when she writes of her encounter with a slaveholder looking for a runaway slave. While she is attending a church conference and eating at a house with friends, a slaveholder interrupts the dinner and searches the house for the runaway. The incident, she remarks, "cast a gloom over the whole Conference" and causes her to lament, "What a terrible thing it was for one human being to have absolute control over another."[30] She recognizes the tragic consequences of such unbridled power

29. Johnson, *God Struck Me Dead*, 40–41.
30. Julia Foote, *A Brand Plucked from the Fire: An Autobiographical Sketch by Mrs. Julia*

and that this absolute control permeates every aspect of the life of the enslaved. Charlie's words to his former enslaver also capture well this vile dimension of slavocracy.

In addition, throughout his narrative about his life under slavery, Charlie emphasizes how his former enslaver and his former enslaver's family often referred to him as a black devil. Such language, as we discussed earlier, derives from the belief that black people were created by the devil and were devils, and it was a theological linguistic method used to deny their humanity. Yet here in his confrontation with his former enslaver Charlie asserts his humanity and his manhood, stating, "I am a man among men," thereby illustrating his complete rejection of his former master's nomenclature for him and the beliefs that undergirded such a classification. The differences that exist between the two do not rest upon Charlie's supposed creation by the devil but upon the fact that his former enslaver "ain't right," because although he goes to church, he does not worship the "God of love," as Charlie does. Charlie, therefore, underscores the hypocritical nature of the slaveholder's religion by drawing a distinct contrast between him and his former enslaver and the two different gods they serve, for as Charlie states to his former enslaver, "What is in me, though, is not in you."

After narrating this exchange, Charlie informs the reader about what exactly *is* in him and how he is able to forgive the former enslaver. God's power and God's love kill the spirit of hate and empower Charlie to love the former slaveholder despite the cruelty he experienced at his hands for many years. As Yolanda Pierce observes, "After his spiritual transformation, Charlie not only turns from sin and toward Christ, but taking on the role of a Christlike figure, he graciously forgives the sins committed against him."[31] Moreover, echoing Pauline language, Charlie speaks of two kinds of death in his explanation of how he could forgive the slave owner, a death that takes place through his conversion experience: he was killed dead and made alive in Christ Jesus, which contradicts and supersedes a death that takes place due to sin's power: sin kills dead.

Charlie's language of being killed dead and made alive in Christ Jesus echoes several Pauline passages. Most notably, his words have resonances with Galatians 2:20, where Paul writes, "I am crucified with Christ: nev-

---

A. J. Foote (Cleveland, OH: Printed for the author by W. F. Schneider, 1879), reprinted in Andrews, *Sisters of the Spirit*, 220.

31. Yolanda Pierce, *Hell without Fires: Slavery, Christianity, and the Antebellum Spiritual Narrative* (Gainesville: University Press of Florida, 2005), 4.

ertheless I live; yet not I, but Christ liveth in me." To be killed dead means to be united with Christ's death of crucifixion, and in doing so the believer shares in his death to the old age order and partakes in his resurrection to life anew. Indeed, Christ's death becomes the believer's experience and so too his resurrection. The new life that the believer experiences is the new life of the risen Christ living in him. Charlie's language of killed dead and made alive fleshes out what he means by "what is in him"; the risen Christ makes him alive and lives in him, empowering him to love his former enslaver.

Charlie's emphasis on being killed dead corresponds with Paul's focus on God's action of crucifying him. The passive nature of Paul's crucifixion indicates that God is the agent behind the deed.[32] Similarly, in Charlie's case, the death he undergoes comes about through divine power. The death Charlie endures includes the killing of hate in his heart, an execution that only God could perform. At the same time, it is important to note what Pierce states about this death of hate: "While the manifestation of religious faith for Charlie allows him to forgive, he does not forget. Charlie's spiritual conversion is of such a fundamentally singular kind that he is able to live with a memory of hate, *but not with the hate itself.*"[33] God's assassination of the spirit of hate within Charlie's heart does not erase the years of torture and pain he endures under his former enslaver, but it does allow him, as he says, to leave "the past behind me."

In addition, 1 Corinthians 15:22 and Romans 6:2–11 form the background of Charlie's declaration. In 1 Corinthians 15:22 Paul writes, "For as in Adam all die, even so in Christ shall all be made alive." Whereas Adam brought death to humanity, Christ brings life so that where death abounds, life abounds all the more, including in Charlie's life, where he is made alive in Christ. Paul's language in Romans 6:2–11 regarding death, life, sin, and grace also reverberates in Charlie's words, shaping and informing his own experience of God and God's power at work in him. In these verses Paul speaks of believers sharing in Christ's death, and by doing so, believers' former selves are "replaced by a new status as God's beloved" and are given an awareness of

---

32. A number of scholars have noted the passive nature of the term σύνσταυρόω in Gal. 2:19 (συνεσταύρωμαι), which is understood as a divine passive. God's action in Paul's life leads to a total transformation of the apostle. J. Louis Martyn, *Galatians: A New Translation with Introduction and Commentary*, Anchor Yale Bible 33A (New York: Doubleday, 1997), 258, remarks, "It is Christ who now lives in Paul, but that does not mean that there is no longer an I. The I has been crucified and re-created."

33. Pierce, *Hell without Fires*, 4.

"Christ living in them."[34] Similar to Paul, who declares his death along with all believers' death to sin, Charlie experiences death and new life in Christ Jesus. Because of this death and resurrection experience, Charlie is no longer a servant of the devil but of the Lord.[35]

Charlie adopts Paul's stance of sin as a power with the ability to kill and juxtaposes it with the Spirit, which makes alive. In his phrase "Sin kills dead" Charlie echoes the apostle's words in Romans 5:12, 21; 6:23, where Paul writes that sin brings death, and 7:11, where he declares that sin slew him. Two powers are at work upon human beings—sin, which brings death, and the Spirit, which opposes sin's death agenda, by bringing forth life, as the apostle writes in Romans 8:6, 10–11. As this scriptural analysis demonstrates, at a pivotal moment in his narrative Charlie takes up Pauline language and utilizes it to describe his conversion, transformation, new stance toward his former enslaver, and the existence of two powers that affect humanity, the Holy Spirit and sin.

Charlie's conversion, which he describes later in his narrative, offers a deepening understanding of his forgiving response to his former enslaver; his conversion profoundly transforms his life. His first experience of God's power takes place in the woods while praying. Later, upon invitation from a preacher to attend a revival, Charlie attends the meeting for four nights, and before going on the fourth night, he prays once again in the woods: "Lord I have neither father nor mother. Have mercy on me."[36] Later on, as the people at church pray for him, he encounters God.

> I went on to church, and the brothers and sisters prayed around me. Then, like a flash, the power of God struck me. It seemed like something struck me in the top of my head and then went on out through the toes of my feet. I jumped, or rather, fell back against the back of the seat. I lay on the floor of the church. A voice said to me, "You are no longer a sinner. Go and tell the world what I have done for you. If you are ashamed of me, I will be ashamed of you before my father." I looked about me and saw a deep pit that seemed to be bottomless. I couldn't hear nobody pray. I began to pray for myself. Again the voice said to me, "Go tell the world what great things the Lord

34. Robert Jewett, *Romans*, Hermeneia (Minneapolis: Fortress, 2007), 395.

35. Pierce, *Hell without Fires*, 4, believes that with the phrase "servant of the devil" Charlie indicates "not just a reference to the spiritual bondage of Satan, but to the physical bondage he experiences under a human devil."

36. Johnson, *God Struck Me Dead*, 45.

has done for you." I rose from the floor shouting; a voice on the inside cried, "Mercy! Lord, have mercy!" . . . Never had I felt such a love before. It just looked like I loved everything and everybody. I went on to work that day shouting and happy. . . . I can't tell you what religion is, only that it is love.[37]

This divine encounter of conversion transforms Charlie's life and bestows upon him an experience with God's power and love that affects his entire being. God's power touches him and grants him a commission to proclaim the gospel to the world. To proclaim the things God has done for him is to proclaim the reality of God's love for everyone, including enslaved persons. Charlie becomes a witness to God's inclusion of all human beings in God's salvific plan, and he has a new identity as a proclaimer of the gospel whose experience of divine love transforms and renews his purpose and life. It is this experience that allows Charlie to forgive his former enslaver. This divine encounter with God endows Charlie with the ability and the courage to face his former enslaver and declare his manhood, his equality, and his new identity.

I Saw Jesus

In another ex-slave conversion narrative, the author begins the account by telling of life before conversion. "I don't know why it was I got converted, because I had been doing nearly everything they told me I ought not to do. I danced, played cards, and done just like I wanted to do."[38] Yet one day the author becomes very heavy and begins to pray. The heaviness and the prayer precede a vision of Jesus. "And there I saw Jesus. He turned my face to the east and said, 'Go and declare my name to the world, and I will fill your heart with song.' While I was laying there I saw the city. It was the prettiest place that I ever saw." Although the author does not state that the city is heaven, the vision of angels that fly around the city suggests as much. This experience is both the author's conversion experience and his commissioning episode, for afterward the author relates the event's transformative nature in Pauline language. "After I passed through this experience I lost all worldly cares. The things I used to enjoy don't interest me now. *I am a new creature* [2 Cor. 5:17] in Jesus, *the workmanship* [Eph. 2:10] of his hand saved from the foundation of the world. I was a *chosen vessel* [Acts 9:15] before the wind ever blew or

37. Johnson, *God Struck Me Dead*, 45–46.
38. Johnson, *God Struck Me Dead*, 111.

before the sun ever shined. Religion is not a work but a *gift from God. We are saved by grace, and it is not of ourselves but the gift of God* [Eph. 2:8]."[39]

The Pauline language of new creature points to the author's perceived difference between a past self and a new self. What was once important to the narrator is no longer important. Similarly, the language of workmanship demonstrates that conversion enabled enslaved Africans to see themselves as God's creation, and neither a creation of the devil nor a child of Ham but a human being whom God creates with divine attention and care. The author's status as "a chosen vessel before the wind ever blew or before the sun ever shined" indicates a divine plan that always included the ex-slave. There was never a time in which God did not have this ex-slave's life in the divine mind and purpose. In highlighting the gift nature of salvation, the author affirms the beginning statement of the narrative—"I don't know why it was I got converted . . ." God comes to the author through divine initiative and agency, and illustrates what Radin observes is a common occurrence in these narratives, which is that it is "God who sought the Negro."[40] God's act of seeking the author and then granting a vision of Jesus solidifies the gift nature of salvation. God's grace seeks humanity and transforms those it finds.

Traveling to the Third Heaven

Terminology akin to death and Paul's ascent to the third heaven appears in the account of another enslaved African in which the seer provides several episodes of divine encounters. The first account this seer outlines begins in this manner: "When the Lord freed my soul I was sitting out praying, and he told me that the sun was going down and said, 'This day you got to die.' And I said, 'If I die I want to go with a prayer in my mouth.' And while I was trusting him he carried me away in the spirit. He told me he was God, and there is none before him nor behind him."[41] God tells the narrator that he is the enslaved's Father and that the enslaved person is his child. The ramifications of this divine recognition cannot be underestimated. God's statement refutes the common beliefs during this time that the enslaved have no god,[42]

---

39. Johnson, *God Struck Me Dead*, 111.

40. Radin, foreword to *God Struck Me Dead*, xi.

41. Johnson, *God Struck Me Dead*, 167.

42. See John Jea's narrative above in chap. 1, in which he relates how this notion was preached to the enslaved.

that they are children of Ham,[43] and are therefore worthy of subjugation. The statement of divine paternity underscores the enslaved African's humanity and creation by God. God then tells the enslaved African to "Go and go in my name."[44] In other words, God authorizes the seer to take on his name and to reject and resist the name given to him by white enslavers and those that support the slavocracy. The seer no longer needs to take on the identity of descendant of Ham but can now take on the name "child of God."

After narrating this episode, the seer reports another event in which travel to the third heaven takes place.

> He told me to look and behold, because he was God. He carried me to the *third heaven* [2 Cor. 12:2] year before last, and I shouted that place over, and I saw angels flying from place to place. In the first heaven I seen people who'd been there for years and years. I saw my mother, sister, and brother, sitting as far back as possible. I saw angels in the second heaven and the Lord spoke to me. He told me, "I am God the Messiah, I am God Almighty. There is none before me nor behind me. I made everything on this green earth. I even made the serpents, even the worms and birds." If he wanted water he wouldn't ask me for it, because he was God and made everything.[45]

Here the seer adopts Paul's cosmological framework in which the seer, as in Paul's description of his journey in 2 Corinthians 12:1–10, travels to the third heaven. However, unlike the apostle, the seer provides details about the sights and sounds distinct to each heavenly realm.[46] The first heaven contains those who have died, and in the second and third realms, angels exist. The seer's ascent to the heavenly realms provides the background for the affirmation of God's role as Creator of all things. God's declaration that he "made everything on this green earth" includes the creation of the enslaved African to whom he speaks and all the enslaved. Here again a divine

---

43. See the discussion of Josiah Priest in chap. 1.

44. Johnson, *God Struck Me Dead*, 167.

45. Johnson, *God Struck Me Dead*, 167.

46. In some ancient Jewish texts, seers and biblical figures are known to travel to different heavens. Some of these texts posit as many as seven heavens, others as few as three, as in this seer's account and in Paul's own narration of his ascent in 2 Cor. 12:1–10. See, for example, The Life of Adam and Eve, Martyrdom and Ascension of Isaiah, as well as The Book of Watchers. The seer in this narrative follows the pattern of the ancient seers in describing the journey. Paul's account is quite laconic in this regard.

encounter serves as a counternarrative to a distorted white theology that maintains blacks were created by the devil.

Meeting God in the Blackberry Patch

In another narrative from this collection of conversion stories, an enslaved African American woman recounts her conversion experience, which includes her travel to hell and heaven. She begins by describing her mother. "I was born in Huntsville, Alabama, during slavery time. When the war broke out I was married and had one child. My mother was a good old-time Christian woman. Me and my sister used to lay in the bed at night and listen to her and my aunt talk about what God had done for them. From this I began to feel like I wanted to be a Christian."[47] This woman goes on to speak about her first divine encounter: "The first time I heard God's voice I was in the blackberry patch. It seemed like I was all heavy and burdened down more than common. I had got so I prayed a lot, and the more I prayed it look like the worse off I got. So while I was picking blackberries I said, 'Lord, what have I done; I feel so sinful.' A voice said to me, 'You have prayed to God, and he will bring you out *more than conqueror* [Rom. 8:37].'"[48] Eventually this woman narrates an experience in which she reaches heaven. Before arriving in heaven, however, she wakes up "in hell" and sees "all kinds of animals and people" who "looked like they wanted to devour" her.[49] Once she overcomes all the obstacles before her, she and her guide come to a gate. "The gate opened. We went in. We stood before the throne of God. The little man said, 'Here is one come from the lower parts of the world.' God spoke, but he didn't open his mouth. 'How did she come?' 'She came through hard trials with the hellhounds on her trail.'"[50] The account highlights the hard trials and opposition faced by this woman, since the guide's response to God's query carries more than one meaning. On the one hand, the hard trials refer to her existence as an enslaved woman. On the other hand, the words also refer to her experience before she came to heaven's gate, which includes the heavy burdens she felt during her conversion experience as well as her experience of waking up in hell. Moreover, the angel's reply that "she came

47. Johnson, *God Struck Me Dead*, 169.
48. Johnson, *God Struck Me Dead*, 169.
49. Johnson, *God Struck Me Dead*, 170.
50. Johnson, *God Struck Me Dead*, 171.

through hard trials" indicates a divine recognition of this woman's struggles, an acknowledgment that not all she suffers escapes divine notice. Thus, the guide's words allude to her earthly difficulties as well as her supernatural trials in her otherworldly encounter. Her earthly and supernatural tribulations mirror each other and converge as obstacles that only God enables her to overcome.

Nevertheless, she receives protection, escapes the clutches of those who want to "devour" her, and ultimately hears a divine commissioning. "A voice said, 'You are born of God. My son delivered your soul from hell, and you must go and help carry the world. You have been chosen out of the world, and hell can't hold you.' When I came back to myself I was just like somebody foolish. I felt like I wanted to run away. I cried and shouted for joy, so glad to be one of the elect children. This is why I say that a child that has been truly born of God knows it."[51] The divine assurance she receives that God "will bring you out *more than conqueror*" leads to her throne-room meeting with God and gestures to her victory over spiritual obstacles as well as her conquest of the present horrendous realities she faces on a daily basis. Her attainment to the throne signals her triumph over the difficulties of an enslaved life. Like so many other narrators in this collection of conversion stories, she is told that she must die, language that points to her impending conversion experience. Yet the declaration of becoming more than a conqueror encourages her throughout the entire ordeal. The Pauline formulation foreshadows her climactic, triumphant episode in heaven and her ultimate salvation as she goes through her conversion experience and receives a heavenly commission. This commission God seals with the promise that "hell can't hold you."

Pauline Language Permeates the Conversion Narratives of the Enslaved

Throughout these conversion narratives Pauline language appears. Language, in phrases like God's "workmanship" and "chosen vessel," focuses on the enslaved's divine creation in Christ. In addition, these experiences are filled with visions that these seers encounter and contain references to God's power and authority. The authors see God, the heavenly throne, Jesus, angels, Satan, and hell. For a people constantly denied education and information, these divine visions demonstrate a reversal of such a practice. God

---

51. Johnson, *God Struck Me Dead*, 171.

grants these seers access and information regarding the divine realms, access that bestows upon them knowledge. Although they may not be able to control their own circumstances or the larger vicissitudes of societal existence, God is ultimately in control of all things, and these revelations provide them with "privileged insight" into the events of the heavenly realms. As a result, the implication is that what these seers see in the earthly realm is not all there is to their existence. The activities in the supernatural realm illustrate that a greater narrative is unfolding, a story in which they are a part.[52]

As one seer put it, "[God] never leaves me in ignorance. Neither does he leave any that trust him in ignorance."[53] The bestowal of visions and dreams points to God as the ultimate arbiter of knowledge and indicates that this God reveals divine knowledge to those forgotten and deemed unworthy by society.

In other conversion accounts in *God Struck Me Dead*, the narrators point to God's power and authority by using additional Pauline passages: God works all things after the counsel of his own will (Eph. 1:11), God removes the sting of death and robs the grave of its victory (1 Cor. 15:55–56), and God finishes what he starts (Phil. 1:6). Such passages underscore God's sovereignty, wisdom, and power over death, creation's cruel enemy. These conversion episodes depict this sovereign God as one who bestows power to the recipients and describes this granting of divine power in Pauline language in that God's power makes them more than a conqueror (Rom. 8:37), shoes them with the gospel of peace (Eph. 6:15), clothes them with spiritual armor (Eph. 6:11–17), and assures them of the sufficiency of divine grace (2 Cor. 12:9) as they go forth to proclaim the gospel; God extends divine aid and assistance to the seers of these encounters.

Why are these conversion experiences important for African American Pauline hermeneutics? First, they illustrate how Paul's language is used to depict heavenly encounters; this indicates that the enslaved see themselves as part of the apostle's story and in turn make him part of their own story. The God who revealed God's self to Paul now reveals God's self to them in a similar manner.

---

52. These divine experiences of the enslaved have analogues with the seers in Jewish apocalyptic literature, literature believed by some scholars to originate out of oppressed communities. See my brief discussion of Daniel in Bowens, *An Apostle in Battle*, 181–83; John Collins, *The Apocalyptic Imagination: An Introduction to Jewish Apocalyptic Literature* (Grand Rapids: Eerdmans, 1998); Mitchell Reddish, ed., *Apocalyptic Literature: A Reader* (Nashville: Abingdon, 1990), 19–38.

53. Johnson, *God Struck Me Dead*, 156.

Second, and relatedly, sharing these conversion stories is an act of resistance to the dominant interpretations of Pauline Scripture. By recounting these divine episodes, the slaves in effect proclaim that their experiences invalidate whites' textual interpretations or text-based interpretations of the apostle. The reality of their conversions and heavenly encounters provides them with testimonies of resistance in which they bear witness to the God who acts in and for them, not a God who wills their enslavement.

Third, these conversion experiences give rise to a body hermeneutic—their bodies, which were often the locus of their masters' domination, torture, and violence, now become the sites of divine engagement. Here the observations of Diana Hayes on the meaning of violence are important. She writes that violence includes physical abuse, but also entails more than that, for

> Violence is a violation: "Whatever violates another in the sense of infringing upon or disregarding or abusing or denying that other, whether physical harm is involved or not, can be understood as an act of violence. The basic overall definition of violence would then become *violation of personhood*," an attack on the very being of a person created, as all are, in the image and likeness of God. . . . Depersonalizing a person—making him or her a thing unworthy of notice or consideration—can destroy in more critical ways than simply sticks or stones battering flesh can. . . . Names do hurt, because they steal our identities as human beings and make us things that can be manipulated according to the whims and wishes of the namer—it is a theft of one's very soul.[54]

These enslaved Africans' conversion stories often contain episodes of or references to violence perpetrated upon their minds and bodies along with stories of divine encounters with God. It is significant that bodies that experienced physical, mental, emotional, and verbal violence receive visitations from the divine realm. The actions of white slave owners carried out upon their bodies and minds sought to steal their souls, but these divine encounters, to paraphrase the words of the psalmist, "restored their bodies and souls" (Ps. 23:4). For example, after the angel touches him, Morte describes the transformation of his body: "I looked new. I looked at my hands and they were new; I looked at my feet and they were new." A divine touch transforms Morte's view of his body; a body that had suffered so much and which he repeatedly referred to in the narrative as subject to his master's

---

54. Diana L. Hayes, "My Hope Is in the Lord," in Townes, *Embracing the Spirit*, 19–20.

whipping was now the object of God's love and affection, resulting in his being called "a chosen vessel" and "salt of the earth"—new names to replace the depersonalized names placed upon him. Indeed, God not only touches his body but even takes over his speech, for he begins to shout and preach, acknowledging that "the words seemed to flow from my lips."

Similarly, the other enslaved Africans in their narratives highlight the effect of God's presence upon their bodies. Divine power strikes Charlie in the top of his head and then goes through the toes of his feet. Others see themselves as new creations, workmanship of God's hands, and for many the experience of being killed dead and made alive involves their bodies. They fall to the ground, go into a trance, or begin shouting or preaching. Their divine Pauline-like experiences give them another way to interpret and understand their black bodies: their bodies that were degraded by physical whips and by emotional and mental whips with words such as "ugly" and "devil" were now bodies touched by angels, called "chosen" by God, and made a new creation. Their ears that were often filled with the cries of fellow slaves were now filled with angels' songs and God's own voice. Their eyes that beheld mothers taken from children, fathers sold, and fellow slaves on auction blocks now beheld the throne of God, the glory of Jesus, and in some cases family members that had made it successfully to heaven.[55] The body hermeneutic highlighted in these conversion stories illustrates that conversion not only took place in the soul but was a totalizing transformation that involved the body as well, resisting the powers that sought to rob their "very souls."

These experiences enabled a relocation of power and authority; the power and authority of the enslaver were undermined and relativized in the conversion experiences of the enslaved. The slaveholders did not have the final word about to whom they belonged. The divine encounters indicated that the enslaved belonged to God, not the slave owner. This relocation of power and authority also involved scriptural interpretation, for their bodies now enabled them to interpret Scripture for themselves. They did not need to rely upon the enslaver's scriptural interpretation of their bodies. Whites interpreted black bodies as demonic, cursed, evil, soulless, and a devilish creation. But these liberating experiences of God's power and Spirit upon the bodies of the enslaved enabled them to see that their bodies

---

55. These conversion experiences did not stop the atrocities that these enslaved Africans witnessed. They did, however, provide what I have termed in this chapter "divine interruptions of the demonic."

were holy, created by God, possessors of souls, and blessed. Such encounters enabled the enslaved to separate the notion of sin from their black bodies. Sin was an outside force from which they could be delivered; it was not associated with their blackness.[56] The God of the Bible loved their bodies and did not curse them.

Fourth, these conversion narratives illustrate divine interruptions of the demonic, God's incursion into human oppressive structures, such as slavery. God shows up in inexplicable ways in moments and times of deep oppression and suffering, and such encounters give formidable examples of the counternarratives that existed among the enslaved. In many instances, these divine interruptions took place during ordinary, everyday events, such as Morte's encounter while plowing in the field, Charlie's experience in the woods, or the enslaved seer's encounter with God while lying on the bed. The weaving of these religious experiences into ordinary life demonstrates that for the enslaved, a unity between the sacred and the profane exists; God could meet them anywhere and respond to their needs.[57] Raboteau remarks about the importance of understanding "the profound connection between the other world and this world in the religious consciousness of the slaves. . . . Following African and biblical tradition, [the slaves] believed that the supernatural continually impinged on the natural, that divine action constantly took place within the lives of men, in the past, present, and future."[58] Although his comments regarding the enslaved's connection between the other world and this world occur in his discussion of spirituals sung by the slaves, his statements are apropos for conversion accounts as well. For the enslaved the natural world and the supernatural world were intricately linked.

Fifth, these conversion stories confirm enslaved Africans' identity as spiritual beings with souls with whom God almighty communicated, souls that visited paradise and beheld the heavenly realms. As Yolanda Pierce observes, "religious conversion provided proof that a slave had a saveable, redeemable soul. Endowed with a soul, the slave could no longer be chattel."[59] These conversion experiences reaffirm the God-given humanity of the

56. See the discussion of Jupiter Hammon above in chap. 1, where he emphasizes in his speeches that all have sinned, both blacks and whites, not just blacks, and so all need salvation.

57. Kimberly Rae Connor, *Conversions and Visions in the Writings of African-American Women* (Knoxville: University of Tennessee Press, 1994), 24.

58. Raboteau, *Slave Religion*, 250.

59. Pierce, *Hell without Fires*, 53.

enslaved, a humanity that refused to allow them to believe the distorted gospel of their slaveholders. Such divine events also illustrated that the enslaved could communicate with God and God could communicate with them. In a society where their voices were muted and their cries were ignored, the power to speak with God and the power to have God speak with them relocated authority. As we have seen in these narratives, these mystical happenings bestowed upon them agency: God tells them to go and proclaim the Word; they are given the ability and the power to speak to others on behalf of God.

That God could come to them and use the same words God spoke to the apostle, such as "You are my chosen vessel" and "My grace is sufficient for you," and that they could have similar experiences as the apostle, such as traveling to the third heaven, also shifts authority regarding how Paul should be interpreted. If the enslaved are having similar experiences as the apostle, and if God is speaking to them just as God spoke to him, then Paul can be understood in a different way than how he is taught and preached to them by white interpreters. In other words, apostle-like divine encounters with God mean that these experiences become the lens through which to read Paul, not the slave minister's sermons. The touch of the numinous transports them to the heavenly realms, indicating the shared social space between human and divine, between ἄνθρωπος (man) and θέος (God), in which both realms remain dynamically related and connected.

Sixth, these accounts share an underlying theme, which is an implicit Pauline understanding of the life of faith and one's encounter with God: "I have been crucified with Christ, nevertheless I live." The repeated language of "You must die," "I was killed dead," "I died but now I'm alive" echoes Paul and his understanding of the necessity of death in that the believer dies to self, to sin, to the world, and receives resurrection to new life in Christ. Pauline language permeates these narratives, indicating the apostle's significance to the religious experiences of the enslaved.

This brief exploration of the reception of Paul's language and the function of this language in enslaved Africans' conversion and commissioning stories demonstrates the integral nature of the apostle's language to blacks' understanding of God and God's power at work on their behalf. Indeed, scriptural language and imagery permeate these accounts and illustrate a divine interruption in the lives of the enslaved. As Cheryl Sanders writes, "[The enslaved] believed that the same God who transformed the sinful status of their souls in the conversion experience would transform the sinful structures of the society. The God who had freed their souls from sin could certainly free their bodies from slavery."[60] Sanders's observation points to the deep relationship the enslaved perceived between spiritual and physical freedom; for both were to the enslaved indissolubly linked.

Paul and his experiences were a "religious source" for the African Americans in these conversion narratives.[61] The God who dealt with Paul, called him on the Damascus road, and took him to the third heaven likewise dealt with them. Such encounters reinforced their dignity and self-worth and undermined the idea that their existence depended upon slavery. They were, in fact, privileged seers, enabled by divine initiative to see and hear the world beyond them. The apostle's language gave them the words to connect their experiences to his and at the same time make these experiences their own.

60. Cheryl Sanders, "African Americans, the Bible and Spiritual Formation," in *African Americans and the Bible: Sacred Texts and Social Textures*, ed. Vincent L. Wimbush (New York: Continuum, 2000), 590.

61. Venable-Ridley, "Paul and the African American Community," 214.

CHAPTER 5

African American Pauline Hermeneutics and the Art of Biblical Interpretation

"Honey, it 'pears when I can read dis good book I shall be nearer to God. . . . I only wants to read dis book, dat I may know how to live; den I hab no fear 'bout dying."[1]

God will not suffer us, always to be oppressed. Our sufferings will come to an end.[2]

In his work, Martin Mittelstadt distinguishes between historical criticism, literary criticism, and reception history in the field of biblical studies. He writes that historical criticism attempts to re-create the world behind the text, whereas literary criticism strives to encounter the Bible as story. Reception history focuses on what the text has meant and "revisit[s] stories of the Scriptures read, interpreted, viewed, and performed through the centuries." In fact, as Mittelstadt states, those engaged in reception history "search for lost voices, interpreters both new and old, and place these voices in the grand symphony of interpretations, a never-ending succession of perfor-

1. Harriet Jacobs, *Incidents in the Life of A Slave Girl*, ed. L. Maria Child (Boston: Published for the author, 1861), reprinted in *I Was Born a Slave: An Anthology of Classic Slave Narratives*, vol. 2, *1849–1866*, ed. Yuval Taylor (Chicago: Lawrence Hill Books, 1999), 591.

2. David Walker, *Walker's Appeal, In Four Articles, Together with A Preamble To The Coloured Citizens of the World, But in Particular and Very Expressly, to Those of The United States of America, Written in Boston, State of Massachusetts, September 28, 1829* (Boston: Revised and published by David Walker, 1830), reprinted in *David Walker's Appeal: In Four Articles* (Mansfield Centre, CT: Martino Publishing, 2015), 15.

mances on the biblical story."[3] The analysis in the previous chapters has accomplished all the aspects that Mittelstadt recognizes as important to the task of reception history. The previous investigation has revisited Pauline Scripture as read, interpreted, viewed, and performed through the centuries by black interpreters. It has also explored black hermeneuts—some well known, others not so well known—and attempted to highlight their voices as significant for black interpretive history of Scripture in regard to Paul. Their voices deserve placement in the "grand symphony" of biblical hermeneutics overall, and especially in relation to black understandings and appropriations of Pauline Scripture. Indeed, as the previous study has shown, the *Nachleben* (afterlife, posthistory) of Pauline Scripture has overwhelmingly positive dimensions in black scriptural interpretive history.[4]

Vincent Wimbush once asked, "How might putting African Americans at the center of the study of the Bible affect the study of the Bible?"[5] This study has reframed his question slightly by exploring how putting African Americans' *reception* of Paul at the center of Pauline hermeneutics might affect the study of Paul. What happens when African Americans are at the center of Pauline interpretation? What might be the implications and ramifications of construing the study of Paul through African American lenses?

These questions inevitably lead us back to the extensive analysis in the previous chapters and to the primary question that began this volume: How have African Americans from the 1700s to the mid-twentieth century interpreted Paul and his letters? As demonstrated by the survey of the black hermeneuts in this monograph, this question, along with the other questions—how might putting African Americans' reception of Paul at the center of Pauline hermeneutics affect the study of Paul? what happens when African Americans are at the center of Pauline interpretation? and what might be the implications of such a reading?—can be answered in numerous ways. African American Pauline hermeneutics is not monolithic. Interpreters employ a variety of Pauline passages and read them in different ways. Yet their aim is consistent in that they utilize Scripture to speak to their contexts and to the larger issues of society. This chapter will offer brief commentary on

3. Martin W. Mittelstadt, "Receiving Luke-Acts: The Rise of Reception History and a Call to Pentecostal Scholars," *Pneuma* 40, no. 3 (2018): 367.

4. Mittelstadt, "Receiving Luke-Acts," 367.

5. Vincent Wimbush, ed., *African Americans and the Bible: Sacred Texts and Social Structures* (New York: Continuum, 2000), 2.

several recurring themes that permeate the above investigation, and how these themes engage these questions and the larger topic of biblical interpretation. The themes in this chapter do not portend to be comprehensive and to include every aspect of the analyses above, but instead will highlight some persistent motifs. The chapter will conclude with some epigrammatic comments regarding possible areas of future research in African American Pauline hermeneutics.

Paul as a Figure of Liberation and Equality, and of Shared Experience

As early as 1774, African American petitioners utilized Paul to argue against slavery and its repeated practice of separating black families. In fact, the apostle's admonitions for husbands to love their wives and children to obey their parents as well as the imperative to bear one another's burdens were central to petitioners' requests early on. In addition, the Paul of Acts 17:26, who declared that God has made of one blood all the nations of the earth, was a central figure for black resistance to white supremacist readings of Paul. Additional examples could be cited, but the overwhelming reality is that for numerous black interpreters, Paul was an advocate for freedom, not for slavery, an advocate for racial justice, not for segregation. His words became a means to critique and call for the overthrow of unjust systems. Black female preachers employed his words about his female colaborers who were preachers, prophets, and ministers in the early church to speak of their own rightful place as preachers. In this volume we have seen that black interpreters employed Paul to protest slavery, the slave trade, racism, sexism, lynching, segregation, war, unequal job and education opportunities, sexual violence, and rape. For these interpreters, Paul's voice mattered in the struggle for justice, equality, and freedom. He becomes their companion in the liberation fight.

What does the idea of Paul as a figure of liberation and equality mean for biblical interpretation? Such a trajectory raises awareness of Scripture, including Pauline Scripture, as a resource for justice, equality, and liberation. It also underscores the possibility of liberative readings of what may seem like difficult figures in the text or difficult texts themselves. Many of these interpreters, who had every right to reject Paul and Pauline Scripture, by and large did not do so. Instead they demonstrate that Pauline Scripture can bring life and healing as well as become a source for resistance to injustice. They also demonstrate that Scripture can speak to current issues and debates, as they utilized Paul to critique slavery, white supremacy, and racism in their own contexts.

To be sure, Howard Thurman and Albert Cleage Jr. did not see Paul as a figure useful for the struggle of liberation and equality. Therefore, they chose to focus on Jesus and Jesus's teaching in the Gospels. Although Thurman acknowledged that Paul did speak for liberation at times, for him Paul's Roman citizenship made him irrelevant to the black struggle and made the apostle more susceptible to oppressive interpretations by whites. For Cleage, Paul's individualization of the gospel made him irrelevant to the project of black nation building. Thurman's and Cleage's readings of Paul raise the issue of how to think about issues of privilege when reading Scripture. Their readings of Paul highlight what it means to think about the apostle as one with privilege and in ways that see him as not so liberative. Their interpretations of Paul were also reactions to how Paul was used against black people throughout history. Hence, their rejection of Paul is another response to white interpretations of the apostle that sought to erase his liberative possibilities. These voices illustrate the complex and complicated layers within African American reception of Paul and reveal that while many blacks gravitated toward Paul as a figure for black liberation, some did not.

Although for Thurman and Cleage Jesus and Jesus's life were more akin to African American experiences than Paul, many blacks maintained that Paul, too, shared their realities. One theme that reappears continuously in the autobiographies, sermons, and essays surveyed above is that Paul shares and gives voice to the various facets of African American existence.[6] Of course, different authors narrate this sharing in different ways. In some instances, the sharing takes place in the realm of divine encounters, such as for Jarena Lee, who, like Paul, during her divine encounter heard words that could not be repeated, and Zilpha Elaw, whose transport to the divine realm was so similar to Paul's that she could not, like him, tell whether she was in or outside of the body when it happened. In the conversion narratives examined above, the enslaved were taken to the third heaven, saw God and the heavenly throne, and had other supernatural episodes. These shared di-

6. Abraham Smith calls this identification with Paul a typological correlation. See his "Paul and African American Biblical Interpretation," in *True to Our Native Land: An African American New Testament Commentary*, ed. Brian Blount et al. (Minneapolis: Fortress, 2007), 31–42, and "Putting 'Paul' Back Together Again: William Wells Brown's *Clotel* and Black Abolitionist Approaches to Paul," *Semeia* 83–84 (1998): 251–62.

vine occurrences, through conversion, sanctification, and journeys into the supernatural realm, illustrate that the Pauline experiences of such divine events transcend time, space, and gender. Likewise, the apostle's focus on the Spirit and spiritual gifts such as glossolalia, healing, and prophecy was central to the Pentecostal movement and its leaders, who saw the Spirit's presence as one that fostered racial unity and transmitted power to transform society. Indeed, for many of the black interpreters in this volume, the apostle was a figure that shared their divine encounters and upheld their call for social transformation.

In addition, shared ministerial experience provided some African Americans with a means to connect to the apostle. Just like the apostle, who chose to work with his hands so that he would not be burdensome to his congregations, John Jea chose to work with his hands during his preaching tours so that he would not be a financial weight to the church either. Martin Luther King Jr. likens himself and his ministry to Paul, who answers the Macedonians' call for aid, when he answers Birmingham's call for help against segregation in their city.

Furthermore, the suffering that Paul undergoes for the sake of the gospel becomes a shared experience for many African Americans. For example, Jupiter Hammon takes up Paul's lament over his fellow Jews in Romans 9:1–3 and 10:1 to mourn over the plight of his fellow enslaved Africans. David Walker uses the apostle's farewell discourse in Acts to forecast his own untimely death, a death that some believe was brought about because he dared to proclaim judgment upon America and to speak out against its racist ways. Martin Luther King Jr. characterizes the suffering that he and other civil rights workers undergo as similar to what Paul had to endure because he preached a gospel of liberation. The apostle's *peristasis* catalogues, also known as hardship lists, become a means by which King interprets the many vicissitudes of a life lived to insure the freedom of others. In his commentary on 2 Corinthians, Guy Nave writes about Paul's emphasis on his sufferings, and he also sees the intersection King makes between the apostle's suffering and that of King and the civil rights workers. "Paul does not expect his believers to play the part of passive victims. The sufferer is an active agent of justice. Those who suffered during the Civil Rights Movement were not passive victims; they were agents for justice. . . . The suffering that Paul refers to is 'redemptive suffering'—suffering that the sufferer chooses to endure as a result of his or her actions for the redemption, liberation, and well-being of others. Paul chooses—and even welcomes—this type of suffering (2 Cor 12:10; cf. Rom

5:3)."[7] To be sure, many of the black interpreters in this monograph saw in Paul's suffering experiences a connection with their own experiences of affliction. They shared a bond with him, for he reflected their experiences and they in turn reflected his experiences.

When these black interpreters merge Paul's divine encounters and sufferings with their own lives, however, they go beyond the idea of adoption and adaptation of Pauline language, although this is certainly part of what is taking place. What this merge signifies is the fusion of black history with sacred history, for African Americans who were repeatedly told that they had no god and that they were not created by God but by the devil, have lives whose divine encounters and physical sufferings coalesce with the apostle's own life story, demonstrating a sacred confluence in which black lives are seen as part of God's history with the world. This sacred confluence, however, is not in the sense that some white supremacist interpreters, like Josiah Priest, argued, in that God ordained blacks for slavery, but is rather to the contrary, that African Americans participate in the divine life of God, whose power delivers them, speaks to and through them, and frees them from both physical and spiritual oppression. Their participation in this divine life demonstrates their humanity and their significance in the divine economy.

These explicators interpret Paul with a *dialectic of experience*, that is, they bring their experiences as African Americans to the text while at the same time allowing the text, specifically Paul's words, to interpret their experiences. There is a dynamic interplay between black lives and the biblical text. Accordingly, this dialectic of experience enables black interpreters to critique their oppressive experiences as not in line with God's will for humanity. For example, Charlie, whose conversion narrative is explored above, recognizes that although he witnesses his enslaver worshiping and going to church, the slaveholder "ain't right" and does not worship the same "God of love" that Charlie does. In another instance, Paul's words about the Fatherhood of God and the unity of humanity enable Ida Robinson to address the real experience of lynching taking place in America and to critique the nation's silence regarding it. These interpreters demonstrate that experience can play a role in biblical interpretation when interpreters bring their experiences to the text and at the same time allow the text to interpret their experience.

---

7. Guy Nave, "2 Corinthians," in Blount, *True to Our Native Land*, 326.

Paul and the Hermeneutic of Trust

An overwhelming number of the interpreters discussed in this volume employed Paul in a hermeneutic of trust; that is, these interpreters saw Scripture as God's sacred word and believed that it mattered for them, for their communities, and for the nation. Interestingly, they applied a hermeneutic of suspicion to the white interpreters of the text, such as the slaveholders, proponents of slavery, and advocates of segregation, and not to the text itself. They did not allow the way Paul was preached or explained to them to make them suspicious of Paul, but rather, more often than not, such interpretations made them suspicious of the white interpreter, as indicated by the following quote from Frederick Douglass.

> For in the United States men have interpreted the Bible against liberty. They have declared that Paul's epistle to *Philemon* is a full proof for the enactment of that hell-black Fugitive Slave Bill which has desolated my people for the last ten years in that country. They have declared that the Bible sanctions slavery. What do we do in such a case? What do you do when you are told by the slaveholders of America that the Bible sanctions slavery? Do you go and throw your Bible into the fire? Do you sing out, "No union with the Bible!" Do you declare that a thing is bad because it has been misused, abused, and made bad use of? Do you throw it away on that account? No! You press it to your bosom all the more closely; you read it all the more diligently; and prove from its pages that it is on the side of liberty—and not on the side of slavery.[8]

In revisiting Frederick Douglass's words from chapter 2, one finds an example of such trust toward Scripture in his denouncement of the misuse of the Bible to justify slavery. Since many black hermeneuts believed God authored the biblical text, they saw the text as life giving and affirming of their value, worth, and dignity. Correspondingly, they believed that Paul's voice spoke to their current context because for them Scripture was a living and breathing

8. Frederick Douglass, "The American Constitution and the Slave: An Address Delivered in Glasgow, Scotland, on 26 March 1860," in *The Frederick Douglass Papers: Series One: Speeches, Debates, and Interviews*, vol. 3, 1855–63, ed. John Blassingame (New Haven: Yale University Press, 1985), 362–63. Also quoted in J. Albert Harrill, "The Use of the New Testament in the American Slave Controversy: A Case History in the Hermeneutical Tension between Biblical Criticism and Christian Moral Debate," *Religion and American Culture: A Journal of Interpretation* 10, no. 2 (2000): 161.

document with relevance for their lives. Even Thurman and Cleage, who did exhibit a hermeneutic of suspicion toward Paul, showed a hermeneutic of trust toward other parts of the scriptural text. For them Scripture was an integral part of the black struggle for justice and equality.[9]

Cosmological Paul and "Canonical" Paul

Many of these interpreters considered the cosmological feature of Paul's theology to be important because they, like Paul, believed in a supernatural world filled with God, angels, Satan, satanic beings, and the Holy Spirit. For instance, Zilpha Elaw and Maria Stewart discuss the supernatural realm in terms of opposition to their preaching and to their speaking out against the injustices of their time. Stewart takes up Paul's language regarding weapons for this spiritual warfare and depicts herself as a woman warrior fighting for truth and freedom.

In addition, the apostle's emphasis on sin as a power resonates with some of the interpreters covered in this monograph, for they see the cosmic nature of sin creating systemic injustices in the nation. Against one of the dominant understandings of their time, in which sin was seen as merely personal, between an individual and God, these interpreters recognized that sin was not just individual but social as well. James Pennington takes a classic Pauline text, Romans 7:21, understood to be about an individual wrestling with sin in his inner nature, and expands the interpretive range of the verse to include systems of evil, writing that for the enslaved African this text means "How, when he [the slave] would do good, evil is thrust upon him."[10] Pennington takes the text and broadens it from one in which evil is present within the self to one in which evil comes from outside the self, and for him this evil is the system of slavery. Likewise, for Reverdy Ransom, Paul's emphasis on the cross as the center of the gospel becomes the basis for the reconstruction of society, that is, the concrete program of social salvation. Ransom maintained that Christian faith links the individual and the social,

9. For more on the hermeneutic of trust in interpreting Scripture, see Richard B. Hays, "Salvation by Trust? Reading the Bible Faithfully," *Christian Century* 114 (February 1997): 218–23.

10. James Pennington, *The Fugitive Blacksmith; or, Events in the History of James W. C. Pennington, Pastor of Presbyterian Church, New York, Formerly A Slave in the State of Maryland, United States* (London: Charles Gilpin, 1850; reprint, Westport, CT: Negro Universities Press, 1971), 30.

for a person's individual experience of salvation will have societal implications, which include the transformation of unjust power structures and systems. For Ransom, salvation liberates not just the individual but also the social—the community, the society, and the nation—since prejudice and oppression permeate all these entities.

While they take up a cosmic understanding of sin and evil, these interpreters do not allow it to negate human agency in the struggle for liberation. God and Satan are powers, albeit unequal, but human beings still have agency and will have to give account for their actions in this life. Walker, Pennington, and Stewart utilize judgment language in their writings and proclaim that human beings, including slaveholders, will be held accountable for their behavior. King also includes judgment language in his work. And similar to Walker, King emphasizes divine and human agency, adopting the Pauline language of partnering with God, and so views human beings as coworkers with God, working together with the Divine to create a more just society.

Many of these interpreters dared to read Paul as a figure of reconciliation and not as a figure of division and separation. As we have seen time and again in the above analysis, Acts 17:26, in which Paul states that God has made of one blood all the nations of the earth, is the *sine qua non* for many African Americans in their understanding of who Paul is and what he believes. Similarly, his words in Ephesians regarding the abolishment of the dividing wall between Jews and gentiles become a paradigm for black hermeneuts to speak of Christ's destruction of the dividing wall between whites and blacks (Eph. 2:14).

Yet this reconciliation does not happen without repentance. James Pennington, in his letter to his former enslaver, urges him to repent for all that he has done; this repentance is integral to Pennington's understanding of judgment and reconciliation. Echoing Ephesians 2:14 and 2 Corinthians 5:20–21, Pennington contends that reconciliation happens through Jesus's blood but is absent without judgment and repentance, which he calls for throughout his correspondence to the slaveholder. For him, for reconciliation to occur there must be justice, an admission of sin, and an accounting for past wrongs. Judgment, repentance, and reconciliation go hand in hand for Pennington and are deeply intertwined.

Another important theme that appears throughout the foregoing analysis is that these interpreters read Paul as he appeared in Scripture to them, whether he was a character in the book of Acts or was the writer of Ephesians, Colossians, and Hebrews. Although demarcations exist in modern biblical scholarship between the undisputed Pauline letters, the deutero-Paulines, and the Paul of Acts, the all-embracing approach that these interpreters utilized in biblical interpretation raises the question of what it means to read Scripture canonically, that is, to read Scripture holistically. These black interpreters insisted that there was a depth and richness to Paul's words that could not be consigned to certain sections of Ephesians, Colossians, or 1 Timothy. As Abraham Smith observes, early black interpreters understood that "the pro-slavers' use of Paul did not entail a comprehensive accounting of 'Paul's' own views"[11] and that "The goal for the pro-slavers was not to produce a fuller picture of 'Paul' in which 'Paul' might speak to a *variety* of challenges and concerns in antebellum times. Rather, the goal for them was to bring premature closure to 'Paul' as an endorser of slavery."[12] These black hermeneuts insisted on looking at and discussing other parts of Paul's writings, thereby demonstrating the significance of the entire "canon" of Paul, and by extension, the importance of reading Scripture comprehensively.[13] Their interpretive approach raises the question for biblical interpretation of whether readings of Paul "bring premature closure to Paul" if they do not take into account all the "Pauline" writings. These interpreters insist that Scripture needs to be in conversation with all of Scripture.

Paul and the Spirit

Early on, the Spirit language that resides in Paul's letters resonated with black interpreters. Hammon emphasizes to his audience that "For as many as are led by the Spirit of God, they are the sons of God" (Rom. 8:14), to illustrate that God's Spirit, which lives within them, provides his hearers with a new existence; their identities do not derive from slaveholders but from God. Black women preachers, like Elaw, embraced the apostle's "Spirit of adoption" language because their own intimate experiences with the Spirit demonstrated that they were loved by God. The Holy Spirit, which

11. Smith, "Putting 'Paul' Back Together," 257.
12. Smith, "Putting 'Paul' Back Together," 260.
13. I am not suggesting that modern biblical criticism abandon the categories of disputed Paul, undisputed Paul, and the Paul of Acts. What I am raising, however, is the larger question that these black hermeneuts raise for biblical interpretation in their reading of Paul: What perspectives, ideas, or understandings of Scripture do we miss if we concentrate only on one section of Scripture and do not explore others? Are there opportunities for liberative readings that get overlooked?

adopted them, also led them to affirm their divine right to proclaim the gospel. Walker, in article 4 of his *Appeal,* repeatedly informs his readers that the enslaved "belong to the Holy Ghost" and are the "property of the Holy Ghost." Since the Holy Spirit is their "rightful owner," they should not be enslaved to any white person, for they have the divine and natural right of freedom. In the opening of his narrative, Jea merges the Spirit's intercession with the groans of the enslaved, fusing the Spirit's voice with that of the oppressed slave. And for the leaders of the Pentecostal movement covered in this volume, the Spirit's presence meant individual and communal empowerment for service, protest, and unity.

The apostle's words about the Spirit, spiritual gifts, and the social implications of the Spirit's presence represented significant counternarratives to the dominant culture. God's Spirit is a transformative power that breaks down barriers, unifies what society deems separate, and bestows upon believers a different way to see the world. For African American interpreters to be adopted by God's Spirit and called God's own children meant that black lives mattered.

To use Paul to speak the language of unity in the midst of a nation filled with racial division was in a sense to speak another language, a type of glossolalia, speech that contradicted the racist and segregationist discourses of the time periods in which these hermeneuts lived. Paul's words were sacred to these interpreters, and as such they needed to be engaged, interpreted, and proclaimed in a way that brought liberation, not enslavement; social transformation, not the social status quo; and racial unity, not division. Interpreting Paul rightly mattered to the faith of these African American interpreters, for they knew the power of Paul's words to shape reality and to give voice to the voiceless. And hermeneuts like Seymour interpreted his language about the power of the Holy Spirit as a "powerful empire" to speak of the location of real power in this world. Real power does not lie with the American empire but lies within the believer and has the capacity to transform and liberate.

Body Language: A Pauline Body Hermeneutic

Throughout this monograph we have traced the importance of a body hermeneutic to an African American Pauline hermeneutic and discussed how this body hermeneutic appears in various ways in the writings of these interpreters. This body hermeneutic rests upon two questions that these interpreters bring to Paul, which are: Can my black body interpret Paul, and can Paul interpret my black body? As we have seen, these questions resulted in a myriad of answers, some of which follow. In a context in which enslaved persons were consistently told that their salvation rested upon obedience to the slaveholders, Hammon insisted in one of his uses of Paul that African Americans work out their own salvation (Phil. 2:12) and use their bodies— their mouths to *"confess the Lord Jesus"* and their *"hearts to believe unto righteousness"* (Rom. 10:9–10). In this insistence Hammon emphasized black agency and the importance of black bodies in the salvific process. Moreover, the fact that God includes African Americans in his language of resurrection, *"we shall all be changed"* (1 Cor. 15:51), indicates that black bodies belong to God and that these bodies too are worthy of divine transformation.

Walker employs Pauline body language to emphasize black unity, noting that all must work together for the salvation of the whole body (1 Cor. 12:12–27), and Jacobs uses Acts 17:26 to critique the sexual violence done to female black bodies. Elaw takes up Paul's maternal imagery regarding being in labor for the Galatians (Gal. 4:19) to speak of her own labor for unbelievers, thereby speaking to the painful bodily reality of giving birth and applying it to the hard labor required to give birth to spiritual transformation. In addition, the Azusa Street revival's emphasis on being one body of Christ, so much so that one participant stated that the physical color line was washed away in the blood, provides another glimpse into an African American Pauline hermeneutic in which Paul's body language signifies the incorporation of black and white into one body of Christ. For Ransom and Robinson, this body hermeneutic included utilizing Paul to protest lynchings of blacks, and for Mason it included protecting black bodies from dying in war. And finally, the repeated emphasis throughout these writings on God and the Holy Spirit's work upon black bodies, causing African Americans to see into the divine realms, hear divine speech, speak in unknown languages, and experience Christ washing their bodies in baptismal waters, demonstrates also that they are daughters and sons of God, bodies touching and being touched by the Holy.

(The) Text Matters: "Findin' Out Different"

This book is an attempt to delve deeply into African American reception and interpretations of Pauline texts. One of the primary outcomes of this investigation is that the text matters. The following statement by a formerly enslaved African American woman, Jenny Proctor, will highlight this important element.

> Dey wasn't no church for de slaves but we goes to de white folks arbor on Sunday evenin' and a white man he gits up dere to preach to de [n——]. He say, "Now I takes my text, which is '[n——] obey your marster and your mistress,' 'cause what you git from dem in here in dis world am all you ev'r goin' to git, 'cause you jes' like de hogs and de other animals, when you dies you ain't no more, after you been throwed in dat hole.' I guess we believed dat for a while 'cause we didn' have no way findin' out different. We didn' see no Bibles.[14]

Jenny acknowledges that for a time she and the other enslaved Africans believed what the white man said because they "didn' see no Bibles." The implication is that if they had Bibles, there would have been an opportunity of "findin' out different" than what was being taught to them. By extrapolation, this quote underscores how important the text was to the enslaved and to African Americans in general, including the interpreters in this volume, for the text was the means of "findin' out different" and unmasking the hypocritical nature of a white supremacist Christianity. The biblical text, including Pauline texts, enabled African Americans to refute such words as proclaimed by this white preacher and facilitated a vision of themselves as connected to the divine life of God.

As stated above, reception history is about recovering "lost voices, interpreters new and old," and so this monograph has sought to do that and to allow interpreters to speak in their own voices about their understandings of Paul. This exploration is an exercise in investigating the many layers of black interpretations of Paul and to demonstrate the variety of ways in which Paul was used and understood throughout American history. Whereas some white interpreters used Paul to say black bodies did not matter and were relegated to slavery and segregation, most of the black interpreters covered in this book used Paul to proclaim that the bodies and lives of black people did matter. For example, Charles Mason used the apostles' words to speak out against a war that would conscript black bodies to fight for freedom in another country when they were denied such freedoms in their own country.

14. George P. Rawick, ed., *The American Slave: A Composite Autobiography*, 41 vols. (Westport, CT: Greenwood, 1972), *Texas Narratives*, vol. 5, pt. 3 (213).

Audrey Lorde, renowned writer and activist, once stated, "The master's tools will never dismantle the master's house."[15] This true and powerful statement speaks to the difficult struggles of the oppressed and sheds light on earlier chapters in this book. One of the important lessons the black interpreters in this book teach us is that the Bible, specifically Paul and Pauline Scripture, never belonged to the master or the "master's minister,"[16] although many white proponents of slavery and segregation insisted that it did. The fact that these black interpreters utilize the apostle so extensively in their petitions, sermons, writings, essays, and autobiographies indicates that Paul did not belong to white interpreters who employed him for their own agendas.

Although white preachers and ministers utilized Paul for their own racist and immoral aims, these black hermeneuts argued that Paul belonged to a higher authority, the God of liberation and freedom, and so should be interpreted with this hermeneutical posture. Many of these African American interpreters refused to believe that Paul advocated white supremacy and enslavement of black bodies; they demonstrated instead that such racist interpretations of the apostle could not and should not be the final word. In doing so, their works make possible the dismantling of the white supremacist house of Pauline interpretation. These hermeneuts have left a rich legacy, which chronicles the importance of Paul for a protest and resistance biblical hermeneutic aimed toward liberation.[17]

Our journey in this volume has allowed us to see how Paul was used and interpreted in a white supremacist manner, in order to dehumanize and oppress. One way to think about African American reception history, particularly of Paul and his writings, is in terms of reclaiming or rescuing Paul, if you will, from the ways in which he was erroneously preached and proclaimed by some white Christians.[18] Another way to think about it is that many blacks

15. Audrey Lorde, "The Master's Tools Will Never Dismantle the Master's House," in *Sister Outsider: Essays and Speeches* (Berkeley, CA: Crossing, 1984, 2007), 110–14.

16. The phrase "master's minister" comes from Howard Thurman's grandmother and her description of the preacher that the slaveholder would often get to preach to the slaves whose text would always be, "Slaves, obey your master." See the introduction to this volume.

17. These interpreters foreground what Brian Blount, *Then the Whisper Put on Flesh: New Testament Ethics in an African American Context* (Nashville: Abingdon, 2001), calls the "boundary-breaking intentions" of Paul (129), and they demonstrate that "the liberative benefits that can be gleaned from his counsel are legion" (156).

18. C. Michelle Venable-Ridley, "Paul and the African American Community," in *Embracing the Spirit: Womanist Perspectives on Hope, Salvation, and Transformation*, ed. Emilie M. Townes (Maryknoll, NY: Orbis, 1997), 214, says the objective of her work is not to

were engaged in a method of *counterreception* in their use of Paul. They did not allow the way Paul was presented to them by whites to be the way they received the apostle, so they engaged in their own counterreception. While Thurman and Cleage's counterreception of Paul included dismissing the apostle to a great extent, a majority of African American interpreters saw Paul as a figure of unity and as a figure whose words led to empowerment, not dehumanization.

These "hidden figures," so often overlooked and neglected when talking about Christian history and Pauline hermeneutics, deserve to be heard, for they offer strategies on how believers can continue to utilize resistance hermeneutics to protest injustice. They offer powerful legacies of what true faith entails. All of these African American interpreters provide a glimpse of the many ways African Americans have utilized Paul in their petitions, autobiographies, speeches, and sermons to address their context, their time, and their historical situation.

Where Do We Go from Here?

One of the questions this volume raises is, "How can we learn from the past?"[19] This is an important question for American Christianity and American churches, since in many ways both have been complicit in supporting racist structures and systems. Another way to ask this question is, "What can these previous Pauline interpreters teach Pauline interpreters today?" They can teach a modern hermeneut quite a lot, if one is open to use Jenny's phrase, to "findin' out different." Their use of Paul can inspire readings of the apostle in the present that appropriate him in ways that speak to present contexts.

Numerous African Americans utilize Paul in their work, so many that all of them could not be included in this volume. This reality means that the need for further research in this area exists. Which additional interpreters employ Paul in a resistance and protest hermeneutic? Where else can one turn to find subversive uses of Paul that speak against racism and oppres-

---

"redeem but to reclaim the writings of Paul." I think that many of the hermeneuts in this volume are engaging in this same project.

19. This section heading echoes the title of Martin Luther King Jr.'s final book, *Where Do We Go from Here: Chaos or Community?* (New York: Harper & Row, 1967), and places the same query to African American Pauline hermeneutics.

sion of women? Exploration of additional African American texts, such as autobiographies, essays, sermons, and political speeches, will provide further understanding of Pauline reception among African Americans. Such explorations can also examine blacks' use of Paul in literature and music, including black spirituals. The interdisciplinary nature of this field would foster important conversations around the intersections of Scripture, history, theology, literature, and music.

The apostle plays a huge role in the theological, political, and social discourses of African Americans throughout history, and further explorations of his role will add to an understanding of his lasting influence. Connected to these possible areas of more research is investigating how interpreters utilize Paul in relation to other scriptural texts. Are there scriptural texts in the primary sources that appear alongside Pauline texts more frequently than others? All such studies are significant for gaining understanding of how the words of this "apostle to the Gentiles" (Rom. 11:13; Gal. 2:8) achieved influence in African American communities and how he continues to influence these communities. Additionally, more research is important for documenting black religious life within American religiosity, because black religious life and experience are integral to the American landscape.

AFTERWORD

by Beverly Roberts Gaventa
Baylor University

Augustine, Luther, Calvin, Wesley, Barth.

When scholarly introductions to the letters of Paul consider his interpreters, these names routinely appear, give or take a few. Some will add Origen or Chrysostom or Aquinas; others may tend toward Baur and Wrede and Schweitzer. Thanks to the labors of Marion Taylor and others, we have begun to ask about women interpreters of Paul in earlier generations, delighting for example in the subtle treatment of 1 Corinthians 14:34 ("Let the women keep silence in the churches") by Margaret Fell and Dorothy Newberry Gott, to name only a few.

In *African American Readings of Paul*, Lisa Bowens has opened up another vein in the reception history of Paul. To the illustrious names of Augustine and company, she adds others. Lemuel Haynes, Maria Stewart, Julia Foote, and Reverdy Ransom take their place alongside the better-known Howard Thurman and Martin Luther King Jr. Surveying works ranging from petitions to the governor of Massachusetts for the termination of slavery (1774) to King's powerful Pauline letter to American Christians (1968), Bowens demonstrates that, while there exist continuities among the preoccupations of African American interpreters of Paul, there are also considerable diversities, even conflicts, in their varied perspectives.

The assumptions of these readings of Paul differ from those of many contemporary scholars. Here "Paul" means the full Pauline corpus, with no quibbling about authorship. Even the book of Hebrews is assumed to have been written by Paul. In the same way, Luke's portrait of Paul is accepted without question, making frequent reference to the assertion that God has made from one ancestor "all nations to inhabit the whole earth" (Acts 17:26). There is also no concern about separating Paul's views from those of the gospel writers or the psalmists or the prophets. Such concerns may well have been unknown to the Pauline interpreters reflected in these pages. Even had they known of such discussions, I suspect they would have found fine distinctions between Paul and not-Paul to be luxury goods, far too flimsy for the hard work necessary for their struggle against bigotry and oppression. What is central here is Paul's preoccupation with the Spirit, with freedom, with divine power.

The results are startling, especially to those of us who may have imagined that Nancy Ambrose, Howard Thurman's grandmother, spoke for the African American majority when she warned against reading Paul's letters because of their use to defend slavery. To be sure, I imagined that there would be counterarguments to the arguments for slavery. The incessant white recourse to a very particular interpretation of "Slaves be subject" requires an equally incessant, or rather, a more articulate and wise display of Paul's convictions. But I did not anticipate the argument of Lemuel Haynes, who countered the preaching of submission by slaves with a pointed understanding of Romans 6:1, "Shall you continue in sin, that is, participate in slavery and the slave trade?" Neither did I expect to read of James Pennington's contention, in the face of white claims that people of color are inherently evil, that slavery itself originates with Satan (a contention I find entirely coherent with Paul's understanding of the gospel).

I was delighted to find African American women who, far from succumbing to the silencing misuse of Paul, explicitly identify their own vocations with that of Paul. Jarena Lee and Zilpha Elaw draw extensively on Paul's letters as they give voice to their own vocations. Elaw even takes from Paul's maternal imagery in Galatians 4:19 words to depict her own evangelistic endeavors. Indeed, writing in 1879, Julia Foote correctly observes that Paul's reference to Phoebe as a *diakonos* puts her in the same company as Tychicus in Ephesians 6:21. She goes on to point out that 1 Corinthians 11 assumes that women and men both take active leadership roles in public worship. (These points have still to be acknowledged in many Christian communities, much less integrated into practice.)

At several points, what interpreters of Paul may regard as recent insights are shown to have long-standing antecedents among African American interpreters. Elaw, for one, contextualizes 1 Corinthians 14:34 as words spoken to a particular group characterized by "disorders and excess," rather than to "the" church at large. And numerous writers Bowens studies reject personal, spiritualized interpretations of sin in favor of a systemic, corporate view, anticipating a move from individualistic to corporate interpretation usually traced to the late twentieth century.

There is more work to be done. As Bowens acknowledges, many authors remain to be explored, along with many additional documents. But hers is a large and inspiring step in the right direction. In short, Lisa Bowens's work provides a glimpse into the life and thought of people for whom the interpretation of Paul has been nothing less than a matter of life and death. They deserve our attention, our respect, our emulation.

BIBLIOGRAPHY

Adams, Nehemiah. *A South-Side View of Slavery, or Three Months at the South in 1854*. Port Washington, NY: Kennikat, 1969.

Alexander, Estrelda. *Limited Liberty: The Legacy of Four Pentecostal Women Pioneers*. Cleveland, OH: Pilgrim, 2008.

Ambrose, Douglas. "Of Stations and Relations: Proslavery Christianity in Early National Virginia." In *Religion and the Antebellum Debate over Slavery*, edited by John R. McKivigan and Mitchell Snay. Athens: University of Georgia Press, 1998.

Andrews, William L., ed. *African American Autobiography: A Collection of Critical Essays*. Englewood Cliffs, NJ: Prentice Hall, 1993.

———, ed. *Sisters of the Spirit: Three Black Women's Autobiographies of the Nineteenth Century*. Bloomington: Indiana University Press, 1986.

Aptheker, Herbert, ed. *A Documentary History of the Negro People in the United States*. 3 vols. New York: Citadel, 1951.

Bailey, Randall, ed. *Yet with a Steady Beat: Contemporary U.S. Afrocentric Biblical Interpretation*. Semeia Studies. Atlanta: Society of Biblical Literature, 2003.

Baldwin, Lewis. *Behind the Public Veil: The Humanness of Martin Luther King, Jr.* Minneapolis: Fortress, 2016.

Bartleman, Frank. *Azusa Street: The Roots of Modern-Day Pentecost*. Introduction by Vinson Synan. Gainesville, FL: Bridge-Logos, 1980.

Berwanger, Eugene H. "Negrophobia in Northern Proslavery and Antislavery Thought." *Phylon* 33, no. 3 (Fall 1972): 266–75.

Blount, Brian. *Then the Whisper Put on Flesh: New Testament Ethics in an African American Context*. Nashville: Abingdon, 2001.

Blount, Brian, Cain Hope Felder, Clarice J. Martin, and Emerson Powery, eds. *True to Our Native Land: An African American New Testament Commentary*. Minneapolis: Fortress, 2007.

Bly, Antonio. "'Pretends He Can Read': Runaways and Literacy in Colonial America, 1730–1776." *Early American Studies* 6, no. 2 (Fall 2008): 261–94.

Bostic, Joy. *African American Female Mysticism: Nineteenth-Century Religious Activism.* New York: Palgrave Macmillan, 2013.

Bowens, Lisa. *An Apostle in Battle: Paul and Spiritual Warfare in 2 Corinthians 12:1–10.* Wissenschaftliche Untersuchungern zum Neuen Testament 2.433. Tübingen: Mohr Siebeck, 2017.

———. "God and Time: Exploring Black Notions of Prophetic and Apocalyptic Eschatology." In *T&T Clark Handbook of African American Theology*, edited by Antonia Daymond, Frederick Ware, and Eric Williams, 213–24. New York: T&T Clark, 2019.

———. "Liberating Paul: African Americans' Use of Paul in Resistance and Protest." In *Practicing with Paul: Reflections on Paul and the Practices of Ministry in Honor of Susan G. Eastman*, edited by Presian Burroughs, 57–73. Eugene, OR: Wipf & Stock, 2018.

———. "Painting Hope: Formational Hues of Paul's Spiritual Warfare Language in 2 Corinthians 10–13." In *Practicing with Paul: Reflections on Paul and the Practices of Ministry in Honor of Susan G. Eastman*, edited by Presian Burroughs, 107–23. Eugene, OR: Wipf & Stock, 2018.

———. "Spirit-Shift: Paul, the Poor, and the Holy Spirit's Ethic of Love and Impartiality in the Eucharist Celebration." In *The Holy Spirit and Social Justice Interdisciplinary Global Perspectives: Scripture and Theology*, edited by Antipas Harris and Michael Palmer, 218–38. Lanham, MD: Seymour, 2019.

Braxton, Brad. *No Longer Slaves: Galatians and African American Experience.* Collegeville, MN: Liturgical Press, 2002.

Braxton, Joanne. *Black Women Writing Autobiography: A Tradition within a Tradition.* Philadelphia: Temple University Press, 1989.

Brown, Henry Box. *Narrative of the Life of Henry Box Brown, Written by Himself.* Edited by John Ernest. Chapel Hill: University of North Carolina Press, 2008; original Manchester: Lee & Glynn, 1851.

Brown, Michael Joseph. *Blackening of the Bible: The Aims of African-American Biblical Scholarship.* Harrisburg, PA: Trinity Press International, 2004.

Brucia, Margaret. "The African-American Poet, Jupiter Hammon: A Home-Born Slave and His Classical Name." *International Journal of the Classical Tradition* 7, no. 4 (2001): 515–22.

Burrow, Rufus, Jr. *Martin Luther King, Jr., and the Theology of Resistance.* Jefferson, NC: McFarland, 2015.

Butler, Anthea. *Women in the Church of God in Christ: Making a Sanctified World.* Chapel Hill: University of North Carolina Press, 2007.

Butterfield, Stephen. *Black Autobiography in America*. Amherst: University of Massachusetts Press, 1974.

Callahan, Allen Dwight. *Embassy of Onesimus: The Letter of Paul to Philemon*. New Testament in Context. Valley Forge, PA: Trinity Press International, 1997.

————. *The Talking Book: African Americans and the Bible*. New Haven: Yale University Press, 2006.

Calmet, Augustin. *Calmet's Great Dictionary of the Holy Bible*. 4 vols. Charlestown: Samuel Etheridge, 1812.

Cannon, Katie. "Slave Ideology and Biblical Interpretation." *Semeia* 47 (1989): 9–23.

Carby, Hazel V. "'Hear My Voice, Ye Careless Daughters': Narratives of Slave and Free Women before Emancipation." In *African American Autobiography: A Collection of Critical Essays*, edited by William Andrews, 59–76. Englewood Cliffs, NJ: Prentice Hall, 1993.

Carter, J. Kameron. *Race: A Theological Account*. New York: Oxford University Press, 2008.

Charlesworth, James, ed. *Old Testament Pseudepigrapha: Apocalyptic Literature and Testaments*. New York: Doubleday, 1983.

Clark, Jawanza Eric, ed. *Albert Cleage Jr. and the Black Madonna and Child*. New York: Palgrave Macmillan, 2016.

————. "Introduction: Why a White Christ Continues to Be Racist: The Legacy of Albert B. Cleage Jr." In *Albert Cleage Jr. and the Black Madonna and Child*, edited by Jawanza Eric Clark, 1–18. New York: Palgrave Macmillan, 2016.

Cleage, Albert B., Jr. *The Black Messiah*. Kansas City, MO: Sheed & Ward, 1968.

Clemmons, Ithiel C. *Bishop C. H. Mason and the Roots of the Church of God in Christ*. Bakersfield, CA: Pneuma Life Publishing, 1996.

Collier-Thomas, Bettye. *Daughters of Thunder: Black Women Preachers and Their Sermons, 1850–1979*. San Francisco: Jossey-Bass, 1998.

Collins, John. *The Apocalyptic Imagination: An Introduction to Jewish Apocalyptic Literature*. Grand Rapids: Eerdmans, 1998.

Cone, James H. "Calling the Oppressors to Account: Justice, Love, and Hope in Black Religion." In *The Courage to Hope: From Black Suffering to Human Redemption*, edited by Quinton Dixie and Cornel West, 74–85. Boston: Beacon, 1999.

————. *The Cross and the Lynching Tree*. Maryknoll, NY: Orbis, 2011.

Conner, Kimberly Rae. *Conversions and Visions in the Writings of African-American Women*. Knoxville: University of Tennessee Press, 1994.

Cooper, Valerie. *Maria Stewart, the Bible, and the Rights of African Americans.* Charlottesville: University of Virginia Press, 2011.

Copher, Charles B. *Black Biblical Studies: An Anthology of Charles B. Copher; Biblical and Theological Issues on the Black Presence in the Bible.* Chicago: Black Light Fellowship, 1993.

———. "Three Thousand Years of Biblical Interpretation with Reference to Black Peoples." In *African American Religious Studies: An Interdisciplinary Anthology*, edited by Gayraud S. Wilmore, 105–28. Durham, NC: Duke University Press, 1989.

Cornelius, Janet Duitsman. *When I Can Read My Title Clear: Literacy, Slavery, and Religion in the Antebellum South.* Columbia: University of South Carolina Press, 1991.

Crowder, Stephanie. *When Momma Speaks: The Bible and Motherhood from a Womanist Perspective.* Louisville: Westminster John Knox, 2016.

Daniels, David D., III. "'Doing All the Good We Can': The Political Witness of African American Holiness and Pentecostal Churches in the Post–Civil Rights Era." In *New Day Begun: African American Churches and Civic Culture in Post–Civil Rights America*, 164–82. Durham, NC: Duke University Press, 2003.

Douglass, Frederick. "The American Constitution and the Slave: An Address Delivered in Glasgow, Scotland, on 26 March 1860." In *The Frederick Douglass Papers: Series One; Speeches, Debates, and Interviews*, vol. 3, 1855–63, edited by John Blassingame. New Haven: Yale University Press, 1985.

———. "Baptists, Congregationalists, the Free Church, and Slavery: An Address Delivered in Belfast, Ireland, on 23 December 1845." In *The Frederick Douglass Papers: Series One; Speeches, Debates, and Interviews*, vol. 1, 1841–46, edited by John Blassingame. New Haven: Yale University Press, 1979.

———. "Narrative of the Life of Frederick Douglass, an American Slave, Written by Himself." In *I Was Born a Slave: An Anthology of Classic Slave Narratives*, vol. 1, *1772–1849*, edited by Yuval Taylor, 523–600. Chicago: Lawrence Hill Books, 1999.

DuPree, Sherry Sherrod. *A Compendium: Bishop C. H. Mason Founder of the Church of God in Christ.* Gainesville, FL: Sherry Sherrod DuPree, 2017.

DuPree, Sherry Sherrod, and Herbert DuPree. *Exposed!!! Federal Bureau of Investigation Unclassified Reports on Churches and Church Leaders.* Washington, DC: Middle Atlantic Regional Press, 1993.

Eastman, Susan. "Galatians 4:19: A Labor of Divine Love." In *Recovering Paul's Mother Tongue: Language and Theology in Galatians*, 89–126. Grand Rapids: Eerdmans, 2007.

Elaw, Zilpha. *Can I Get a Witness? Prophetic Religious Voices of African American Women; An Anthology*. Edited by Marcia Riggs. Maryknoll, NY: Orbis, 1997.

———. *Memoirs of the Life, Religious Experience, Ministerial Travels and Labours of Mrs. Zilpha Elaw, an American Female of Colour: Together with Some Account of the Great Religious Revivals in America [Written By Herself]*. London: Published by the authoress, 1846. Reprinted in *Sisters of the Spirit: Three Black Women's Autobiographies of the Nineteenth Century*. Edited by William L. Andrews. Bloomington: Indiana University Press, 1986.

Ernest, John. Introduction to *Narrative of the Life of Henry Box Brown Written by Himself*, edited by John Ernest, 1–38. Chapel Hill: University of North Carolina Press, 2008.

Faulkner, Juanita Williams, and Raynard D. Smith, eds. *It Is Written: Minutes of the General Assembly Church of God in Christ Held at Memphis Tennessee, 1919–1932*. Memphis, TN: COGIC Publishing House, 2017.

Felder, Cain Hope. "The Letter to Philemon: Introduction, Commentary, and Reflections." In *New Interpreter's Bible Commentary* 11. Nashville: Abingdon, 2000.

———. *Race, Racism, and the Biblical Narratives*. Minneapolis: Fortress, 2002.

———, ed. *Stony the Road We Trod: African American Biblical Interpretation*. Minneapolis: Fortress, 1991.

———. *Troubling Biblical Waters: Race, Class, and Family*. Bishop Henry McNeal Turner Studies in North American Black Religion, vol. 3. Maryknoll, NY: Orbis, 1989.

Finkenbine, Roy E. "Boston's Black Churches: Institutional Centers of the Antislavery Movement." In *Courage and Conscience: Black and White Abolitionists in Boston*, edited by Donald M. Jacobs, 169–90. Bloomington: Indiana University Press, 1993.

Fluker, Walter Earl, and Catherine Tumber, eds. *A Strange Freedom: The Best of Howard Thurman on Religious Experience and Public Life*. Boston: Beacon, 1998.

Foote, Julia. *A Brand Plucked from the Fire: An Autobiographical Sketch by Mrs. Julia A. J. Foote*. Cleveland, OH: Printed for the author by W. F. Schneider, 1879. Reprinted in *Sisters of the Spirit: Three Black Women's Autobiographies of the Nineteenth Century*. Edited by William Andrews. Bloomington: Indiana University Press, 1986.

Gates, Henry Louis, Jr. *The Signifying Monkey: A Theory of African-American Literary Criticism*. New York: Oxford University Press, 1988.

Gaventa, Beverly. *Our Mother Saint Paul*. Louisville: Westminster John Knox, 2007.

Gilbert, Kenyatta. *A Pursued Justice: Black Preaching from the Great Migration to Civil Rights*. Waco, TX: Baylor University Press, 2017.

Gilkes, Cheryl Townsend. *If It Wasn't for the Women . . . : Black Women's Experience and Womanist Culture in Church and Community*. Maryknoll, NY: Orbis, 2001.

Glaude, Eddie. *Exodus! Religion, Race, and Nation in Early Nineteenth-Century Black America*. Chicago: University of Chicago Press, 2000.

Gorman, Michael. *Elements of Biblical Exegesis: A Basic Guide for Students and Ministers*. Rev. and expanded ed. Peabody, MA: Hendrickson, 2009.

Grant, Jacquelyn. *White Women's Christ and Black Women's Jesus: Feminist Christology and Womanist Response*. Atlanta: Scholars Press, 1989.

Green, J. D. *Narrative of the Life of J. D. Green, A Runaway Slave, Containing an Account of His Three Escapes*. Huddersfield, UK: Henry Fielding, Pack Horse Yard, 1864. Reprinted in *I Was Born a Slave: An Anthology of Classic Slave Narratives*. Vol. 1, *1772–1849*. Edited by Yuval Taylor. Chicago: Lawrence Hill Books, 1999.

Harrill, Albert. "The Use of the New Testament in the American Slave Controversy: A Case History in the Hermeneutical Tension between Biblical Criticism and Christian Moral Debate." *Religion and American Culture: A Journal of Interpretation* 10, no. 2 (2000): 149–86.

Hayes, Diana L. "My Hope Is in the Lord." In *Embracing the Spirit: Womanist Perspectives on Hope, Salvation, and Transformation*, edited by Emilie M. Townes, 9–29. Maryknoll, NY: Orbis, 1997.

Haynes, Lemuel. "The Sufferings, Support, and Reward of Faithful Ministers Illustrated: Being the Substance of Two Valedictory Discourses, delivered at Rutland, West Parish, May 24th, A.D. 1818." In *Sketches of the Life and Character of the Rev. Lemuel Haynes, A.M., For Many Years Pastor of A Church in Rutland, VT and Late in Granville, New-York*. Edited by Timothy Mather Cooley. New York: Harper & Brothers, 1837.

Hays, Richard B. "Salvation by Trust? Reading the Bible Faithfully." *Christian Century* 114 (1997): 218–23.

Haywood, Chanta. "Prophesying Daughters: Nineteenth-Century Black Religious Women, the Bible, and Black Literary History." In *African Americans and the Bible: Sacred Texts and Social Textures*, edited by Vincent Wimbush, 355–66. New York: Continuum, 2000.

Henderson, Christina. "Sympathetic Violence: Maria Stewart's Antebellum Vision of African American Resistance." In "New Registers for the Study of Blackness," edited by Martha J. Cutter, special issue, *MELUS* 38, no. 4 (December 2013): 52–75.

Hendricks, Obery M., Jr. "An MLK Birthday Sermon." In *The Universe Bends toward Justice: Radical Reflections on the Bible, the Church, and the Body Politic.* Maryknoll, NY: Orbis, 2011.

Higginbotham, Evelyn Brooks. "African-American Women's History and the Metalanguage of Race." In *"We Specialize in Wholly Impossible": A Reader in Black Women's History*, edited by Darlene Clark Hine, Wilma King, and Linda Reed, 3–24. Brooklyn, NY: Carlson Publishing, 1995.

Hodge, Charles. *A Commentary on Ephesians.* 1856. Reprint, Edinburgh: First Banner of Truth, 1964, 1991.

Hodges, Graham Russell, ed. *Black Itinerants of the Gospel: The Narratives of John Jea and George White.* Madison, WI: Madison House, 1993.

Holte, James Craig. *The Conversion Experience in America: A Sourcebook on Religious Conversion Autobiography.* New York: Greenwood, 1992.

Horton, James Oliver, and Lois E. Horton. "The Affirmation of Manhood: Black Garrisonians in Antebellum Boston." In *Courage and Conscience: Black and White Abolitionists in Boston*, edited by Donald M. Jacobs, 127–54. Bloomington: Indiana University Press, 1993.

Horton, James O., and Amanda Kleintop, eds. *Race, Slavery, and the Civil War: The Tough Stuff of American History and Memory.* Richmond: Virginia Sesquicentennial of the American Civil War Commission, 2011.

Houchins, Sue E. *Spiritual Narratives.* Schomburg Library of Nineteenth Century Black Women Writers. New York: Oxford University Press, 1988.

Jackson, Rebecca Cox. *Gifts of Power: The Writings of Rebecca Cox Jackson, Black Visionary, Shaker Eldress.* Edited by Jean McMahon Humez. Amherst: University of Massachusetts Press, 1981.

Jacobs, Donald M. "David Walker and William Lloyd Garrison." In *Courage and Conscience: Black and White Abolitionists in Boston*, edited by Donald M. Jacobs, 1–20. Bloomington: Indiana University Press, 1993.

Jacobs, Harriet. *Incidents in the Life of A Slave Girl.* Edited by L. Maria Child. Boston: Published for the author, 1861. Reprinted in *I Was Born a Slave: An Anthology of Classic Slave Narratives.* Vol. 2, *1849–1866.* Edited by Yuval Taylor. Chicago: Lawrence Hill Books, 1999.

Jacobsen, Douglas, ed. *A Reader in Pentecostal Theology: Voices from the First Generation.* Bloomington: Indiana University Press, 2006.

Jasper, David. *A Short Introduction to Hermeneutics.* Louisville: Westminster John Knox, 2004.

Jea, John. *The Life, History, and Unparalleled Sufferings of John Jea, the African Preacher.* Documenting the American South. University of North Carolina at Chapel Hill Digitization Project. https://docsouth.unc.edu/neh/jea john/jeajohn.html.

Jefferson, Thomas. *Notes on the State of Virginia*. Philadelphia: Pritchard & Hall, 1787.

Jewett, Robert. *Romans*. Hermeneia. Minneapolis: Fortress, 2007.

Johnson, Clifton, ed. *God Struck Me Dead: Religious Conversion Experiences and Autobiographies of Ex-Slaves*. Philadelphia: Pilgrim, 1969.

Kaalund, Jennifer T. *Reading Hebrews and 1 Peter with the African American Great Migration: Diaspora, Place, and Identity*. London: T&T Clark, 2019.

Kasemann, Ernst. *Commentary on Romans*. Translated by Geoffrey W. Bromiley. Grand Rapids: Eerdmans, 1980.

King, Martin Luther, Jr. "Letter from Birmingham City Jail." In *A Testament of Hope: The Essential Writings and Speeches of Martin Luther King, Jr.*, edited by James Melvin Washington. San Francisco: HarperSanFrancisco, 1986.

———. *Strength to Love*. New York: Harper & Row, 1968.

———. *Where Do We Go from Here: Chaos or Community?* New York: Harper & Row, 1967.

———. "'Why Jesus Called a Man a Fool,' Sermon Delivered at Mount Pisgah Missionary Baptist Church." August 27, 1967?. Stanford University Martin Luther King, Jr., Research and Education Institute. https://kinginstitute .stanford.edu/king-papers/documents/why-jesus-called-man-fool -sermon-delivered-mount-pisgah-missionary-baptist.

Klauck, Hans-Josef, ed. *Encyclopedia of the Bible and Its Reception*. Berlin: de Gruyter, 2009.

LaRue, Cleophus J. *The Heart of Black Preaching*. Louisville: Westminster John Knox, 2000.

———. *I Believe I'll Testify: The Art of African American Preaching*. Louisville: Westminster John Knox, 2011.

Lee, Jarena. *The Life and Religious Experience of Jarena Lee, A Coloured Lady, Giving An Account of Her Call to Preach the Gospel. Revised and Corrected from the Original Manuscript, Written by Herself.* Philadelphia: Printed and published for the author, 1836. Reprinted in *Sisters of the Spirit: Three Black Women's Autobiographies of the Nineteenth Century*. Edited by William Andrews. Bloomington: Indiana University Press, 1986.

Lewis, Lloyd A. "An African American Appraisal of the Philemon-Paul-Onesimus Triangle." In *Stony the Road We Trod: African American Biblical Interpretation*, edited by Cain Hope Felder. Minneapolis: Fortress, 1991.

Lincoln, C. Eric. *Sounds of the Struggle: Persons and Perspectives in Civil Rights*. New York: Friendship, 1968.

Lindley, Susan. "'Neglected Voices' and Praxis in the Social Gospel." *Journal of Religious Ethics* 18, no. 1 (1990): 75–102.

Lischer, Richard. *The Preacher King: Martin Luther King, Jr. and the Word That Moved America.* New York: Oxford University Press, 1995.

Lorde, Audrey. "The Master's Tools Will Never Dismantle the Master's House." In *Sister Outsider: Essays and Speeches*, 110–13. Berkeley, CA: Crossing, 1984, 2007.

Lovejoy, Joseph C. *The North and the South! Letter from J. C. Lovejoy, Esq to His Brother, Hon. Owen Lovejoy, M. C., with remarks by the Editor of the Washington Union.* Washington, DC, 1859.

Luker, Ralph. *The Social Gospel in Black and White: American Racial Reform, 1885–1912.* Chapel Hill: University of North Carolina Press, 1991.

MacLam, Helen. "Introduction: Black Puritan on the Northern Frontier; The Vermont Ministry of Lemuel Haynes." In *Black Preacher to White America: The Collected Writings of Lemuel Haynes, 1774–1833*, edited by Richard Newman. Brooklyn, NY: Carlson Publishing, 1990.

Marbury, Herbert. *Pillars of Cloud and Fire: The Politics of Exodus in African American Biblical Interpretation.* New York: New York University Press, 2015.

Martin, Larry, ed. *Azusa Street Sermons by William J. Seymour.* Joplin, MO: Christian Life Books, 1999.

Martyn, J. Louis. *Galatians: A New Translation with Introduction and Commentary.* Anchor Yale Bible 33A. New York: Doubleday, 1997.

Mason, E. W. *The Man . . . Charles Harrison Mason: Sermons of His Early Ministry (1915–1929) and a Biographical Sketch of His Life.* Memphis, TN: Church of God in Christ Publishing House, 1979.

Mason, Mary C., ed. and comp. *The History and Life Work of Bishop C. H. Mason.* 1924. Reprint, Memphis, TN: Church of God in Christ, 1987.

May, Cedrick, and Julie McCown. "'An Essay on Slavery': An Unpublished Poem by Jupiter Hammon." *Early American Literature* 48, no. 2 (2013): 457–71.

McKivigan, John R., and Mitchell Snay, eds. Introduction to *Religion and the Antebellum Debate over Slavery*, 1–35. Athens: University of Georgia Press, 1998.

Miller, Samuel. *The Life of Samuel Miller, D.D. LL.D.* 2 vols. Philadelphia: Clayton, Remsen & Haffelfinger, 1869.

———. *A Sermon Preached at March 13th, 1808, For the Benefit of the Society Instituted In The City of New York, For The Relief Of Poor Widows With Small Children.* New York: Hopkins & Seymour, 1808.

————. *A Sermon Preached at Newark, October 22d, 1823 Before the Synod of New Jersey*. Trenton, NJ: George Sherman, 1823.

Mitchell, Henry H. *Black Preaching*. San Francisco: Harper & Row, 1979.

Mitchell, Laura L. "'Matters of Justice between Man and Man': Northern Divines, the Bible and the Fugitive Slave Act of 1850." In *Religion and the Antebellum Debate over Slavery*, edited by John R. McKivigan and Mitchell Snay, 134–66. Athens: University of Georgia Press, 1998.

Mittelstadt, Martin W. "Receiving Luke-Acts: The Rise of Reception History and a Call to Pentecostal Scholars." *Pneuma* 40, no. 3 (2018): 367–88.

Moorhead, James H. *Princeton Seminary in American Religion and Culture*. Grand Rapids: Eerdmans, 2012.

Morris, Calvin S. *Reverdy C. Ransom: Black Advocate of the Social Gospel*. Lanham, MD: University Press of America, 1990.

Moses, Wilson Jeremiah. *Black Messiahs and Uncle Toms: Social and Literary Manipulations of a Religious Myth*. University Park: Pennsylvania State University Press, 1982.

Nave, Guy. "2 Corinthians." In *True to Our Native Land: An African American New Testament Commentary*, edited by Brian Blount, Cain Hope Felder, Clarice J. Martin, and Emerson Powery, 307–32. Minneapolis: Fortress, 2007.

Nelson, D. Kimathi. "The Theological Journey of Albert B. Cleage, Jr.: Reflections from Jaramogi's Protégé and Successor." In *Albert Cleage Jr. and the Black Madonna and Child*, edited by Jawanza Eric Clark, 21–38. New York: Palgrave Macmillan, 2016.

Newman, Richard. "Preface: The Paradox of Lemuel Haynes." In *Black Preacher to White America: The Collected Writings of Lemuel Haynes, 1774–1833*, edited by Richard Newman. Brooklyn, NY: Carlson Publishing, 1990.

Noll, Mark. *The Civil War as a Theological Crisis*. Chapel Hill: University of North Carolina Press, 2006.

Nydam, Arien. "Numerological Tradition in the Works of Jupiter Hammon." *African American Review* 40, no. 2 (Summer 2006): 207–20.

O'Neale, Sondra. *Jupiter Hammon and the Biblical Beginnings of African-American Literature*. Metuchen, NJ: ATLA and Scarecrow Press, 1993.

Owens, Rosalie S. *Bishop Ida Bell Robinson: The Authoritarian Servant Leader*. Middletown, DE: Rosalie Owens, 2019.

Page, Hugh, and Randall Bailey, eds. *The Africana Bible: Reading Israel's Scriptures from Africa and the African Diaspora*. Minneapolis: Fortress, 2010.

Paris, Peter. "The Bible and the Black Churches." In *The Bible and Social Reform*, edited by Ernest R. Sandeen, 133–54. Philadelphia: Fortress, 1982.

———. *Black Religious Leaders: Conflict in Unity.* Louisville: Westminster John Knox, 1991.

Payne, Daniel Alexander. *Recollections of Seventy Years.* Nashville: Publishing House of the AME Sunday School Union, 1888.

———. *Sermons and Addresses, 1853–1891: Bishop Daniel A. Payne.* Edited by Charles Killian. New York: Arno, 1972.

Pennington, James. *The Fugitive Blacksmith; or, Events in the History of James W. C. Pennington, Pastor of Presbyterian Church, New York, Formerly A Slave in the State of Maryland, United States.* London: Charles Gilpin, 1850. Reprint, Westport, CT: Negro Universities Press, 1971.

Petition of 1779 by Slaves of Fairfield County. Revolutionary War Papers. Connecticut State Library.

Pierce, Yolanda. *Hell without Fires: Slavery, Christianity, and the Antebellum Spiritual Narrative.* Gainesville: University Press of Florida, 2005.

Powery, Emerson. "'Rise Up, Ye Women': Harriet Jacobs and the Bible." *Postscripts* 5, no. 2 (2009): 171–84.

Powery, Emerson, and Rodney Sadler. *The Genesis of Liberation: Biblical Interpretation in the Antebellum Narratives of the Enslaved.* Louisville: Westminster John Knox, 2016.

Priest, Josiah. *Slavery as It Relates to the Negro or African Race.* Albany, NY: C. Van Benthuysen & Co., 1843.

Raboteau, Albert. *American Prophets: Seven Religious Radicals and Their Struggle for Social and Political Justice.* Princeton: Princeton University Press, 2016.

———. *A Fire in the Bones: Reflections on African-American Religious History.* Boston: Beacon, 1995.

———. *Slave Religion: The "Invisible Institution" in the Antebellum South.* New York: Oxford University Press, 1978.

Randolph, Peter. *Sketches of Slave Life; or, Illustrations of the "Peculiar Institution" by Peter Randolph, An Emancipated Slave.* Boston: Published for the author, 1855. Reprinted in *"Sketches of Slave Life" and "From Slave Cabin to the Pulpit."* Edited by Katherine Clay Bassard. Morgantown: West Virginia University Press, 2016.

Ransom, Reverdy. "The Coming Vision." In *Making the Gospel Plain: The Writings of Bishop Reverdy Ransom,* edited by Anthony B. Pinn, 215–22. Harrisburg, PA: Trinity Press International, 1999.

———. *Making the Gospel Plain: The Writings of Bishop Reverdy C. Ransom.* Edited by Anthony Pinn. Harrisburg, PA: Trinity Press International, 1999.

———. *The Negro: The Hope or the Despair of Christianity.* Boston: Ruth Hill, 1935.

———. *The Pilgrimage of Harriet Ransom's Son*. Nashville: Sunday School Union, 1949.

Rawick, George P., ed., *The American Slave: A Composite Autobiography*. 41 vols. Westport, CT: Greenwood, 1972.

Reddish, Mitchell, ed. *Apocalyptic Literature: A Reader*. Nashville: Abingdon, 1990.

Richards, Philip. "Nationalist Themes in the Preaching of Jupiter Hammon." *Early American Literature* 25, no. 2 (1990): 123–38.

Richardson, Marilyn. "What If I Am a Woman? Maria Stewart's Defense of Black Women's Political Activism." In *Courage and Conscience: Black and White Abolitionists in Boston*, edited by Donald M. Jacobs. Bloomington: Indiana University Press, 1993.

Riggs, Marcia, ed. *Can I Get a Witness? Prophetic Religious Voices of African American Women, an Anthology*. Maryknoll, NY: Orbis, 1997.

Saillant, John. *Black Puritan, Black Republican: The Life of Lemuel Haynes, 1753–1833*. New York: Oxford University Press, 2003.

———. "Lemuel Haynes and the Revolutionary Origins of Black Theology, 1776–1801." *Religion and American Culture* 2, no. 1 (1992): 79–102.

———. "Origins of African American Biblical Hermeneutics in Eighteenth-Century Black Opposition to the Slave Trade and Slavery." In *African Americans and the Bible: Sacred Texts and Social Structures*, edited by Vincent L. Wimbush, 236–50. New York: Continuum, 2000.

———. " 'Remarkably Emancipated from Bondage, Slavery, and Death': An African American Retelling of the Puritan Captivity Narrative, 1820." *Early American Literature* 29 (1994): 122–40.

———. "Traveling in Old and New Worlds with John Jea, the African Preacher, 1773–1816." *Journal of American Studies* 33 (1999): 473–90.

Sanders, Cheryl. "African Americans, the Bible and Spiritual Formation." In *African Americans and the Bible: Sacred Texts and Social Textures*, edited by Vincent L. Wimbush, 588–602. New York: Continuum, 2000.

Schweninger, Loren, and Robert Shelton, eds. *Race, Slavery, and Free Blacks: Series I, Petitions to Southern Legislatures, 1777–1867*. A Microfilm project of University Publications of America. Bethesda, MD.

Sechrest, Love. *A Former Jew: Paul and the Dialectics of Race*. New York: T&T Clark, 2009.

Sernett, Milton, ed. *African American Religious History: A Documentary Witness*. Durham, NC: Duke University Press, 1999.

Seymour, William. "Apostolic Address." In *A Reader in Pentecostal Theology:*

Voices from the First Generation, edited by Douglas Jacobsen. Bloomington: Indiana University Press, 2006.

———. *The Doctrines and Discipline of the Azusa Street Apostolic Faith Mission of Los Angeles, California by William J. Seymour Its Founder and General Overseer*. Complete Azusa Street Library, vol. 7, edited by Larry Martin. Joplin, MO: Christian Life Books, 2000.

———. "Gifts of the Spirit." In *Azusa Street Sermons by William J. Seymour*, edited by Larry Martin. Joplin, MO: Christian Life Books, 1999.

———. "In Money Matters." In *Azusa Street Sermons by William J. Seymour*, edited by Larry Martin. Joplin, MO: Christian Life Books, 1999.

———. "Receive Ye the Holy Ghost." In *Azusa Street Sermons by William J. Seymour*, edited by Larry Martin. Joplin, MO: Christian Life Books, 1999.

———. "Sanctified on the Cross." In *Azusa Street Sermons by William J. Seymour*, edited by Larry Martin. Joplin, MO: Christian Life Books, 1999.

Simmons, Martha, and Frank A. Thomas, eds. *Preaching with Sacred Fire: An Anthology of African American Sermons, 1750 to the Present*. New York: Norton, 2010.

Slave Petition for Freedom during the Revolution, 1773–1779. Petition (b). Boston, April 20, 1773.

Slave Petition for Freedom during the Revolution, 1773–1779. Petition (d). January 13, 1777.

Smith, Abraham. "Paul and African American Biblical Interpretation." In *True to Our Native Land: An African American New Testament Commentary*, edited by Brian Blount, Cain Hope Felder, Clarice J. Martin, and Emerson Powery, 31–42. Minneapolis: Fortress, 2007.

———. "Putting 'Paul' Back Together Again: William Wells Brown's *Clotel* and Black Abolitionist Approaches to Paul." *Semeia* 83–84 (1998): 251–62.

Smith, Mitzi J. "'This Little Light of Mine': The Womanist Biblical Scholar as Prophetess, Iconoclast, and Activist." In *I Found God in Me: A Womanist Biblical Hermeneutics Reader*, edited by Mitzi J. Smith. Eugene, OR: Cascade, 2015.

———. "'Unbossed and Unbought': Zilpha Elaw and Old Elizabeth and a Political Discourse of Origins." *Black Theology: An International Journal* 9, no. 3 (2011): 287–311.

Smith, Raynard D. "Seeking the Just Society: Charles Harrison Mason's Quest for Social Equality." In *With Signs Following: The Life and Ministry of Charles Harrison*, edited by Raynard Smith. St. Louis: Christian Board Publication, 2015.

Smith, Shanell T. *The Woman Babylon and the Marks of Empire: Reading Reve-*

lation with a Postcolonial Womanist Hermeneutics of Ambivalence. Emerging Scholars. Minneapolis: Fortress, 2014.

Smith, Shively. *Strangers to Family: Diaspora and 1 Peter's Invention of God's Household.* Waco, TX: Baylor University Press, 2016.

Smith, Timothy L. "Slavery and Theology: The Emergence of Black Christian Consciousness in Nineteenth Century America." *Church History* 41 (December 1972): 497–512.

South Carolina Department of Archives and History. "Race, Slavery, and Free Blacks Petition." Race & Slavery Petitions Project. https://library.uncg.edu/slavery/petitions/details.aspx?pid=1645.

"Spirit and Power—a 10-Country Survey of Pentecostals." Pew Research Center, October 5, 2006. http://www.pewforum.org/2006/10/05/spirit-and-power/.

Stampp, Kenneth. *The Peculiar Institution: Slavery in the Ante-Bellum South.* New York: Knopf, 1978.

Stewart, James Brewer. "Abolitionists, the Bible, and the Challenge of Slavery." In *The Bible and Social Reform,* edited by Ernest Sandeen. Philadelphia: Fortress, 1982.

———. "Boston, Abolition, and the Atlantic World, 1820–1861." In *Courage and Conscious: Black and White Abolitionists in Boston,* edited by Donald M. Jacobs, 101–26. Bloomington: Indiana University Press, 1993.

Stewart, Maria W. *Maria W. Stewart, America's First Black Woman Political Writer: Essays and Speeches.* Edited by Marilyn Richardson. Bloomington: Indiana University Press, 1987.

Stuckenbruck, Loren T. "Prayers of Deliverance from the Demonic in the Dead Sea Scrolls and Related Early Jewish Literature." In *The Changing Face of Judaism, Christianity, and Other Greco-Roman Religions in Antiquity,* edited by Ian H. Henderson and Gerbern S. Oegema, 146–65. Studien zu den Jüdischen Schriften aus hellenistisch-römischer Zeit 2. Gutersloh: Gutersloher Verlagshaus, 2006.

Taylor, Yuval, ed. *I Was Born a Slave: An Anthology of Classic Slave Narratives.* Vol. 1, *1772–1849.* Vol. 2, *1849–1866.* Chicago: Lawrence Hill Books, 1999.

Theissen, Gerd. *The Social Setting of Pauline Christianity: Essays on Corinth.* Edited and translated with an introduction by John H. Schutz. Philadelphia: Fortress, 1982.

Thurman, Howard. *Jesus and the Disinherited.* Richmond, IN: Friends United, 1981; original Nashville: Abingdon, 1949.

———. *The Papers of Howard Washington Thurman.* Edited by Walter Fluker. Columbia: University of South Carolina Press, 2009–2017.

Turner, William C., Jr. "Preaching the Spirit: The Liberation of Preaching." *Journal of Pentecostal Theology* 14, no. 1. (2005): 3–16.

———. *The United Holy Church of America: A Study in Black Holiness-Pentecostalism*. Piscataway, NJ: Gorgias, 2006.

Venable-Ridley, C. Michelle. "Paul and the African American Community." In *Embracing the Spirit: Womanist Perspectives on Hope, Salvation, and Transformation*, edited by Emilie M. Townes, 212–33. Maryknoll, NY: Orbis, 1997.

Walker, David. *Walker's Appeal, In Four Articles, Together with A Preamble To The Coloured Citizens of the World, But in Particular and Very Expressly, to Those of The United States of America, Written in Boston, State of Massachusetts, September 28, 1829*. Boston: Revised and published by David Walker, 1830. Reprinted in *David Walker's Appeal: In Four Articles*. Mansfield Centre, CT: Martino Publishing, 2015.

Ware, Frederick L. *African American Theology: An Introduction*. Louisville: Westminster John Knox, 2016.

Weems, Renita J. *Just a Sister Away: A Womanist Vision of Women's Relationships in the Bible*. San Diego: LuraMedia, 1988.

White, Calvin, Jr. *The Rise to Respectability: Race, Religion, and the Church of God in Christ*. Fayetteville: University of Arkansas Press, 2012.

White, Deborah Gray. *Ar'n't I a Woman? Female Slaves in the Plantation South*. New York: Norton, 1985.

Williams, Demetrius. "The Acts of the Apostles." In *True to Our Native Land: An African American New Testament Commentary*, edited by Brian Blount, Cain Hope Felder, Clarice J. Martin, and Emerson Powery, 213–48. Minneapolis: Fortress, 2007.

Williams, Eric Lewis. "'Mad with Supernatural Joy': On Representations of Pentecostalism in the Black Religious Imagination." *Journal of the Interdenominational Theological Center* 44 (Fall–Spring 2016): 81–97.

Wimbush, Vincent, ed. *African Americans and the Bible: Sacred Texts and Social Structures*. New York: Continuum, 2000.

Yellin, Jean Fagan. *Harriet Jacobs: A Life*. New York: Basic Civitas Books, 2004.

———. "Harriet Jacobs in the Refugee Camps." In *Race, Slavery, and the Civil War: The Tough Stuff of American History and Memory*, edited by James O. Horton and Amanda Kleintop, 92–98. Richmond: Virginia Sesquicentennial of the American Civil War Commission, 2011.

Yetman, Norman R., ed. *Voices from Slavery: The Life of American Slaves—in the Words of 100 Men and Women Who Lived It and Many Years Later Talked about It*. New York: Holt, Rinehart & Winston, 1970.

SCRIPTURE INDEX